TREASURY OF LITERATURE

INTEGRATED SPELLING

Teacher's Edition

GRADE 2

HARCOURT BRACE & COMPANY

Orlando   Atlanta   Austin   Boston   San Francisco   Chicago   Dallas   New York
Toronto   London

Printed in the United States of America

ISBN 0-15-302576-X

3 4 5 6 7 8 9 10   022 97 96 95

Contents

Unit 1

Unit 2

Philosophy of *Integrated Spelling*

Integrated Spelling is spelling and vocabulary instruction that is developmental in sequence, complete in scope, and fully integrated with the literature-based instruction in *Treasury of Literature.* Based on extensive research, the program offers teachers useful and practical strategies for maximizing children's learning of spelling and provides numerous opportunities for children to learn and apply a variety of spelling strategies to all of their writing.

Integrated Spelling is based upon these beliefs:

 Spelling instruction is most effective when it takes place within the broader context of reading and writing.

 There is a meaning basis for spelling: knowledge of spelling and word meaning should be developed through reading and responding to literature.

 Use of an organized, developmental spelling curriculum and purposeful activities promotes spelling growth.

 A diagnostic tool that gives teachers insight into each child's stage of development is an integral part of an effective spelling program.

 A spelling program should help children develop a spelling consciousness—an ability to examine their own writing and identify misspelled words.

 Allowing young children to invent or use temporary spelling in their writing, while gradually helping them arrive at more standard spellings, is reflective of the natural developmental process for learning spelling.

 Knowledge of the history and heritage of the English language, along with language play, is an essential component of a spelling program.

Integration with *Treasury of Literature*

For each selection in *Treasury of Literature,* a corresponding spelling lesson links reading, writing, vocabulary development, and spelling, providing a more meaningful approach to spelling instruction.

Integrated Spelling provides instruction and practice for every day of the week. Each core lesson, which can be combined with a pretest and a posttest, includes

* a spelling generalization.
* a corresponding list of Spelling Words prompted by the literature and gathered from research.
* a *Strategy Workshop* with one or more graphophonic, visual, or morphemic spelling strategies that children practice and apply to learn to be strategic spellers.
* a *Vocabulary WordShop* that includes Words to Explore from the literature children have read, with vocabulary activities and exercises to develop and broaden children's concepts and word knowledge.
* word origin and history features, spelling activities related to story themes and concepts from *Treasury of Literature,* motivating games for a variety of practice, and writing applications that encourage response to literature.

Review Lessons

The last lesson of each unit in *Integrated Spelling* is a review lesson that connects to the writing forms and language skills featured in the corresponding *Treasury of Literature* unit. By reviewing spelling and vocabulary in the context of reading and writing, children reinforce spelling in a natural way.

Developmental Levels of Spellers

Children benefit most from instruction that is appropriate to their developmental levels. The developmental levels of most second graders, as shown below, may be determined using the Spelling Placement Inventory on page T333 of this Teacher's Edition. See pages T248–T249 for information on developmental levels of spellers, Grades 1-8.

DEVELOPMENTAL LEVEL	CHARACTERISTICS
Semi-Phonetic Spellers *(Below-Level)*	• use knowledge of sounds represented by letters to invent spellings. • may omit major sounds, particularly vowel sounds in some words; e.g., *camr* for *camera*. • write some words that are decipherable. • understand the concept of word and left-to-right progression.
Phonetic Spellers *(On-Level)*	• refine their invented spellings. • use a phonetic or letter-name system of spelling in which they make a one-to-one match between each of the sequential sounds they hear in words. • spell words the way words sound. Athough the spelling may be unconventional, the words are usually readable. • may or may not be aware of word segmentation—breaking words into smaller parts.
Transitional Spellers *(Above-Level)*	• move from concrete to more abstract representation, one that requires greater reliance on visual memory—spelling words the way they look rather than the way they sound. • develop a sense of when a particular spelling looks correct. • may still invent spellings but have learned many of the conventions of English spelling. • may include all the letters in a word but may reverse some letters, such as in *taod* for *toad* or *fete* for *feet*.

ASSIGNMENT GUIDE page T250

The Assignment Guide presents suggestions for tailoring instruction to fit the needs of children at each developmental level. Within each lesson plan are opportunities for teacher choice and guidance for meeting individual needs that can further help you shape instruction.

SPELLING PLACEMENT INVENTORY page T333

Determining a child's developmental level can best be done through a combination of observation, evaluation of written work, and administration and interpretation of a placement instrument. In addition to providing guidelines for observing children effectively and analyzing written work, *Integrated Spelling* provides a Spelling Placement Inventory, procedures for administering the Inventory, and guidelines for interpreting the results for each grade level.

This Inventory establishes a benchmark of spelling awareness for each child and serves as an indicator of his or her developmental level at a specific time. Progress throughout the year can be determined by comparing performance on lesson assignments to performance on the Inventory, or you may want children to take the Placement Inventory periodically to demonstrate progress.

At the end of the year, you may want to have children take the Spelling Placement Inventory again to demonstrate the progress they have made.

WORD LISTS pages T344-T345

In a spelling program, a significant factor in making instruction match developmental levels is the quality of the word lists around which instruction centers. At every level children should concentrate on learning to spell words they encounter most often in their reading and use most frequently in their writing.

The lists of words to be taught in *Integrated Spelling* were compiled from no fewer than nine research-generated word lists, in addition to lists of words that appear in *Treasury of Literature*. Three of these research-based lists rank words by frequency of occurrence in reading. Four others rank words by frequency of occurrence in children's writing. The others rank words according to how often they are misspelled.

In *Integrated Spelling*, the instructional plan of the developmental lessons is both consistent and flexible:

- Skill development takes place in the context of reading, writing, listening, and speaking.

- Each developmental lesson has four parts that may be taught in 3–5 days.

- Children progress through these stages in each lesson: discovery of spelling patterns through sorting, consideration of relevant rules and strategies, application of these rules and strategies, and confirmation of understanding.

- Opportunities for teacher choice allow instruction to be tailored to fit the various developmental levels of the children in the class.

- Suggestions for meeting individual needs help ensure that every child benefits from every lesson.

- An Assignment Guide is provided on page T250 of this Teacher's Edition. Use it to adjust assignments to the developmental levels of individual children.

Part 1

Introduction

The first page of each Teacher's Edition lesson provides tools for making instruction appropriate for children and includes the objectives and lesson-planning information, an informal assessment procedure, and second-language support guidance. Pretest/Posttest Context Sentences also appear on this page.

The second page of each Teacher's Edition lesson, labeled *Introduction*, shows the first pupil page. It also offers a pretest and a Self-Check procedure; a choice of an open-sort or a closed-sort activity, either of which may be used to help children discover patterns and common elements in the Spelling Words; a summarizing-the-learning activity (In Summary); and an extension activity (Your Own Words).

Home Activities Master A, provided for each lesson, presents the open-sort activity. It may be used in class or may be distributed to be completed as homework.

Part 2

Strategy Workshop

This Teacher's Edition page and its corresponding Pupil's Edition page present useful strategies and structural information about the Spelling Words. Children immediately put this new knowledge to use in the workshop activities, which they may work on cooperatively or independently.

Part 3

Vocabulary WordShop

These two pupil pages guide children to think critically about the spellings and meanings of high-utility words and topically related words from the literature.

Opportunities for you to model dictionary use are often indicated, and optional writing activities are provided. Additional practice is provided on Practice Activities Master B.

Part 4

Lesson Wrap-Up

On the final day of the lesson sequence, children have the opportunity to demonstrate proficiency by taking the posttest. A Reteach procedure structured to help children with learning differences is provided on the final teacher page. In addition, the teacher page suggests one or more activities that integrate the curriculum areas. These lively activities involve all three modalities and encourage creativity.

Review Lessons At the end of each unit, a review lesson gives children another opportunity to work with the words, review strategies and rules, and apply their accumulated knowledge in writing activities as well as practice using a standardized test format.

Spelling Log

A Spelling Log provides an excellent opportunity for children to record new words they learn, keep an ongoing record of words they have misspelled on pretests or in other writing, and note troublesome words as an aid to writing and proofreading. A Spelling Log also encourages children to record words that are of special interest to them, such as words having to do with a favorite activity, place, or topic. The Pupil's Edition of *Integrated Spelling* includes a Spelling Log in which children may record words from the spelling lessons, words they have misspelled in pretests and posttests, and words they acquire from other sources.

Introducing the Spelling Log

Ask children to name some different ways they learn new words. *(reading books, signs, menus; listening to the radio; watching TV; talking with friends)* To introduce the idea of a Spelling Log, ask children to name some things they can do to remember new words they learn. Explain that there is a special section of their spelling book that they can use for recording new words. Have children read page 5 of the Pupil's Edition silently. Then invite volunteers to read aloud the dialogue in the speech balloons.

Introduce the Spelling Log by having children look at pages 6 and 7 in their books. Explain that there are three parts to the Spelling Log: **Words to Study, Words to Explore,** and **My Own Word Collection.** Then read pages 6 and 7 with the children to find out about these parts. Ask the following questions:

- What is the first part of your Spelling Log for? What kinds of words will you write in this part of the Log?

- Where will you find the words to write in the second part of the Log? Name some words that might go on the pages labeled *Art and Music Words.*
- What words will you write in the third part of your Spelling Log? What are some groups you might create?

Invite children to examine the Spelling Log in their books. Have volunteers identify the three parts of the Spelling Log and tell on which page each begins and ends.

Creating Spelling Logs

You might also help children create additional or separate individual Spelling Logs. Suggest that they use sheets of lined paper which they can keep in a notebook. To be useful, each Spelling Log should be organized so that children can easily find words they have written and systematically add new words. Children might organize their logs alphabetically, with one page for each letter of the alphabet.

Encourage children to include these items in their logs:

- troublesome words such as *to, too,* and *two,* along with context sentences or definitions that help children remember which word to use.
- words that share a spelling pattern or common structure.
- interesting word facts about word origins and history.

Set aside some time for children to create or decorate the covers for their individual Spelling Logs.

See pages T239–T240 for additional information about the Spelling Log.

Page 5

Page 6

Page 7

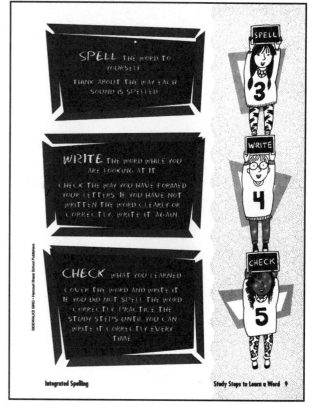

Study Steps to Learn a Word

Study Steps to Learn a Word will help children become successful, independent spellers. The strategy utilizes visual, auditory, and kinesthetic modalities.

- The *first* step has children say the word and think about its meaning, reinforcing the meaning basis for spelling.
- The *second* step asks children to look at the word, think about words that are related in meaning or resemble it, and visualize it. (This step develops the use of analogy as a spelling cue.)
- The *third* step has children spell the word silently and think about sound/letter relationships, reinforcing sound/letter cues.
- The *fourth* step utilizes a kinesthetic mode—writing—to develop children's visual memory of the word. Children write the word, check the clarity of the letters, and then rewrite the word if necessary. (This step reminds children to write legibly to avoid spelling errors.)

- The *fifth* step strengthens children's visual memory of the word by having them cover the word, rewrite it, and check its spelling.

Introducing the Study Steps

Before children begin their work in the Pupil's Edition, introduce them to Study Steps to Learn a Word. Read pages 8 and 9 to the children. Ask volunteers to reread the individual steps aloud. Guide children through the steps, using an example.

Ways to Use the Study Steps

Discuss with children when they might use Study Steps to Learn a Word. Here are some suggestions:

- when they encounter unfamiliar words or words they are unsure how to spell.
- when they misspell words in their writing.
- when they misspell words on the pretest or posttest.

Words with Short *a*

Objective
To spell words with short *a*

Lesson Planner
Assign words based on the developmental levels of individual children. See the Assignment Guide on page T250.

Informal Assessment
Children's writing may show that they have difficulty with short *a*.

MODEL

pad

Where is the (pod) of paper?

Use this lesson to introduce the spelling of words with the short *a* vowel sound. Encourage children to apply what they have learned to help them spell other words in which they hear the short *a* sound. After children have completed the lesson, have them proofread their writing and correct any errors they may have made spelling words with the short *a* sound.

SECOND-LANGUAGE SUPPORT Many second-language speakers have difficulty distinguishing the short *a* sound from the short *e* and the short *u* sounds. Have children practice listening for the short *a* sound in pairs of words such as the following: *man, men; bad, bed; pat, pet; fan, fun; bag, bug; ran, run.* COMPARING AND CONTRASTING

Pretest/Posttest Context Sentences
You may want to test Semi-Phonetic Spellers on words 1–6 only.

1. **an**   We saw **an** old car.
2. **bad**   I have a **bad** cut on my leg.
*3. **bat**   He hit the ball with the **bat**.
4. **map**   Can you find this city on the **map**?
*5. **had**   We **had** a good time at the zoo.
6. **dad**   Her **dad** is at home.

*7. **sat**   Kelly **sat** in the big chair.
8. **sad**   Was the boy happy or **sad**?
9. **cat**   Is your pet a dog or a **cat**?
10. **mad**   I was **mad** when I lost my ball.

*Words appearing in "Ronald Morgan Goes to Bat." Some additional story words following the generalization are *asked, at, man, fast, and, that, grass, catch, ran,* and *can.*

RESOURCES: HOME
ACTIVITIES MASTER **1A**

NOTE: Fill in the teacher's note on the Home Activities Master before sending it home with children. See the Assignment Guide on page T250 for assigning lists of words.

INTRODUCTION page 10

Pretest Administer the pretest. Say each word, use it in the sentence provided on page T15, and then repeat the word. ACCESSING PRIOR KNOWLEDGE

Self-Check Have children check their own pretests by referring to their lists of Spelling Words. For each misspelled word on the pretest, remind children to use the **Study Steps to Learn a Word** on pages 8–9 of the Pupil's Edition. STUDENT SELF-ASSESSMENT

Introducing the Lesson Using your informal assessment and children's pretests as a guide, choose either the open sort or the closed sort as an introductory activity for the lesson. To use the open sort, copy Home Activities Master 1A in the Copying Masters section.

Open Sort: Distribute the word cards to children and have them individually or cooperatively select criteria for sorting. Ask children to read their groups of words. Have others tell how the

words in each group are alike. You may want to send home the word cards so that children can complete the Home Activities Master.

Closed Sort: Read aloud with children the lesson title and the Spelling Words on Pupil's Edition page 10.

- Write the words *pad, rat, tap,* and *pan* as headings on the board.
- As you say each of the following words, have children tell under which word to list it: *man, lad, cap,* and *hat.*
- Have children name other words for each group. List their responses under the appropriate headings. SORTING WORDS

In Summary You may want children to summarize the lesson in their own words. Point out that knowing that short *a* can be spelled with an *a* can help children spell other words.

Your Own Words You may want to have children list in their Spelling Logs other words with the short *a* vowel sound. RECOGNIZING PATTERNS

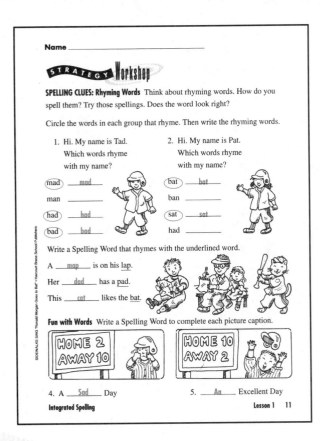

Name _____

STRATEGY Workshop

SPELLING CLUES: Rhyming Words Think about rhyming words. How do you spell them? Try those spellings. Does the word look right?

Circle the words in each group that rhyme. Then write the rhyming words.

1. Hi. My name is Tad. Which words rhyme with my name?

(mad) _mad_
man _____
(had) _had_
(bad) _bad_

2. Hi. My name is Pat. Which words rhyme with my name?

(bat) _bat_
ban _____
(sat) _sat_
had _____

Write a Spelling Word that rhymes with the underlined word.

A _map_ is on his lap.

Her _dad_ has a pad.

This _cat_ likes the bat.

Fun with Words Write a Spelling Word to complete each picture caption.

HOME 2 AWAY 10

HOME 10 AWAY 2

4. A _Sad_ Day

5. _An_ Excellent Day

Integrated Spelling

Lesson 1   11

Standardized spelling for words in English had not yet been formulated as late as the seventeenth century. According to the Oxford dictionary, the following spellings for *cat* were all in use at that time: *catt, catte, kat, katt, katte.*

STRATEGY WORKSHOP page 11

Spelling Clues: Rhyming Words

Tell children that rhyming words are often spelled alike. Ask children to name any two Spelling Words that rhyme. Write the words on the board and have a volunteer underline the letters that are the same in both words. Point out that the letter *a* stands for the short *a* sound. Ask what letter stands for the final sound. Explain that if children know how to spell a word, they can often figure out how to spell a rhyming word by changing only the first letter. Demonstrate by changing the first letter of one of the words on the board to spell another rhyming word. APPLYING SPELLING STRATEGIES

 SECOND-LANGUAGE SUPPORT Have children work with partners to find and read rhyming words for *Tad* and *Pat* on Pupil's Edition page 11. Then help children tell about the pictures to check their understanding of word meanings. USING RHYMING WORDS

 SEMI-PHONETIC SPELLERS Make a word card for *mad* and letter cards for *h, b, d,* and *s.* Have children read and spell *mad.* Then as you cover the *m* with each letter, ask children to read and spell the rhyming word.

Fun with Words

Discuss the pictures with children. Ask how the child in each picture feels. Then have children complete the activity independently.

Practice Activities

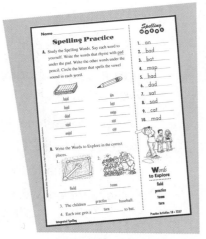

RESOURCES: PRACTICE ACTIVITIES MASTER 1B

Use as extra practice or as a homework activity.

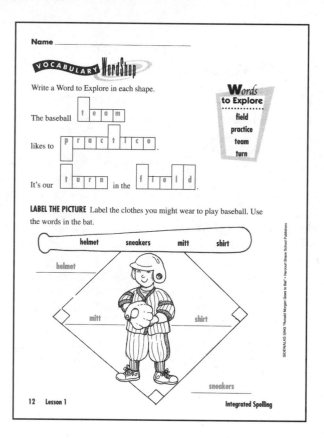

VOCABULARY WORDSHOP pages 12–13

Words to Explore Write the Words to Explore on the board: *field, practice, team, turn.* Discuss their meanings with children. Have children look at the word shapes to help them figure out which word completes each sentence.

Spelling Log Have children add the Words to Explore to their Spelling Logs.

TRANSITIONAL SPELLERS Assign the Words to Explore. As a practice activity, have children write each Word to Explore on a word card. Help them cut apart the letters of each word. Ask children to put the letters back together to spell the words.

Label the Picture Have children point to and identify their clothing. Then ask whether they would wear this clothing for other activities they do. Have them discuss what they wear when they do such things as swim, ride a bike, or play baseball.

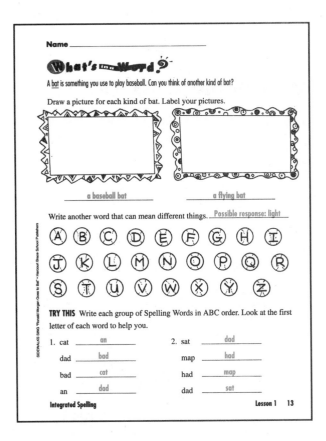

What's in a Word? Read the directions with children. Then ask them to tell about another kind of bat. If possible, display pictures of both types of bats. Encourage children to describe the pictures.

Ask children to name other words that can mean more than one thing. Write their responses on the board. Discuss the meanings. MULTIPLE-MEANING WORDS

Try This Model putting a group of words, such as *and, can, did,* and *fun,* in alphabetical order by identifying the beginning letters and pointing them out in the alphabet. USING ALPHABETICAL ORDER

 Working Together Suggest that children work in pairs. As one child says each letter in the alphabet, the other can tell which, if any, word begins with the letter.

Posttest To check children's mastery of the Spelling Words, use the context sentences on page T15 to administer the posttest.

Vocabulary Activities

Optional Writing Idea: Description Have children write a description of each type of bat. Use webs like the following to record their ideas for describing bats. Encourage children to use words from the webs in their writing.

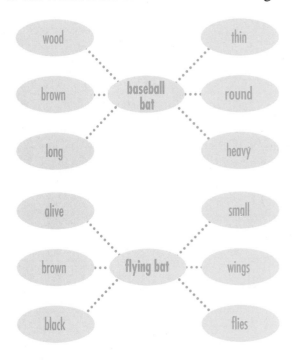

LESSON WRAP-UP

Words to Explore and Context Sentences

1. **field**   We play baseball in a **field**.
2. **practice**   I **practice** the piano so I can play better.
3. **team**   How many players are on a soccer **team**?
4. **turn**   Everyone will have a **turn** to play.

Reteach

LEARNING DIFFERENCES Help children make word cards for the Spelling Words. Then have children trace over the *a* in each word in a different color. Encourage pairs of children to work together to read and spell each word. AUDITORY/ KINESTHETIC MODALITIES

INTEGRATED CURRICULUM ACTIVITY

Language Arts

Word Hunt Write the following twenty-four words on self-stick notes and stick them in various locations in the classroom:

Organize children into four teams. Give each team one of the following "Secret Words":

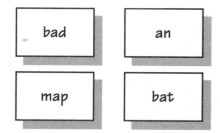

Have each team find and collect all six words that rhyme with their Secret Word. Encourage each team to use its words in a story or a poem. Ask each team to choose a Recorder to write the story or poem as the others tell it. Ask children to find and circle the short *a* words in their writing.

LESSON 2

Words with Short *e*

Objective
To spell words with short *e*

Lesson Planner
Assign words based on the developmental levels of individual children. See the Assignment Guide on page T250.

Informal Assessment
Children's writing may show that they have difficulty with short *e*.

MODEL

pen

I used a (pin) to write this letter.

Use this lesson to introduce the spelling of words with the short *e* vowel sound. Encourage children to apply what they have learned to help them spell other words in which they hear the short *e* sound. After children have completed the lesson, have them proofread their writing and correct any errors they may have made spelling words with the short *e* sound.

 SECOND-LANGUAGE SUPPORT Short vowel sounds often present the greatest difficulty for children. Many children have problems distinguishing between the sounds of short *e* and short *a*. Have them practice listening to and repeating pairs of words such as *ten, tan; pet, pat; bed, bad.*

In addition, speakers of Vietnamese, Spanish, or Tagalog may find it difficult to distinguish the sound of short *e* from the long *a* sound. These children may benefit from practice with word pairs such as *get, gate; let, late; men, mane.* COMPARING AND CONTRASTING

Pretest/Posttest Context Sentences
You may want to test Semi-Phonetic Spellers on words 1–6 only.

1. **bet**   I **bet** you will have fun.
2. **men**   I see two **men** in the car.
3. **egg**   The hen laid an **egg**.
4. **yes**   Did you say **yes** or no?
5. **ten**   A person has **ten** toes.
*6. **mess**   Let's clean up this **mess**.

7. **wet**   She got **wet** in the rain.
8. **leg**   Your knee is part of your **leg**.
9. **set**   Jamie **set** the table.
10. **yet**   Did the rain stop **yet**?

*Word appearing in "Matthew and Tilly." Some additional story words following the generalization are *them, best, when, ever,* and *well.*

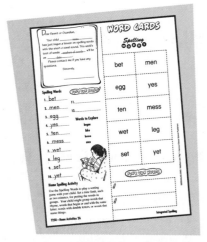

RESOURCES: HOME ACTIVITIES MASTER 2A

NOTE: Fill in the teacher's note on the Home Activities Master before sending it home with children. See the Assignment Guide on page T250 for assigning lists of words.

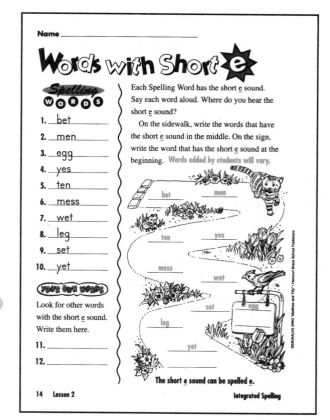

INTRODUCTION page 14

Pretest Administer the pretest. Say each word, use it in the sentence provided on page T21, and then repeat the word. ACCESSING PRIOR KNOWLEDGE

Self-Check Have children check their own pretests by referring to their lists of Spelling Words. For each misspelled word on the pretest, remind children to use the **Study Steps to Learn a Word** on pages 8–9 of the Pupil's Edition. STUDENT SELF-ASSESSMENT

Introducing the Lesson To use the open sort, copy Home Activities Master 2A in the Copying Masters section.

Open Sort: Distribute the word cards to children and have them individually or cooperatively select criteria for sorting. Then ask children to name their categories. Have others tell which words could go in each category named. You may want to send home the word cards so that children can complete the Home Activities Master.

Closed Sort: Read aloud with children the lesson title and the Spelling Words on Pupil's Edition page 14.

• Write the words *end, hen, net,* and *elk* on the board. Read the words and have children listen for the short *e* sound.
• Have children sort the words according to whether they hear the short *e* sound at the beginning or in the middle.
• Encourage children to name other words that could fit into each group. SORTING WORDS

In Summary Ask children what letter can spell the short *e* sound. *(e)* Point out that knowing this spelling for the short *e* sound can help children spell other words.

Your Own Words As children read environmental print, magazines, newspapers, or maps, have them find and list in their Spelling Logs other words with the short *e* vowel sound. RECOGNIZING PATTERNS

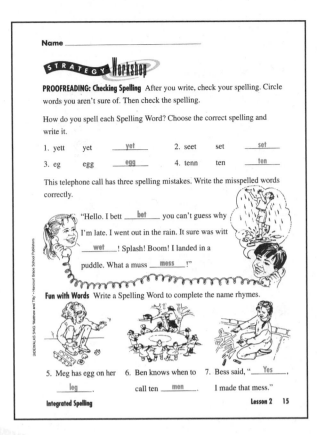

Name _____

STRATEGY Workshop

PROOFREADING: Checking Spelling After you write, check your spelling. Circle words you aren't sure of. Then check the spelling.

How do you spell each Spelling Word? Choose the correct spelling and write it.

1. yett   yet   _yet_   2. seet   set   _set_

3. eg   egg   _egg_   4. tenn   ten   _ten_

This telephone call has three spelling mistakes. Write the misspelled words correctly.

"Hello. I bett ____bet____ you can't guess why I'm late. I went out in the rain. It sure was witt ____wet____! Splash! Boom! I landed in a puddle. What a muss ____mess____!"

Fun with Words Write a Spelling Word to complete the name rhymes.

5. Meg has egg on her ____leg____.

6. Ben knows when to call ten ____men____.

7. Bess said, "____Yes____, I made that mess."

Integrated Spelling   Lesson 2   15

In a word sort, a child or group of children categorizes words written on cards by physically grouping them. The features a word may have in common with others can be shared letters, similarities in letter sounds, structural elements, grammatical functions, or related meaning.
(Jean Wallace Gillet and M. Jane Kita)

STRATEGY WORKSHOP page 15

Proofreading: Checking Spelling Suggest that after children circle a word whose spelling they are unsure of, they might try writing the word in different ways. Explain that children should use the spelling that looks correct, ask someone who knows the correct spelling, or look up the word in a dictionary. APPLYING SPELLING STRATEGIES

 SECOND-LANGUAGE SUPPORT Have children work in pairs. Suggest that they use paper cups for "telephones." Have them take turns repeating the conversation shown in the middle of Pupil's Edition page 15. Encourage children to continue the conversation by adding other things the children pictured might say. ROLE-PLAYING

 SEMI-PHONETIC SPELLERS Help children copy their Spelling Words onto a strip of paper. Have them use the strip as they complete Pupil's Edition page 15. They can find the correctly spelled word on their strip, compare that word to those on the page, and then copy the correctly spelled word.

Fun with Words Write the names *Meg, Ben,* and *Bess* on the board. As you point to each word, have children give rhyming words for it. Then have children complete the activity independently. Ask them to name all the rhyming words in each sentence.

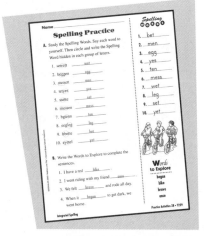

RESOURCES: PRACTICE ACTIVITIES MASTER 2B

Use as extra practice or as a homework activity.

VOCABULARY WORDSHOP pages 16–17

Words to Explore Write the Words to Explore on the board: *began, bike, brave, once.* Discuss their meanings with children. Then invite children to discuss times when they have been brave or adventures they may have had on a bike. Encourage them to use the Words to Explore.

Spelling Log Have children add the Words to Explore to their Spelling Logs.

TRANSITIONAL SPELLERS Assign the Words to Explore. As a practice activity, provide alphabet noodles for children. Have them glue the noodles onto a sheet of paper to spell each Word to Explore. Next to each word, have children use it in a sentence.

What's in a Word? Explain to children that many words in English come from words in other languages. Ask why the word *friend* may have come from a word that means "to love." Then have children tell some reasons they love having friends. WORD ORIGINS

Synonyms Remind children that a synonym is a word with almost the same meaning as another word. Then make a word web for *friend.* Write children's synonyms for *friend* in the web. Children can use these synonyms or ones of their own to write under the pictures. USING SYNONYMS

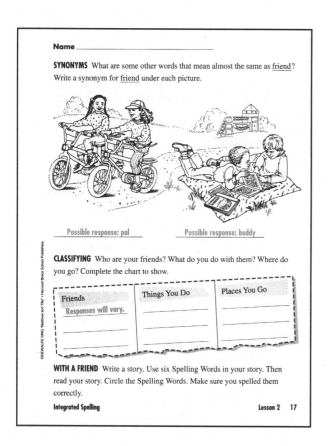

Name _____

SYNONYMS What are some other words that mean almost the same as <u>friend</u>? Write a synonym for <u>friend</u> under each picture.

Possible response: pal   Possible response: buddy

CLASSIFYING Who are your friends? What do you do with them? Where do you go? Complete the chart to show.

Friends	Things You Do	Places You Go
Responses will vary.		

WITH A FRIEND Write a story. Use six Spelling Words in your story. Then read your story. Circle the Spelling Words. Make sure you spelled them correctly.

Integrated Spelling   Lesson 2   17

Classifying Ask children to name things that could go under each heading. List their responses on the board. CLASSIFYING IDEAS

 Working Together Children could work in groups of three to complete the chart. Each group member can take a turn being the Recorder for a column of the chart.

With a Friend Suggest that children begin by planning what the story will be about and listing the Spelling Words they will use. Children may want to take turns being the Storyteller and the Recorder. After children have written their stories, have them circle the Spelling Words. USING SPELLING STRATEGIES

Posttest To check children's mastery of the Spelling Words, use the context sentences on page T21 to administer the posttest.

Optional Writing Idea: Rhyming Poem Have children use rhyming Spelling Words, or words that rhyme with the Spelling Words, to write a rhyming poem. You may want to suggest that children group rhyming words together as a prewriting activity.

bet	men	egg	yes
wet	ten	leg	mess
let	hen	beg	less
set	pen	peg	
yet	then		
get			
jet			
net			
pet			

Vocabulary Activities

LESSON WRAP-UP

Words to Explore and Context Sentences

1. **began**   He opened the book and **began** to read.
2. **bike**   You can ride your **bike** on the path.
3. **brave**   Firefighters must be very **brave**.
4. **once**   I have heard this story **once** before.

Reteach

 LEARNING DIFFERENCES Make two sets of word cards for the Spelling Words. Omit the letter *e* in one set and the final or double consonant in the other set. Have volunteers write the missing letters on the cards as you say the words aloud. Then have children take turns picking cards and reading aloud the words. AUDITORY/KINESTHETIC MODALITIES

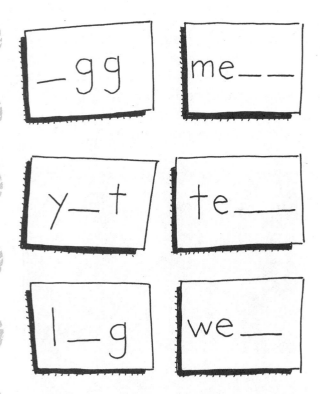

INTEGRATED CURRICULUM ACTIVITIES

Language Arts

Quick Skits Write the Spelling Words on slips of paper, fold them, and place them in a box or other container. Have children form small groups. Have each group pick at random two words from the box. Set a time limit, such as two minutes, during which the groups can create brief skits using the two Spelling Words they picked. When the time is up, groups take turns presenting their quick skits.

Social Studies

Famous People Have children name *ten* famous women or *men*. Encourage them to tell why each person became well-known.

Words with Short *i*

Objective
To spell words with short *i*

Lesson Planner
Assign words based on the developmental levels of individual children. See the Assignment Guide on page T250.

Informal Assessment
Children's writing may show that they have difficulty with short *i*.

 MODEL

fit

This hat doesn't ⟨fet⟩ me.

Use this lesson to introduce the spelling of words with the short *i* vowel sound. Encourage children to apply what they have learned to help them spell other words in which they hear the short *i* sound. After children have completed the lesson, have them proofread their writing and correct any errors they may have made spelling words with the short *i* sound.

 SECOND-LANGUAGE SUPPORT Spanish-speaking children often replace the short *i* vowel sound with the long *e* sound. Have them practice listening to and pronouncing word pairs such as *bit, beet; dip, deep; sit, seat.* Children who speak Chinese, Vietnamese, or Tagalog may have similar difficulties and can benefit from the same kind of practice. COMPARING AND CONTRASTING

Pretest/Posttest Context Sentences
You may want to test Semi-Phonetic Spellers on words 1–6 only.

1. **pin**   There is a **pin** in the sewing box.
2. **sit**   Which chair will you **sit** in?
*3. **if**   We'll be on time **if** we hurry.
*4. **fix**   She tried to **fix** the broken toy.
5. **hid**   The cat **hid** inside the box.
6. **him**   Dad took me with **him**.

7. **hill**   The ball rolled down the **hill**.
8. **six**   An ant has **six** legs.
9. **win**   Which team will **win** the game?
10. **bit**   There's only a little **bit** left.

*Words appearing in "Arthur's Pet Business." Some additional story words following the generalization are *big, will, is, rid, it, his, miss, did, in,* and *sick.*

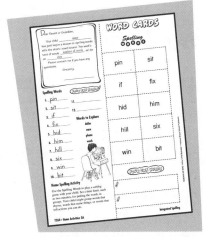

RESOURCES: HOME ACTIVITIES MASTER **3A**

NOTE: Fill in the teacher's note on the Home Activities Master before sending it home with children. See the Assignment Guide on page T250 for assigning lists of words.

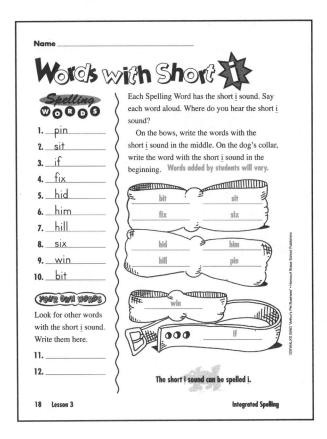

Name _____

Words with Short i

Spelling WORDS

1. pin
2. sit
3. if
4. fix
5. hid
6. him
7. hill
8. six
9. win
10. bit

YOUR OWN WORDS
Look for other words with the short i sound. Write them here.

11. _____
12. _____

Each Spelling Word has the short i sound. Say each word aloud. Where do you hear the short i sound?

On the bows, write the words with the short i sound in the middle. On the dog's collar, write the word with the short i sound in the beginning. *Words added by students will vary.*

| bit | sit |
| fix | six |

| hid | him |
| hill | pin |

| win |
| if |

The short i sound can be spelled i.

18   Lesson 3

Integrated Spelling

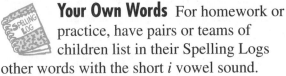

- -

INTRODUCTION page 18

Pretest Administer the pretest. Say each word, use it in the sentence provided on page T27, and then repeat the word. ACCESSING PRIOR KNOWLEDGE

Self-Check Have children check their own pretests by referring to their lists of Spelling Words. For each misspelled word on the pretest, remind children to use the **Study Steps to Learn a Word** on pages 8–9 of the Pupil's Edition. STUDENT SELF-ASSESSMENT

Introducing the Lesson To use the open sort, copy Home Activities Master 3A in the Copying Masters section.

Open Sort: Distribute the word cards to children and have them individually or cooperatively select criteria for sorting. As children hold up and read a word, have others tell a word that could be grouped with it and why. You may want to send home the word cards so that children can complete the Home Activities Master.

Closed Sort: Read aloud with children the lesson title and the Spelling Words on Pupil's Edition page 18.
- Write the words *in* and *Tim* as column heads on the board. Read the words. Have children tell where they hear the short *i* sound. (beginning; middle)
- As you say each of the following words, ask children to tell under which column you should write it: *it, mix, fin, is,* and *bit.*
- Ask children to name other words for each column. SORTING WORDS

In Summary You may want children to summarize the lesson in their own words. Point out that knowing how to spell the short *i* sound can help children spell many words.

Your Own Words For homework or practice, have pairs or teams of children list in their Spelling Logs other words with the short *i* vowel sound. RECOGNIZING PATTERNS

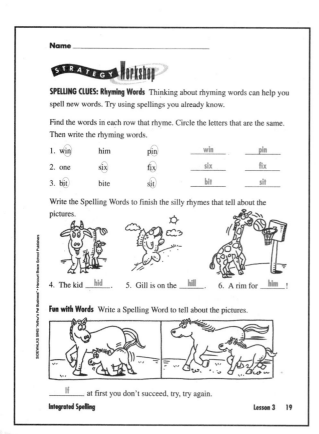

The English language, as written and spoken in the United States, is characterized by a consistent system of spelling, but not a consistent system of pronunciation. Many speakers, for example, pronounce *pen* and *pin* with distinctly different vowel sounds. In some parts of the United States, however, the two words are homophones.

STRATEGY WORKSHOP page 19

Spelling Clues: Rhyming Words Remind children that rhyming words are often spelled with the same ending letters. Explain that children can use the spelling of words they already know to help them figure out how to spell rhyming words. APPLYING SPELLING STRATEGIES

 SECOND-LANGUAGE SUPPORT Discuss the art on Pupil's Edition page 19. Make sure children understand that a *kid* is a baby goat, that a *gill* is part of a fish, and that a *rim* is often round and made of metal or tin. Have children name rhyming words for *kid*, *gill*, and *rim*. USING RHYMING WORDS

SEMI-PHONETIC SPELLERS Remind children that all the Spelling Words have an *i* in them. Then have children work in pairs to spell aloud and to write the words to complete the page.

Fun with Words Discuss the illustrations. Then give examples to demonstrate the meaning of *succeed*. After children have completed the activity, they might enjoy drawing their own pictures for the sentence.

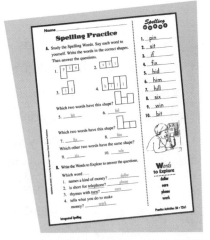

RESOURCES: PRACTICE ACTIVITIES MASTER 3B

Use as extra practice or as a homework activity.

VOCABULARY WORDSHOP pages 20–21

Words to Explore Write the Words to Explore on the board: *dollar, earn, phone, work.* Discuss their meanings with children. Then discuss the chart. Ask questions such as the following: *What happened on Wednesday of Week 1? On what day did this person earn three dollars? Which week was that?*

Spelling Log Have children add the Words to Explore to their Spelling Logs.

TRANSITIONAL SPELLERS Assign the Words to Explore. As a practice activity, have children work in pairs to play a game. One child thinks of a Word to Explore and, on a sheet of paper, makes a blank for each letter in the word. The other guesses letters. The first writes correct letters where they belong in the word. When all the letters have been added, children should read the word and use it in a sentence.

What's in a Word? Ask what chores, or odd jobs, children do around the house. List their responses on the board. Then discuss the responses, which might include vacuuming, feeding pets, or making beds. Ask why these might be called "odd jobs." UNDERSTANDING IDIOMS

Working Together Children can work in pairs to complete their charts for the What's in a Word? activity. Encourage partners to check that all their words are spelled correctly.

Vocabulary Activities

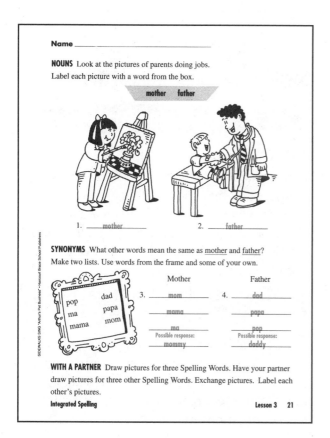

Name _____

NOUNS Look at the pictures of parents doing jobs. Label each picture with a word from the box.

mother   father

1. _____mother_____   2. _____father_____

SYNONYMS What other words mean the same as <u>mother</u> and <u>father</u>? Make two lists. Use words from the frame and some of your own.

pop   dad
ma   papa
mama   mom

Mother	Father
3. _____mom_____	4. _____dad_____
_____mama_____	_____papa_____
_____ma_____	_____pop_____
Possible response:	Possible response:
_____mommy_____	_____daddy_____

WITH A PARTNER Draw pictures for three Spelling Words. Have your partner draw pictures for three other Spelling Words. Exchange pictures. Label each other's pictures.

Integrated Spelling   Lesson 3   21

Nouns Discuss the picture. Ask what job each person is doing and what each person would be called. (artist, doctor) Then have children discuss other jobs people do and what the people who do them are called. WORD MEANINGS

Synonyms Ask children to name other words for *mother* and for *father.* List their responses on the board in two columns. Explain that the words in one column are synonyms for *mother* and the words in the other are synonyms for *father.* UNDERSTANDING SYNONYMS

With a Partner Draw a pin on the board and ask a volunteer to label it with a Spelling Word. Then draw a person winning a race and have it labeled. Ask children to complete the activity by drawing and labeling pictures. WORD MEANINGS

Posttest To check children's mastery of the Spelling Words, use the context sentences on page T27 to administer the posttest.

Optional Writing Idea: Personal Story
Have children write about a job in school or at home. Help children make a chart in which they can organize their ideas before they write.

What	When	Where
feeding fish	last week	at home
glasses fell in fish tank		

Encourage children to illustrate their stories and to share the stories by reading them aloud.

Vocabulary Activities   Lesson 3   T31

LESSON WRAP-UP

Words to Explore and Context Sentences

1. **dollar** He gave me ten dimes for my **dollar.**
2. **earn** My sister washes cars to **earn** money.
3. **phone** I called my friend on the **phone.**
4. **work** I like to do my **work.**

Reteach

LEARNING DIFFERENCES Have children write their Spelling Words with yarn. Children can glue yarn onto a sheet of paper in the shape of each letter to spell each word. Then have children trace the letters with their fingers as they spell the words aloud. VISUAL/KINESTHETIC MODALITIES

INTEGRATED CURRICULUM ACTIVITIES

Language Arts

Six to Win Organize children into teams of two or three. Have each team find and list six words, other than the Spelling Words, that have a short *i* vowel sound. The first team to find six short *i* words wins. After the game, list all the words to see how many different words were found.

Math

Pet Problems Have children pretend they will *sit* for *six* pets. Help them list each pet and the amount of money they will earn for taking care of it. Then encourage children to ask and answer questions like these:

- How much money will I earn altogether?
- If I need to earn $6.00, which two pets must I take care of?

Words with Short *o*

Objective
To spell words with short *o*

Lesson Planner
Assign words based on the developmental levels of individual children. See the Assignment Guide on page T250.

Informal Assessment
Children's writing may show that they have difficulty with short *o*.

MODEL

mop
Use the (map) to wash the floor.

Use this lesson to introduce the spelling of words with the short *o* vowel sound. Encourage children to apply what they have learned to help them spell other words in which they hear the short *o* sound. After children have completed the lesson, have them proofread their writing and correct any errors they may have made spelling words with the short *o* sound.

SECOND-LANGUAGE SUPPORT Children who speak Spanish, Chinese, Vietnamese, Tagalog, or Thai may have difficulty distinguishing between the short *o* and the short *u* vowel sounds. Provide opportunities for them to hear and identify the difference between the vowel sounds in words such as *hot, hut; not, nut;* and *cot, cut.* COMPARING AND CONTRASTING

Pretest/Posttest Context Sentences
You may want to test Semi-Phonetic Spellers on words 1–6 only.

*1.	**top**	Can you reach the **top** shelf?
*2.	**lot**	We'll have a **lot** of fun.
3.	**mom**	I asked my **mom** to help me.
*4.	**doll**	We bought a **doll** and a teddy bear.
*5.	**rock**	Will you **rock** the baby?
*6.	**box**	Put the puzzle pieces in the **box.**
7.	**stop**	The dog would not **stop** barking.
8.	**pond**	Fish and frogs live in this **pond.**
9.	**job**	Luis did a good **job** cleaning up.
10.	**fox**	A **fox** has a bushy tail.

*Words appearing in "I Have a Sister—My Sister Is Deaf." Some additional story words following the generalization are *on, not, clock,* and *dog.*

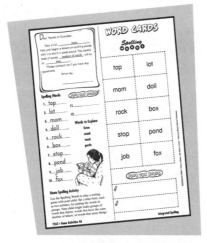

RESOURCES: HOME ACTIVITIES MASTER 4A

NOTE: Fill in the teacher's note on the Home Activities Master before sending it home with children. See the Assignment Guide on page T250 for assigning lists of words.

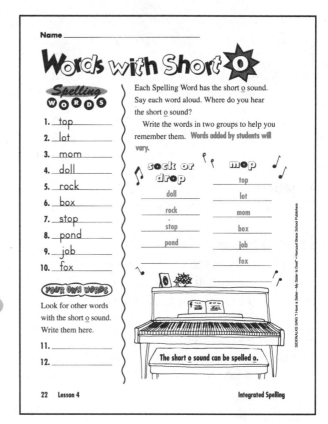

INTRODUCTION page 22

Pretest Administer the pretest. Say each word, use it in the sentence provided on page T33, and then repeat the word. ACCESSING PRIOR KNOWLEDGE

Self-Check Have children check their own pretests by referring to their list of Spelling Words. For each misspelled word on the pretest, remind children to use the **Study Steps to Learn a Word** on pages 8–9 of the Pupil's Edition. STUDENT SELF-ASSESSMENT

Introducing the Lesson To use the open sort, copy Home Activities Master 4A in the Copying Masters section.

Open Sort: Distribute word cards to children and have them individually or cooperatively select criteria for sorting. Ask children to read their groups of words and tell how the words are alike. You may want to send home the word cards so that children can complete the Home Activities Master.

Closed Sort: Read aloud with children the lesson title and the Spelling Words on Pupil's Edition page 22.
- Write the words *hop, sock, dot,* and *shop* on the board.
- Have children tell which words can be grouped together because they have the CVC pattern. List *hop* and *dot.*
- Write *sock* and *shop* in another list.
- Have children name other short *o* words for each group. SORTING WORDS

In Summary You may want children to summarize the lesson in their own words. Point out that the CVC pattern can be used to help them spell other words.

Your Own Words For homework or practice, you may want to have pairs or teams of children list in their Spelling Logs other words with the short *o* sound. RECOGNIZING PATTERNS

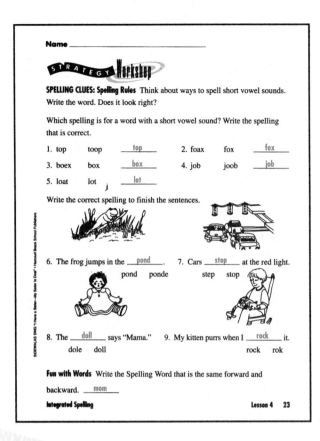

Name _____

STRATEGY Workshop

SPELLING CLUES: Spelling Rules Think about ways to spell short vowel sounds. Write the word. Does it look right?

Which spelling is for a word with a short vowel sound? Write the spelling that is correct.

1. top   toop   _top_   2. foax   fox   _fox_
3. boex   box   _box_   4. job   joob   _job_
5. loat   lot   _lot_

Write the correct spelling to finish the sentences.

6. The frog jumps in the _pond_.   7. Cars _stop_ at the red light.
   pond   ponde   step   stop

8. The _doll_ says "Mama."   9. My kitten purrs when I _rock_ it.
   dole   doll   rock   rok

Fun with Words Write the Spelling Word that is the same forward and backward. _mom_

Integrated Spelling   Lesson 4   23

A more sensible approach to the teaching of spelling should be based on two main aspects: learning about the written language and learning to use the strategies that competent spellers use.
(Diane Snowball)

STRATEGY WORKSHOP page 23

Spelling Clues: Spelling Rules
Point out that many short vowel words have a CVC pattern. Use the word *top* as an example. Then ask the following questions:

- How many vowel letters usually stand for a short vowel sound? (one)
- Do words with short vowel sounds usually end with *e*? (no)
- What letter usually stands for the short *o* sound? *(o)*

APPLYING SPELLING STRATEGIES

 SECOND-LANGUAGE SUPPORT Discuss the art on Pupil's Edition page 23. Check children's understanding of the words *frog, pond, stop, red light*, and *doll*. Make sure children understand that *rock* can mean "a stone" or "to move gently back and forth." Have them demonstrate *rock* by rocking something in their arms. WORD MEANINGS

 SEMI-PHONETIC SPELLERS Write the following on the board:

_ o _
_ _ o _
_ o _ _

Explain that the lines stand for consonants. Have children use these patterns of short vowel words to help them as they complete the page.

Fun with Words
Write the word *dad* on the board. Then as you spell it backward, write the letters. Point out that *dad* is spelled the same backward and forward.

RESOURCES: PRACTICE ACTIVITIES MASTER 4B

Use as extra practice or as a homework activity.

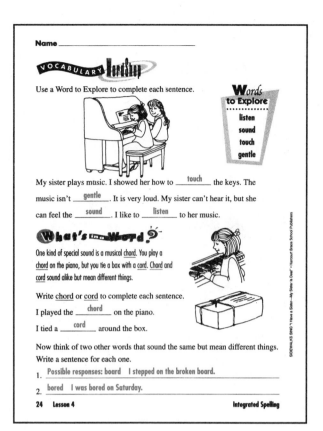

VOCABULARY WORDSHOP pages 24–25

Words to Explore Write the Words to Explore on the board: *listen, sound, touch, gentle.* Discuss their meanings with children. Then ask what the girls in the picture are doing. Have children name words they think of when they think about piano music. Then have them use the Words to Explore to complete the sentences about the picture.

Spelling Log Have children add the Words to Explore to their Spelling Logs.

TRANSITIONAL SPELLERS Assign the Words to Explore. As a practice activity, have children work in pairs to take turns giving clues for the Words to Explore and spelling the answers.

What's in a Word? Write *chord* and *cord* on the board. Explain that the words sound the same but are spelled differently and have different meanings. Discuss the meanings. Then have children name other words that sound the same but are spelled differently. List their responses, which might include *I* and *eye, blue* and *blew,* or *here* and *hear.* IDENTIFYING HOMOPHONES

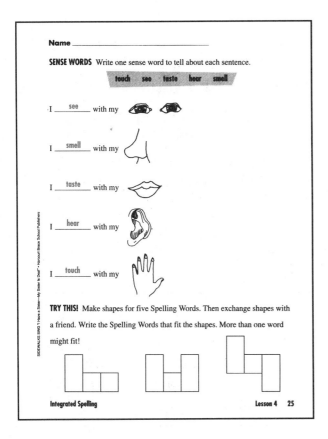

Sense Words Have children name the five senses (seeing, hearing, tasting, touching, smelling) and tell which part of the body goes with each. Then have them name other words they think of when they think of each sense. USING DESCRIBING WORDS

Try This! Draw a Spelling-Word shape on the board. Have children identify several lowercase letters that could fit each letter shape. Then ask a volunteer to write a Spelling Word that fits in the shape. Have children complete the activity by making their own shapes. APPLYING SPELLING STRATEGIES

 Working Together Have children work in groups of five. Each group member should make a different word shape and find the Spelling Words that have that shape. Then group members can share their results.

Posttest To check children's mastery of the Spelling Words, use the context sentences on page T33 to administer the posttest.

Optional Writing Idea: Description Have children write a description of something, such as a favorite food. Make sure that they use describing words for all five senses in their writing. Help children make a chart of sense words they might use in their writing. Point out that some words can be used to describe more than one sense. Then you may want to have children share their descriptions in small groups.

See	Hear	Touch	Smell	Taste
red shiny	crunchy when I bite it	smooth	not much smell sweet	sweet juicy

LESSON WRAP-UP

Words to Explore and Context Sentences

1. **listen** Did you **listen** to the new tape?
2. **sound** I hear the **sound** of rain on the roof.
3. **touch** Your fingers feel cold when you **touch** ice.
4. **gentle** Be **gentle** with the kitten.

Reteach

 LEARNING DIFFERENCES Say each Spelling Word aloud, emphasizing the vowel sound. Then dictate the spelling as children write the word in large letters. Next, spell the word aloud with children as they write it again. Have children trace the word for additional reinforcement. Then ask children to write the word from memory. AUDITORY/ KINESTHETIC MODALITIES

INTEGRATED CURRICULUM ACTIVITY

Language Arts

Fox in a Box Have children prepare to play this game by making fourteen word cards, as shown:

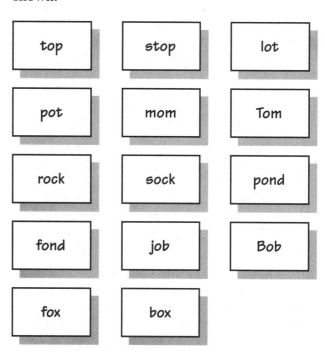

Children can play this game in groups of two to four. Mix up the cards and place them face down in a pile. The first player takes the top card and then turns over cards from the pile until he or she finds the card that rhymes with it. The words that rhyme are set aside. The other cards are returned to the pile and mixed again. Then the second player takes the top card and turns over cards until he or she finds the matching card, and so on. The player who finds the match *fox/box* calls out, "Fox in a box!" This child wins the game.

Objectives

To review spelling patterns and strategies in Lessons 1–4; to give children the opportunity to recognize and use these spelling patterns and the Spelling Words in their writing

Review of Spelling Strategies

Review with children the spelling strategies presented in Lessons 1–4.

USING RHYMING WORDS Write the word *ten* on the board and have children read it aloud. Remind children that rhyming words end with the same sounds but have different beginning sounds. Ask children to spell aloud words that rhyme with *ten*. Write their responses on the board under *ten*. Then work with children to circle the words on the board that rhyme with *ten* and are spelled correctly.

CHECKING SPELLING Write on the board the sentence *Are you done yat?* Ask children to read the sentence and identify the misspelled word. Have a volunteer circle the word and spell it correctly. Then ask children how they can check the spelling to see if it is right. (Ask someone who knows the correct spelling or look it up in a dictionary.) Model how to look up *yet* in a dictionary.

USING SPELLING RULES Write the words *top* and *toop* on the board. Have children look at the two spellings, and ask volunteers to explain how they can use the rules for spelling short vowel sounds to decide which spelling is correct for the word *top*. Remind children that many short vowel words have a CVC pattern. Write *C* under the consonants and *V* under the vowels in *top* and *toop*. Point out that *t-o-p* follows the CVC pattern and is the correct spelling of the word *top*.

Unit 1 Words

The following words from Unit 1 are reviewed in this lesson:

Lesson 1 Words with Short *a:* bad, dad, had, mad

Lesson 2 Words with Short *e:* leg, men, wet

Lesson 3 Words with Short *i:* sit, six, win

Lesson 4 Words with Short *o:* job, lot, mom, stop, top

❝Word families are, in effect, spelling patterns. Children who learn many common word families also learn something more important—to look carefully at the spelling pattern of a new word and search through the words they already know for words with the same spelling pattern. **❞**

(Patricia M. Cunningham)

UNIT REVIEW

Name _____

Practice Test

A. Read each pair of sentences. Circle the underlined word that is spelled correctly in the sentence.

1. My (dad) took me to a baseball game.
   My did took me to a baseball game.

2. The mon on the team wore striped pants.
   The (men) on the team wore striped pants.

3. We hoped our team would wen.
   We hoped our team would (win).

4. Being a baseball player is a great jab.
   Being a baseball player is a great (job).

5. One player got (mad) when he struck out.
   One player got med when he struck out.

6. Another player fell and hurt his lag.
   Another player fell and hurt his (leg).

7. The best player batted in sox runs.
   The best player batted in (six) runs.

26   Lesson 5   Integrated Spelling

PRACTICE TEST pages 26–27

Options for Administering the Practice Test

The Practice Test provides an opportunity to review Spelling Words and spelling generalizations.

Option 1: Have children review their **Words to Study** in the Spelling Log for Unit 1. If they need extra help, review the spelling generalizations on Pupil's Edition pages 10, 14, 18, and 22. Then administer both parts of the Practice Test on Pupil's Edition pages 26–27 to determine whether children have mastered the spelling generalizations.

Option 2: Administer Part A of the Practice Test, which is on Pupil's Edition page 26, as a pretest. Have children check their pretests and study the words they misspelled. On another day, administer Part B of the Practice Test, which is on Pupil's Edition page 27, as a posttest.

Options for Evaluation

• Have children check their own Practice Tests by referring to their lists of Spelling Words. The list on page T39 provides references to the lessons where children will find the words on the Practice Test.

• You may prefer to assign partners and have them check each other's Practice Tests. Have children use their own lists of Spelling Words to check their partners' tests.

For each word misspelled on the Practice Test, remind children to follow the **Study Steps to Learn a Word** on pages 8–9 of the Pupil's Edition. Be sure to have them write the words they missed in the Unit 1 **Words to Study** box in the Spelling Log. STUDENT SELF-ASSESSMENT

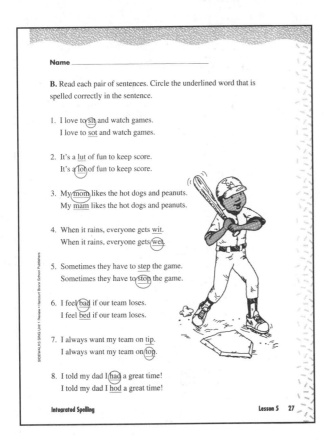

Name _____

B. Read each pair of sentences. Circle the underlined word that is spelled correctly in the sentence.

1. I love to sit and watch games.
   I love to sot and watch games.

2. It's a lut of fun to keep score.
   It's a lot of fun to keep score.

3. My mom likes the hot dogs and peanuts.
   My mam likes the hot dogs and peanuts.

4. When it rains, everyone gets wit.
   When it rains, everyone gets wet.

5. Sometimes they have to step the game.
   Sometimes they have to stop the game.

6. I feel bad if our team loses.
   I feel bed if our team loses.

7. I always want my team on tip.
   I always want my team on top.

8. I told my dad I had a great time!
   I told my dad I hod a great time!

Integrated Spelling   Lesson 5   27

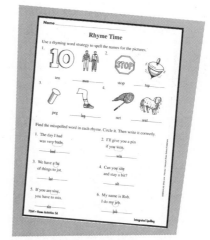

RESOURCES: HOME ACTIVITIES MASTER 5A

Use as an extra activity to reinforce spelling strategies.

Review of Spelling Strategies Review with children the spelling strategies discussed on pages 176–177 of the Pupil's Edition. Then distribute Home Activities Master 5A.

The Reteach section of each Lesson Wrap-Up provides suggestions for helping children who are still having difficulty with the concepts taught in that lesson.

RESOURCES: PRACTICE ACTIVITIES MASTER 5B

Use as an extra activity to provide children with an opportunity to combine spelling and writing.

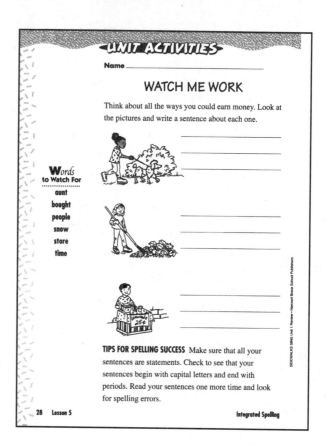

UNIT 1 ACTIVITIES pages 28–29

Activities on pages 28 and 29 of the Pupil's Edition emphasize writing (Watch Me Work), reading (Children in Books), and word play (Word Doodles). The **Tips for Spelling Success** point out the importance of standard spelling and give children hints for proofreading and for applying spelling strategies.

Watch Me Work Read the directions with children. Ask what they could do to earn money. Then discuss the pictures and ask what those children are doing to earn money. Have children complete the activity. Encourage them to share and discuss their sentences and the pictures.

Have children read aloud the **Tips for Spelling Success.** Then point out the **Words to Watch For.** These are words children often use in writing. Explain that children can use the list to help them spell these words correctly. When children proofread their work, provide them

with the checklist below or with the proofreading checklist on page 175 of the Pupil's Edition. **WRITING/PROOFREADING**

Proofreading Checklist

✔ Did I spell words correctly?
✔ Did I write sentences that tell complete thoughts?
✔ Did I begin each sentence with a capital letter?
✔ Did I end each sentence with the correct end mark?

 If children need help with writing sentences about the pictures, refer them to pages 10–11 of the *Language Handbook.*

Children in Books Read the directions with children. Then have children name story characters they have read about. List the characters' names on the board. Point out that children should choose two characters and make a list for each one. Allow time for children to share and discuss their lists.

Have children read the **Tips for Spelling Success** and encourage them to proofread their work. COMPARING AND CONTRASTING/ PROOFREADING

Word Doodles Write the word *tin* on the board. Tell children they will change the vowel in *tin* to make a word that names a number. Have children name the number *(ten)* and spell *ten* as you write it on the board. Then have children complete the activity individually or in pairs.

Read the **Tips for Spelling Success.** Remind children that many words with short vowels follow the CVC pattern. Encourage children to use this information to help them complete the activity. LANGUAGE PLAY

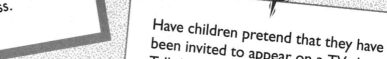

Have children use the review words listed on page T39 to play a guessing game. Write the words on slips of paper and place them in a bag. Have children take turns picking a slip of paper and acting out the meaning of the word for others to guess.

Have children pretend that they have been invited to appear on a TV show. Tell them they are going to explain to children in the TV audience how to use a rhyming-words strategy to help them spell words. Suggest to children that they write on the board or draw pictures to help them demonstrate the strategy.

For children who need a reteaching activity, have them write each review word listed on page T39 on a word card. Then have children sort the cards into four groups according to the vowel sound in each word. Ask children to identify the short vowel sound in each group.

Children may enjoy using the review words listed on page T39 to make up their own Word Doodles like those on page 29 of the Pupil's Edition.

LESSON 6

Words with Short *u*

Objective
To spell words with short *u*

Lesson Planner
Assign words based on the developmental levels of individual children. See the Assignment Guide on page T250.

Informal Assessment
Children's writing may show that they have difficulty spelling words with the short *u* sound.

MODEL

> nuts
> Do squirrels eat (nots)?

Use this lesson to introduce the spelling of words with the short *u* vowel sound. Encourage children to apply what they have learned to help them spell other words in which they hear the short *u* sound. After children have completed the lesson, have them proofread their writing and correct any errors they may have made spelling words with the short *u* sound.

 SECOND-LANGUAGE SUPPORT There are many languages in which the short *u* sound does not exist. Children may have difficulty differentiating this sound from short *a* and short *e*. Give children practice listening to and pronouncing groups of words such as *nut, nap, net; run, ran, red;* and *bud, bad, bed.*

In addition, children whose primary language is Spanish, Chinese, Vietnamese, Tagalog, or Thai may confuse the short *u* and short *o* sounds. Have them listen to and repeat word pairs such as *cut, cot; nut, not;* and *pup, pop.* COMPARING AND CONTRASTING

Pretest/Posttest Context Sentences
You may want to test Semi-Phonetic Spellers on words 1–6 only.

1. **us**   They played tag with **us.**
2. **cup**   I would like a **cup** of milk.
3. **dug**   Ben **dug** a deep hole.
4. **much** She ate too **much** food.
5. **duck** The **duck** swam on the pond.
6. **mud**   My dog digs in the **mud.**

7. **bus**   I take a **bus** to school.
8. **cut**   He **cut** the paper in half.
*9. **must** We **must** be home before dark.
*10. **jump** How far can you **jump**?

*Words appearing in "The Wolf's Chicken Stew." Some additional story words following the generalization are just, suddenly, uncle, but, shucks, hundred, *and* scrumptious.

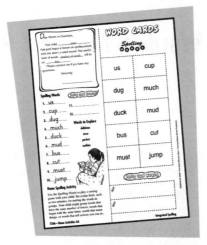

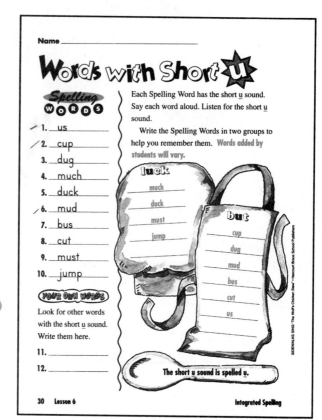

**RESOURCES: HOME
ACTIVITIES MASTER** 6A

NOTE: Fill in the teacher's note on the Home
Activities Master before sending it home with
children. See the Assignment Guide on
page T250 for assigning lists of words.

INTRODUCTION page 30

Pretest Administer the pretest. Say each
word, use it in the sentence provided on page
T45, and then repeat the word. ACCESSING
PRIOR KNOWLEDGE

Self-Check Have children check their
own pretests by referring to their list of
Spelling Words. For each misspelled word on
the pretest, remind children to use the **Study
Steps to Learn a Word** on pages 8–9 of the
Pupil's Edition. STUDENT SELF-ASSESSMENT

Introducing the Lesson To use the open sort,
copy Home Activities Master 6A in the
Copying Masters section.
Open Sort: Distribute word cards to children and
have them individually or cooperatively select
criteria for sorting. Ask children to read their
groups of words and tell how the words are
alike. You may want to send home the word
cards so that children can complete the Home
Activities Master.

Closed Sort: Read aloud with children the lesson
title and the Spelling Words on Pupil's Edition
page 30.
- Write the words *hug* and *pup* on the board.
  Say the words. Point out that both words
  have the short *u* sound and the CVC pattern.
  Have children name other short *u* words that
  would fit in this group.
- Write the words *up, luck, dust,* and *lump* on
  the board. Say the words and have children
  listen for the short *u* sound. Ask children
  which three could be grouped together
  because they follow the CVCC pattern.
  SORTING WORDS

In Summary Ask children to tell one way they
can spell the short *u* sound. *(u)* Point out that
knowing how to spell the short *u* vowel sound
can help them spell many words.

Your Own Words As children view
movies, videos, or television shows,
have them look for and list in their
Spelling Logs other words with the short *u*
vowel sound. RECOGNIZING PATTERNS

Name _____

STRATEGY Workshop

SPELLING CLUES: Sounds and Letters Say the word. Listen for the vowel sound. Did you spell the sound correctly?

Change the vowel to <u>u</u> in each word.
Write the Spelling Word.

1. cot ___cut___ 2. is ___us___
3. dog ___dug___ 4. mast ___must___

Answer the riddles. Change the vowels to make Spelling Words.

5. I can fly.
   I can swim.
   I am a de<u>c</u>k. ___duck___

6. I'm dirt when I'm dry.
   When I'm wet, I'm <u>m</u>ad. ___mud___

7. I hold water.
   You drink from me.
   I'm a cap. ___cup___

Fun with Words Do the math. Write a Spelling Word.

8. j + u t + m p − t = ___jump___
9. a b − a + u s = ___bus___
10. s + m u + c − s + h = ___much___

Integrated Spelling   Lesson 6   31

STRATEGY WORKSHOP page 31

Spelling Clues: Sounds and Letters
Remind children that when they spell a word, they should listen for the letter sounds and then write the letters that stand for the sounds. Slowly say *cut.* Have children tell what letter stands for each sound they hear. Write the letters to spell the word. If children say the wrong vowel, have them listen again for the short *u* sound. APPLYING SPELLING STRATEGIES

SECOND-LANGUAGE SUPPORT Review the meanings of *deck, duck, mad, mud, cap,* and *cup.* Then have children tell which words have the short *u* sound. Ask them to draw pictures for the words *duck, mud,* and *cup* and to label the pictures with the correct words. WORD MEANINGS

SEMI-PHONETIC SPELLERS Write *cot* on a word card. Make a letter card for *u.* Have children put the *u* over the *o* to get *cut.* Ask them to say and then spell *cut.* Follow a similar procedure for other words on Pupil's Edition page 31.

Fun with Words
Write the following on the board:

$$c + up − p + t =$$

Then show children how to solve the equation to get the word *cut.* Encourage children to work in pairs to complete the activity.

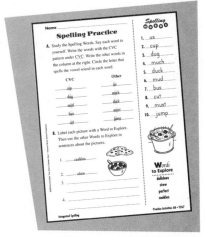

RESOURCES: PRACTICE ACTIVITIES MASTER 6B
Use as extra practice or as a homework activity.

VOCABULARY WORDSHOP pages 32–33

Words to Explore Write the Words to Explore on the board: *delicious, stew, perfect, cookies.* Discuss their meanings with children. Then discuss the illustrations at the top of Pupil's Edition page 32 and have children tell what each animal is doing.

Spelling Log Have children add the Words to Explore to their Spelling Logs.

TRANSITIONAL SPELLERS Assign the Words to Explore. As a practice activity, have children write their own conversation about a meal. Make sure they use all four Words to Explore in their writing. Ask them to underline the Words to Explore.

What's in a Word? Have children listen for the expression *food for thought* in these sentences:

> This book was *food for thought.*
> Harry's ideas give me *food for thought.*

Ask whether *food for thought* is something to eat. Explain, if necessary, that *food for thought* means "something to think about." FIGURATIVE LANGUAGE

Name _____

DICTIONARY Put the words in ABC order to make the table of contents for a cookbook.

Contents

Applesauce 2

Bread 5

Hamburger 9

Muffins 12

Page 2

Contents

Noodles 20

Potatoes 26

Salad 30

Yams 35

Page 3

Contents
Page 2
Hamburger
Applesauce
Muffins
Bread
Page 3
Salad
Potatoes
Noodles
Yams

WORD SEARCH Look at the picture. Find five Spelling Words. Write them under the picture.

mud   jump   cup   duck   bus

Integrated Spelling   Lesson 6   33

The word *cookies* came into the English language from Dutch. Other food words have come into English from languages spoken all over the world. *Broccoli* and *spaghetti* come from the Italian language; *pretzels* and *noodle* come from the German. *Pecan* and *squash* come from Native American languages.

Dictionary Have children tell how they put words in alphabetical order. (They look at the first letter or letters.) Point out that reciting the alphabet aloud or looking at an alphabet can help them figure out how to put the words in alphabetical order. You may want children to circle the first letter of each word in the box. This will help them isolate and focus on the initial letter. USING ALPHABETICAL ORDER

 Working Together Have children work together to put their spelling words in alphabetical order and to check them.

Word Search Discuss the picture with children. Ask them to find and name as many objects as they can before they complete the activity. USING PICTURE CLUES

Posttest To check children's mastery of the Spelling Words, use the context sentences on page T45 to administer the posttest.

Optional Writing Idea: Recipe Have children work in small groups to write their own recipes for Delicious Stew, Delicious Cookies, Perfect Stew, or Perfect Cookies. Discuss with them the ingredients in stews or cookies they have eaten and the cooking methods with which they are familiar. Encourage them to use their imaginations to create new recipes.

Suggest that children begin by brainstorming a list of possible ingredients to help them decide what to include in their recipes. You may want to have children copy their finished recipes onto recipe cards and put them in a class recipe box in a Reading Center.

Delicious Stew
meat
carrots
sugar
potatoes
apples
salt
beans

Vocabulary Activities

LESSON WRAP-UP

Words to Explore and Context Sentences

1. **delicious**   The pears taste **delicious.**
2. **stew**   We will eat **stew** for dinner.
3. **perfect**   This is the **perfect** jacket for me!
4. **cookies**   We baked oatmeal **cookies.**

Reteach

LEARNING DIFFERENCES Play an echo game to help children remember the spelling of the words in this lesson. Point to one of the Spelling Words, say it aloud, and have children repeat it after you. Point to each letter as you spell the word. Have children echo you. Then say the word again and have children repeat it. Follow the same procedure with the other Spelling Words. VISUAL/ AUDITORY MODALITIES

INTEGRATED CURRICULUM ACTIVITY

Language Arts

All of Us on the Bus To prepare for this activity, set up double rows of chairs with an aisle between them to look like the seats on a bus. Put one chair in front for the "driver." Display the Spelling Words where the driver and passengers can see them easily. Explain that the driver and passengers are going to tell a story about a bus trip. Each child in turn will add a sentence to the story. Each sentence must have one of the Spelling Words in it. Children can use the Spelling Words more than once but they should include all the words by the end of the story. The bus driver will check off each Spelling Word when it is used for the first time.

Begin the story for children with this sentence: *One day we went for a funny bus ride.* Have the bus driver add the next sentence. Then go up and down the rows of passengers, asking each child to add another sentence.

LESSON 7

Words with Long *e, i,* and *o*

Objective
To spell words with long *e,* long *i,* and long *o*

Lesson Planner
Assign words based on the developmental levels of individual children. See the Assignment Guide on page T250.

Informal Assessment
Children's writing may show that they have difficulty spelling words with long vowel sounds.

MODEL

> he
> Will ⓗⓘ help you?

Use this lesson to introduce the spelling of words with the long *e,* long *i,* and long *o* vowel sounds. Encourage children to apply what they have learned to help them spell other words. After children have completed the lesson, have them proofread their writing and correct any errors they may have made spelling words with these vowel sounds.

 SECOND-LANGUAGE SUPPORT Some children may have difficulty differentiating the long *i* sound from the short *a* sound. Give children practice in listening to and pronouncing pairs of words such as *bite, bat; fine, fan;* and *hide, had.* COMPARING AND CONTRASTING

Pretest/Posttest Context Sentences
You may want to test Semi-Phonetic Spellers on words 1–6 only.

*1. **by**   A bus went **by** the house.
 2. **told**   Mom **told** us to come home.
*3. **me**   You can sit with **me.**
 4. **try**   I will **try** to do well.
 5. **kind**   What **kind** of vegetables do you like?
 6. **cold**   I wear mittens when it's **cold.**

*7. **my**   Can you play at **my** house today?
 8. **most**   Sara has read **most** of these books.
 9. **child**   The **child** walked to school.
10. **both**   Hold up **both** hands.

*Words appearing in "Everett Anderson's Friend." Some additional story words following the generalizations are *he, she, be, why, find,* and *go.*

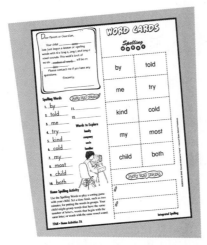

**RESOURCES: HOME
ACTIVITIES MASTER** **7A**

NOTE: Fill in the teacher's note on the Home
Activities Master before sending it home
with children. See the Assignment Guide
on page T250 for assigning lists of words.

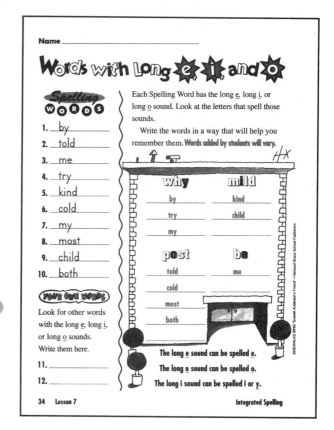

INTRODUCTION page 34

Pretest Administer the pretest. Say each word,
use it in the sentence provided on page T51,
and then repeat the word. ACCESSING PRIOR
KNOWLEDGE

Self-Check Have children check their
own pretests by referring to their list of
Spelling Words. For each misspelled word on
the pretest, remind children to use the **Study
Steps to Learn a Word** on pages 8–9 of the
Pupil's Edition. STUDENT SELF-ASSESSMENT

Introducing the Lesson To use the open sort,
copy Home Activities Master 7A in the
Copying Masters section.

Open Sort: Distribute word cards to children and
have them individually or cooperatively select
criteria for sorting. Encourage children to read
their words and then to add at least one word to
each category. You may want to send home the
word cards so that children can complete the
Home Activities Master.

Closed Sort: Read aloud with children the lesson
title and the Spelling Words on Pupil's Edition
page 34.

- Write the words *cry, both,* and *she* as
headings on the board. Have children identify
the vowel sound as you say each word.
- As you say each of these words, have
children tell which column it belongs in:
mind, why, bold, he, host, fly, be, and *wild.*
Write the words in the correct columns.
- Point out the two spellings of long *i.* Ask
children to sort the long *i* words into two
groups. SORTING WORDS

In Summary Ask children to summarize the
lesson. Help children conclude that the long *e*
sound may be spelled with the letter *e,* the long
i sound may be spelled with the letter *y* or *i,*
and the long *o* sound with the letter *o.*

Your Own Words Have pairs of
children think of and list in their
Spelling Logs other words with the
long *e,* long *i,* or long *o* vowel sound.
RECOGNIZING PATTERNS

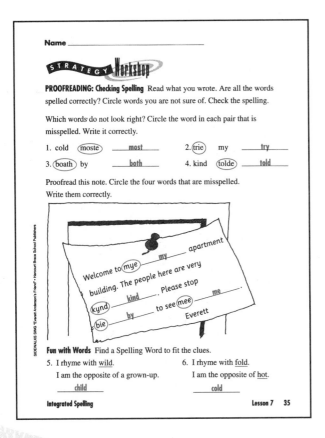

Name _____

STRATEGY Workshop

PROOFREADING: Checking Spelling Read what you wrote. Are all the words spelled correctly? Circle words you are not sure of. Check the spelling.

Which words do not look right? Circle the word in each pair that is misspelled. Write it correctly.

1. cold (moste) ___most___ 2. (trie) my ___try___
3. (boath) by ___both___ 4. kind (tolde) ___told___

Proofread this note. Circle the four words that are misspelled. Write them correctly.

Welcome to (mye) my apartment building. The people here are very (kynd) kind. Please stop (bie) by to see (mee) me.

Everett

Fun with Words Find a Spelling Word to fit the clues.

5. I rhyme with <u>wild</u>.
   I am the opposite of a grown-up.
   ___child___

6. I rhyme with <u>fold</u>.
   I am the opposite of <u>hot</u>.
   ___cold___

Integrated Spelling   Lesson 7   35

STRATEGY WORKSHOP page 35

PROOFREADING: Checking Spelling
Suggest that children check their spelling when they proofread their own writing. Point out the following hints:

- If the long *i* sound is at the end of a word, it is often spelled with a *y*.
- If the long *i* sound is in the middle of a word, it is sometimes spelled with an *i* followed by *ld* or *nd*. APPLYING SPELLING STRATEGIES

SECOND-LANGUAGE SUPPORT Write *my*, *kind*, *by*, and *me* on the board. As you point to each word, have volunteers read it. Then have children say sentences for the words to show that they understand the word meanings. WORD MEANINGS

SEMI-PHONETIC SPELLERS Encourage children to work in pairs. As one child reads a word from the page, the other can look it up on the Spelling Word list and spell the word aloud.

Fun with Words
Make sure that children understand the meaning of *opposite*. Have them give opposites for these words: *light*, *old*, and *short*. (*dark* or *heavy*, *young* or *new*, *tall* or *long*) Then ask children to complete the activity independently. After they have finished, challenge children to think of other words that rhyme with *child* and *cold*.

Practice Activities

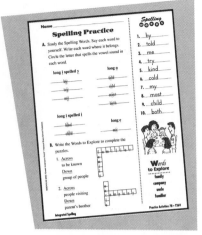

RESOURCES: PRACTICE ACTIVITIES MASTER 7B

Use as extra practice or as a homework activity.

VOCABULARY WORDSHOP pages 36–37

Words to Explore Write the Words to Explore on the board: *family, company, uncle, familiar.* Discuss their meanings with children. Then ask children to name some family members and to discuss when people might have their families as company.

 Spelling Log Have children add the Words to Explore to their Spelling Logs.

TRANSITIONAL SPELLERS Assign the Words to Explore. As a practice activity, have children use the Words to Explore in sentences, but instead of actually writing the Words to Explore, have them leave blanks for the letters. Then have children exchange papers and complete each other's sentences.

What's in a Word? Write *boy* on the board. Discuss with children the words on Pupil's Edition page 36 that mean *boy* in other languages. Ask what other words children might know from other languages. COMPARING AND CONTRASTING

Antonyms Remind children that *antonyms* are words with opposite meanings. Write the words *up, hard,* and *little* on the board and have children give antonyms for them. Then tell children that the sentences they will complete are part of a poem. USING ANTONYMS

 Working Together Partners can work together to choose antonyms to complete the poem. Then have them read aloud the completed poem together and use the spelling list to check the Spelling Words.

Name _____

ANTONYMS Use a Spelling Word to write the opposite of each underlined word.

Friends

Friends are <u>mean</u> ___kind___

I like mine.

My friend is a <u>grown-up</u> ___child___.

We play outside when it's mild.

We play outside when it's <u>hot</u> ___cold___

Because we are not too old!

I like my friend—A LOT!

ACTION WORDS Look at the friends in the pictures. Write an action word to tell what they are doing.

riding   reading   throwing

___reading___   ___throwing___   ___riding___

WITH A FRIEND Use four Spelling Words to make a word search puzzle. Write the words across or down. Fill in the empty spaces with other letters. Then trade papers and find the words.

Integrated Spelling

Lesson 7   37

In English-speaking countries, water faucets with the letter *C* dispense cold water. In some countries, however, water faucets with the letter *C* dispense hot water. The words *caliente* in Spanish, *caldo* in Italian, and *chaud* in French all mean "hot."

Action Words Remind children that action words tell what you can do. Have them act out action words for others to guess. Ask what two Spelling Words are action words. *(try, told)* USING ACTION VERBS

With a Friend You may want to supply grid paper for children to work on. Suggest that children construct their puzzles by looking for words that begin with the same letter, like *most* and *me* in the sample puzzle on page 37 of the Pupil's Edition.

Posttest Have children study the words they misspelled on the pretest. To check children's mastery of the Spelling Words, use the context sentences on page T51 to administer the posttest.

Optional Writing Idea: Personal Story
Ask children to write about having company. Encourage them to think about favorite friends or relatives whose visits they enjoy. Suggest that children draw pictures to help them think about details they want to include in their writing. After children finish, they may want to put their pictures and their stories into a class scrapbook.

LESSON WRAP-UP

Words to Explore and Context Sentences

1. **family** — There are five people in my **family.**
2. **company** — I like it when **company** comes for dinner.
3. **uncle** — My dad's brother is my **uncle.**
4. **familiar** — This story sounded **familiar** because I'd heard it before.

Reteach

LEARNING DIFFERENCES You may want to prepare an audiotape for children. On the tape, pronounce a Spelling Word, spell it slowly, and repeat it. Have children turn off the tape to write the word. Leave a folder with a list of the Spelling Words near the tape player so that children can check their work. VISUAL/AUDITORY/KINESTHETIC MODALITIES

INTEGRATED CURRICULUM ACTIVITIES

Math

Add a Word Make flashcards for the following math problems. Write the answers on the back.

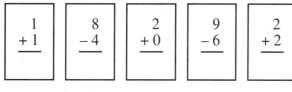

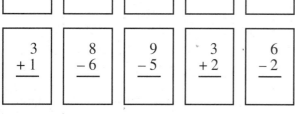

Then write the Spelling Words on separate word cards. Children choose a flashcard, figure out the answer, and then match the flashcard to a Spelling Word with the same number of letters.

Language Arts

About Me Tell children that each of them is going to write some clues that will help the others figure out who they are. Share examples of clues that children might give:

> My hair is long.
> Both of my front teeth fell out!

Encourage children to use the Spelling Words in their clues. Have them write their clues under the heading *About Me*. Display children's clues and challenge children to figure out who the clues tell about.

Objective
To spell words with long *a* spelled *ay* or *ai*

Lesson Planner
Assign words based on the developmental levels of individual children. See the Assignment Guide on page T250.

Informal Assessment
Children's writing may show that they have difficulty spelling words in which the letters *ay* or *ai* stand for the long *a* vowel sound.

MODEL

pail
Put the sand in the (pal).

Use this lesson to introduce the spelling of words with the long *a* vowel sound spelled *ay* or *ai*. Encourage children to apply what they have learned to help them spell other words. After children have completed the lesson, have them proofread their writing and correct any errors they may have made spelling words in which the letters *ay* or *ai* stand for the long *a* sound.

SECOND-LANGUAGE SUPPORT Children who speak Vietnamese, Spanish, or Tagalog may find it difficult to differentiate between the long *a* and short *e* vowel sounds. Give children practice in listening to and pronouncing pairs of words such as *sale, sell; gate, get;* and *tale, tell.*
COMPARING AND CONTRASTING

Pretest/Posttest Context Sentences
You may want to test Semi-Phonetic Spellers on words 1–6 only.

1. **may**   You **may** open the box now.
2. **rain**   She got wet in the **rain.**
3. **say**   Let's **say** hello to Mr. Garcia.
*4. **wait**   We **wait** for the bus here.
5. **pay**   Paul has money to **pay** for his lunch.
6. **train** The **train** stopped at the station.

7. **lay**   The hen will **lay** an egg.
8. **laid**   The hen **laid** an egg yesterday.
9. **way**   Which **way** shall we turn?
*10. **tail**   The dog wagged its **tail.**

*Words appearing in "Mitchell Is Moving." Some additional story words following the generalization are *away, day, stay, anyway, maybe, birthday, waited,* and *nails.*

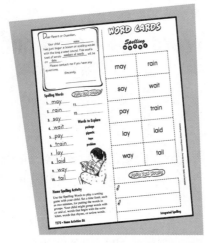

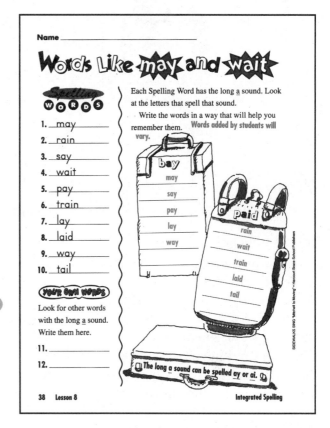

RESOURCES: HOME ACTIVITIES MASTER (8A)

NOTE: Fill in the teacher's note on the Home Activities Master before sending it home with children. See the Assignment Guide on page T250 for assigning lists of words.

INTRODUCTION page 38

Pretest Administer the pretest. Say each word, use it in the sentence provided on page T57, and then repeat the word. ACCESSING PRIOR KNOWLEDGE

 Self-Check Have children check their own pretests by referring to their list of Spelling Words. For each misspelled word on the pretest, remind children to use the **Study Steps to Learn a Word** on pages 8–9 of the Pupil's Edition. STUDENT SELF-ASSESSMENT

Introducing the Lesson To use the open sort, copy Home Activities Master 8A in the Copying Masters section.

Open Sort: Distribute word cards to children and have them individually or cooperatively select criteria for sorting. Have children read aloud each group of words. Ask others to name the category. You may want to send home the word cards so that children can complete the Home Activities Master.

Closed Sort: Read aloud with children the lesson title and the Spelling Words on Pupil's Edition page 38.

• Make word cards for these words: *day, pail, nail, stay, hay,* and *maid.* Make letter cards for *ai* and *ay.*

• Display the *ai* and *ay* cards. Have children put the word cards into the appropriate groups.

• Have children read the words in each group and tell whether the long *a* sound comes in the middle or at the end. Ask how the long *a* sound is spelled in the middle *(ai)* or at the end *(ay)* of these words. SORTING WORDS

In Summary Ask children to tell two ways to spell the long *a* sound. (with the letters *ay* or the letters *ai)*

Your Own Words For homework or practice, you may want to have pairs or teams of children list in their Spelling Logs other words in which the letters *ay* or *ai* spell the long *a* vowel sound. RECOGNIZING PATTERNS

Name ____________________

STRATEGY Workshop

SPELLING STRATEGY: Rhyming Words Think about how to spell a rhyming word you know. Try that spelling. Does it look right?

Write five Spelling Words that rhyme with day. Circle the letters that are the same in each word.

day

pay way say lay may

Finish the poem with Spelling Words.

The Squirrel's Song
What a pain
To be caught in the rain.
I'll make a sail
With the help of my tail.

Fun with Words Write Spelling Words to tell what the chicken says.

I wait.
I get on the train
I laid my egg!

Integrated Spelling Lesson 8 39

> Learning to spell can be a joy to the learner, and observing the results of their students' unfolding concepts about how to spell can be a delight to the teacher.
> (Ethel Buchanan)

STRATEGY WORKSHOP page 39

Spelling Strategy: Rhyming Words Remind children that rhyming words often end the same but have different beginning sounds. Write the word *day* on the board. Ask volunteers to use the spelling of *day* to help them spell these words: *way, hay, bay,* and *play.* APPLYING SPELLING STRATEGIES

SEMI-PHONETIC SPELLERS To remind children to include the vowels and to reinforce the two spellings of long *a,* suggest that children write the Spelling Words with *ay* in one color and the Spelling Words with *ai* in a different color.

SECOND-LANGUAGE SUPPORT Have children draw pictures of rain, a sail, and a tail. Help them label their pictures. They can use these pictures to help them complete the poem about the squirrel on Pupil's Edition page 39. USING PICTURE CLUES

Fun with Words Have children tell briefly what the chicken is doing in each illustration. Children might enjoy working with partners to decide on the best Spelling Word to complete the sentence in each speech balloon.

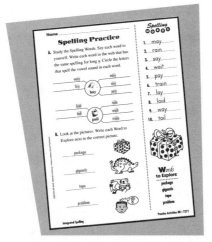

RESOURCES: PRACTICE
ACTIVITIES MASTER (8B)

Use as extra practice or as a homework activity.

VOCABULARY WORDSHOP pages 40–41

Words to Explore Write the Words to Explore on the board: *package, gigantic, tape, problem.* Discuss their meanings with children. Then have children look at the first picture of dinosaurs on Pupil's Edition page 40. Ask them to use the Words to Explore to tell about the picture. Then have children use the words to complete the sentences that tell about the picture.

Spelling Log Have children add the Words to Explore to their Spelling Logs.

TRANSITIONAL SPELLERS Assign the Words to Explore. As a practice activity, have children choose two words. Tell them to write one word with blanks for the vowels and the other with blanks for the consonants. Have children trade words and fill in the missing letters.

What's in a Word? Read the directions with children. Then have them name dinosaurs with which they are familiar. Write the names on the board. Ask which part of *dinosaur, dino* or *saur,* children think comes from the Greek word for *lizard.* (*Saur* comes from *sauros,* meaning "lizard.") WORD ORIGINS

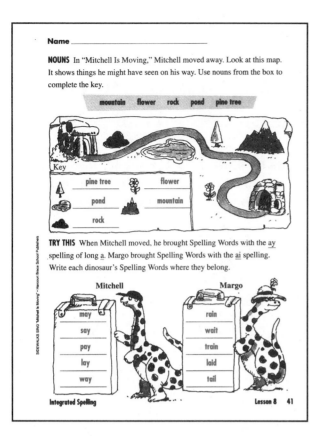

Name _____

NOUNS In "Mitchell Is Moving," Mitchell moved away. Look at this map. It shows things he might have seen on his way. Use nouns from the box to complete the key.

| mountain | flower | rock | pond | pine tree |

Key

pine tree	flower
pond	mountain
rock	

TRY THIS When Mitchell moved, he brought Spelling Words with the _ay_ spelling of long _a_. Margo brought Spelling Words with the _ai_ spelling. Write each dinosaur's Spelling Words where they belong.

Mitchell
may
say
pay
lay
way

Margo
rain
wait
train
laid
tail

Integrated Spelling   Lesson 8   41

SIDEWALKS SING "Mitchell Is Moving" • Harcourt Brace School Publishers

---

Nouns Remind children that a noun is a word that names a person, an animal, a place, or a thing. Then ask children to name things they see on the map. Have them find the map key, and discuss what a map key is. Make sure they understand that they will write nouns from the box next to the symbols to complete the map key. USING NOUNS

Try This Suggest that children write their Spelling Words in a list. Have them circle the _ay_ words in red and the _ai_ words in blue before writing them on the correct suitcase. CLASSIFYING

Working Together Suggest that children work in pairs to complete Try This. One child can be Mitchell and the other can be Margo. Have them write all the Spelling Words on cards. Then Mitchell can take the _ay_ words and Margo can take the _ai_ words.

Posttest To check children's mastery of the Spelling Words, use the context sentences on page T57 to administer the posttest.

Optional Writing Idea: Writing About a Picture Have children write about the picture of the dinosaurs wrapping the box on Pupil's Edition page 40. Tell them to use as many Spelling Words and Words to Explore as they can. Children might enjoy writing dialogue to tell what the dinosaurs might be saying. Help children write notes as they look at the picture. Explain that they can refer to their notes as they write. Then children may want to work together to act out their finished writing.

gigantic package
lots of paper
tape and string
big mess

Vocabulary Activities

LESSON WRAP-UP

Words to Explore and Context Sentences

1. **package** What is in that **package**?
2. **gigantic** Dinosaurs were **gigantic.**
3. **tape** Can we **tape** this sign to the door?
4. **problem** If you have a **problem,** ask for help.

Reteach

LEARNING DIFFERENCES Have children work in pairs to paint their Spelling Words. Children might enjoy taking turns painting the letters of each word. As one child names the first letter, the second child paints it. Suggest that they switch roles for each letter. When children have finished painting, have them read and spell each word.
AUDITORY/KINESTHETIC MODALITIES

INTEGRATED CURRICULUM ACTIVITY

Physical Education

Spelling Word Toss Prepare for this game by writing the Spelling Words in boxes on a large sheet of butcher paper or newsprint.

may	rain
wait	say
pay	train
laid	lay
way	tail

Have children play this game in two teams of two or three players each. One team is the *ay* team and the other is the *ai* team. Place the paper on the floor. Players from the two teams take turns tossing a beanbag onto the game board. Players for the *ay* team try to have the beanbag land on words spelled with *ay,* while players for the other team try to land on words spelled with *ai.*

When a team member lands on a word with the correct spelling for his or her team, he or she uses the word in a sentence and writes the word on the board. The first team to have the beanbag land on all five of its own words wins the game.

Words Like *keep* and *team*

Objective
To spell words with long *e* spelled *ee* or *ea*

Lesson Planner
Assign words based on the developmental levels of individual children. See the Assignment Guide on page T250.

Informal Assessment
Children's writing may show that they have difficulty spelling words in which the letters *ee* or *ea* stand for the long *e* vowel sound.

MODEL

> meet
> I will ~~met~~ you at ten.

Use this lesson to introduce the spelling of words with the long *e* vowel sound spelled *ee* or *ea*. Encourage children to apply what they have learned to help them spell other words. After children have completed the lesson, have them proofread their writing and correct any errors they may have made spelling words in which the letters *ee* or *ea* stand for the long *e* sound.

SECOND-LANGUAGE SUPPORT Help children understand the meanings of the Spelling Words by emphasizing the words when they are used in context. Ask volunteers to act out the meanings of words such as *read, eat, feet, feel,* or *seat.* MAKING INFERENCES/ROLE-PLAYING

Pretest/Posttest Context Sentences
You may want to test Semi-Phonetic Spellers on words 1–6 only.

*1.	**need**	It's cold, so I **need** a hat.
2.	**read**	I'm going to **read** this book.
3.	**deep**	Mike dug a **deep** hole in the sand.
4.	**eat**	We **eat** our lunch at noon.
*5.	**keep**	I **keep** my pencil in my desk.
*6.	**team**	Our **team** has won three games.
7.	**feet**	Put your sneakers on your **feet.**
8.	**each**	She gave **each** child an apple.
9.	**feel**	Does the water **feel** too cold?
10.	**seat**	Please go to your **seat** and sit down.

*Words appearing in "Jamaica Tag-Along." Some additional story words following the generalization are *meet, see, feelings,* and *sneaked.*

RESOURCES: HOME ACTIVITIES MASTER 9A

NOTE: Fill in the teacher's note on the Home Activities Master before sending it home with children. See the Assignment Guide on page T250 for assigning lists of words.

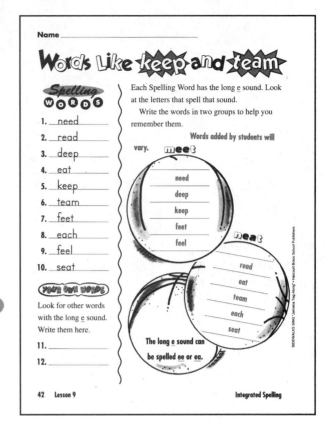

Name _____

Words Like keep and team

Spelling Words

1. need
2. read
3. deep
4. eat
5. keep
6. team
7. feet
8. each
9. feel
10. seat

YOUR OWN WORDS
Look for other words with the long e sound. Write them here.

11. _____
12. _____

Each Spelling Word has the long e sound. Look at the letters that spell that sound.

Write the words in two groups to help you remember them.

Words added by students will vary.

meet
need
deep
keep
feet
feel

neat
read
eat
team
each
seat

The long e sound can be spelled ee or ea.

42 Lesson 9   Integrated Spelling

INTRODUCTION page 42

Pretest Administer the pretest. Say each word, use it in the sentence provided on page T63, and then repeat the word. ACCESSING PRIOR KNOWLEDGE

☑ Self-Check Have children check their own pretests by referring to their list of Spelling Words. For each misspelled word on the pretest, remind children to use the **Study Steps to Learn a Word** on pages 8–9 of the Pupil's Edition. STUDENT SELF-ASSESSMENT

Introducing the Lesson To use the open sort, copy Home Activities Master 9A in the Copying Masters section.

Open Sort: Distribute word cards to children and have them individually or cooperatively select criteria for sorting. Have children name their categories. Ask others to tell which words fit into them. You may want to send home the word cards so that children can complete the Home Activities Master.

Closed Sort: Read aloud with children the lesson title and the Spelling Words on Pupil's Edition page 42.

- Write *ee* and *ea* as headings on the board. Then display the word *seed*. Ask whether *seed* would go in a group of words with the *ee* or *ea* spelling for long *e*. Write *seed* under *ee*. Follow a similar procedure for *bead*.
- Display the following words: *peel, beach, peach, feed, weed,* and *heat*. Ask children to read each word and to write it in the correct column on the board. SORTING WORDS

In Summary Ask children to summarize the lesson. Then ask two ways in which the long *e* sound can be spelled. (with the letters *ee* or the letters *ea*)

Your Own Words Have pairs of children work together to list in their Spelling Logs other words in which the letters *ee* or *ea* stand for the long *e* vowel sound. RECOGNIZING PATTERNS

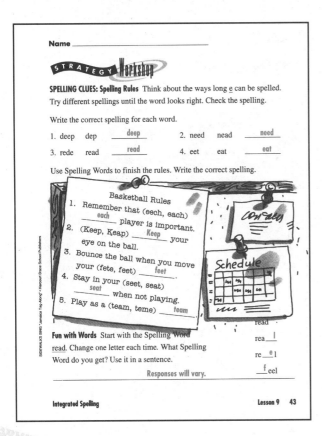

Name _____

STRATEGY Workshop

SPELLING CLUES: Spelling Rules Think about the ways long e can be spelled. Try different spellings until the word looks right. Check the spelling.

Write the correct spelling for each word.

1. deep   dep   _deep_   2. need   nead   _need_

3. rede   read   _read_   4. eet   eat   _eat_

Use Spelling Words to finish the rules. Write the correct spelling.

Basketball Rules
1. Remember that (eech, each) _each_ player is important.
2. (Keep, Keap) _Keep_ your eye on the ball.
3. Bounce the ball when you move your (fete, feet) _feet_.
4. Stay in your (seet, seat) _seat_ when not playing.
5. Play as a (team, teme) _team_.

Fun with Words Start with the Spelling Word _read_. Change one letter each time. What Spelling Word do you get? Use it in a sentence.

read
rea_l_
re_e_l
_f_eel

Responses will vary.

Integrated Spelling   Lesson 9   43

> The single best method for studying words to be learned is based on research supporting a visual imagery and visual memory approach.
> (Elton G. Stetson)

STRATEGY WORKSHOP page 43

Spelling Clues: Spelling Rules
Remind children that if a word has a long *e* vowel sound, they can try writing the word with different spellings for long *e* to see which one looks correct. On the board, write *teeth* and *teath*. Ask which looks correct. Point out to children that if they are not sure, they should look up the words in a dictionary. APPLYING SPELLING STRATEGIES

SECOND-LANGUAGE SUPPORT Review the meanings of the Spelling Words. Play a guessing game in which you give clues for each Spelling Word. Have children guess the Spelling Word answer. An example might be as follows: *You have two of me. I'm attached to your legs. (feet)* WORD MEANINGS

SEMI-PHONETIC SPELLERS To reinforce the two spellings of long *e,* have children write the Spelling Words. They can use one color for the vowels and another for the consonants.

Fun with Words
Before children do this activity, work through the following puzzle with them.

hit
h(a)t
(b)at

You may also want to discuss the spellings and meanings of *reel* and *real*.

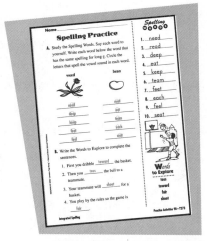

RESOURCES: PRACTICE ACTIVITIES MASTER 9B

Use as extra practice or as a homework activity.

VOCABULARY WORDSHOP pages 44–45

Words to Explore Write the Words to Explore on the board: *toss, toward, fair, shoot.* Discuss their meanings with children. Have children act out the meanings of *toss, toward,* and *shoot.* Ask what would be *fair* and what might not be *fair* in a game of basketball. Then have children complete the activity.

 Spelling Log Have children add the Words to Explore to their Spelling Logs.

 TRANSITIONAL SPELLERS Assign the Words to Explore. As a practice activity, have children write each letter of each Word to Explore on a separate card or self-stick note. Then have them use the letters to spell the words.

What's in a Word? Remind children that compound words, like *basketball,* are made up of two words. Give clues like the following to help children think of other compound words:

> You put mail in a box. *(mailbox)*
> You clean each tooth with your brush. *(toothbrush)*

Then have children complete the activity.
UNDERSTANDING COMPOUND WORDS

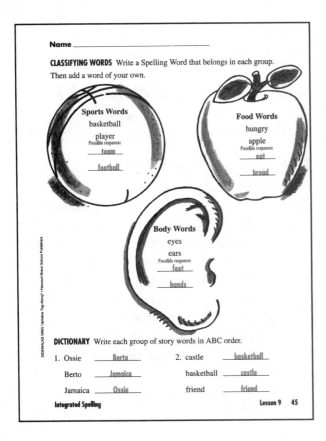

Name _____

CLASSIFYING WORDS Write a Spelling Word that belongs in each group. Then add a word of your own.

Sports Words
basketball
player
Possible response:
___team___
___football___

Food Words
hungry
apple
Possible response:
___eat___
___bread___

Body Words
eyes
ears
Possible response:
___feet___
___hands___

DICTIONARY Write each group of story words in ABC order.

1. Ossie   ___Berto___
   Berto   ___Jamaica___
   Jamaica   ___Ossie___

2. castle   ___basketball___
   basketball   ___castle___
   friend   ___friend___

Integrated Spelling   Lesson 9   45

Classifying Words Have children read aloud the names of the categories and the items in each category. Check children's understanding by asking why the two items listed for each category go together. Then ask children to name other words for each category. List their responses on the board. EXPANDING VOCABULARY

Dictionary Remind children that they should look at the first letter of each word in the list to put the words in alphabetical order. Suggest that children circle the first letter of each word to help them isolate and focus on that letter. USING ALPHABETICAL ORDER

 Working Together Suggest that children work in groups of three to alphabetize the words in the Dictionary activity. Have each child write one of the words to be alphabetized on a sheet of paper. Then have them hold their words as they arrange themselves in alphabetical order.

Posttest Review the Spelling Words with children. Then, to check children's mastery of the words, use the context sentences on page T63 to administer the posttest.

Optional Writing Idea: Description Have children write a description of a basketball. If possible, provide a real basketball that children can look at and touch. Have children tell how it looks and feels. Suggest that they make a chart to organize their ideas.

See	Hear	Feel	Smell
round big orange	smack when it bounces	bumpy	like rubber

You could arrange a display of children's descriptions with the basketball. Cut away one side of a cardboard carton, place the basketball inside, and tape the descriptions to the carton.

LESSON WRAP-UP

Words to Explore and Context Sentences

1. **toss**   Just **toss** your jacket on the chair.
2. **toward**   The dog ran **toward** me.
3. **fair**   The game will be **fair** if we obey the rules.
4. **shoot**   You **shoot** the basketball into the hoop.

Reteach

LEARNING DIFFERENCES Help children make a small card, about 2 x 2 inches, for each Spelling Word. Then make a set of larger cards, about 5 x 2 inches, for each Spelling Word, but omit the letter combination *ee* or *ea*. Have children find the small card that matches each larger card. Then have them read aloud and spell each word. VISUAL/KINESTHETIC MODALITIES

INTEGRATED CURRICULUM ACTIVITIES

Physical Education

On Your Feet, In Your Seat Have children play this game at their seats. Choose one child to be the Leader. Give the Leader a list of the Spelling Words from this lesson. Then have the Leader stand in front of the group. The Leader slowly reads the words from the spelling list in random order. When the Leader reads a word in which the long *e* sound is spelled *ee* as in *feet,* children should stand. When the long *e* sound is spelled *ea* as in *seat,* children should sit down. Let children take turns being the Leader.

Language Arts

Riddles Have children write riddles about different sports. Tell them to use three Spelling Words in each riddle. Then, on a separate sheet of paper, ask children to draw a picture of themselves playing the sport to answer the riddle. You could display the riddles and pictures in a class riddle book.

> I need a bat. There are nine people on my team. Sometimes I hit a fly ball deep into left field. What sport do I play?

Words Like *boat* and *show*

Objective
To spell words with long *o* spelled *oa* or *ow*

Lesson Planner
Assign words based on the developmental levels of individual children. See the Assignment Guide on page T250.

Informal Assessment
Children's writing may show that they have difficulty spelling words in which the letters *oa* or *ow* stand for the long *o* vowel sound.

MODEL

> goat
> A goat is an animal.

Use this lesson to introduce the spelling of words with the long *o* vowel sound spelled *oa* or *ow*. Encourage children to apply what they have learned to help them spell other words. After children have completed the lesson, have them proofread their writing and correct any errors they may have made spelling words in which the letters *oa* or *ow* stand for the long *o* sound.

SECOND-LANGUAGE SUPPORT Use pictures to help children understand the meanings of Spelling Words such as *boat, coal, coat, coast,* and *road.* Ask volunteers to demonstrate the meanings of other Spelling Words, such as *slow* and *low.*
USING PICTURE CLUES/ROLE-PLAYING

Pretest/Posttest Context Sentences
You may want to test Semi-Phonetic Spellers on words 1–6 only.

*1.	**boat**	The **boat** sailed on the river.
2.	**row**	Can we **row** across the lake?
3.	**show**	I'll **show** you the picture I drew.
4.	**coal**	People get **coal** from the mine.
5.	**coat**	Put on your **coat** if you're cold.
6.	**slow**	Rabbits are fast, but turtles are **slow.**
7.	**coast**	The ship sailed along the **coast.**
8.	**own**	Kevin wants a puppy of his **own.**
9.	**low**	The fence was **low** enough to step over.
10.	**road**	A few cars went by on the **road.**

*Word appearing in "Abuela." Some additional story words following the generalization are *loading, unload,* and *sailboat.*

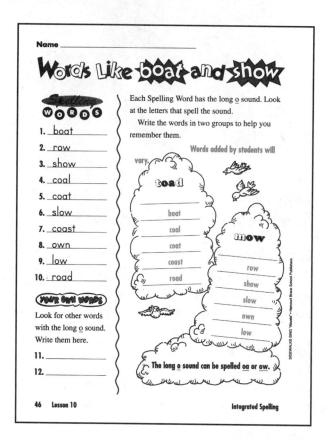

RESOURCES: HOME ACTIVITIES MASTER 10A

NOTE: Fill in the teacher's note on the Home Activities Master before sending it home with children. See the Assignment Guide on page T250 for assigning lists of words.

INTRODUCTION page 46

Pretest Administer the pretest. Say each word, use it in the sentence provided on page T69, and then repeat the word. ACCESSING PRIOR KNOWLEDGE

 Self-Check Have children check their own pretests by referring to their list of Spelling Words. For each misspelled word on the pretest, remind children to use the **Study Steps to Learn a Word** on pages 8–9 of the Pupil's Edition. STUDENT SELF-ASSESSMENT

Introducing the Lesson To use the open sort, copy Home Activities Master 10A in the Copying Masters section.

Open Sort: Distribute word cards to children and have them individually or cooperatively select criteria for sorting. After they finish sorting, have children share and discuss the categories they chose. You may want to send home the word cards so that children can complete the Home Activities Master.

Closed Sort: Read aloud with children the lesson title and the Spelling Words on Pupil's Edition page 46.

- Write the words *toad, grow, goal,* and *flow* on the board. Have children group words by the spelling for long *o*.
- Ask children to identify the letters that spell the long *o* sound in each group. Then ask children to suggest other words that could fit into each group. SORTING WORDS

In Summary Have children summarize the lesson. Ask them how the long *o* sound can be spelled. (with the letters *oa* or the letters *ow*)

Your Own Words Have children search the classroom to find long *o* words spelled with *oa* or *ow*. They might use maps, globes, advertisements, newspapers, or magazines. Ask children to list their words in their Spelling Logs. RECOGNIZING PATTERNS

STRATEGY Workshop

PROOFREADING: Checking Spelling Read what you wrote. Do any words look funny? Circle them. Then check the spelling.

Which word in each pair is misspelled? Circle it. Then write it correctly.

1. (coale)   show   _coal_
2. row   (rowd)   _road_
3. boat   (sloa)   _slow_
4. (coate)   coast   _coat_

Circle the words that are misspelled. Write them correctly to complete the letter.

Dear Abuela,

I loved our adventure. Do you remember the (bowt) _boat_ we saw? Well, I got to (roa) _row_ one of my (oan) _own_ ! The next time you visit, I will take you to the (coste) _coast_ and (showe) _show_ you how well I can row!

Love, Rosa

Fun with Words Find the Spelling Word hidden in these words. Write it in the shape.

glow
blow
flow

| l | o | w |

Integrated Spelling

Lesson 10   47

• •

STRATEGY WORKSHOP page 47

Proofreading: Checking Spelling
Remind children to proofread what they write. Then write the words *goat* and *gowte* on the board. Ask a volunteer to circle the one that looks wrong. Ask children how they could check the spelling. Then ask a volunteer to write the word correctly. *(goat)* APPLYING SPELLING STRATEGIES

SECOND-LANGUAGE SUPPORT Write the words *boat, row, own, coast,* and *show* on the board. Have children use each word in a sentence to show its meaning. Encourage children to refer to the words as they complete the letter on Pupil's Edition page 47. WORD MEANINGS

SEMI-PHONETIC SPELLERS Have children write the Spelling Words on word cards. Encourage them to use the word cards to check the spelling of the words on Pupil's Edition page 47.

Fun with Words
Write *grow* and *throw* on the board. Circle the Spelling Word *row* in each word. Have children follow a similar procedure to complete the activity.

Practice Activities

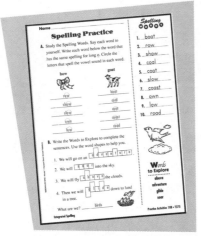

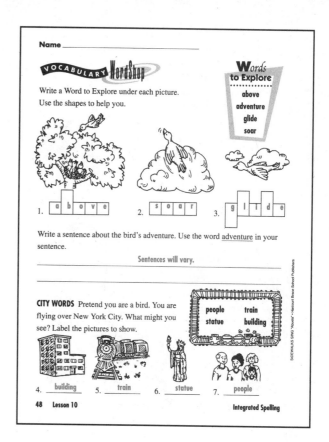

RESOURCES: PRACTICE ACTIVITIES MASTER 10B

Use as extra practice or as a homework activity.

- -

VOCABULARY WORDSHOP pages 48–49

Words to Explore Write the Words to Explore on the board: *above, adventure, glide, soar*. Discuss their meanings with children. Have children tell what the bird is doing in each picture. Then have children write each word under its picture. Suggest that they use the word shapes to help them.

Have children tell about the bird's adventure. Then ask them to write their sentences independently.

 Spelling Log Have children add the Words to Explore to their Spelling Logs.

 TRANSITIONAL SPELLERS Assign the Words to Explore. As a practice activity, have children give letter clues for the Words to Explore. Other children should guess and then spell the answers. An example might be as follows: *This word starts with the first two letters in the alphabet. (above)*

City Words Ask children what they might see in a city. List their responses on the board. After children have completed the activity, invite them to write or tell a story about a family's visit to the city. Encourage them to use all four city words.

 Working Together Have children work in small groups to brainstorm more city words. They could list the words under categories such as Buildings, Transportation, Interesting Sights, and People. Have each group choose a Recorder to list the words. Children can use these words in their stories.

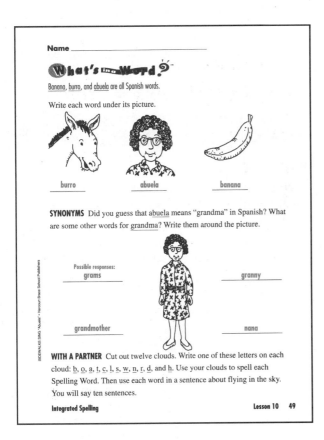

Name _____

What's in a Word?

Banana, burro, and abuela are all Spanish words.

Write each word under its picture.

burro   abuela   banana

SYNONYMS Did you guess that abuela means "grandma" in Spanish? What are some other words for grandma? Write them around the picture.

Possible responses:
grams   granny

grandmother   nana

WITH A PARTNER Cut out twelve clouds. Write one of these letters on each cloud: b, o, a, t, c, l, s, w, n, r, d, and h. Use your clouds to spell each Spelling Word. Then use each word in a sentence about flying in the sky. You will say ten sentences.

Integrated Spelling   Lesson 10   49

SIDEWALKS SING "Abuela" • Harcourt Brace School Publishers

Words introduced in the feature What's in a Word? on page 49 of the Pupil's Edition have been adopted into English from Spanish. Another such word is *rodeo*, which means in Spanish "to go around" or "a cattle ring."

· ·

What's in a Word? Point out to children that two of the Spanish words, *banana* and *burro*, are also English words. Explain that they were Spanish words first and that they later became English words, too. WORD ORIGINS

Synonyms Have children work cooperatively to complete this activity. Encourage them to share different words they use for *grandma*. You might want to list some of their responses on the board for children to use as they complete this activity. USING SYNONYMS

With a Partner Provide paper, crayons or markers, and a cloud pattern. Have children write the letters *o*, *a*, and *w* on clouds of one color and the other letters on clouds of another color. WORD MEANINGS

Posttest Have children study the words they misspelled on the pretest. To check children's mastery of the Spelling Words, use the context sentences on page T69 to administer the posttest.

Optional Writing Idea: Sentences About a Picture Have children look again at the pictures and the Spanish words in What's in a Word? on Pupil's Edition page 49. Tell children that they are going to choose one of the pictures and write sentences describing it. Suggest that they begin by writing the Spanish word and making a web of their ideas.

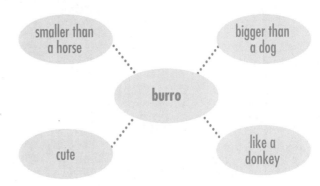

Vocabulary Activities

Lesson 10   T73

LESSON WRAP-UP

Words to Explore and Context Sentences

1. **above**   The jet flew in the sky **above** us.
2. **adventure** This book is about Kim's **adventure** in space.
3. **glide**   Watch the skater **glide** across the ice.
4. **soar**   This paper plane will **soar** through the air.

Reteach

LEARNING DIFFERENCES Write one of the Spelling Words on the board. Have children study the word for about thirty seconds. Then erase the word. Have children write the word on their papers. When they have finished, write the word on the board again. Have children check their spelling and correct it, if necessary. Repeat this procedure for each Spelling Word. VISUAL MODALITY

INTEGRATED CURRICULUM ACTIVITIES

Language Arts

Boat Show Have children use scrap materials such as margarine tubs and small boxes to make toy boats. Set up a boat show to display the boats. Then have children write about their boats. Encourage them to use Spelling Words to tell a story about an adventure they might have in their boats.

Science

Boat or Coast? On a large sheet of butcher paper, write the column headings *On the Coast* and *In a Boat*. Ask what plants or animals children might see if they were on the coast or in a boat. Have children record their responses. Encourage children to add illustrations and to continue to add words to the lists.

Objectives

To review spelling patterns and strategies in Lessons 6–10; to give children the opportunity to recognize and use these spelling patterns and the Spelling Words in their writing

Review of Spelling Strategies

Review with children the spelling strategies presented in Lessons 6–10.

USING SOUND/LETTER RELATIONSHIPS Write *moch* on the board. Then say *much* and have children listen for the short *u* sound. Point to *moch* and ask if it is the correct spelling for *much*. Explain that children should listen to the sounds and then use the letters that stand for the sounds to spell a word. Repeat *much* and have a volunteer correct the spelling.

CHECKING SPELLING Write the sentence *Our tem won the game* on the board. Ask children to read the sentence and identify the misspelled word. Ask them to tell how they knew that *t-e-m* is not the correct spelling. (Possible responses: It doesn't look right; I read the word *team* in a story and it was spelled *t-e-a-m*.) Have a volunteer circle the word and respell it. Then ask children how they can check the spelling to see if it is right. (Ask someone who knows the correct spelling or look up the word in a dictionary.)

USING RHYMING WORDS Write the word *cold* on the board and have children identify it. Review how they can use a rhyming strategy to spell the word *gold*. First, have children identify the letter that stands for the beginning sound of *cold*. Then, have children show how they can substitute the letter *g* for the letter *c* in *cold* to spell the rhyming word *gold*.

USING SPELLING RULES Write the words *deep* and *seat* on the board. Have a child circle the two ways that the long *e* sound can be spelled. Then write *keep* and *keap* on the board, and ask which word is spelled correctly. Ask children to tell how thinking of ways to spell a vowel sound can help them write a word when they aren't sure of the spelling.

Unit 2 Words

The following words from Unit 2 are reviewed in this lesson:

Lesson 6 Words with Short *u*: jump, bus, cut

Lesson 7 Words with Long *e, i,* and *o:* kind, most, told

Lesson 8 Words with /ā/ *ay, ai:* wait, may, rain

Lesson 9 Words with /ē/ *ee, ea:* eat, feel, each

Lesson 10 Words with /ō/ *oa, ow:* coast, show, low

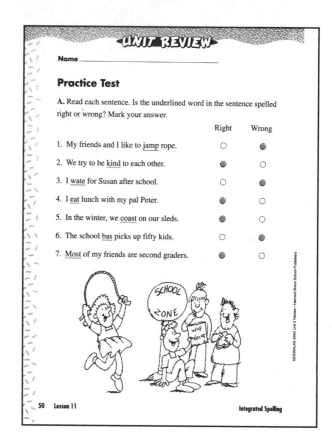

> **Students are willing to risk spelling new words using cues from known words, meaning units within words, and their level of understanding about how the spelling system works.**
>
> (Ethel Buchanan)

PRACTICE TEST pages 50–51

Options for Administering the Practice Test

The Practice Test provides an opportunity to review Spelling Words and spelling generalizations in a standardized test format.

Option 1: Have children review the **Words to Study** in the Spelling Log for Unit 2. If they need extra help, review the spelling generalizations on Pupil's Edition pages 30, 34, 38, 42, and 46. Then administer both parts of the Practice Test on Pupil's Edition pages 50–51 to determine whether children have mastered the spelling generalizations.

Option 2: Administer both parts of the Practice Test on Pupil's Edition pages 50–51 as a pretest, and then on another day, dictate the Spelling Words on both parts of the Practice Test as a posttest.

 ### Options for Evaluation

- Have children check their own Practice Tests by referring to their lists of Spelling Words. The list on page T75 provides references to the lessons where children will find the words on the Practice Test.
- You may prefer to assign partners and have them check each other's Practice Tests. Refer children to their own lists of Spelling Words to use as they check their partners' tests.

For each word that children misspelled on the Practice Test, remind them to follow the **Study Steps to Learn a Word** on pages 8–9 of the Pupil's Edition. Be sure to have them write the misspelled words in the Unit 2 **Words to Study** box in the Spelling Log. STUDENT SELF-ASSESSMENT

Name _____

B. Read each sentence. Is the underlined word in the sentence spelled right or wrong? Mark your answer.

	Right	Wrong
1. We <u>may</u> play ball on Saturday.	●	○
2. I <u>feal</u> good about my friends.	○	●
3. Putting on a <u>sho</u> with a friend is fun.	○	●
4. We <u>cat</u> hats from a newspaper.	○	●
5. My best friend <u>tolde</u> me a secret.	○	●
6. We splash through puddles in the <u>rain</u>.	●	○
7. We swing together on the <u>low</u> bars.	●	○
8. We see <u>eech</u> other every day.	○	●

Integrated Spelling   Lesson 11   51

RESOURCES: HOME ACTIVITIES MASTER 11A

Use as an extra activity to reinforce spelling strategies.

Review of Spelling Strategies Review with children the spelling strategies discussed on pages 176–177 of the Pupil's Edition. Then distribute Home Activities Master 11A.

The Reteach section of each Lesson Wrap-Up provides suggestions for helping children who are still having difficulty with the concepts taught in that lesson.

Practice Test

RESOURCES: PRACTICE ACTIVITIES MASTER 11B

Use as an extra activity to provide children an opportunity to combine spelling and writing.

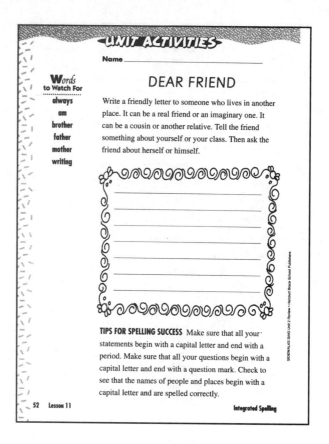

UNIT 2 ACTIVITIES pages 52–53

Activities on pages 52 and 53 of the Pupil's Edition emphasize writing (Dear Friend), reading (Come for Supper), and word play (Word Doodles). The **Tips for Spelling Success** point out the importance of standard spelling and give children hints for proofreading and for applying spelling strategies.

Dear Friend Review the form of a friendly letter with children. Then ask to whom children might like to write a letter. Encourage them to think not only of friends or relatives but also of story or movie characters. Have children share and discuss ideas about what they might tell in their letters. Then read the directions with children. Have them complete the activity independently.

Have children read the **Tips for Spelling Success.** Point out the **Words to Watch For.** These are words children often use in writing. Explain that children can use the list to help them spell the words correctly. When children

proofread their work, provide them with the following checklist or the proofreading checklist on page 175 of the Pupil's Edition. WRITING/PROOFREADING

Proofreading Checklist

✔ Did I spell words correctly?
✔ Did I begin each sentence with a capital letter?
✔ Did I end each sentence with the correct end mark?
✔ Did I begin people's names and special words with capital letters?
✔ Did I remember the comma after the greeting?

If children need help with writing a friendly letter, refer them to pages 12–13 of the *Language Handbook.*

COME FOR SUPPER

Pretend you could invite a character from a story you have read to supper. What would you talk about? Write down some questions you would ask. Then write a menu and a list of games to play. Choose food and games that you and your friend would both like.

TIPS FOR SPELLING SUCCESS Make sure that all your questions end with a question mark. Check your writing and your spelling.

WORD DOODLES

Use the clues to make new words.

1. Add a letter or letters to make a word.
   The ⟨raindrops⟩ __r__ __a__ __i__ __n__ sounds like "drip-drop."

   The ⟨train⟩ __t__ __r__ __a__ __i__ __n__ sounds like "choo choo."

2. Add the first and last letters to make a word.

   Take off your ⟨coat⟩ __c__ __o__ __a__ __t__

   Walk down a ⟨road⟩ __r__ __o__ __a__ __d__ .

TIPS FOR SPELLING SUCCESS Use what you know about long vowel sounds to help you spell new words.

Integrated Spelling   Lesson 11   53

Come for Supper Read the directions with children. Then have children name story characters they might like to invite to supper. List the names on the board. Before children begin work on the activity, have them list the steps they will complete: choosing a character, writing a list of questions they would ask the character, writing a menu, and listing games.

Have children read the **Tips for Spelling Success** and encourage them to proofread their work. WRITING/PROOFREADING

 Children may find it helpful to use pages 50–51 of the *Language Handbook* when writing their questions.

Word Doodles Read the directions with children. Explain that for the first sentence in number 1, children will write a letter to make a word and for the second sentence, they will add a letter to that word to make a new word. Point out that the illustrations will help them.

Then explain that for number 2, children will write two letters to make a word to complete the first sentence and then change the first letter and the last letter of that word to make a different word to complete the second sentence.

Read the **Tips for Spelling Success** and encourage children to recall the spellings of long vowel sounds and to apply what they learned to spelling new words. USING PICTURE CLUES AND SOUND/LETTER RELATIONSHIPS

For children who need a reteaching activity, make word cards for the review words listed on page T75. Ask pairs of children to work together, and have each partner take half of the cards. Then have children take turns reading words aloud for each other to spell. When all of the words have been spelled, have partners trade cards.

Challenge children to use the review words listed on page T75 to make up their own Word Doodles like those on Pupil's Edition page 53 by adding a letter to the beginning of *eat* and *each* or by changing the first and last letters of *wait* or *boat.* To help children get started, ask them to find the pairs of review words that can be used together in the Word Doodles. (*wait* and *rain, bus* and *cut*)

Have children write each of the review words listed on page T75 on a separate word card. Then have them work in pairs to sort the words into five groups according to the vowel sound in each word (short *u*, long *i*, long *o*, long *a*, long *e*). Finally, ask children to sort the long *o*, long *a*, and long *e* groups according to the spelling pattern of each word in the group.

Have children write sentences using the review words listed on page T75 and then illustrate them. Encourage children to use at least two review words in each sentence.

LESSON 12

Words Like *make* and *five*

Objective
To spell words with long *a* spelled *a-e* or with long *i* spelled *i-e*

Lesson Planner
Assign words based on the developmental levels of individual children. See the Assignment Guide on page T250.

Informal Assessment
Children's writing may show that they have difficulty spelling long *a* or long *i* words that have a CVCe pattern.

MODEL

lake
We swim at the laik.

Use this lesson to introduce the spelling of words with the long *a* vowel sound spelled *a-e* or the long *i* vowel sound spelled *i-e*. Encourage children to apply what they have learned to help them spell other words with a long *a* or long *i* vowel sound and the CVCe spelling pattern. After children have completed the lesson, have them proofread their writing and correct any errors they may have made spelling words with long vowel sounds that are spelled *a-e* or *i-e*.

SECOND-LANGUAGE SUPPORT Children who speak Vietnamese, Spanish, or Tagalog may find it difficult to differentiate between the long *a* and short *e* vowel sounds. Give children practice listening to and pronouncing pairs of words such as *sale, sell; gate, get;* and *tale, tell*.

Some children may have difficulty distinguishing the long *i* vowel sound from the short *a* vowel sound. Give children practice in listening to and repeating pairs of words such as *bite, bat; fine, fan;* and *hide, had*. COMPARING AND CONTRASTING

Pretest/Posttest Context Sentences
You may want to test Semi-Phonetic Spellers on words 1–6 only.

*1.	**take**	Did you **take** the pencil from the box?
2.	**fire**	Stay away from the hot **fire.**
3.	**made**	She **made** noodles for supper.
*4.	**five**	I counted **five** birds in the tree.
5.	**game**	Which team won the **game**?
*6.	**life**	I have lived here all my **life.**
7.	**late**	Cara got to school **late** today.
8.	**nice**	It's a **nice** day to play outside.
*9.	**make**	You can **make** a puppet from a sock.
*10.	**side**	Turn your paper to the other **side.**

*Words appearing in "Six-Dinner Sid." Some additional story words following the generalizations are *places, safe, like,* and *twice.*

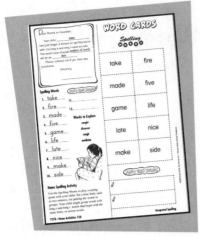

RESOURCES: HOME ACTIVITIES MASTER 12A

NOTE: Fill in the teacher's note on the Home Activities Master before sending it home with children. See the Assignment Guide on page T250 for assigning lists of words.

INTRODUCTION page 54

Pretest Administer the pretest. Say each word, use it in the sentence provided on page T81, and then repeat the word. ACCESSING PRIOR KNOWLEDGE

Self-Check Have children check their own pretests by referring to their list of Spelling Words. For each misspelled word on the pretest, remind children to use the **Study Steps to Learn a Word** on pages 8–9 of the Pupil's Edition. STUDENT SELF-ASSESSMENT

Introducing the Lesson To use the open sort, copy Home Activities Master 12A in the Copying Masters section.

Open Sort: Distribute word cards to children and have them individually or cooperatively select criteria for sorting. Then, as you name each Spelling Word, ask which categories it might fit in. You may want to send home the word cards so that children can complete the Home Activities Master.

Closed Sort: Read aloud with children the lesson title and the Spelling Words on Pupil's Edition page 54.

- Write the words *rake, mice, hive,* and *gate* on the board. Ask children how the four words are alike. (CVCe pattern)
- Have children identify the vowel sound in each word.
- As children sort the words by vowel sounds, write the two lists on the board. Encourage children to add their own words to each list. SORTING WORDS

In Summary Ask children what kind of vowel sound a word with the CVCe pattern often has. (long) Elicit that long *a* can be spelled *a-e* and long *i, i-e.*

Your Own Words Ask children to brainstorm and list in their Spelling Logs other the CVCe words that have the long *a* or long *i* vowel sound. RECOGNIZING PATTERNS

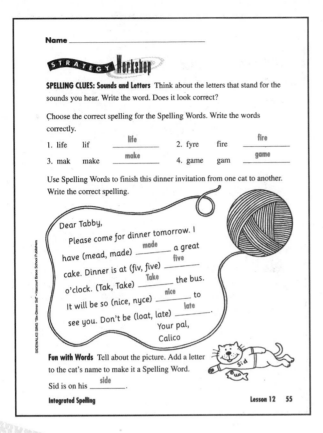

Name _____

STRATEGY Workshop

SPELLING CLUES: Sounds and Letters Think about the letters that stand for the sounds you hear. Write the word. Does it look correct?

Choose the correct spelling for the Spelling Words. Write the words correctly.

1. life   lif   _life_   2. fyre   fire   _fire_
3. mak   make   _make_   4. game   gam   _game_

Use Spelling Words to finish this dinner invitation from one cat to another. Write the correct spelling.

Dear Tabby,
  Please come for dinner tomorrow. I
have (mead, made) _made_ a great
cake. Dinner is at (fiv, five) _five_
o'clock. (Tak, Take) _Take_ the bus.
It will be so (nice, nyce) _nice_ to
see you. Don't be (loat, late) _late_.
          Your pal,
          Calico

Fun with Words Tell about the picture. Add a letter to the cat's name to make it a Spelling Word.

Sid is on his _side_.

Integrated Spelling   Lesson 12   55

STRATEGY WORKSHOP page 55

Spelling Clues: Sounds and Letters Ask
children what vowel sound they hear in the word *bake*. (long *a*) Then have children think about letters that can stand for the long *a* sound. (*a-e, ai, ay*) Have children use what they know about letter sounds to spell *bake*. Write their spelling on the board. Ask if it looks right. If it doesn't, help children spell the word correctly. Follow a similar procedure for long *i*. Use the word *ride*. APPLYING SPELLING STRATEGIES

 SEMI-PHONETIC SPELLERS To reinforce long vowel sounds with final *e*, make cards for the following words: *mad, kit, cap, pin*. Then make four letter *e* cards. As you display each word, have it identified. Then add the *e* and have the new word identified. Point out the long vowel sounds.

Fun with Words Write *Sam* on the board. Ask
what letter children can add to *Sam* to get a new word. (*e*) Write *same* and have it identified. Ask how the vowel sound changed when *e* was added to *Sam*. Then have children complete the activity independently.

SECOND-LANGUAGE SUPPORT Have children point to their fronts, backs, and sides. Then ask whether the cat in the picture is on its front, back, or side. USING PICTURE CLUES

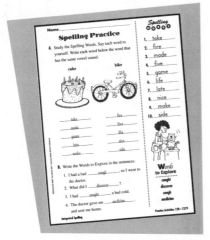

RESOURCES: PRACTICE ACTIVITIES MASTER 12B

Use as extra practice or as a homework activity.

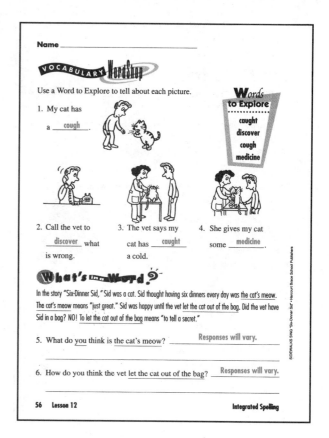

VOCABULARY WORDSHOP pages 56–57

Words to Explore Write the Words to Explore on the board: *caught, discover, cough, medicine.* Discuss their meanings with children. Then ask what is happening in each picture on Pupil's Edition page 56. Have children use the words from the box to complete the sentences about the pictures.

Spelling Log Have children add the Words to Explore to their Spelling Logs.

TRANSITIONAL SPELLERS Assign the Words to Explore. As a practice activity, have children trace the shape of each Word to Explore on a separate sheet of paper. Under the shape, ask them to write a clue for the word. Have children exchange papers and use the clues to write the correct words in the shapes.

What's in a Word? Tell children that some expressions don't mean exactly what the words say. Write on the board the sentence *Jane is "on the ball."* Read the sentence. Then ask whether it means Jane is really standing on a ball. (no) Explain that it means Jane is smart, or knows what is going on. Ask what other expressions children know that don't mean exactly what the words say. Then have them complete the activity independently. FIGURATIVE LANGUAGE

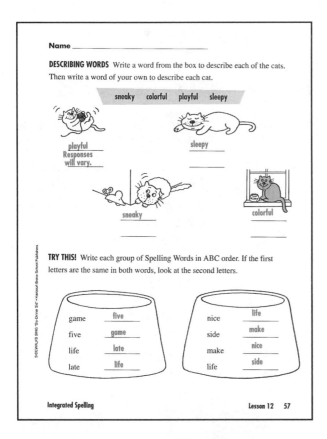

Name _____

DESCRIBING WORDS Write a word from the box to describe each of the cats. Then write a word of your own to describe each cat.

| sneaky | colorful | playful | sleepy |

playful
Responses
will vary.

sleepy

sneaky

colorful

TRY THIS! Write each group of Spelling Words in ABC order. If the first letters are the same in both words, look at the second letters.

game	five
five	game
life	late
late	life

nice	life
side	make
make	nice
life	side

Integrated Spelling

Lesson 12   57

Over a period of time, many words in the English language have taken on meanings very different from their original meanings. A striking example is the word *nice*, which once meant "stupid."

Describing Words

Write *cat* on the board. Have children name words they can think of when they think of cats. Write them in a web around the word *cat*. Then have children tell how they might describe the cats pictured. Add those words to the web. USING DESCRIBING WORDS

 Working Together Have children work in pairs to draw their own pictures of cats. Then ask them to write describing words for their cats around the pictures. Children might enjoy using their words to write a poem about cats.

Try This!

Write the words *cat* and *cute* on the board. Ask which would come first in alphabetical order and why. Remind children that if words begin with the same letter, children should look at the second letter to put the words in alphabetical order. USING ALPHABETICAL ORDER

Posttest

To check children's mastery of the Spelling Words, use the context sentences on page T81 to administer the posttest.

Optional Writing Idea: Description

Have children choose one of the cats pictured in the Describing Words activity on Pupil's Edition page 57 to write about. Point out that they have already written two describing words that they can use in their descriptions. Before children write, suggest that they list those two words and brainstorm other words and phrases that describe their chosen cats.

playful
small
has spots
cute

LESSON WRAP-UP

Words to Explore and Context Sentences

1. **caught**   She **caught** the ball with both hands.
2. **discover**   You can **discover** interesting shells at the beach.
3. **cough**   Mike had a cold and a **cough.**
4. **medicine**   I took **medicine** when I was sick.

Reteach

LEARNING DIFFERENCES Write the Spelling Words from this lesson on a sheet of paper. Leave out the vowel *a* or *i* from each word. Tell children that a vowel is missing from each word. Say the first word aloud and have children repeat it after you. Then have children write in the missing vowel and read the word aloud. Follow the same procedure with each of the remaining words.
VISUAL/AUDITORY MODALITIES

| t**a**ke |
| f**i**re |
| m**a**de |
| f**i**ve |
| g**a**me |
| l**i**fe |
| l**a**te |
| n**i**ce |
| m**a**ke |
| s**i**de |

INTEGRATED CURRICULUM ACTIVITIES

Language Arts

Rhyme Time Children can play this game in pairs or groups of three. Write each of the Spelling Words from this lesson on a card. Mix up the cards and place them face down in a pile. The first player picks the top card and tries to think of a word that rhymes with the word on the card. If the player can name a rhyming word with the same spelling pattern, he or she gets to keep the card. If the player cannot think of a rhyming word with the same spelling pattern, the card is returned to the pile. The game continues until no cards are left in the pile.

Social Studies

What Do You Do? Write the following Spelling Words on cards: *fire, game, life, make, take.* Have children work in groups of five. Give one word to each group. Have children think of a profession that their word makes them think of. Then have them use the word in a riddle about the profession. Ideas might include the following:

fire—firefighter, forest ranger
game—athlete, baseball player
life—doctor, lifeguard
make—chef, dressmaker
take—bus driver, garbage collector

Words Like *note* and *cute*

Objective
To spell words with long *o* spelled *o-e* or long *u* spelled *u-e*

Lesson Planner
Assign words based on the developmental levels of individual children. See the Assignment Guide on page T250.

Informal Assessment
Children's writing may show that they have difficulty spelling words that have the long *o* or long *u* vowel sound.

MODEL

rose
A (ros) is a flower.

Use this lesson to introduce the spelling of words with the long *o* vowel sound spelled *o-e* or the long *u* vowel sound spelled *u-e*. Encourage children to apply what they have learned to help them spell other words that end with *e* and have a long *o* or long *u* vowel sound. After children have completed the lesson, have them proofread their writing and correct any errors they may have made spelling words with long vowel sounds that are spelled *o-e* or *u-e*.

SECOND-LANGUAGE SUPPORT Discuss the meanings of the Spelling Words. Ask children to demonstrate or illustrate the meanings of the words *nose, rope, bone, mule, huge,* and *note.* MAKING INFERENCES

Pretest/Posttest Context Sentences
You may want to test Semi-Phonetic Spellers on words 1–6 only.

1.	**bone**	The dog buried the **bone.**
2.	**mule**	I rode a **mule** at the Grand Canyon.
3.	**nose**	The rabbit has a pink **nose.**
4.	**huge**	An elephant is a **huge** animal.
5.	**use**	May I **use** your pencil?
*6.	**note**	Mom wrote a **note** to my teacher.
7.	**rope**	Ben tied a knot in the **rope.**
8.	**cute**	The kittens are so **cute**!
9.	**woke**	Rosa **woke** up early this morning.
10.	**hope**	I **hope** you can come to my party.

*Word appearing in "Old Henry." Some additional story words following the generalizations are *wrote* and *excuse.*

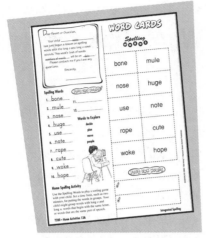

RESOURCES: HOME ACTIVITIES MASTER 13A

NOTE: Fill in the teacher's note on the Home Activities Master before sending it home with children. See the Assignment Guide on page T250 for assigning lists of words.

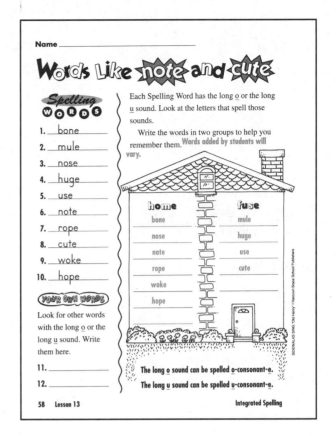

INTRODUCTION page 58

Pretest Administer the pretest. Say each word, use it in the sentence provided on page T87, and then repeat the word. ACCESSING PRIOR KNOWLEDGE

Self-Check Have children check their own pretests by referring to their list of Spelling Words. For each misspelled word on the pretest, remind children to use the **Study Steps to Learn a Word** on pages 8–9 of the Pupil's Edition. STUDENT SELF-ASSESSMENT

Introducing the Lesson To use the open sort, copy Home Activities Master 13A in the Copying Masters section.

Open Sort: Distribute word cards to children and have them individually or cooperatively select criteria for sorting. Have children tell why they grouped the words as they did. You may want to send home the word cards so that children can complete the Home Activities Master.

Closed Sort: Read aloud with children the lesson title and the Spelling Words on Pupil's Edition page 58.

- Write the words *fuse, cone, dome,* and *cute* on the board. Ask children how the four words are alike. (CVCe pattern; long vowel sound)
- Have children identify the vowel sound in each word.
- As children sort the words by vowel sounds, write the two lists on the board. Encourage children to add their own words to each list. SORTING WORDS

In Summary Ask children to summarize the lesson in their own words. Elicit that the long *o* vowel sound can be spelled with *o-e* and the long *u* vowel sound can be spelled with *u-e*.

Your Own Words For homework or practice, you may want to have children list in their Spelling Logs other words that have the long *o* or long *u* vowel sound. RECOGNIZING PATTERNS

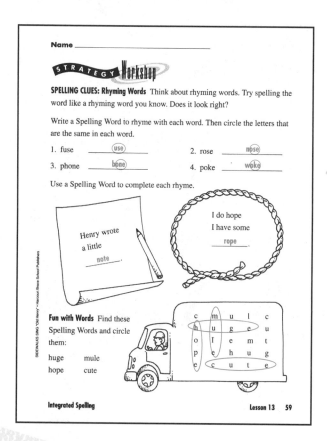

Final *e* that is "silent" is, in fact, a pattern marker. In words such as *hop* and *hope* or *cut* and *cute* that have the same spellings except for final *e*, final *e* indicates which of the two sounds the vowel stands for in the word.

STRATEGY WORKSHOP page 59

Spelling Clues: Rhyming Words
Have children tell how thinking about rhyming words can help them spell words when they are writing. Ask children to give examples of some rhyming words and to tell how to spell them. APPLYING SPELLING STRATEGIES

SEMI-PHONETIC SPELLERS Remind children that rhyming words often end alike. As children read each word on Pupil's Edition page 59, have them look for a Spelling Word with the same ending sound.

SECOND-LANGUAGE SUPPORT Write the words *wrote* and *hope* on the board and have them read aloud. Point out that in the middle of Pupil's Edition page 59, children will be looking for words that rhyme with *wrote* and *hope*. Ask children to suggest possible answers. RHYMING WORDS

Fun with Words
Tell children that the letters of the Spelling Words hidden in this puzzle may be written across or down. Then have children complete the activity independently.

Practice Activities

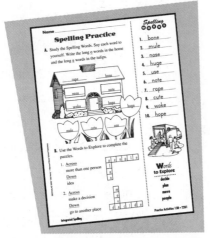

RESOURCES: PRACTICE ACTIVITIES MASTER 13B

Use as extra practice or as a homework activity.

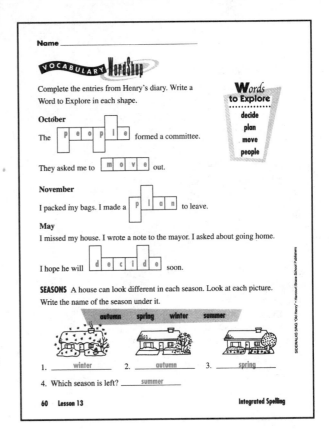

VOCABULARY WORDSHOP pages 60–61

Words to Explore Write the Words to Explore on the board: *decide, plan, move, people.* Discuss their meanings with children. Then explain that the word shapes will help children figure out which Word to Explore completes each sentence.

Spelling Log Have children add the Words to Explore to their Spelling Logs.

TRANSITIONAL SPELLERS Assign the Words to Explore. As a practice activity, have children write the Words to Explore in alphabetical order. Encourage them to use each word in a sentence.

Seasons Ask children to name the four seasons. Have them tell which season is their favorite and why. Ask how their street might look during each season. Then have children complete the activity independently.

Vocabulary Activities

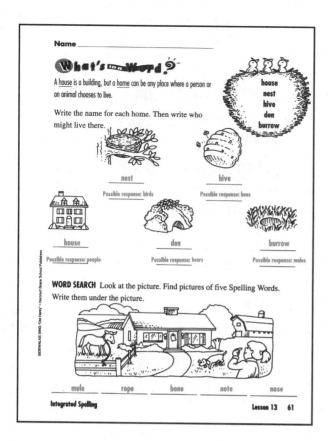

What's in a Word? Have children name different homes that animals or people live in. List their responses on the board. Encourage children to draw one kind of home and the animal or person who lives there. WORD MEANINGS

 Working Together Have children work together to make a home collage. Encourage them to cut out pictures of homes from magazines or to draw homes. Have them use their collage to discuss different kinds of homes with their classmates.

Word Search Ask children what kind of home the picture shows. (a farmhouse) Encourage children to circle the pictures for the five Spelling Words before writing the Spelling Words on the lines. USING PICTURE CLUES

Posttest To check children's mastery of the Spelling Words, use the context sentences on page T87 to administer the posttest.

Optional Writing Idea: Paragraphs Tell children to choose two of the homes pictured in the What's in a Word? activity on Pupil's Edition page 61. Have them write a comparison of the two homes. Suggest that they organize their ideas by making a Venn diagram that shows how the two homes are alike and how they are different.

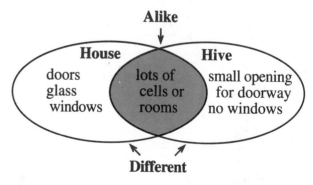

After children have completed their diagrams, suggest that they draft two paragraphs. In the first paragraph, they can tell how the two homes are alike. In the second paragraph, they can tell how the two are different.

Vocabulary Activities

LESSON WRAP-UP

Words to Explore and Context Sentences

1. **decide**   She had to **decide** whether to get a red or a green hat.
2. **plan**   They have a **plan** for getting out of the house in case of fire.
3. **move**   We will **move** the table to the wall.
4. **people**   A lot of **people** came to the show.

Reteach

LEARNING DIFFERENCES Write the Spelling Words from this lesson on a sheet of paper. Omit the vowel *o* or *u*. Tell children that a vowel is missing from each word. Say the first word aloud and have children repeat it after you. Then have children write in the missing vowel on a self-stick note, place it where it belongs, and read the word aloud. Follow the same procedure with each of the remaining words. VISUAL/AUDITORY MODALITIES

o b[o]ne
m[u]le
n_se
h_ge
o _se
n_te
r_pe
c_te
o w_ke
h_pe

INTEGRATED CURRICULUM ACTIVITIES

Language Arts

Parts of Speech Have children work in small groups to decide whether each of the Spelling Words in this lesson is a noun, a describing word, or a verb. Ask children to list the words in three columns on a sheet of paper. After children have completed their lists, have them take turns selecting a noun, a describing word, and a verb to use in a silly sentence.

Nouns	Describing Words	Verbs
bone	huge	use
mule	cute	woke
nose		hope
note		
rope		

Music

B-O-N-E Have children work in small groups to spell Spelling Words to the tune of "Frère Jacques." For each verse, encourage children to first spell the word and then to make up the last lines to tell what the word means. A sample follows:

B-O-N-E, B-O-N-E,
That spells *bone!*
That spells *bone!*
A bone is in my body.
A bone is in my body.
Yes, it is!
Yes, it is!

Invite children to sing their songs.

Consonant Clusters

Objective
To spell words with consonant clusters with *l*, *r*, or *t*

Lesson Planner
Assign words based on the developmental levels of individual children. See the Assignment Guide on page T250.

Informal Assessment
Children's writing may show that they have difficulty spelling words with initial or final consonant clusters.

MODEL

stop
We (sop) for the red light.

Use this lesson to introduce the spelling of words with consonant clusters. Encourage children to apply what they have learned to help them spell other words that begin or end with consonant clusters. After children have completed the lesson, have them proofread their writing and correct any errors they may have made spelling words with these clusters.

SECOND-LANGUAGE SUPPORT Children who speak Chinese or other Asian languages may experience difficulty distinguishing *fr* from *fl*. Provide opportunities for them to listen to and repeat pairs of words such as *free, flee; frame, flame;* and *fry, fly.*

Speakers of Chinese and Vietnamese may also have problems differentiating between initial *gr* and *dr*. Have children listen to and repeat pairs of words such as *grain, drain; grip, drip;* and *grew, drew.*

Because the clusters *st* and *sl* do not appear at the beginnings of words in Spanish, these initial clusters may cause problems for Spanish-speaking children. You may notice that children tend to add the short *e* sound in front of words with initial *st* or *sl*. Write words such as *stop, stay, slip,* and *slow* on the board. Say each word aloud and have children repeat it. Have children underline and identify the letters that stand for the beginning sounds. Then say the word again.

Some children acquiring English may have difficulty distinguishing final *st* from final *s* or *ss*. Provide practice in listening to and repeating pairs of words such as *last, lass; mist, miss;* and *past, pass.* COMPARING AND CONTRASTING

Pretest/Posttest Context Sentences
You may want to test Semi-Phonetic Spellers on words 1–6 only.

*1.	**from**	I walked **from** my house to the store.
2.	**dry**	I got wet in the rain, but now I'm **dry.**
3.	**still**	Did the car move, or did it sit **still**?
4.	**fast**	How **fast** can that boat go?
*5.	**blow**	You **blow** into the horn to play it.
6.	**grass**	Cows eat **grass.**
7.	**sled**	They went down the snowy hill on their **sled.**
8.	**stood**	We **stood** up and cheered.
9.	**last**	The **last** letter of the alphabet is *z.*
10.	**fly**	We **fly** down the hill on our bikes.

*Words appearing in "Little Penguin's Tale." Some additional story words following the generalization are *trouble, friends, break, cried, place, glass, clever, sliding, best,* and *just.*

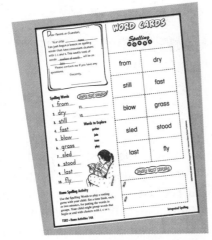

RESOURCES: HOME ACTIVITIES MASTER 14A

NOTE: Fill in the teacher's note on the Home Activities Master before sending it home with children. See the Assignment Guide on page T250 for assigning lists of words.

Name _____

Consonant Clusters

Spelling WORDS

1. from
2. dry
3. still
4. fast
5. blow
6. grass
7. sled
8. stood
9. last
10. fly

YOUR OWN WORDS

Look for other words with consonant clusters. Write them here.

11. _____
12. _____

62   Lesson 14

Each Spelling Word has a consonant cluster. Look at the letters that spell the consonant clusters. Do you see the clusters with l, r, and t?

Write the Spelling Words in groups to help you remember them. Words added by students will vary.

freeze
- from
- dry
- grass

stop or past
- still
- stood
- fast
- last

play
- blow
- sled
- fly

The letters l, r, and t can be parts of consonant clusters.

Integrated Spelling

INTRODUCTION page 62

Pretest Administer the pretest. Say each word, use it in the sentence provided on page T93, and then repeat the word. ACCESSING PRIOR KNOWLEDGE

Self-Check Have children check their own pretests by referring to their list of Spelling Words. For each misspelled word on the pretest, remind children to use the **Study Steps to Learn a Word** on pages 8–9 of the Pupil's Edition. STUDENT SELF-ASSESSMENT

Introducing the Lesson To use the open sort, copy Home Activities Master 14A in the Copying Masters section.

Open Sort: Distribute word cards to children and have them individually or cooperatively select criteria for sorting. Then as you name different categories, ask which words could fit in them. You may want to send home the word cards so that children can complete the Home Activities Master.

Closed Sort: Read aloud with children the lesson title and the Spelling Words on Pupil's Edition page 62.

- Write the words *frog, blue, stop, past, flat,* and *grow* on the board. Have children identify initial or final consonant clusters.
- Have children sort into groups the words that have consonant clusters with *l, r,* and *t.* Ask them to name other words for each group. Write their responses in groups on the board.
- Ask children to sort words with consonant clusters with *t* according to whether the words begin or end with the cluster. SORTING WORDS

In Summary Ask how all the words in the lesson are alike. (All have consonant clusters.) Then point out that all the clusters have the letter *l, r,* or *t* in them.

Your Own Words As children read billboards and other environmental print, encourage them to list in their Spelling Logs other words with initial or final consonant clusters. RECOGNIZING PATTERNS

Sorting Activities

Name _____

STRATEGY Workshop

SPELLING CLUES: Rhyming Words Think of rhyming words. Then spell the word like a rhyming word you know. Does it look right?

Circle the two rhyming words. Then write the Spelling Word.

1. cast land (last) ___last___
2. (grass)(brass) grape ___grass___
3. drip (dry)(try) ___dry___
4. (stood) said (hood) ___stood___

Write a rhyming Spelling Word to complete the ad.

Come to the Land of Ice and Snow

Rent a (bed) ___sled___. (My) ___Fly___

down a snowy hill as (last) ___fast___

as you can go. Then hear the wind

(glow) ___blow___. You won't want to

sit (hill) ___still___! You'll want to go,

go, go!

Fun with Words Write a Spelling Word to tell about the penguin.

I am a penguin ___from___ the South Pole.

Integrated Spelling   Lesson 14   63

> Goals of a spelling program include developing independent spellers who can spell many words and developing writers who will edit their written communications.
>
> (Maryann Murphy Manning and Gary L. Manning)

STRATEGY WORKSHOP page 63

Spelling Clues: Rhyming Words Have children tell how thinking about rhyming words can help them spell words when they are writing. Write these words on the board: *dog, frog, free.* Have children tell which two rhyme. Then ask them to spell other words that rhyme with *dog* and *frog.* APPLYING SPELLING STRATEGIES

SEMI-PHONETIC SPELLERS Make, or have children make, word cards for the rhyming words on Pupil's Edition page 63. Have them mix the cards and then use them to play a matching game. Children should match and spell the rhyming words.

Fun with Words Have children tell what the penguin in the picture is doing. Then have them write the Spelling Word to complete the sentence.

SECOND-LANGUAGE SUPPORT Discuss the meaning of the words *South Pole* and point out the location on a globe. Ask children whether they think there is really a pole at the South Pole. DRAWING CONCLUSIONS

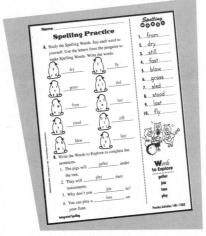

RESOURCES: PRACTICE ACTIVITIES MASTER 14B

Use as extra practice or as a homework activity.

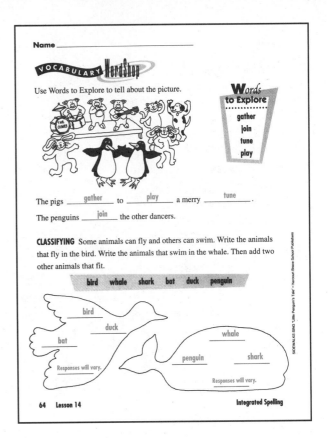

- -

VOCABULARY WORDSHOP pages 64–65

Words to Explore Write the Words to Explore on the board: *gather, join, tune, play.* Discuss their meanings with children. Then have children tell what the animals in the picture are doing. Encourage children to use the Words to Explore in their discussion of the picture.

Spelling Log Have children add the Words to Explore to their Spelling Logs.

TRANSITIONAL SPELLERS Assign the Words to Explore. As a practice activity, have children play the following game: Write the Words to Explore on the board. Then organize children into two teams. Say a sentence, but leave out the Word to Explore. The first two children from each team write the word on the board to complete the sentence. Each player to finish correctly scores a point for his or her team.

Classifying When children have completed the activity, encourage them to make a collage of animals that can fly or animals that can swim. Have them cut pictures of the animals from magazines or draw their own pictures. As children show their collages, have others tell which category the animals fit in.

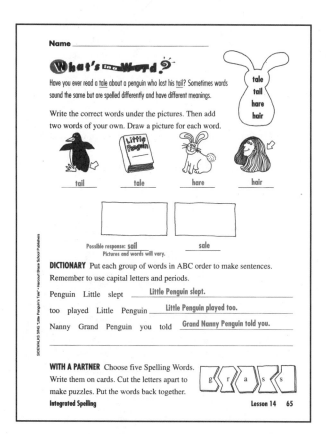

What's in a Word? Write the words *eight* and *ate* on the board. Point out that the words sound alike but have different spellings. Have children use the words in sentences to show their meanings. USING HOMOPHONES

 Working Together Have children work together to make a list of homophones. Encourage children to write or draw a definition for each word.

Dictionary Review with children how to put words in alphabetical order. Then have them put these words in alphabetical order to make a sentence: *cat, with, yarn, plays, A.* Write the sentence. Point out the capital letter at the beginning and the period at the end. USING ALPHABETICAL ORDER

With a Partner Provide tagboard cards for children to use for their puzzles. Have children exchange puzzles to put back together. WORD PLAY

Posttest To check children's mastery of the Spelling Words, use the context sentences on page T93 to administer the posttest.

Optional Writing Idea: Invitation Have children write an invitation to the party pictured on Pupil's Edition page 64. You may want to provide them with an invitation frame that they can copy and complete. Then have children use crayons or markers to decorate their invitations.

> ☀ JOIN THE PARTY! ☀
>
> You are invited to join our party!
> Date: _____
> Time: _____
> Place: _____
> Here's what we will do: _____
>
> Your friend,

Vocabulary Activities

LESSON WRAP-UP

Words to Explore and Context Sentences

1. **gather**   We will **gather** at the front steps.
2. **join**   We asked him to **join** us at the table.
3. **tune**   Bill can play this **tune** on the fiddle.
4. **play**   Can you **play** a song on the piano?

Reteach

LEARNING DIFFERENCES Have children make a tape recording of the Spelling Words. Suggest that they refer to the Spelling Word list as they say each word, spell it, and then repeat it on the tape. Then have children listen to their tape. Encourage them to stop the tape after each word and write the word from memory. AUDITORY MODALITY

INTEGRATED CURRICULUM ACTIVITY

Language Arts

Opposites Attract An even number of children can play this game. Write the following six Spelling Words on cards.

On another set of cards, write the following six words that are opposites of the Spelling Words.

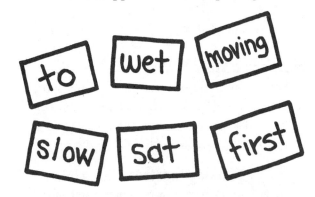

If more than twelve children will be playing the game, make two cards for each additional pair of children. Use Spelling Words from past lessons and their opposites. Words you might use include *huge, tiny; cold, hot; top, bottom; stop, go; sad, happy;* and *bad, good.* Mix the cards and distribute them at random to the children. Have children find classmates with the opposites of their words. Ask pairs of children to read aloud their words and to use them in sentences.

LESSON 15

Final Double Consonants

Objective
To spell words that end with double consonants

Lesson Planner
Assign words based on the developmental levels of individual children. See the Assignment Guide on page T250.

Informal Assessment
Children's writing may show that they have difficulty spelling words that end in double consonants.

MODEL

will

I ⟨wil⟩ be home late.

Use this lesson to introduce the spelling of words with the final double consonants *ll, ss,* and *dd.* Encourage children to apply what they have learned to help them spell other words that end with these double consonants. After children have completed the lesson, have them proofread their writing and correct any errors they may have made spelling words with final *ll, ss,* or *dd.*

SECOND-LANGUAGE SUPPORT Final consonants can cause difficulty for children whose first language does not emphasize them. Only a few consonants appear at the ends of words in Spanish, for example, and many Spanish-speaking people tend to drop final consonants in conversation. Write the Spelling Words that end with *ss* on the board and read them to children. Have volunteers underline the letters that stand for the ending sound in each word and identify the letters. Have children repeat each word aloud with you. SOUND/LETTER RELATIONSHIPS

Pretest/Posttest Context Sentences
You may want to test Semi-Phonetic Spellers on words 1–6 only.

*1.	**ball**	Kick the **ball** into the goal.
*2.	**add**	Let's **add** some apples to the fruit salad.
3.	**miss**	Hurry so we won't **miss** the bus.
*4.	**all**	She used **all** the paint.
5.	**dress**	Gina wore her new **dress** today.
6.	**fall**	Be careful not to **fall** down.
7.	**less**	There is **less** milk in this cup than in that one.
*8.	**call**	Will you **call** me on the phone?
9.	**pass**	I **pass** his house on my way to school.
10.	**glass**	Windows are made of **glass.**

*Words appearing in "Fiesta!" Some additional story words following the generalization are *yell, smell(s),* and *fill(s).*

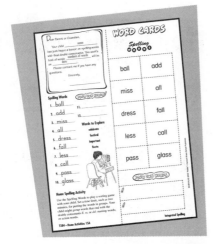

RESOURCES: HOME ACTIVITIES MASTER **15A**

NOTE: Fill in the teacher's note on the Home Activities Master before sending it home with children. See the Assignment Guide on page T250 for assigning lists of words.

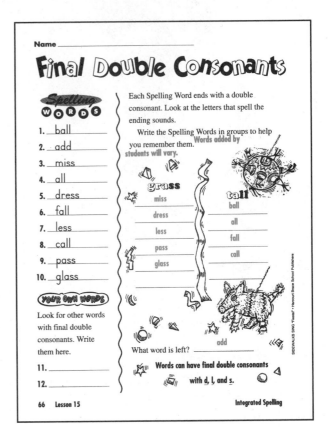

INTRODUCTION page 66

Pretest Administer the pretest. Say each word, use it in the sentence provided on page T99, and then repeat the word. ACCESSING PRIOR KNOWLEDGE

Self-Check Have children check their own pretests by referring to their list of Spelling Words. For each misspelled word on the pretest, remind children to use the **Study Steps to Learn a Word** on pages 8–9 of the Pupil's Edition. STUDENT SELF-ASSESSMENT

Introducing the Lesson To use the open sort, copy Home Activities Master 15A in the Copying Masters section.

Open Sort: Distribute word cards to children and have them individually or cooperatively select criteria for sorting. Have children tell why they grouped words as they did. You may want to send home the word cards so that children can complete the Home Activities Master.

Closed Sort: Read aloud with children the lesson title and the Spelling Words on Pupil's Edition page 66.

- Write the words *hall, grass, odd, tall, dress,* and *add* on the board. Have children identify the final consonants in each word.
- Have children tell which words are alike because they end with the same letters. Write the words in groups on the board.
- Have children tell which group each of these words belongs in: *fuss, still, doll, brass.* SORTING WORDS

In Summary Ask children to summarize the lesson in their own words. Elicit that all of the words end with double consonants.

Your Own Words For homework or practice, you may want to have pairs or teams of children list in their Spelling Logs other words with final double consonants. RECOGNIZING PATTERNS

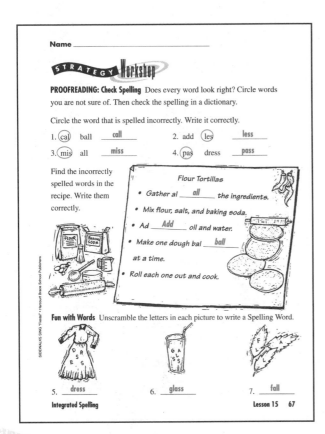

Name _____

STRATEGY Workshop

PROOFREADING: Check Spelling Does every word look right? Circle words you are not sure of. Then check the spelling in a dictionary.

Circle the word that is spelled incorrectly. Write it correctly.

1. (cal) ball _____call_____   2. add (les) _____less_____

3. (mis) all _____miss_____   4. (pas) dress _____pass_____

Find the incorrectly spelled words in the recipe. Write them correctly.

Flour Tortillas

- Gather al _____all_____ the ingredients.
- Mix flour, salt, and baking soda.
- Ad _____Add_____ oil and water.
- Make one dough bal _____ball_____ at a time.
- Roll each one out and cook.

Fun with Words Unscramble the letters in each picture to write a Spelling Word.

5. _____dress_____   6. _____glass_____   7. _____fall_____

Integrated Spelling   **Lesson 15   67**

> Spelling makes sense only in the context of the written word, where it serves the needs of both writers and readers. Viewed in its proper perspective, spelling is a tool to assist writers in expressing themselves effectively.
> (Texas Education Agency)

STRATEGY WORKSHOP page 67

Proofreading: Check Spelling
Write this sentence on the board: *The dgg barked.* Have children read the sentence and tell which word does not look right. Circle *dgg*. Cross it out and write *dog* correctly. Have children use this strategy as they complete Pupil's Edition page 67. APPLYING SPELLING STRATEGIES

 SECOND-LANGUAGE SUPPORT As you read aloud each step in the recipe on Pupil's Edition page 67, have children act it out to show they understand the meaning. Discuss any meanings that are not clear. Before children complete the activity, read aloud the recipe again and emphasize the misspelled words. WORD MEANINGS

Fun with Words
Remind children that each word ends with a double consonant. Have children use this as a clue in figuring out the words.

SEMI-PHONETIC SPELLERS If children need help unscrambling the words in Fun with Words, supply them with the last letter for each word. Remind them that each word ends with a double consonant.

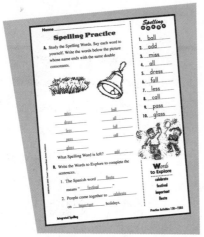

RESOURCES: PRACTICE ACTIVITIES MASTER 15B

Use as extra practice or as a homework activity.

VOCABULARY WORDSHOP pages 68–69

Words to Explore Write the Words to Explore on the board: *celebrate, festival, important, fiesta.* Discuss their meanings with children. Point out that *fiesta* is a Spanish word. Ask which other Word to Explore tells what *fiesta* means. *(festival)* You might want to point out that either *fiesta* or *festival* can be used in sentence 1 or 4.

Spelling Log Have children add the Words to Explore to their Spelling Logs.

TRANSITIONAL SPELLERS Assign the Words to Explore. As a practice activity, have children make a word search puzzle for the Words to Explore. Give children graph paper. They should put one letter of each word in each square and use other letters to fill empty squares. Have children exchange puzzles to solve.

Musical Nouns Have children name and tell about musical instruments with which they are familiar. List the instrument names on the board. If necessary, add *maracas* to the list. Explain that maracas might be played at a fiesta.

What's in a Word? Discuss with children some of the things they might celebrate, such as holidays and birthdays. Ask what they do at their celebrations. Encourage them to tell about games they play or foods they eat. Then have children complete the activity independently. WORD MEANINGS

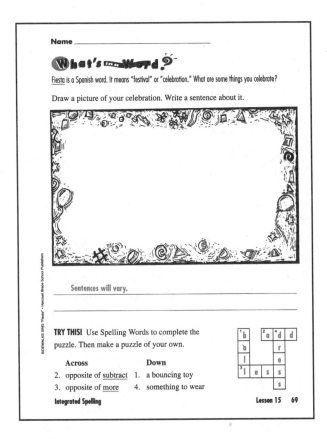

Name _____

What's the Word?

Fiesta is a Spanish word. It means "festival" or "celebration." What are some things you celebrate?

Draw a picture of your celebration. Write a sentence about it.

Sentences will vary.

TRY THIS! Use Spelling Words to complete the puzzle. Then make a puzzle of your own.

Across
2. opposite of <u>subtract</u>
3. opposite of <u>more</u>

Down
1. a bouncing toy
4. something to wear

	¹b	²a	⁴d	d
	a		r	
	l		e	
³l	e	s	s	
			s	

Integrated Spelling

Lesson 15   69

- -

Try This! Read the puzzle clues aloud with children. If necessary, help them locate the number in the puzzle that matches each clue. Supply grid paper for children to use when they make their own puzzles. WORD MEANINGS

 Working Together Have children work in pairs to make their crossword puzzles. Provide tagboard squares or small self-stick notes. Suggest that children write each letter for each word on a square. They can then use the squares to build word puzzles.

Posttest To check children's mastery of their Spelling Words, use the context sentences on page T99 to administer the posttest.

Optional Writing Idea: Personal Story Have children write about the picture they drew of a celebration. (See Pupil's Edition page 69.) Help children make a chart, such as the one shown below, to organize their writing. Children may want to put their stories into a class celebrations book for a Reading Center.

What	4th of July picnic
Who	my whole family
When	last summer
Where	at my grandma's house
What Happened	Muffin and her puppies ate all the hot dogs.

Vocabulary Activities

LESSON WRAP-UP

Words to Explore and Context Sentences

1. **celebrate**   I **celebrate** my birthday every year.
2. **festival**   People danced at the **festival.**
3. **important**   It's **important** to know the rules when you play a game.
4. **fiesta**   Roberto told us about the **fiesta** for Cinco de Mayo.

Reteach

LEARNING DIFFERENCES Write each Spelling Word at the top of a sheet of paper. Each day, have children use a different style to spell the words on the papers. Possible ways for writing are with paint, with alphabet noodles, with colored glue, or with different-colored crayons. VISUAL/KINESTHETIC MODALITIES

INTEGRATED CURRICULUM ACTIVITIES

Physical Education

Pass the Ball Play this game with a foam or a soft rubber ball that children can pass from hand to hand. Have children sit in a circle and pass the ball around as music plays on a tape. Stop the tape at random. When the music stops, give the child holding the ball a Spelling Word to spell aloud. Continue the game until children have spelled all of the Spelling Words correctly.

Language Arts

Riddle Time Write the Spelling Words on cards and put the cards in a paper bag or other container. Ask volunteers to choose a word, to read it silently, and to tell a riddle about the word or act out its meaning. Ask the rest of the group to think about the clues and to guess the Spelling Word.

LESSON 16

Words with *sh* and *ch*

Objective
To spell words that begin or end with the digraph *sh* or *ch*

Lesson Planner
Assign words based on the developmental levels of individual children. See the Assignment Guide on page T250.

Informal Assessment
Children's writing may show that they have difficulty spelling words with the digraph *sh* or *ch*.

MODEL

dish
The food is on the (dich).

Use this lesson to introduce the spelling of words with initial and final *sh* or *ch*. Encourage children to apply what they have learned to help them spell other words that begin or end with these digraphs. After children have completed the lesson, have them proofread their writing and correct any errors they may have made spelling words that begin or end with *sh* or *ch*.

SECOND-LANGUAGE SUPPORT Because the sound /sh/ is not found in some languages, it causes difficulty for many children. Spanish-speaking children, as well as others, may substitute the sound /ch/ for initial /sh/. Give children practice in listening to and repeating pairs of words such as *ship, chip; shop, chop;* and *shore, chore.*

Children may also have difficulty differentiating between final /ch/ and /sh/. Give practice with pairs of words such as *much, mush; which, wish;* and *rich, fish.* COMPARING AND CONTRASTING

Pretest/Posttest Context Sentences
You may want to test Semi-Phonetic Spellers on words 1–6 only.

1.	**ship**	The **ship** sailed across the ocean.
2.	**rich**	The **rich** king counted his gold.
3.	**wash**	After we eat, we **wash** the dishes.
*4.	**change**	You can **change** the color from red to blue.
5.	**shop**	I bought a sweater in that **shop.**
6.	**chest**	Put the toys away in the **chest.**
7.	**fish**	We saw a **fish** in the pond.
8.	**reach**	Can you **reach** the high shelf?
9.	**wish**	I **wish** the sun would come out.
10.	**shape**	A baseball has a round **shape.**

*Word appearing in "Miss Eva and the Red Balloon." Some additional story words following the generalization are *she, shiny,* and *shook.*

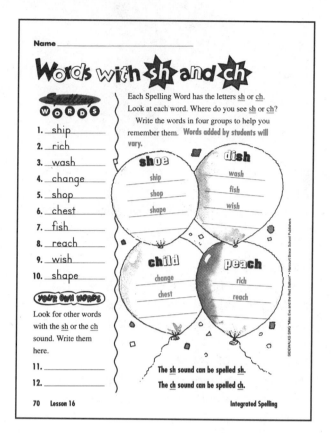

RESOURCES: HOME ACTIVITIES MASTER 16A

NOTE: Fill in the teacher's note on the Home Activities Master before sending it home with children. See the Assignment Guide on page T250 for assigning lists of words.

INTRODUCTION page 70

Pretest Administer the pretest. Say each word, use it in the sentence provided on page T105, and then repeat the word. ACCESSING PRIOR KNOWLEDGE

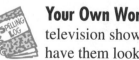 **Self-Check** Have children check their own pretests by referring to their list of Spelling Words. For each misspelled word on the pretest, remind children to use the **Study Steps to Learn a Word** on pages 8–9 of the Pupil's Edition. STUDENT SELF-ASSESSMENT

Introducing the Lesson To use the open sort, copy Home Activities Master 16A in the Copying Masters section.

Open Sort: Distribute word cards to children and have them individually or cooperatively select criteria for sorting. Then have children read their groups of words. Ask how the words are alike. You may want to send home the word cards so that children can complete the Home Activities Master.

Closed Sort: Read aloud with children the lesson title and the Spelling Words on Pupil's Edition page 70.

- Write the letters *sh* and *ch* as headings on the board. As you say these words, have children tell under which heading they belong: *cheek, beach, shade, chin, flash, which, shake,* and *crash.* Write each word in the correct column.
- Have children sort the words on the board into groups with initial *sh*, initial *ch*, final *sh*, and final *ch*. SORTING WORDS

In Summary Ask children how they would spell the sound /sh/ and how they would spell the sound /ch/.

Your Own Words As children view television shows, movies, and videos, have them look for objects whose names begin or end with *sh* or *ch*. Encourage them to write in their Spelling Logs the names of the objects they saw. RECOGNIZING PATTERNS

The alphabet we use to write words in English is a variation on the ancient Roman alphabet. Because the Roman alphabet does not include separate letters for single sounds like /sh/ and /ch/, we write pairs of letters to represent them. Many modern European languages also use the Roman alphabet and have had to make similar adjustments.

STRATEGY WORKSHOP page 71

Spelling Rules: Sounds and Letters Remind children that the sound /sh/ is often spelled with the letters *sh* and that the sound /ch/ is often spelled with the letters *ch*. Then have children tell whether they would use *sh* or *ch* to spell these words: *shine, China, such,* and *leash.* APPLYING SPELLING STRATEGIES

 SEMI-PHONETIC SPELLERS Have children work in pairs to spell and write the Spelling Words on Pupil's Edition page 71. Ask children to take turns saying and spelling aloud a word for the other to write.

 SECOND-LANGUAGE SUPPORT Write the Spelling Words *reach, change,* and *shape* on the board. Discuss their meanings. Then have children draw pictures to show their meanings. WORD MEANINGS

Fun with Words Have children name the things pictured. Tell them to write the Spelling Word that names each picture.

Practice Activities

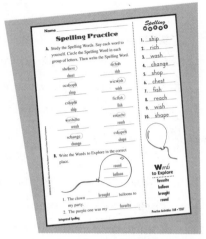

RESOURCES: PRACTICE ACTIVITIES MASTER 16B

Use as extra practice or as a homework activity.

- -

VOCABULARY WORDSHOP pages 72–73

Words to Explore Write the Words to Explore on the board: *favorite, balloon, brought, round.* Discuss their meanings with children. Then have children complete the activity.

 Spelling Log Have children add the Words to Explore to their Spelling Logs.

Dictionary Display a dictionary page. Ask what children notice about the order of the words. (They are in alphabetical order.) Then ask why words in a dictionary are listed in alphabetical order. (so readers can find them more easily) Have children complete the activity independently. USING ALPHABETICAL ORDER

 TRANSITIONAL SPELLERS Assign the Words to Explore. As a practice activity, have children look up the Words to Explore in a dictionary. Ask them to write each word. Next to each word, have children put the page number on which they found it and a definition of the word.

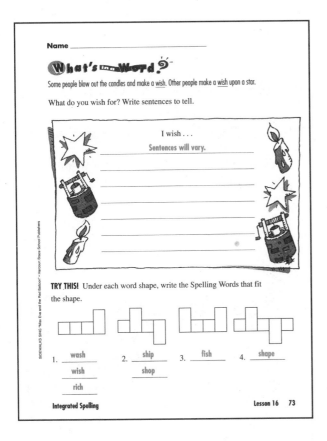

Name _____

What's in a Word?

Some people blow out the candles and make a wish. Other people make a wish upon a star.

What do you wish for? Write sentences to tell.

I wish . . .

Sentences will vary.

TRY THIS! Under each word shape, write the Spelling Words that fit the shape.

1. wash
   wish
   rich

2. ship
   shop

3. fish

4. shape

Integrated Spelling

Lesson 16   73

What's in a Word? Write *wish* on the board. Ask children to tell what they think of when they hear the word *wish*. Write their responses in a web around *wish*. Children can use these responses to help them complete the activity. DEVELOPING VOCABULARY

 Working Together Have children work together to make a group "I Wish" poem. Encourage each group to choose a Recorder to write down the wishes. Then have children illustrate their poem.

Try This! Ask children how many lines they see below the first word shape. (three) Explain that three Spelling Words will fit in that shape. Ask how many words fit each of the other shapes. Then have children complete the activity independently. USING SPELLING STRATEGIES

Posttest To check children's mastery of the Spelling Words, use the context sentences on page T105 to administer the posttest.

Optional Writing Idea: Story Have children write a story from the point of view of a fish who makes a wish. Help them brainstorm a list of wishes a fish might make. Then have each child choose a wish from the list to write about. Remind children to pretend they are the fish and to write as if the fish were telling about the wish. Children may want to wear simple fish costumes as they read their finished stories to their classmates.

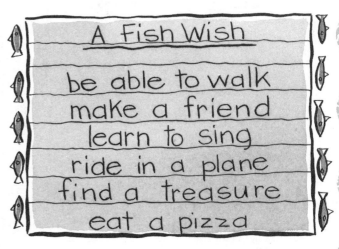

A Fish Wish

be able to walk
make a friend
learn to sing
ride in a plane
find a treasure
eat a pizza

Vocabulary Activities

LESSON WRAP-UP

Words to Explore and Context Sentences
1. **favorite** Summer is my **favorite** season.
2. **balloon** Dad tied a string to my **balloon.**
3. **brought** I **brought** a plant to school.
4. **round** A circle is **round.**

Reteach

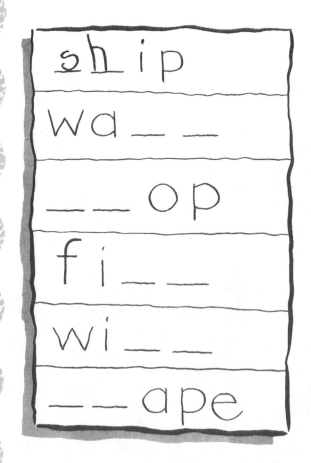

LEARNING DIFFERENCES Write all of the Spelling Words with *sh* on one sheet of paper, but omit *sh.* Say each word aloud and have children write *sh* to complete the word. Then have children read the completed words aloud. Follow a similar procedure for the Spelling Words with *ch.*
AUDITORY/KINESTHETIC MODALITIES

INTEGRATED CURRICULUM ACTIVITY

Language Arts

Wash Out Have children use the following words to make a set of seventeen word cards:

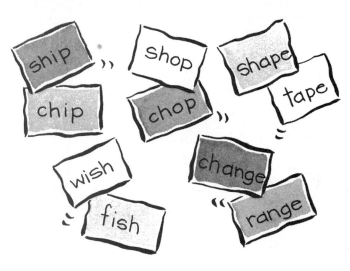

Groups of three or four can use the cards to play a game of "Wash Out." Mix up the cards and give each child three cards. Place the remaining cards face down in a pile. Children will try to make rhyming pairs. During each turn, a player picks a card and tries to make a rhyme with a card he or she holds. If the child makes a rhyming pair, he or she puts those cards aside and takes two more cards from the pile. If the child does not have a rhyming pair, he or she must put one card back in the pile. At the end of the game, one child will be left with the *wash* card, which has no rhyme.

Objectives

To review spelling patterns and strategies in Lessons 12–16; to give children the opportunity to recognize and use these spelling patterns and the Spelling Words in their writing

Review of Spelling Strategies

Review with children the spelling strategies presented in Lessons 12–16.

USING SOUND/LETTER RELATIONSHIPS Write *let* on the board. Then say *late* and have children listen for the long *a* sound. Remind children that to spell a word, they must use letters that stand for the sounds they hear in the word. Ask what letters can stand for the long *a* sound. *(a-e, ay, ai)* Then ask whether *let* spells *late*. Ask children to spell it correctly.

USING RHYMING WORDS Write the word *last* on the board and have children identify it. Review how they can use a rhyming strategy to spell the word *past*. First have children identify the letter that stands for the beginning sound in *last*. Then replace the *l* with a *p* to show children how they can substitute the letter *p* for the *l* in *last* to spell *past*.

CHECKING SPELLING Write on the board the sentence *I wok up and got out of bed.* Ask children to read the sentence and to identify the misspelled word. Have a volunteer circle the word and spell it correctly. Then ask children how they can check the spelling to see if it is correct. (They can ask someone who knows the correct spelling or look the word up in a dictionary.)

Unit 3 Words

The following words from Unit 3 are reviewed in this lesson.

Lesson 12 Words with Long *a* or Long *i*: fire, make, nice, late, five

Lesson 13 Words with Long *o* or Long *u*: mule, nose, use

Lesson 14 Consonant Clusters: fly, blow

Lesson 15 Final Double Consonants: dress, ball, glass

Lesson 16 Words with *sh* and *ch*: reach, rich

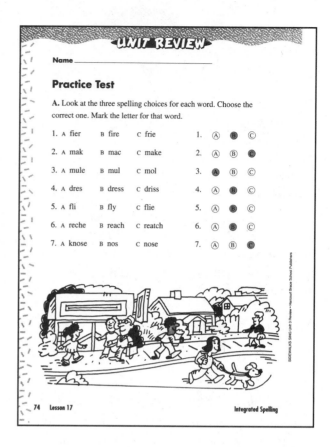

PRACTICE TEST pages 74–75

Options for Administering the Practice Test

The Practice Test provides an opportunity to review Spelling Words and spelling generalizations in a standardized test format.

Option 1: Have children review their **Words to Study** in the Spelling Log for Unit 3. If they need extra help, review the spelling generalizations on Pupil's Edition pages 54, 58, 62, 66, and 70. Then administer both parts of the Practice Test on Pupil's Edition pages 74–75 to determine whether children have mastered the spelling generalizations.

Option 2: You may want to use items 1–7 on Pupil's Edition page 74 as a pretest and 1–8 on Pupil's Edition page 75 as a posttest.

 Options for Evaluation

- Have children check their own Practice Tests by referring to their lists of Spelling Words. The list on the preceding page provides references to the lessons where children will find the words on the Practice Test.
- You may prefer to assign partners and to have them check each other's Practice Tests. Refer children to their own lists of Spelling Words to use as they check their partners' tests.

For each word misspelled on the Practice Test, remind children to follow the **Study Steps to Learn a Word** on pages 8–9 of the Pupil's Edition. Be sure to have them write the words they missed in the Unit 3 **Words to Study** box in the Spelling Log. STUDENT SELF-ASSESSMENT

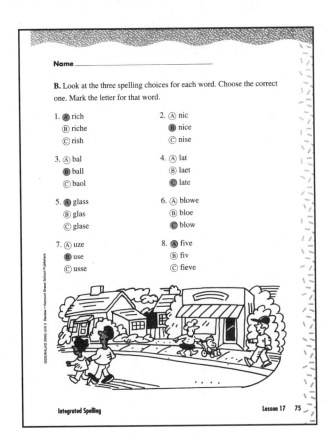

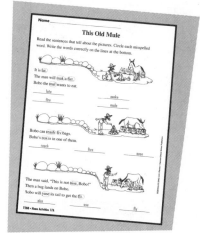

RESOURCES: HOME ACTIVITIES MASTER 17A

Use as an extra activity to reinforce spelling strategies.

Review of Spelling Strategies Review with children the spelling strategies discussed on pages 176–177 of the Pupil's Edition. Then distribute Home Activities Master 17A.

The Reteach section of each Lesson Wrap-Up provides suggestions for helping children who are still having difficulty with the concepts taught in that lesson.

RESOURCES: PRACTICE ACTIVITIES MASTER 17B

Use as an extra activity to provide children an opportunity to combine spelling and writing.

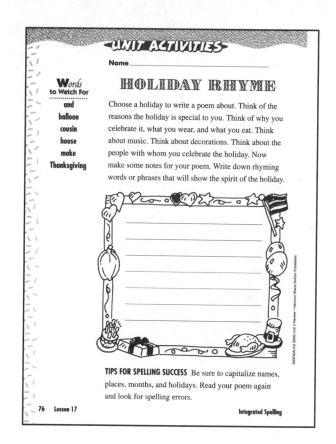

UNIT 3 ACTIVITIES pages 76–77

Activities on pages 76 and 77 of the Pupil's Edition emphasize writing (Holiday Rhyme), reading (Guided Tour), and word play (Word Doodles). The **Tips for Spelling Success** point out the importance of standard spelling and give children hints for proofreading and for applying spelling strategies.

Holiday Rhyme Read the directions with children. Have them share and discuss favorite holidays and how they celebrate them. You may want to write the headings *Why You Celebrate, What You Wear, What You Eat, Music, Decorations,* and *People* on the board. List children's responses under the appropriate headings. Then help children list their notes and rhyming words. Remind them to follow the steps of the Writing Process as they write their poems.

Have children read aloud the **Tips for Spelling Success.** Then point out the **Words to Watch For.** These are words children often use

in writing. Explain that children can use the list as a reference to help them spell the words correctly.

When children proofread their work, provide them with the following checklist or with the proofreading checklist on page 175 of the Pupil's Edition. WRITING/PROOFREADING

Proofreading Checklist

✔ Did I spell words correctly?

✔ Did I write complete sentences?

✔ Did I begin sentences with capital letters?

✔ Did I end sentences with the correct marks?

✔ Did I begin people's names and the names of places, months, and holidays with capital letters?

If children need help with writing a poem, refer them to pages 20–21 of the *Language Handbook.*

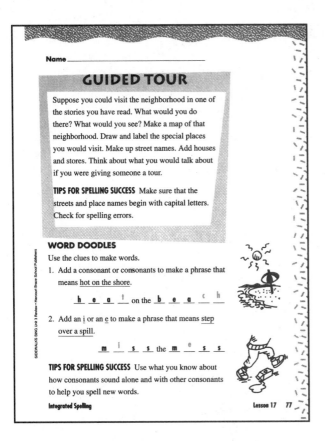

Name _____

GUIDED TOUR

Suppose you could visit the neighborhood in one of the stories you have read. What would you do there? What would you see? Make a map of that neighborhood. Draw and label the special places you would visit. Make up street names. Add houses and stores. Think about what you would talk about if you were giving someone a tour.

TIPS FOR SPELLING SUCCESS Make sure that the streets and place names begin with capital letters. Check for spelling errors.

WORD DOODLES

Use the clues to make words.

1. Add a consonant or consonants to make a phrase that means <u>hot on the shore</u>.

   <u>h</u> <u>e</u> <u>a</u> <u>t</u> on the <u>b</u> <u>e</u> <u>a</u> <u>c</u> <u>h</u>

2. Add an <u>i</u> or an <u>e</u> to make a phrase that means <u>step over a spill</u>.

   <u>m</u> <u>i</u> <u>s</u> <u>s</u> the <u>m</u> <u>e</u> <u>s</u> <u>s</u>

TIPS FOR SPELLING SUCCESS Use what you know about how consonants sound alone and with other consonants to help you spell new words.

Integrated Spelling   Lesson 17   77

Guided Tour Read the directions with children. Then ask them to discuss different neighborhoods they have read about. Use questions like the following to stimulate discussion: *What would you do there? What would you see?*

Provide drawing paper and crayons or markers for children to use to make their maps. Remind them to include places they would like to visit and street names on their maps.

Have children read aloud the **Tips for Spelling Success,** and encourage them to proofread their work. MAKING MAPS/ PROOFREADING

Word Doodles Read the phrase for number 1 with children. Have them think of words that mean almost the same as *hot* and *shore*. Encourage children to use the given letters as clues. Remind them to listen for sounds to help them figure out how to spell the words. Then ask children to complete number 2 independently.

Read aloud the **Tips for Spelling Success** and encourage children to recall and use the strategy. USING LETTER SOUNDS

Suggest that children use these review words, which are listed on page T111, to make up their own Word Doodles like those on page 77 of the Pupil's Edition: *glass, ball, dress, reach, and rich.* Instead of making up phrases, children might draw and label pictures, leaving two blanks for the final consonant pair.

Have children who need a reteaching activity write all the review words, which are listed on page T111, on a sheet of paper. Then ask them to write each review word on a separate word card. Help children cut each word apart between the letters. Then have children use the letters to spell the words. Suggest they use their lists to help them.

Have children write on word cards these review words from page T111: *make, late, fire, nice, five, nose, mule,* and *use.* Then children can sort the words into groups according to the vowel sound they hear in each word. Have children identify the spelling pattern for each group. Then challenge children to write other words to fit in each group.

Ask children to draw pictures of the review words listed on page T111. Have them write the words on word cards. Then children can play a memory game. Have them turn all the pictures and word cards face down. Tell them to find the matching pairs.

Words with *th, wh,* and *ng*

Objective
To spell words that begin or end with *th*, begin with *wh*, or end with *ng*

Lesson Planner
Assign words based on the developmental levels of individual children. See the Assignment Guide on page T250.

Informal Assessment
Children's writing may show that they have difficulty spelling words with *th, wh,* or *ng*.

MODEL

Why
(Wy) are the dogs barking?

Use this lesson to introduce the spelling of words with initial or final *th*, initial *wh*, and final *ng*. Encourage children to apply what they have learned to help them spell other words that begin or end with these consonant digraphs. After children have completed the lesson, have them proofread their writing and correct any errors they may have made spelling words with *th, wh,* or *ng*.

SECOND-LANGUAGE SUPPORT Spanish-speaking children and speakers of some other languages may have difficulty differentiating between the sounds of final *th* and final *t*. Give practice in listening to and repeating word pairs such as *math, mat; bath, bat; tooth, toot.*

Some children acquiring English may confuse /hw/*wh* with /h/*h*. These children need practice distinguishing between words such as *when, hen; wheel, heel; wheat, heat.*

Some children may also have difficulty differentiating final /ng/*ng* from /ngk/*nk*. Use pairs of words such as *sing, sink; ring, rink; thing, think.* COMPARING AND CONTRASTING

Pretest/Posttest Context Sentences
You may want to test Semi-Phonetic Spellers on words 1–6 only.

*1.	**long**	I got a **long** string for my kite.
*2.	**they**	The children said **they** had fun.
*3.	**which**	**Which** bike is yours?
4.	**bath**	Dan gave the dog a **bath**.
5.	**ring**	Alice put the **ring** on her finger.
6.	**them**	My friends asked me to help **them**.
*7.	**while**	What will you do **while** I am gone?
8.	**math**	We add and subtract in **math**.
9.	**those**	Did you eat all of **those** peanuts?
*10.	**than**	A cow is bigger **than** a frog.

*Words appearing in "Awful Aardvark." Some additional story words following the generalization are *then, this, the, that, where, what, when, strong, during,* and *morning.*

RESOURCES: HOME ACTIVITIES MASTER 18A

NOTE: Fill in the teacher's note on the Home Activities Master before sending it home with children. See the Assignment Guide on page T250 for assigning lists of words.

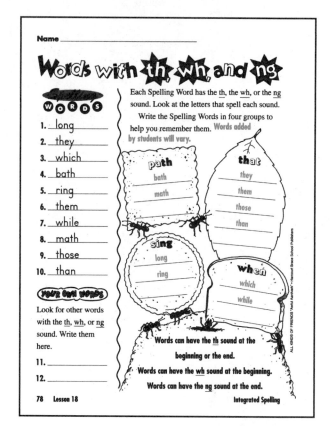

INTRODUCTION page 78

Pretest Administer the pretest. Say each word, use it in the sentence provided on page T117, and then repeat the word. ACCESSING PRIOR KNOWLEDGE

☑ Self-Check Have children check their own pretests by referring to their lists of Spelling Words. For each misspelled word on the pretest, remind children to use the **Study Steps to Learn a Word** on pages 8–9 of the Pupil's Edition. STUDENT SELF-ASSESSMENT

Introducing the Lesson Using your informal assessment and children's pretests as a guide, choose either the open sort or the closed sort as an introductory activity for the lesson. To use the open sort, copy Home Activities Master 18A in the Copying Masters section.

Open Sort: Distribute word cards to children and have them individually or cooperatively select criteria for sorting. Encourage children to tell why they grouped their words as they did. You may want to send home the word cards so that children can complete the Home Activities Master.

Closed Sort: Read aloud with children the lesson title and the Spelling Words on Pupil's Edition page 78.

- Write the words *that* and *when* on the board. Circle the *th* and *wh.* Then as you say each of these words, have children tell under which word you should write it: *these, white, whale,* and *this.*
- Follow a similar procedure for final *th* and *ng.* Write the words *path* and *sing* on the board. Say these words: *both, sang, with,* and *rang.* SORTING WORDS

In Summary Ask what letters children learned about in this lesson. Point out that the sounds for *th, wh,* and *ng* can be spelled with the letters *th, wh,* and *ng,* respectively.

Your Own Words Encourage children to record words with *th, wh,* or *ng* that they see in their reading and to list the words in their Spelling Logs. RECOGNIZING PATTERNS

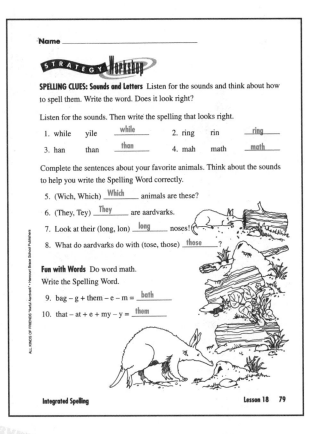

Name _____

STRATEGY Workshop

SPELLING CLUES: Sounds and Letters Listen for the sounds and think about how to spell them. Write the word. Does it look right?

Listen for the sounds. Then write the spelling that looks right.

1. while   yile   _while_
2. ring   rin   _ring_
3. han   than   _than_
4. mah   math   _math_

Complete the sentences about your favorite animals. Think about the sounds to help you write the Spelling Word correctly.

5. (Wich, Which) _Which_ animals are these?

6. (They, Tey) _They_ are aardvarks.

7. Look at their (long, lon) _long_ noses!

8. What do aardvarks do with (tose, those) _those_ ?

Fun with Words Do word math. Write the Spelling Word.

9. bag – g + them – e – m = _bath_

10. that – at + e + my – y = _them_

Integrated Spelling   Lesson 18   79

The ancient Vikings, who came from Denmark to invade England and eventually settle down there, added some words to the English language that we still use today. Three of them are words that begin with *th—they, them,* and *their.*

STRATEGY WORKSHOP page 79

Spelling Clues: Sounds and Letters
Remind children that knowing the letters that sounds stand for can help them figure out how to spell words correctly. Have children listen for the beginning sound in *this.* Then ask what letters spell that sound. Follow a similar procedure with *whale* and the end sound in *hang.*
APPLYING SPELLING STRATEGIES

SECOND-LANGUAGE SUPPORT Have children practice listening to and saying words with *th, wh,* and *ng.* Have them make letter cards for *th, wh,* and *ng.* Then as you say each Spelling Word, have children repeat it and hold up the appropriate letter card.
SOUND-LETTER RELATIONSHIPS

SEMI-PHONETIC SPELLERS Have children write the Spelling Words on a strip of paper. Have them check the spelling of each activity word on Pupil's Edition page 79 against the spelling on their lists.

Fun with Words
Write the following word equation on the board. Have children solve it with you. Suggest that they use a similar procedure to complete the activity.

$$lot - t + sing - si = long$$

Practice Activities   Lesson 18   T119

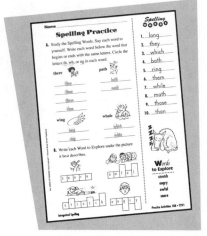

RESOURCES: PRACTICE ACTIVITIES MASTER 18B

Use as extra practice or as a homework activity.

VOCABULARY WORDSHOP pages 80–81

Words to Explore Write the Words to Explore on the board: *stretch, angry, awful, snore.* Discuss their meanings with children. Ask what is happening in each picture. Encourage children to pretend to be Lion and Aardvark and to act out each picture. Then have them use the Words to Explore to complete the sentences.

Spelling Log Have children add the Words to Explore to their Spelling Logs.

TRANSITIONAL SPELLERS Assign the Words to Explore. As a practice activity, have children write the Words to Explore on word cards. Ask a volunteer to choose a word to act it out. Then have other children hold up the word that is being acted out.

What's in a Word? Write the word *grasshopper* on the board and have children tell how the name describes the insect. Then ask children to rename with descriptive names other animals they know. Examples for a dog might be "four-legged friend" or "barking machine." WORD ORIGINS

Classifying Have children identify the animals in the pictures. Ask how the first group of animals is alike. If necessary, ask when these animals sleep and when they are awake. Follow a similar procedure for the second group of animals. If necessary, ask where all the animals are. (in a tree)

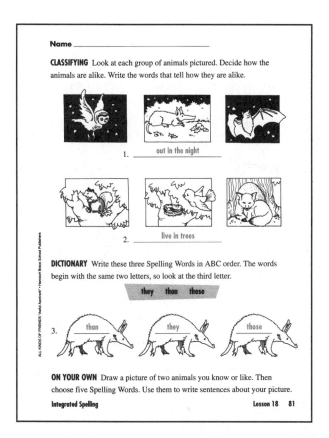

Name _____

CLASSIFYING Look at each group of animals pictured. Decide how the animals are alike. Write the words that tell how they are alike.

1. _____ out in the night _____

2. _____ live in trees _____

DICTIONARY Write these three Spelling Words in ABC order. The words begin with the same two letters, so look at the third letter.

they   than   those

3. than   they   those

ON YOUR OWN Draw a picture of two animals you know or like. Then choose five Spelling Words. Use them to write sentences about your picture.

Integrated Spelling   Lesson 18   81

Dictionary Write the words *which, what,* and *when* on the board. Have children tell which word comes first, next, and last in alphabetical order. Point out, if necessary, that when the first two letters are the same, children must look at the third letter. ALPHABETICAL ORDER

 Working Together Have children work in groups of three to alphabetize the words. Have each child write one word on a card. Then have them arrange the cards in alphabetical order. You might want children to put other Spelling Words in alphabetical order as well.

On Your Own Ask children to name some animals. Write their responses on the board. As you point to each animal name, ask children to use a Spelling Word in a sentence about the animal. Then have them complete the activity. WORD MEANINGS

Posttest To check children's mastery of the Spelling Words, use the context sentences on page T117 to administer the posttest.

Optional Writing Idea: Description Have children write a description of an aardvark. If possible, provide a picture of an aardvark from an encyclopedia or a magazine. Help children organize their ideas in a web.

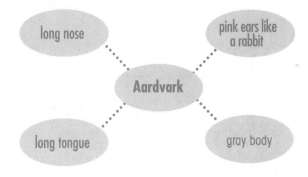

LESSON WRAP-UP

Words to Explore and Context Sentences

1. **stretch** I **stretch** up and then bend low.
2. **angry** Dad gets **angry** when I am late.
3. **awful** The alarm made an **awful** noise.
4. **snore** Do you **snore** in your sleep?

Reteach

LEARNING DIFFERENCES Have children work with one group of Spelling Words at a time. On one day, for example, have children write the words that begin with *th.* Ask them to circle the letters *th* in each word and to pronounce the words aloud. On other days, follow a similar procedure for final *th,* initial *wh,* and final *ng.* AUDITORY/KINESTHETIC MODALITIES

INTEGRATED CURRICULUM ACTIVITIES

Language Arts

Aardvark Chow Have children work in small groups to make up advertisements for a new brand of aardvark food. Encourage children to include Spelling Words in their ads. Invite children to illustrate the ads. Then ask volunteers to share their work. Have children find and identify the Spelling Words in one another's ads.

Science

Animal Facts Make an animal matching game. On sentence strips, write facts about animals. Use a Spelling Word in each fact. On word cards, write the animals' names. Have children match the facts to the animals. Then have them identify the Spelling Words.

Words Like *car, book,* and *track*

Objective

To spell words with the sound /k/ spelled *c, k,* or *ck.*

Lesson Planner

Assign words based on the developmental levels of individual children. See the Assignment Guide on page T250.

Informal Assessment

Children's writing may show that they have difficulty spelling words with the sound /k/ spelled *c, k,* or *ck.*

MODEL

cat
Our ⟨kat⟩ is gray and white.

Use this lesson to introduce the spelling of words in which *c, k,* or *ck* stand for the sound /k/ at the beginning or the end of a word. Encourage children to apply what they have learned to help them spell other words that begin or end with /k/. After children have completed the lesson, have them proofread their writing and correct any errors they may have made spelling words with initial or final /k/ spelled *c, k,* or *ck.*

SECOND-LANGUAGE SUPPORT Children who speak Korean, Samoan, Vietnamese, Thai, or Indonesian languages may have difficulty differentiating initial /k/ spelled *c* or *k* from initial /g/ spelled *g.* Give children practice listening to and repeating pairs of words such as *coat, goat; cold, gold;* and *cap, gap.* COMPARING AND CONTRASTING

Pretest/Posttest Context Sentences

You may want to test Semi-Phonetic Spellers on words 1–6 only.

*1.	**car**	Mom drove us in her **car.**
2.	**book**	We read a story from this **book.**
3.	**stick**	Don threw a **stick** for his dog to chase.
4.	**kick**	I'll **kick** the ball into the goal.
5.	**took**	She **took** a crayon from the box.
*6.	**care**	The cat takes **care** of her kittens.
*7.	**track**	The tire left a **track** in the mud.
8.	**black**	This zebra has **black** and white stripes.
9.	**neck**	A giraffe has a long **neck.**
10.	**pack**	I carry my books in a **pack** on my back.

*Words appearing in "It's an Armadillo!" Some additional story words following the generalization are *can, cozy, cool, camera, collects, comes, called, keeps, kinds,* and *look.*

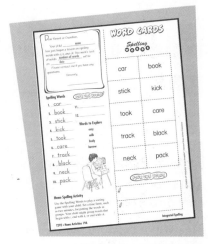

RESOURCES: HOME ACTIVITIES MASTER 19A

NOTE: Fill in the teacher's note on the Home Activities Master before sending it home with children. See the Assignment Guide on page T250 for assigning lists of words.

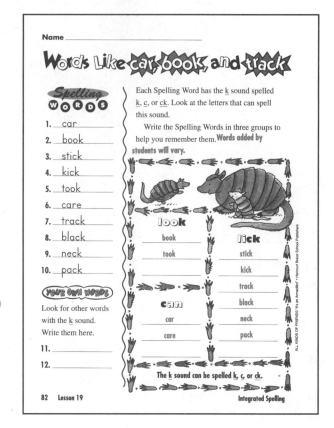

INTRODUCTION page 82

Pretest Administer the pretest. Say each word, use it in the sentence provided on page T123, and then repeat the word. ACCESSING PRIOR KNOWLEDGE

Self-Check Have children check their own pretests by referring to their list of Spelling Words. For each misspelled word on the pretest, remind children to use the **Study Steps to Learn a Word** on pages 8–9 of the Pupil's Edition. STUDENT SELF-ASSESSMENT

Introducing the Lesson To use the open sort, copy Home Activities Master 19A in the Copying Masters section.

Open Sort: Distribute word cards to children and have them individually or cooperatively select criteria for sorting. As children read their groups of words, have other children tell how the words are alike. You may want to send home the word cards so that children can complete the Home Activities Master.

Closed Sort: Read aloud with children the lesson title and the Spelling Words on Pupil's Edition page 82.
- Write these words on the board: *trick, hook, cane, cave, leak,* and *block.* Ask children to group words according to the letters that spell the /k/ sound. Write the words in the appropriate groups on the board.
- Ask volunteers to circle the letters that spell the /k/ sound. Then ask children to suggest other words that could fit into each group. SORTING WORDS

In Summary Ask children to summarize the lesson. Elicit that the /k/ sound can be spelled with the letters *c, k,* or *ck.*

Your Own Words Have pairs or teams of children list in their Spelling Logs other words with the /k/ sound spelled *c, k,* or *ck.* RECOGNIZING PATTERNS

Name _____

STRATEGY Workshop

SPELLING CLUES: Sounds and Letters Think about letters that can spell the sounds. Try each letter or pair of letters. Does the word look right?

Add _k_ or _ck_ to complete each Spelling Word. Write the Spelling Words.

1. boo __k__   ___book___
2. ki __ck__   ___kick___
3. ne __ck__   ___neck___
4. too __k__   ___took___

Add letters to complete the Spelling Words. Then write the Spelling Words to tell about the pictures.

pa __ck__

sti __ck__

5. Put on a ___pack___.
6. Walk with a ___stick___.

tra __ck__

bla __ck__

7. See this animal ___track___.
8. It belongs to a ___black___ bear.

Fun with Words Add a vowel to one Spelling Word to make another Spelling Word.

___car___

___care___

Integrated Spelling

Lesson 19   83

(side text, vertical) ALL KINDS OF FRIENDS "It's an Armadillo!" Harcourt Brace School Publishers

---

The spellings of many words in English have changed over the years. Since about 1650, the word *book* has had its modern spelling. Before that, the spellings *booke, boke, bok,* and *buk* were used. The earliest known spelling, from about the year 938, is *boc*.

STRATEGY WORKSHOP page 83

Spelling Clues: Sounds and Letters Discuss the spelling strategy with children. Point out that the /k/ sound is spelled with the letter *k* at the ends of some of the Spelling Words and that the same sound is spelled with *ck* at the ends of others. Suggest that children write the letter or letters they think are correct for each word in items 1–4 on Pupil's Edition page 83. Then tell them to look at the word to see if it looks right. APPLYING SPELLING STRATEGIES

 SEMI-PHONETIC SPELLERS Have children write the two Spelling Words that end with *k* and count how many vowels are in each word. (two vowels) Then have children write the Spelling Words that end with *ck* and count how many vowels are in each of these words. (one vowel) Point out that looking at the number of vowels can help children remember whether to use *k* or *ck* to spell the words in this lesson.

 SECOND-LANGUAGE SUPPORT Discuss the four illustrations in the middle of Pupil's Edition page 83. Ask children to point to the pack, the stick, a track, and the black bear. USING PICTURES CLUES

Fun with Words Write *cap* on the board and read it aloud with children. Then write *cape* and read it aloud with children. Ask what letter was added to *cap* to make a new word. Then have children complete the activity independently.

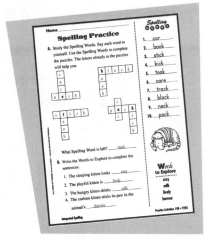

**RESOURCES: PRACTICE
ACTIVITIES MASTER 19B**
Use as extra practice or as a
homework activity.

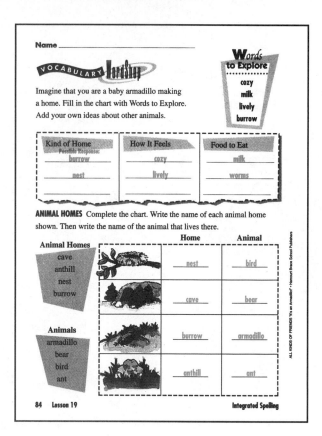

VOCABULARY WORDSHOP pages 84–85

Words to Explore Write the Words to Explore
on the board: *cozy, milk, lively, burrow.*
Discuss their meanings with children. Then
have volunteers read the headings on the chart.
Discuss things that could fit under each
heading. Ask children to complete the activity
independently.

Spelling Log Have children add
the Words to Explore to their
Spelling Logs.

TRANSITIONAL SPELLERS Assign the Words
to Explore. As a practice activity,
have children draw a picture for each
Word to Explore. Then have them label each
picture with the correct word. Encourage
children to use the words in sentences to tell
about their pictures.

Animal Homes Draw a house on the board.
Ask what the name of this kind of home is.
Then write *house* next to the picture. Ask who
lives in houses. Write *people* next to *house.*
Have children name other homes and tell who
or what lives in them. Then have them
complete the activity independently.

What's in a Word? Tell children that
armadillo is a Spanish word. Ask them to
name other Spanish words that they have read
or that they know. *(abuela, fiesta)* Then have
them complete this activity independently.
WORD ORIGINS

Name _____

What's in a Word?

Armadillo is a Spanish word. It means "little armored one." Here are some other Spanish words.

Write each word under its picture.

| banana | abuela | piñata | burro |

1. burro   2. abuela   3. piñata   4. banana

QUESTION WORDS Write question words to complete the questions. Then write words to answer them.

| What | Where | When |

5. __What__ animal is in the picture? __an armadillo__

6. __Where__ is it sleeping? __in a burrow__

7. __When__ does it go out? __at night__

WITH A PARTNER Write the Spelling Words on cards. Then put them in ABC order. As you take turns reading each word, use it in a sentence about an armadillo or another animal you know about.

Integrated Spelling   Lesson 19   85

ALL KINDS OF FRIENDS "It's an Armadillo" • Harcourt Brace School Publishers

· ·

Question Words Have children identify the armadillo. Ask what the armadillo is doing. Then have children use the words *what, where,* and *when* to ask questions about the picture. UNDERSTANDING QUESTIONS

Working Together Encourage children to work in pairs to write and answer questions about armadillos or other animals. Children can share their work on an Animal Quiz Show.

With a Partner Provide word cards for children to use. Remind them to look at the second, third, or fourth letter, if necessary, when putting words in alphabetical order. USING ALPHABETICAL ORDER

Posttest To check children's mastery of the Spelling Words, use the context sentences on page T123 to administer the posttest.

Optional Writing Idea: Friendly Letter Have children write a letter to a friend or relative to share the Spanish words from What's in a Word? You may want to display the correct format for a friendly letter and remind children to refer to it when they write the final copies of their letters.

heading

> 24 Tampa Way
> Ocala, Florida 32670
> October 23, 1995

greeting

> Dear Kate,

body

> I'm finally getting used to my new school. At first, it was hard. The school is so big, and I didn't know anyone. Now I know my way around. I am making new friends, too. I still miss my old friends, though. Please write!

closing
signature

> Your friend,
> LaTisha

Vocabulary Activities

LESSON WRAP-UP

Words to Explore and Context Sentences

1. **cozy**   The kittens look **cozy** all curled up together.
2. **milk**   I had a glass of **milk** with lunch.
3. **lively**   The **lively** fish swam all around.
4. **burrow**   The rabbit poked its head out of its underground **burrow.**

Reteach

LEARNING DIFFERENCES Have children write one of the Spelling Words on paper as you spell it for them. Check to see that children have written the word correctly. Then have them cover the word with a ruler or a strip of paper, close their eyes, and picture the word. When children open their eyes, have them keep the word covered and write it again on their paper. Ask children to look at their word and compare it with the model, one letter at a time. If the word is misspelled, have the child repeat the activity.
VISUAL MODALITY

INTEGRATED CURRICULUM ACTIVITIES

Language Arts

Riddles Have children write the Spelling Words on slips of paper and place them in a box or another container. Have pairs of children take a word from the box. Each pair must use their word to make up a riddle. The word can be the answer to the riddle, or it can be contained in the riddle itself. You might want to give examples, such as the following:

I am full of words.
You can read me.
What am I? (book)

I am a ball, but I am not round.
People kick me.
What am I? (football)

Have children share their riddles.

Art

Word Pictures Have children make Spelling Word collages. Suggest that they use paint or letters cut from construction paper to spell the words. Encourage children to place the words creatively on their collages.

Words Like *she's* and *you're*

Objective
To spell contractions with *is, are, am,* and *will*

Lesson Planner
Assign words based on the developmental levels of individual children. See the Assignment Guide on page T250.

Informal Assessment
Children's writing may show that they have difficulty spelling contractions with *is, are, am,* and *will*.

MODEL

you'll
Let me know if (youll) be able to help.

Use this lesson to introduce the spelling of contractions with *is, are, am,* and *will*. Encourage children to apply what they have learned to help them spell other contractions. After children have completed the lesson, have them proofread their writing and correct any errors they may have made spelling contractions with *is, are, am,* or *will*.

 SECOND-LANGUAGE SUPPORT The contraction *I'll* may cause particular problems for children acquiring English. Children often use the present-tense form of verbs instead of the future tense. In Spanish, for example, the present tense can often be used to indicate the future. Help children become familiar with the use of *I'll* by having them answer questions such as the following:

Teacher:	Where will you go after school?
Child:	I'll go home.
Teacher:	What will you have for dinner?
Child:	I'll have a hamburger.
Teacher:	What will you do after dinner?
Child:	I'll play a game with my sister.
Teacher:	What will you do tomorrow?
Child:	I'll come to school.

UNDERSTANDING CONTRACTIONS

Pretest/Posttest Context Sentences
You may want to test Semi-Phonetic Spellers on words 1–6 only.

1. **he's**   I hope **he's** ready to go.
2. **we're**   Today **we're** going on a trip.
3. **I'm**   **I'm** glad to see you.
4. **she's**   Do you think **she's** going to win?
5. **they're**   Cats purr when **they're** happy.
6. **I'll**   **I'll** see you again tomorrow.

*7. **you're**   Are you glad **you're** here?
8. **that's**   I think **that's** the last apple.
9. **there's**   It looks like **there's** one more apple in the bag.
10. **what's**   Tell me **what's** going on.

*Word appearing in "The Day Jimmy's Boa Ate the Wash."

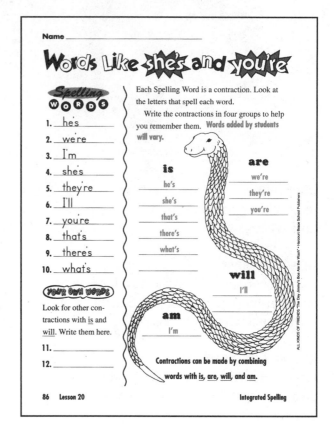

RESOURCES: HOME ACTIVITIES MASTER 20A

NOTE: Fill in the teacher's note on the Home Activities Master before sending it home with children. See the Assignment Guide on page T250 for assigning lists of words.

INTRODUCTION page 86

Pretest Administer the pretest. Say each word, use it in the sentence provided on page T129, and then repeat the word. ACCESSING PRIOR KNOWLEDGE

Self-Check Have children check their own pretests by referring to their list of Spelling Words. For each misspelled word on the pretest, remind children to use the **Study Steps to Learn a Word** on pages 8–9 of the Pupil's Edition. STUDENT SELF-ASSESSMENT

Introducing the Lesson To use the open sort, copy Home Activities Master 20A in the Copying Masters section.

Open Sort: Distribute word cards to children and have them individually or cooperatively select criteria for sorting. Ask children why they sorted the words as they did. You may want to send home the word cards so that children can complete the Home Activities Master.

Closed Sort: Read aloud with children the lesson title and the Spelling Words on Pupil's Edition page 86.

- Write *is*, *are*, *am*, and *will* on the board. As you say each of the following contractions, have children tell under which word you should write it: *here's*, *we're*, *I'm*, and *they'll*.
- Ask children to name other contractions for each group. Note that only *I'm* can go in the *am* group. SORTING WORDS

In Summary Ask children to summarize the lesson. Elicit that contractions with *is*, *are*, *am*, and *will* are spelled with *'s*, *'re*, *'m*, and *'ll*, respectively.

Your Own Words Have children list in their Spelling Logs other contractions with *is* and *will*. RECOGNIZING PATTERNS

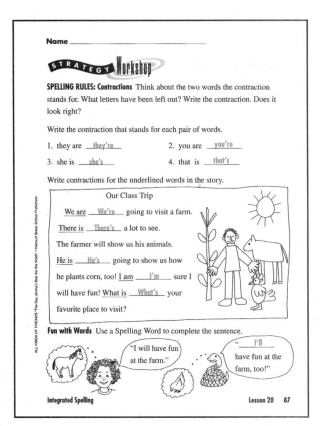

Name _____

STRATEGY Workshop

SPELLING RULES: Contractions Think about the two words the contraction stands for. What letters have been left out? Write the contraction. Does it look right?

Write the contraction that stands for each pair of words.

1. they are __they're__   2. you are __you're__

3. she is __she's__   4. that is __that's__

Write contractions for the underlined words in the story.

Our Class Trip

We are __We're__ going to visit a farm.

There is __There's__ a lot to see.

The farmer will show us his animals.

He is __He's__ going to show us how

he plants corn, too! I am __I'm__ sure I

will have fun! What is __What's__ your

favorite place to visit?

Fun with Words Use a Spelling Word to complete the sentence.

"I will have fun at the farm."

"__I'll__ have fun at the farm, too!"

Integrated Spelling   Lesson 20   87

STRATEGY WORKSHOP page 87

Spelling Rules: Contractions Before children complete the activities on Pupil's Edition page 87, have them tell from what two words each Spelling Word was formed. Remind them that the apostrophe stands for the letter or letters that were left out when the two words were combined. APPLYING SPELLING STRATEGIES

 SEMI-PHONETIC SPELLERS Make word cards for *I, you, he, she, we, they, that, there, what, 's, 'll, 'm,* and *'re.* Have children use the cards to make Spelling Words. Ask them to use the words in sentences.

Fun with Words Discuss the pictures with children. After children have completed the activity, encourage them to use contractions in sentences to tell what they might have fun doing at the farm.

SECOND-LANGUAGE SUPPORT Help children understand contractions in context by using pairs of sentences. For example, say this sentence: *Now we are going to lunch.* Then repeat the sentence, substituting the contraction: *Now we're going to lunch.* Encourage children to repeat the sentences and to make up their own. USING SENTENCE FRAMES

Practice Activities

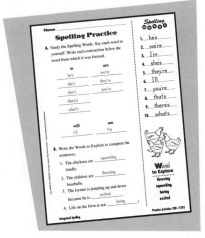

RESOURCES: PRACTICE ACTIVITIES MASTER 20B

Use as extra practice or as a homework activity.

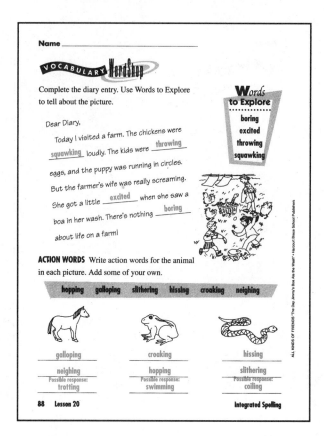

VOCABULARY WORDSHOP pages 88–89

Words to Explore Write the Words to Explore on the board: *boring, excited, throwing, squawking*. Discuss their meanings with children. Have volunteers demonstrate each word by acting it out. Ask other children to tell which word is being acted out and to use it in a sentence.

 Spelling Log Have children add the Words to Explore to their Spelling Logs.

 TRANSITIONAL SPELLERS Assign the Words to Explore. As a practice activity, ask children to write clues for each Word to Explore. Have children write the Words to Explore on separate cards. Then ask children to exchange clues and match the clues to the words they tell about.

Action Words Before children complete the activity, read the action words aloud. Have volunteers show what each word means. Encourage children to demonstrate other action words, and have the rest of the group guess the words. USING ACTION WORDS

What's in a Word? Tell children that someone who plays a game is called a *player.* Write *player* on the board and show how *er* was added to *play* to get *player.* Then ask what someone who jumps could be called. *(jumper)* WORD MEANINGS

 Working Together Have children work together to list other words that end with *er* and tell what people do. Suggest that children write a definition, such as "one who paints," for each word.

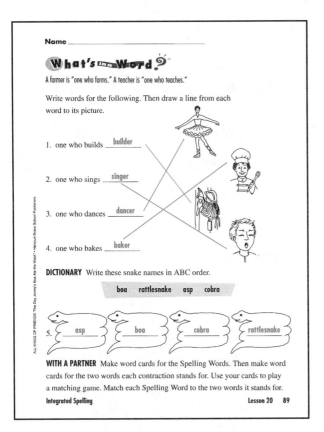

Name _____

What's the Word?

A farmer is "one who farms." A teacher is "one who teaches."

Write words for the following. Then draw a line from each word to its picture.

1. one who builds ___builder___

2. one who sings ___singer___

3. one who dances ___dancer___

4. one who bakes ___baker___

DICTIONARY Write these snake names in ABC order.

| boa | rattlesnake | asp | cobra |

5. ___asp___ ___boa___ ___cobra___ ___rattlesnake___

WITH A PARTNER Make word cards for the Spelling Words. Then make word cards for the two words each contraction stands for. Use your cards to play a matching game. Match each Spelling Word to the two words it stands for.

Integrated Spelling   Lesson 20   89

Dictionary Read the snake names aloud with children. Then have children look up each name in a dictionary or an encyclopedia and share what they learn about the snakes. USING ALPHABETICAL ORDER

With a Partner Each pair of children will need twenty cards, ten for the Spelling Words and ten for the words from which the Spelling Words were formed. Suggest that children play "Concentration." USING WORD MEANINGS

Posttest To check children's mastery of the Spelling Words, use the context sentences on page T129 to administer the posttest.

Optional Writing Idea: Story Have children work in small groups to write an adventure story. Encourage them to use the Words to Explore from this lesson. Remind children that a story needs a beginning, a middle, and an ending. Suggest that they make a story map to help them plan their story.

Beginning	pond is boring snapping turtles go for a walk
Middle	dogs bark hens squawk too noisy
Ending	turtles glad to go back to pond

Vocabulary Activities

LESSON WRAP-UP

Words to Explore and Context Sentences

1. **boring**   The movie was long and **boring.**
2. **excited**   Maria was so **excited** that she jumped up and down.
3. **throwing** We take turns catching and **throwing** the ball.
4. **squawking** The birds are all **squawking** loudly.

Reteach

LEARNING DIFFERENCES Have children work at the board. Write a Spelling Word on the board and ask children to read it aloud. Have children point out the apostrophe and tell the words from which the contraction was formed. Then tell them to trace over the word with colored chalk. After they have traced the word, have them erase it and write it again from memory. If it is not correct, repeat the activity.   VISUAL/KINESTHETIC MODALITIES

INTEGRATED CURRICULUM ACTIVITIES

Language Arts

What's Happening? Help children make telephones by attaching string to paper cups. Then have children use their telephones as they make up conversations. Tell children to use contractions from this lesson in their conversations.

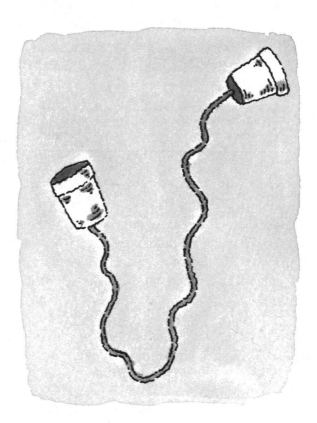

Physical Education

Jump Rope Have children take turns spelling the Spelling Words as they jump rope. Children should say one letter or apostrophe for each jump. Challenge them to try to spell each word without missing a beat or stepping on the rope.

Words Like *food* and *new*

Objective
To spell words with the sound /o͞o/ spelled *oo, ew,* or *ou*

Lesson Planner
Assign words based on the developmental levels of individual children. See the Assignment Guide on page T250.

Informal Assessment
Children's writing may show that they have difficulty spelling words with the /o͞o/ sound spelled *oo, ew,* or *ou.*

MODEL

> blew
> The wind (bleu) my hat off.

Use this lesson to introduce the spelling of words in which the vowel sound /o͞o/ is spelled *oo, ew,* or *ou.* Encourage children to apply what they have learned to help them spell other words with /o͞o/. After children have completed the lesson, have them proofread their writing and correct any errors they may have made spelling words with /o͞o/ spelled *oo, ew,* or *ou.*

SECOND-LANGUAGE SUPPORT Help children understand the meanings of the Spelling Words by using the words in context. Say sentences using the Spelling Words, or have children work together to compose sentences. UNDERSTANDING WORD MEANINGS

Pretest/Posttest Context Sentences
You may want to test Semi-Phonetic Spellers on words 1–6 only.

1.	**soon**	I hope we get home **soon.**
2.	**grew**	The boy **grew** three inches this year.
*3.	**you**	Will **you** sit with me?
4.	**room**	We painted the **room** yellow.
*5.	**new**	He bought a **new** hat at the store.
6.	**group**	There are six children in each **group.**
7.	**school**	We take the bus to **school.**
8.	**flew**	The bird **flew** to its nest in the tree.
*9.	**food**	What kind of **food** do you like to eat?
10.	**drew**	Alex **drew** a picture of his house.

*Words appearing in "A Dinosaur Named after Me." An additional story word following the generalization is *too.*

RESOURCES: HOME ACTIVITIES MASTER 21A

NOTE: Fill in the teacher's note on the Home Activities Master before sending it home with children. See the Assignment Guide on page T250 for assigning lists of words.

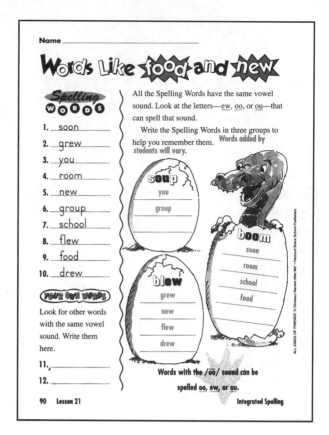

INTRODUCTION page 90

Pretest Administer the pretest. Say each word, use it in the sentence provided on page T135, and then repeat the word. ACCESSING PRIOR KNOWLEDGE

 Self-Check Have children check their own pretests by referring to their list of Spelling Words. For each misspelled word on the pretest, remind children to use the **Study Steps to Learn a Word** on pages 8–9 of the Pupil's Edition. STUDENT SELF-ASSESSMENT

Introducing the Lesson To use the open sort, copy Home Activities Master 21A in the Copying Masters section.
Open Sort: Distribute word cards to children and have them individually or cooperatively select criteria for sorting. As children read each group of words, ask others to add at least one word to each category. You may want to send home the word cards so that children can complete the Home Activities Master.

Closed Sort: Read aloud with children the lesson title and the Spelling Words on Pupil's Edition page 90.

- Write the letters *ew, ou,* and *oo* as headings on the board. Then write the words *blew, knew, soup, broom, group,* and *pool.* Have children read the words and identify the vowels in each.
- Have children tell under which letters you should write each word. SORTING WORDS

In Summary Ask children what letters can spell the vowel sound /oo/. (*oo, ew,* or *ou*) Then have them name a word for each spelling.

Your Own Words As practice, have children list in their Spelling Logs other words with the /oo/ sound spelled *oo, ew,* or *ou.* RECOGNIZING PATTERNS

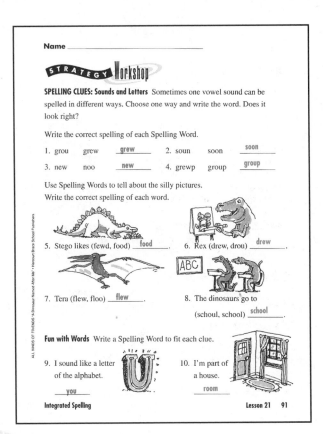

Name _____

STRATEGY Workshop

SPELLING CLUES: Sounds and Letters Sometimes one vowel sound can be spelled in different ways. Choose one way and write the word. Does it look right?

Write the correct spelling of each Spelling Word.

1. grou   grew   _grew_   2. soun   soon   _soon_
3. new   noo   _new_   4. grewp   group   _group_

Use Spelling Words to tell about the silly pictures.
Write the correct spelling of each word.

5. Stego likes (fewd, food) _food_.   6. Rex (drew, drou) _drew_.

7. Tera (flew, floo) _flew_.   8. The dinosaurs go to
   (schoul, school) _school_.

Fun with Words Write a Spelling Word to fit each clue.

9. I sound like a letter of the alphabet.   10. I'm part of a house.
   you   _room_

Integrated Spelling   Lesson 21   91

The modern spelling for the word *new* has been in use since approximately 1450. Previous known spellings include *newe* (1377), *nywe* (1297), *neowe* (1205), and *niwe* (1000).

STRATEGY WORKSHOP page 91

Spelling Clues: Sounds and Letters

Ask how children can spell the vowel sound /oo/. (*ew, oo,* or *ou*) Explain that they should try these letters when they spell words with /oo/. Then write *groo, grue,* and *grew* on the board. Ask which looks right. Tell children that if they are not sure, they should ask someone who knows the correct spelling or look up the word in a dictionary. APPLYING SPELLING STRATEGIES

 SEMI-PHONETIC SPELLERS Have children write the Spelling Words in three different colors. Tell them to use one color for words with the letters *oo,* a second color for words with *ew,* and a third color for words with *ou.* Then have children refer to their colored words to help them complete Pupil's Edition page 91.

Fun with Words

Children might enjoy writing clues for other Spelling Words after they have completed this activity.

 SECOND-LANGUAGE SUPPORT Write the words *are* and *see* on the board. Read aloud each word and ask children what letter it sounds like. Write *r* and *c* next to the appropriate words. Help children read the Spelling Words to find one that sounds like another letter. USING SOUND/LETTER RELATIONSHIPS

RESOURCES: PRACTICE ACTIVITIES MASTER 21B

Use as extra practice or as a homework activity.

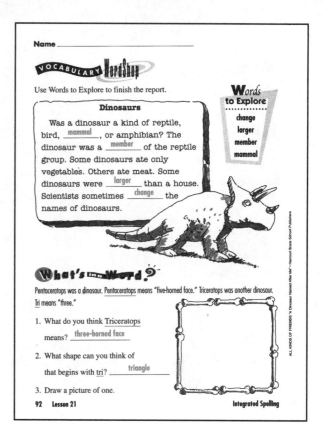

Name _____

VOCABULARY WordShop

Use Words to Explore to finish the report.

Words to Explore
change
larger
member
mammal

Dinosaurs

Was a dinosaur a kind of reptile, bird, __mammal__, or amphibian? The dinosaur was a __member__ of the reptile group. Some dinosaurs ate only vegetables. Others ate meat. Some dinosaurs were __larger__ than a house. Scientists sometimes __change__ the names of dinosaurs.

What's in a Word?

Pentaceratops was a dinosaur. Pentaceratops means "five-horned face." Triceratops was another dinosaur. Tri means "three."

1. What do you think Triceratops means? __three-horned face__

2. What shape can you think of that begins with tri? __triangle__

3. Draw a picture of one.

92   Lesson 21   Integrated Spelling

VOCABULARY WORDSHOP pages 92–93

Words to Explore Write the Words to Explore on the board: *change, larger, member, mammal.* Discuss their meanings with children. After children have completed the activity, ask volunteers to read the report aloud.

Spelling Log Have children add the Words to Explore to their Spelling Logs.

TRANSITIONAL SPELLERS Assign the Words to Explore. As a practice activity, have children draw a picture for each Word to Explore. Ask them to use the words to label their pictures.

What's in a Word? Tell children that many dinosaur names, like Pentaceratops, have meanings that tell something about the dinosaur. Help children find out the meanings of other dinosaur names. Have them record their findings to share and discuss. WORD ORIGINS

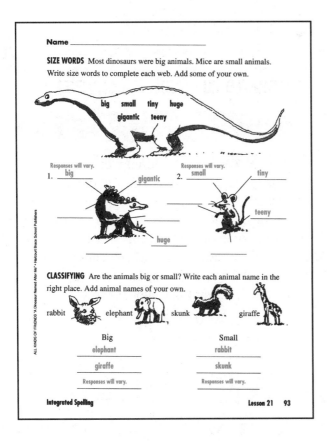

Name _____

SIZE WORDS Most dinosaurs were big animals. Mice are small animals. Write size words to complete each web. Add some of your own.

big   small   tiny   huge
gigantic   teeny

Responses will vary.
1. big
gigantic
huge

Responses will vary.
2. small   tiny
teeny

CLASSIFYING Are the animals big or small? Write each animal name in the right place. Add animal names of your own.

rabbit   elephant   skunk   giraffe

Big	Small
elephant	rabbit
giraffe	skunk
Responses will vary.	Responses will vary.

Integrated Spelling   Lesson 21   93

Size Words Have children read the words in the dinosaur shape. Then ask children to name other size words, such as *large* and *little*. Write their responses on the board. Before children complete the activity, have them use the words to describe animals they know about. USING DESCRIBING WORDS

Classifying Ask children to name big things. Then have them name small things. Record their responses in two webs on the board. Then have children complete the activity. CLASSIFYING

 Working Together Have children work in pairs to think of other categories, such as *Feathers*, *Fur*, and *Two Legs*. Ask them to draw pictures or write the names of animals that could go in each category.

Posttest To check children's mastery of the Spelling Words, use the context sentences on page T135 to administer the posttest.

Optional Writing Idea: Report Have children pick a mammal and write a report about it. Point out that there are a lot of mammals, such as elephants, mice, tigers, pigs, squirrels, and cows. Suggest that children write the name of the mammal they have chosen at the top of a sheet of paper and then list facts they would like to tell about it. Then they can use facts from their list when they write their reports. Children may want to videotape their reports for a class nature documentary about mammals.

> Elephants
> mammals
> large
> thick skin
> long nose—trunk
> eat plants

Vocabulary Activities

Lesson 21   T139

LESSON WRAP-UP

Words to Explore and Context Sentences

1. **change** The leaves **change** color in the fall.
2. **larger** That truck is **larger** than a car.
3. **member** Diane is a **member** of our singing group.
4. **mammal** A cat is a **mammal,** and so are you!

Reteach

 **LEARNING DIFFERENCES** Make word cards for the Spelling Words but leave out the letters *oo, ou,* and *ew.* Make letter cards for *oo, ou,* and *ew.* Have children use the letter cards to complete the Spelling Words. Then have them write each Spelling Word. Ask them to trace over the *oo, ou,* and *ew* in a second color. VISUAL/KINESTHETIC MODALITIES

sch__l

oo

sch|oo|l

INTEGRATED CURRICULUM ACTIVITIES

Language Arts

Puppet Show Have children work in small groups to create a puppet show about a dinosaur's first day in a new dinosaur school. Encourage children to write a short script that includes some of the Spelling Words from this lesson. Then they can make dinosaur puppets from lunch bags and scrap materials to use when they present their puppet show.

Math

Secret Codes Write the following on the board:

6 + 6 = s	8 + 7 = e	6 + 7 = c	3 + 1 = r
7 + 2 = o	5 + 5 = w	3 + 2 = h	7 + 7 = p
9 + 7 = n	9 + 2 = m	9 + 8 = l	4 + 3 = d
4 + 4 = g	4 + 2 = u	9 + 9 = f	1 + 1 = y

Have children do the math to break the secret code to spell Spelling Words. Sample secret code words follow:

$\overline{7}$ $\overline{4}$ $\overline{15}$ $\overline{10}$ $\overline{4}$ $\overline{9}$ $\overline{9}$ $\overline{11}$ $\overline{2}$ $\overline{9}$ $\overline{6}$

LESSON 22

Words Like *fight* and *sky*

Objective
To spell words with the long *i* sound spelled *igh* or *y*

Lesson Planner
Assign words based on the developmental levels of individual children. See the Assignment Guide on page T250.

Informal Assessment
Children's writing may show that they have difficulty spelling words with the long *i* sound spelled *igh* or *y*.

MODEL

> Both birds and airplanes ~~flie~~. fly

Use this lesson to introduce the spelling of words in which the long *i* vowel sound is spelled with the letters *igh* or *y*. Encourage children to apply what they have learned to help them spell other words with the long *i* vowel sound. After children have completed the lesson, have them proofread their writing and correct any errors they may have made spelling words with the long *i* sound spelled *igh* or *y*.

SECOND-LANGUAGE SUPPORT Some children may have difficulty distinguishing the long *i* vowel sound from the short *a* vowel sound. Give children practice in listening to and repeating pairs of words such as *might, mat; sight, sat;* and *fight, fat.* COMPARING AND CONTRASTING

Pretest/Posttest Context Sentences
You may want to test Semi-Phonetic Spellers on words 1–6 only.

1.	**high**	Planes fly **high** above the clouds.
2.	**cry**	The loud noise made the baby **cry**.
*3.	**night**	We see the moon mostly at **night**.
*4.	**sky**	Look up at the blue **sky**.
*5.	**fight**	We get along well and don't **fight**.
*6.	**right**	Tina gave the **right** answer to the question.
7.	**light**	When it's dark, turn on a **light**.
8.	**sight**	A rainbow is a beautiful **sight**.
9.	**bright**	I wear sunglasses when the sun is too **bright**.
*10.	**might**	The cloudy sky makes me think it **might** rain.

*Words appearing in "Tyrone the Horrible." Some additional story words following the generalization are *try, myself, Tyrone, dying, by,* and *my*.

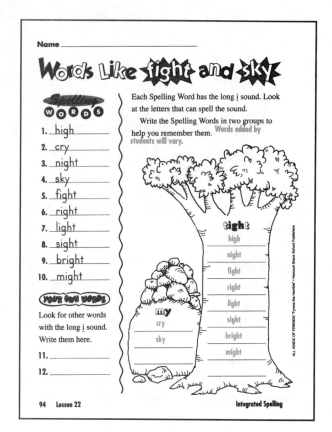

RESOURCES: HOME
ACTIVITIES MASTER **22A**

NOTE: Fill in the teacher's note on the
Home Activities Master before sending it
home with children. See the Assignment
Guide on page T250 for assigning
lists of words.

INTRODUCTION page 94

Pretest Administer the pretest. Say each
word, use it in the sentence provided on page
T141, and then repeat the word. ACCESSING
PRIOR KNOWLEDGE

 Self-Check Have children check their
own pretests by referring to their list of
Spelling Words. For each misspelled word on
the pretest, remind children to use the **Study
Steps to Learn a Word** on pages 8–9 of the
Pupil's Edition. STUDENT SELF-ASSESSMENT

Introducing the Lesson To use the open sort,
copy Home Activities Master 22A in the
Copying Masters section.

Open Sort: Distribute word cards to children and
have them individually or cooperatively select
criteria for sorting. Have children name their
categories. Ask others to tell which words
belong in each category. You may want to send
home the word cards so that children can
complete the Home Activities Master.

Closed Sort: Read aloud with children the lesson
title and the Spelling Words on Pupil's Edition
page 94.

- Write *my, slight, why,* and *tight* on the board.
  Have children circle the letter or the letters
  that stand for the long *i* sound.
- Have children write the words from the
  board on word cards. Ask them to sort the
  words into groups with the spellings *igh*
  and *y.*
- Have children name other words that could
  fit into each group. SORTING WORDS

In Summary Have children summarize the
lesson. Point out that the long *i* vowel sound
can be spelled with the letters *igh* or *y.*

Your Own Words For homework
or practice, you may want to have
pairs of children list in their Spelling
Logs other words with the long *i* sound spelled
igh or *y.* RECOGNIZING PATTERNS

Sorting Activities

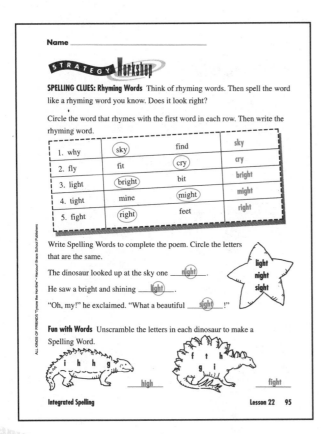

The words *bright, fight, might, night, right,* and *sight* are often pronounced so that they rhyme with *bite*. In some parts of the United States, however, these words are pronounced so that they rhyme with *not*. In Australia, the same words rhyme with *gate*.

STRATEGY WORKSHOP page 95

Spelling Clues: Rhyming Words Discuss the spelling strategy with children. Point out that they can use a rhyming strategy to spell words by writing the letter or letters that stand for the beginning sound or sounds and then using the spelling of a rhyming word that they know. APPLYING SPELLING STRATEGIES

SECOND-LANGUAGE SUPPORT Write the words *night, light,* and *sight* on the board. As you point to and read each word, have children use it in a sentence to show its meaning. WORD MEANINGS

Fun with Words If children need help unscrambling the letters, suggest that they use their list of Spelling Words to help them figure out which letter could be the first letter. Explain, for example, that the letters for the first word are *i, h, h,* and *g.* Tell children that they can look at the spelling list to figure out that no Spelling Word begins with *i* or *g,* so the first letter of the word must be *h.*

SEMI-PHONETIC SPELLERS Have children write each letter from the first dinosaur on a separate card or on a self-stick note. Help them put the letters in order to spell a Spelling Word. Follow a similar procedure for the second dinosaur.

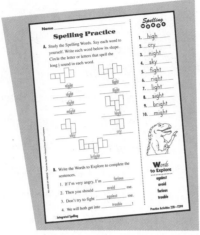

RESOURCES: PRACTICE ACTIVITIES MASTER 22B

Use as extra practice or as a homework activity.

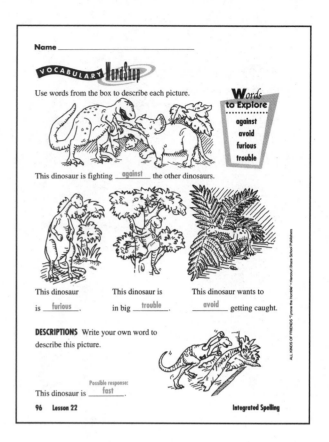

VOCABULARY WORDSHOP pages 96–97

Words to Explore Write the Words to Explore on the board: *against, avoid, furious, trouble.* Discuss their meanings with children. Then ask what is happening in each picture. Have children write the words to complete the sentences.

Spelling Log Have children add the Words to Explore to their Spelling Logs.

TRANSITIONAL SPELLERS Assign the Words to Explore. As a practice activity, write each Word to Explore on a separate sheet of paper. Then make letter cards for the letters in all the words. Put the letters in a bag. Have children take turns choosing letters and placing them where they belong to spell the Words to Explore. Have children read the completed words.

Descriptions Discuss the picture with children. Have them tell what words could describe the dinosaur. Then have children complete the activity independently. USING DESCRIBING WORDS

What's in a Word? Ask children to tell what they know about tyrannosaurs. Ask why tyrannosaurs might have been called "tyrant lizards." Then have children complete the activity independently. WORD ORIGINS

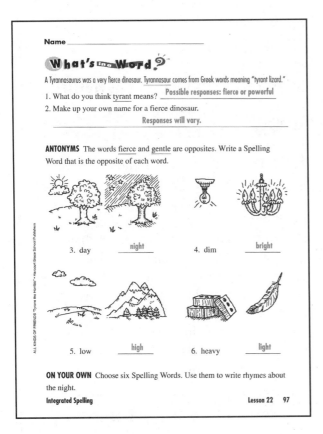

Name_____

What's the Word?

A Tyrannosaurus was a very fierce dinosaur. Tyrannosaur comes from Greek words meaning "tyrant lizard."

1. What do you think <u>tyrant</u> means? **Possible responses: fierce or powerful**
2. Make up your own name for a fierce dinosaur.
                    Responses will vary.

ANTONYMS The words <u>fierce</u> and <u>gentle</u> are opposites. Write a Spelling Word that is the opposite of each word.

3. day <u>night</u>   4. dim <u>bright</u>

5. low <u>high</u>   6. heavy <u>light</u>

ON YOUR OWN Choose six Spelling Words. Use them to write rhymes about the night.

Integrated Spelling   Lesson 22   97

Antonyms Have children give examples of antonyms, such as *happy* and *sad*. They might enjoy playing a game in which one child says a word and other children guess its antonym. USING ANTONYMS

On Your Own Explain to children that they can write several short rhymes or one long rhyme with their six words. Encourage children to illustrate and share their work. LANGUAGE PLAY

Working Together Have children work in pairs to write their rhymes. Suggest that each child write alternate lines for the rhyme.

Posttest To check children's mastery of the Spelling Words, use the context sentences on page T141 to administer the posttest.

Optional Writing Idea: Dialogue Have children draw a picture of two dinosaurs. Then ask what the dinosaurs might talk about if they could speak to one another. Have children write a dialogue to go with their pictures. Children may want to work with a partner to write the dialogue and to act it out for their classmates.

Vocabulary Activities

LESSON WRAP-UP

Words to Explore and Context Sentences

1. **against**   Our team played **against** their team.
2. **avoid**   Try to **avoid** stepping in puddles.
3. **furious**   Dad was **furious** when his car broke down.
4. **trouble**   My dog was in big **trouble** when it chewed on my shoe!

Reteach

LEARNING DIFFERENCES Write all of the Spelling Words with *igh* on one sheet of paper but omit the *igh*. Say each word aloud, and have children write *igh* to complete it. Then have children read the completed words aloud. Follow a similar procedure for the Spelling Words with *y*.
AUDITORY/KINESTHETIC MODALITIES

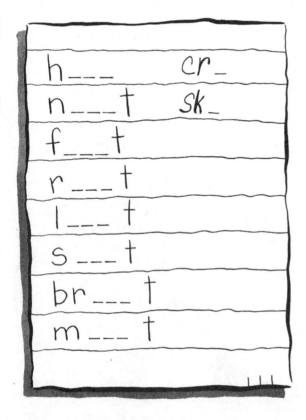

INTEGRATED CURRICULUM ACTIVITIES

Language Arts

Parts of Speech Have children work in groups to classify each of the Spelling Words except *high* as a noun, a verb, or a describing word. Point out that some words have more than one meaning and so may fit into more than one category. Explain, for example, that *cry* and *fight* can be nouns as well as verbs or that *light* and *right* can be describing words as well as nouns. Suggest that children make a chart to classify their Spelling Words. Have groups compare their charts and discuss any differences they find.

Nouns	Verbs	Describing Words
night	cry	light
sky	fight	right
light	might	bright
sight		
fight		

Science

Night Sky Ask children to draw pictures of the night sky. Encourage them to include and label the moon and stars. Then share a book about constellations with the group. Have children choose a constellation to add to their drawings.

Encourage children to use Spelling Words to write about their pictures.

Review of Lessons 18–22

Objectives

To review spelling patterns and strategies in Lessons 18–22; to give children the opportunity to recognize and use these spelling patterns and the Spelling Words in their writing

Review of Spelling Strategies

Review with children the spelling strategies presented in Lessons 18–22.

USING SOUND/LETTER RELATIONSHIPS Write *groo* on the board. Then say *grew* and have children listen for the vowel sound. Point to *groo* and explain that this is an incorrect spelling for *grew*. Ask children what two letters can stand for the vowel sound heard at the end of *grew*. *(ew)* Then have them spell *grew* correctly.

FORMING CONTRACTIONS Write the words *we are* on the board. Ask a volunteer to write the contraction that stands for these two words. *(we're)* Have children tell which letters are the same in both the two words and the contraction and which letter has been left out of the contraction.

USING RHYMING WORDS Write the word *light* on the board and have children read it aloud. Review with children how they can use a rhyming strategy to spell the word *tight*. First have children identify the letter that stands for the beginning sound of *light*. Then have children substitute the letter *t* for the letter *l* in *light* to spell the rhyming word *tight*.

Unit 4 Words

The following words from Unit 4 are reviewed in this lesson.

Lesson 18 Words with *th, wh,* and *ng:* bath, while, long

Lesson 19 Words Like *car, book,* and *track:* track, pack, book

Lesson 20 Words Like *she's* and *you're:* she's, what's, I'll

Lesson 21 Words Like *food* and *new:* school, drew, flew

Lesson 22 Words Like *fight* and *sky:* night, fight, might

Name _____

Practice Test

A. Read each sentence. Find the correctly spelled word to complete it. Mark the letter next to that word.

1. My dog likes to take a _____ in the rain.
   Ⓐ bathe   Ⓑ beth   🅒 bath
2. I like to _____ animals in the woods.
   🅐 track   Ⓑ trak   Ⓒ trake
3. _____ not afraid of lizards or snakes.
   Ⓐ Shes   🅑 She's   Ⓒ Shes'
4. The zookeeper visited our _____.
   Ⓐ skol   Ⓑ schol   🅒 school
5. Bats are mammals that fly at _____.
   🅐 night   Ⓑ nite   Ⓒ nigt
6. The bee stung me _____ I slept.
   Ⓐ wile   🅑 while   Ⓒ whil
7. Wild dogs like to travel in a _____.
   Ⓐ pak   Ⓑ pac   🅒 pack

98   Lesson 23   Integrated Spelling

❝Even in a print-rich environment, spelling development does not just happen for many children. There must be a predictable period of time set aside each day for the specific, intentional study of words and their spellings. ❞

(J. Richard Gentry and
Jean Wallace Gillet)

. . . .

PRACTICE TEST pages 98–99

Options for Administering the Practice Test

The Practice Test provides an opportunity to review Spelling Words and spelling generalizations in a standardized test format.

Option 1: Have children review their **Words to Study** in the Spelling Log for Unit 4. If they need extra help, review the spelling generalizations on Pupil's Edition pages 78, 82, 86, 90, and 94. Then administer both parts of the Practice Test on Pupil's Edition pages 98–99 to determine whether children have mastered the spelling generalizations.

Option 2: Administer Part A of the Practice Test on Pupil's Edition page 98 as a pretest. Have children check their pretests and study the words they misspelled. On another day, administer Part B of the Practice Test on Pupil's Edition page 99 as a posttest.

Options for Evaluation

- Have children check their own Practice Test by referring to their lists of Spelling Words. The list on the preceding page provides references to the lessons where children will find the words on the Practice Test.
- You may prefer to assign partners and have them check each other's Practice Tests. Refer children to their own lists of Spelling Words to use as they check their partners' tests.

For each word that they misspelled on the Practice Test, remind children to follow the **Study Steps to Learn a Word** on pages 8–9 of the Pupil's Edition. Be sure to have them write the words they missed in the Unit 4 **Words to Study** box in the Spelling Log. STUDENT SELF-ASSESSMENT

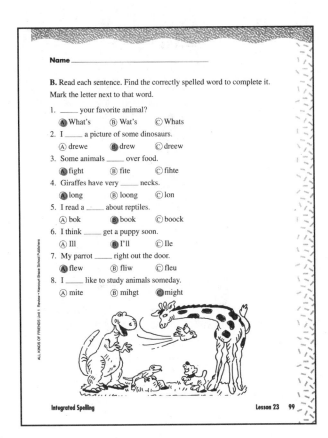

B. Read each sentence. Find the correctly spelled word to complete it. Mark the letter next to that word.

1. _____ your favorite animal?
   - (A) What's
   - (B) Wat's
   - (C) Whats

2. I _____ a picture of some dinosaurs.
   - (A) drewe
   - (B) drew
   - (C) dreew

3. Some animals _____ over food.
   - (A) fight
   - (B) fite
   - (C) fihte

4. Giraffes have very _____ necks.
   - (A) long
   - (B) loong
   - (C) lon

5. I read a _____ about reptiles.
   - (A) bok
   - (B) book
   - (C) boock

6. I think _____ get a puppy soon.
   - (A) Ill
   - (B) I'll
   - (C) Ile

7. My parrot _____ right out the door.
   - (A) flew
   - (B) fliw
   - (C) fleu

8. I _____ like to study animals someday.
   - (A) mite
   - (B) mihgt
   - (C) might

Integrated Spelling
Lesson 23   99

RESOURCES: HOME ACTIVITIES MASTER 23A

Use as an extra activity to reinforce spelling strategies.

· ·

Review of Spelling Strategies Review with children the spelling strategies discussed on pages 176–177 of the Pupil's Edition. Then distribute Home Activities Master 23A.

The Reteach section of each Lesson Wrap-Up provides suggestions for helping children who are still having difficulty with the concepts taught in that lesson.

RESOURCES: PRACTICE ACTIVITIES MASTER 23B

Use as an extra activity to provide children an opportunity to combine spelling and writing.

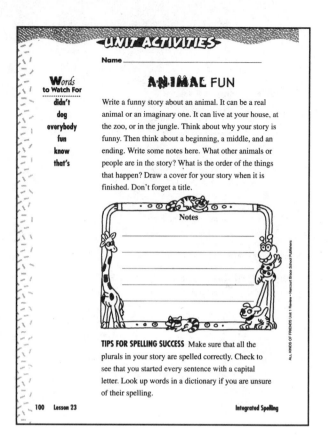

UNIT 4 ACTIVITIES pages 100–101

Activities on pages 100 and 101 of the Pupil's Edition emphasize writing (Animal Fun), reading (Welcome Home), and word play (Word Doodles). The **Tips for Spelling Success** point out the importance of standard spelling and give children hints for proofreading and for applying spelling strategies they have learned.

Animal Fun Read the directions with children. Ask what makes a funny story funny. Encourage them to share funny stories with which they are familiar or funny things that have happened to them. Remind children to list the characters they want to write about and to think about the order in which things will happen in their stories. Suggest that they make notes about the beginning, the middle, and the ending of the story. After children have completed their stories, provide drawing paper and crayons or markers for making covers. Then invite children to share their work.

Have children read aloud the **Tips for Spelling Success.** Then point out the **Words to Watch For.** These are words children often use in writing. Explain that children can refer to the list to help them spell these words correctly.

When children proofread their work, provide them with the checklist below or the proofreading checklist on page 175 of the Pupil's Edition. WRITING/PROOFREADING

Proofreading Checklist

- ✔ Did I spell words correctly?
- ✔ Did I write complete sentences?
- ✔ Did I begin sentences with capital letters?
- ✔ Did I end sentences with the correct marks?
- ✔ Did I spell plurals correctly?

 If children need help in writing a story, refer them to pages 8–9 of the *Language Handbook.*

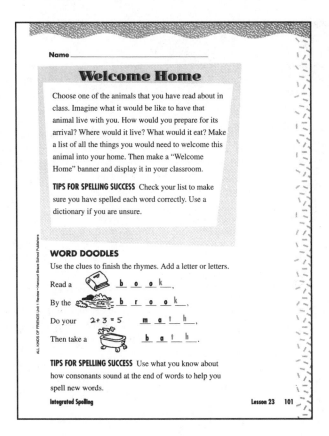

Welcome Home Read the directions with children. Then have them name animals they have read about. List their responses on the board. Ask how children would prepare if the animals were to visit, where the animals would live, and what they would eat. Encourage children to work together on their lists and banners.

Have children read the **Tips for Spelling Success** and encourage them to proofread their work. WRITING/PROOFREADING

Word Doodles Read the directions with children. Tell them that the pictures will help them figure out the words and the number of blanks will show whether they need to write one or two letters to complete the words.

Read the **Tips for Spelling Success** and encourage children to recall and use the strategy. Tell them that they can also use a rhyming strategy to help them spell the words. USING LETTER SOUNDS AND RHYMING WORDS

Assign pairs of children two of the review words listed on page T147. Give children a few minutes to think of a way to act out their words. Then as children act out their words, have others guess them. Ask the guessers to spell aloud the words.

Have children play a variation of the game "Hot Potato." Have children sit in a circle and pass a beanbag or foam ball around as music plays. When the music stops, give the child holding the "hot potato" one of the review words listed on page T147 to spell. Continue until all of the review words have been spelled twice.

For children who need a reteaching activity, play the following game. Attach one of the review words from page T147 to the back of each child. Have children take turns standing with their backs to the group. The group must give clues for each word. The child standing must guess the word, spell it, and use it in a sentence.

Words Like *arm* and *heart*

Objective

To spell words with the sound /är/ spelled *ar* or *ear*

Lesson Planner

Assign words based on the developmental levels of individual children. See the Assignment Guide on page T250.

Informal Assessment

Children's writing may show that they have difficulty spelling words with the sound /är/ spelled *ar* or *ear*.

MODEL

art
I draw pictures in (at).

Use this lesson to introduce the spelling of words in which the sound /är/ is spelled with the letters *ar* or *ear*. Encourage children to apply what they have learned to help them spell other words with this sound. After children have completed the lesson, have them proofread their writing and correct any errors they may have made spelling words with the sound /är/ spelled *ar* or *ear*.

SECOND-LANGUAGE SUPPORT Help children understand the meanings of the Spelling Words by using the words in context. Say a sentence, but leave out the Spelling Word. Have children tell which word completes the sentence. Then encourage children to use the words in sentences of their own. MAKING INFERENCES

Pretest/Posttest Context Sentences

You may want to test Semi-Phonetic Spellers on words 1–6 only.

*1. **arm**   Your elbow is part of your **arm.**
*2. **are**   Puppies **are** baby dogs.
3. **far**   Grandma lives **far** away.
4. **heart**   I drew a big, red **heart** for your valentine.
5. **dark**   It is **dark** at night.
6. **hard**   Are the math problems too **hard**?

7. **farm**   We grow corn on our **farm.**
8. **park**   Do you like to play ball at the **park**?
9. **start**   When will school **start**?
10. **part**   This **part** of the flower is the petal.

*Words appearing in "The Chalk Doll." Some additional story words following the generalization are *party, yard,* and *tar.*

RESOURCES: HOME ACTIVITIES MASTER 24A

NOTE: Fill in the teacher's note on the Home Activities Master before sending it home with children. See the Assignment Guide on page T250 for assigning lists of words.

INTRODUCTION page 102

Pretest Administer the pretest. Say each word, use it in the sentence provided on page T153, and then repeat the word. ACCESSING PRIOR KNOWLEDGE

Self-Check Have children check their own pretests by referring to their list of Spelling Words. For each misspelled word on the pretest, remind children to use the **Study Steps to Learn a Word** on pages 8–9 of the Pupil's Edition. STUDENT SELF-ASSESSMENT

Introducing the Lesson To use the open sort, copy Home Activities Master 24A in the Copying Masters section.

Open Sort: Distribute word cards to children and have them individually or cooperatively select criteria for sorting. Then have children name one of their sorting groups. Ask others what words fit into the group. You may want to send home the word cards so that children can complete the Home Activities Master.

Closed Sort: Read aloud with children the lesson title and the Spelling Words on Pupil's Edition page 102.

- Write the letters *ar* and *ear* as headings on the board. Then write the words *tar, heart, arm,* and *chart.* Have children sort the words into groups spelled with *ar* and *ear.* Write the words in the appropriate columns.
- Have children sort the words in the *ar* column according to whether the *ar* comes in the beginning, the middle, or the end of the word. SORTING WORDS

In Summary Have children summarize the lesson in their own words. Point out that the sound /är/ can be spelled with the letters *ar* or *ear.*

Your Own Words For homework or practice, have pairs or teams of children look in books, newspapers, or magazines to find and then list in their Spelling Logs other words with the sound /är/ spelled *ar* or *ear.* RECOGNIZING PATTERNS

Name _____

S T R A T E G Y Workshop

PROOFREADING: Check Spelling Read what you wrote. If you are not sure how a word is spelled, circle it. Then check the spelling.

Which words do not look right? Circle the misspelled word in each row. Write it correctly.

1. (fa)   are   heart   ___far___

2. part   (peark)   start   ___park___

3. hard   arm   (deark)   ___dark___

4. art   (fearm)   cart   ___farm___

Circle the misspelled words. Write them correctly.

I'm making a rag doll. I will

(steart) ___start___ with a basket of rags.

I will make (peart) ___part___ of my doll

blue. One (earm) ___arm___ will be yellow!

I will sew on eyes, a nose, and a mouth. Then

I will sew on a big red (hart) ___heart___.

Making a rag doll is not (harde) ___hard___ at all!

Fun with Words Write the Spelling Word that sounds like a letter of the alphabet. ___are___

Integrated Spelling   Lesson 24   103

• •

STRATEGY WORKSHOP page 103

Proofreading: Check Spelling
Write on the board the sentence *We drove in the cear.* Ask which word looks wrong. Circle *cear.* Then ask how children can figure out the right way to spell *car.* Write *car* correctly on the board. APPLYING SPELLING STRATEGIES

SEMI-PHONETIC SPELLERS Help children make word cards for their Spelling Words. As they complete the activities on Pupil's Edition page 103, encourage children to find the card for each word on the page. Have them check the spelling and, if necessary, use the card to help them spell the activity word correctly.

Fun with Words After children have completed the activity, have them make a list of words that sound like letters of the alphabet.

SECOND-LANGUAGE SUPPORT As you say each letter of the alphabet, have children tell which words, if any, sound like the letter. Write the words on the board. (*a, bee, sea, I, jay,* and so on) Discuss their meanings. LANGUAGE PLAY

RESOURCES: PRACTICE ACTIVITIES MASTER 24B

Use as extra practice or as a homework activity.

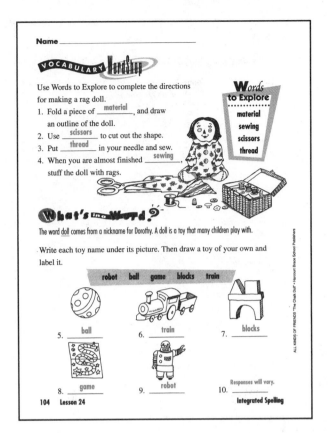

VOCABULARY WORDSHOP pages 104–105

Words to Explore Write the Words to Explore on the board: *material, sewing, scissors, thread.* Discuss their meanings with children. Ask how all the words are related. (They tell about sewing.) Then ask children how they would use material, scissors, and thread if they were making a doll.

Spelling Log Have children add the Words to Explore to their Spelling Logs.

TRANSITIONAL SPELLERS Assign the Words to Explore. As a practice activity, have children write a riddle for each Word to Explore. Then have them write each word on a separate card. As each child reads his or her riddle aloud, have others hold up the word that answers it.

What's in a Word? Ask children what their favorite toys are. Then ask how children think toys got their names. Tell them that teddy bears were named after Theodore Roosevelt, who was a president of the United States. Then have children complete the activity. WORD ORIGINS

Name _____

MULTIPLE MEANINGS The word <u>material</u> can mean "sewing fabric." <u>Material</u> can also mean "what something is made of." List the materials under the correct heading in the outline.

Materials

Wheels	Paint	Thread	Cloth	Wood	Stuffing

Making Toys

1. Wagon
   - A. _Wheels_
   - B. _Wood_
   - C. _Paint_

2. Rag Doll
   - A. _Cloth_
   - B. _Stuffing_
   - C. _Thread_

WITH A PARTNER Cut out five paper-doll shapes. Write a Spelling Word on each doll. Then choose a doll. Read the word, and use it in a sentence.

Integrated Spelling

Lesson 24　105

ALL KINDS OF FRIENDS "The Chalk Doll" • Harcourt Brace School Publishers

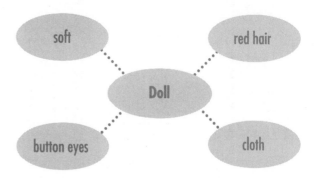

❝ . . . children need to be encouraged to write often using the spelling strategies they have developed. **❞**
(Carol Beers and James Beers)

• •

Multiple Meanings Discuss both meanings of *material* with children. Then discuss the pictures of the wagon and the rag doll. Ask what children think they would need to make each toy. WORD MEANINGS

 Working Together Have children work together to list other words that have multiple meanings. Encourage children to give definitions to show the different meanings of the words. As an example, use the Spelling Word *park,* which can mean "an outdoor place where people can walk or play" or "to leave a car or truck in one place."

With a Partner To help children complete this activity, you may want to provide a paper-doll pattern for children to trace. WORD MEANINGS

Posttest To check children's mastery of the Spelling Words, use the context sentences on page T153 to administer the posttest.

Optional Writing Idea: Description Display a doll and an action figure. Tell children that they are going to write a description of the doll or the action figure. Suggest that they begin by making a web of words and phrases that describe the object.

```
   soft                    red hair
           \        /
            \      /
             Doll
            /      \
           /        \
 button eyes         cloth
```

After children have completed their descriptions, ask them to draw a picture of the object they described. Then encourage children to share their work.

Vocabulary Activities

LESSON WRAP-UP

Words to Explore and Context Sentences

1. **material**   This **material** is made from cotton.
2. **sewing**   Paul is **sewing** a button on his shirt.
3. **scissors**   Use the **scissors** to cut the cloth.
4. **thread**   I used red **thread** to sew my puppet.

Reteach

LEARNING DIFFERENCES Prepare a paper with the nine Spelling Words with the /är/ sound spelled *ar*. Omit the letters *ar* in each word. Remind children that the letters *ar* can stand for the /är/ sound. Tell them that the letters that stand for /är/ are missing from these Spelling Words. Say the first word aloud. Have children repeat the word, write the missing letters, and read the word aloud. Follow the same procedure with each of the other words. Then have children tell what letters stand for the /är/ sound in *heart*. Have children write *heart* as you spell it aloud.
AUDITORY/KINESTHETIC MODALITIES

__ __ m
__ __ e
f __ __
d __ __ k
h __ __ d
f __ __ m
p __ __ k
st __ __ t
p __ __ t

INTEGRATED CURRICULUM ACTIVITIES

Language Arts

Have a Heart   Write each of the Spelling Words on a card. When you write the word *heart,* draw a heart shape around it. Mix up the cards and place them face down in a pile. Children take turns picking a card and using the Spelling Word on the card in a sentence. The child who picks the *heart* card gets another turn.

Science

What Is What?   On a large sheet of butcher paper, draw the outline of a person.

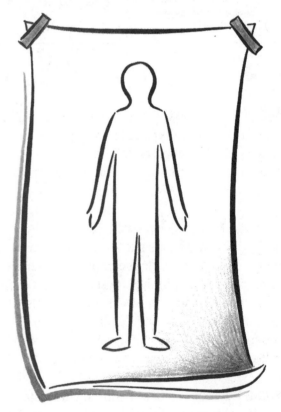

Have children tell which two Spelling Words name parts of a person. *(heart, arm)* Label those parts. Then have children label the other body parts. (head, neck, hand, foot, leg, and so on)

Words Like *door* and *more*

Objective
To spell words with the sound /ôr/ spelled *ore*, *or*, or *oor*

Lesson Planner
Assign words based on the developmental levels of individual children. See the Assignment Guide on page T250.

Informal Assessment
Children's writing may show that they have difficulty spelling words with the sound /ôr/ spelled *ore*, *or*, or *oor*.

MODEL

for
This hat is (foor) you.

Use this lesson to introduce the spelling of words in which the sound /ôr/ is spelled with the letters *ore*, *or*, or *oor*. Encourage children to apply what they have learned to help them spell other words with this sound. After children have completed the lesson, have them proofread their writing and correct any errors they may have made spelling words with the sound /ôr/ spelled *ore*, *or*, or *oor*.

SECOND-LANGUAGE SUPPORT Help children understand the meanings of the Spelling Words by using them in context. Write the words on word cards and distribute them among children. Then say a sentence for each word but leave out the word. Have the child or children with the word stand up and use it to complete the sentence. Then ask children to switch cards and to use the new words in sentences. WORD MEANINGS

Pretest/Posttest Context Sentences
You may want to test Semi-Phonetic Spellers on words 1–6 only.

1.	**store**	We buy milk at the **store.**
2.	**or**	Do you want a red marker **or** a blue one?
*3.	**door**	Come in and then close the **door.**
*4.	**more**	Which glass has **more** in it?
5.	**corn**	I like to eat **corn** on the cob.
6.	**horse**	The **horse** is galloping in the pasture.
7.	**floor**	They put a rug on the **floor.**
8.	**short**	We drew a **short** line and a long one.
9.	**born**	My baby sister was **born** yesterday.
10.	**sort**	What **sort** of toy would you like?

*Words appearing in "The Little Painter of Sabana Grande." Some additional story words following the generalization are *for, morning, important, before,* and *corner.*

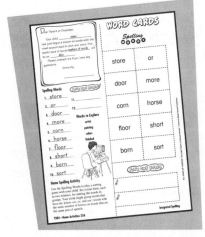

RESOURCES: HOME ACTIVITIES MASTER 25A

NOTE: Fill in the teacher's note on the Home Activities Master before sending it home with children. See the Assignment Guide on page T250 for assigning lists of words.

Name _____

Words Like door and more

Spelling WORDS

1. store
2. or
3. door
4. more
5. corn
6. horse
7. floor
8. short
9. born
10. sort

YOUR OWN WORDS

Look for other words with the same vowel sound. Write them here.

11. _____
12. _____

106   Lesson 25

Each Spelling Word has the same vowel sound. Look at the letters—*ore, or,* or *oor*—that spell that sound. Write the Spelling Words in three groups to help you remember them. Words added by students will vary.

ore
store
more

orn
or
corn
horse
short
born
sort

Words with Two Vowels Together
door
floor

Words with the /ôr/ sound can be spelled *ore, or,* or *oor.*

Integrated Spelling

INTRODUCTION page 106

Pretest Administer the pretest. Say each word, use it in the sentence provided on page T159, and then repeat the word. ACCESSING PRIOR KNOWLEDGE

Self-Check Have children check their own pretests by referring to their list of Spelling Words. For each misspelled word on the pretest, remind children to use the **Study Steps to Learn a Word** on pages 8–9 of the Pupil's Edition. STUDENT SELF-ASSESSMENT

Introducing the Lesson To use the open sort, copy Home Activities Master 25A in the Copying Masters section.

Open Sort: Distribute word cards to children and have them individually or cooperatively select criteria for sorting. As you read each word, have children tell what group or groups the word could be included in. You may want to send home the word cards so that children can complete the Home Activities Master.

Closed Sort: Read aloud with children the lesson title and the Spelling Words on Pupil's Edition page 106.

- Write the letters *ore, or,* and *oor* as headings on the board. Then display these words, one at a time: *tore, door,* and *horn.* Ask which group each word belongs in.
- Ask children to name other words for each group. SORTING WORDS

In Summary Ask what letters children learned about in this lesson. (*or, oor, ore*) Point out that the sound /ôr/ can be spelled with the letters *ore, or,* or *oor.*

Your Own Words Encourage children to find and record in their Spelling Logs other words with the sound /ôr/ spelled *ore, oor,* or *or.* RECOGNIZING PATTERNS

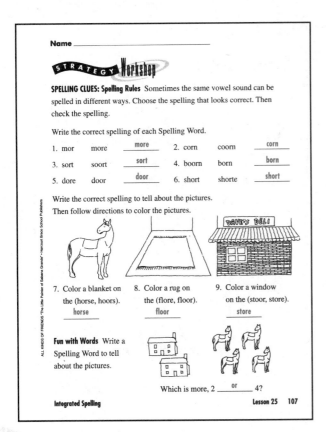

Name _____

STRATEGY Workshop

SPELLING CLUES: Spelling Rules Sometimes the same vowel sound can be spelled in different ways. Choose the spelling that looks correct. Then check the spelling.

Write the correct spelling of each Spelling Word.

1. mor   more   _more_   2. corn   coorn   _corn_

3. sort   soort   _sort_   4. boorn   born   _born_

5. dore   door   _door_   6. short   shorte   _short_

Write the correct spelling to tell about the pictures.
Then follow directions to color the pictures.

DAVEY'S DELI

7. Color a blanket on the (horse, hoors).   _horse_

8. Color a rug on the (flore, floor).   _floor_

9. Color a window on the (stoor, store).   _store_

Fun with Words Write a Spelling Word to tell about the pictures.

Which is more, 2 _or_ 4?

Integrated Spelling   Lesson 25   107

ALL KINDS OF FRIENDS "The Little Painter of Sabana Grande"—Harcourt Brace School Publishers

---

> Word Sorts help to sensitize children to the types of order that exist in English spelling.
>
> (Robert C. Schlagel and Joy H. Schlagel)

STRATEGY WORKSHOP page 107

Spelling Clues: Spelling Rules
Point out that if children are not sure how to spell the sound /ôr/ in a word, they should try the different spellings for the sound to see which spelling looks right. Tell children they can use their Spelling Word list or a dictionary to check the spellings of words. APPLYING SPELLING STRATEGIES

SEMI-PHONETIC SPELLERS Have children follow the directions in the second activity on Pupil's Edition page 107 to paint the three pictures. Then ask children to use paint to write the Spelling Word that tells about each picture.

Fun with Words
Ask how many houses and how many horses children see. Explain that children can complete the question by writing the correct Spelling Word in the blank.

SECOND-LANGUAGE SUPPORT Use the pictures in Fun with Words to help children understand the meanings of the numbers *two* and *four* and the words *more* and *or*. Have children count the houses and the horses. Then ask them to answer the question by telling which is more—two or four. You might want to continue the activity by having children hold up a different number of fingers on each hand. Then ask which number of fingers is more. USING PICTURE CLUES

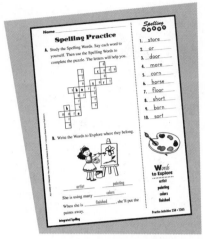

**RESOURCES: PRACTICE
ACTIVITIES MASTER** **25B**

Use as extra practice or as a
homework activity.

- -

VOCABULARY WORDSHOP pages 108–109

Words to Explore Write the Words to Explore
on the board: *artist, painting, colors, finished.*
Discuss their meanings with children. Then
have children use the words in sentences about
a painting.

Spelling Log Have children add
the Words to Explore to their
Spelling Logs.

TRANSITIONAL SPELLERS Assign the Words
to Explore. As a practice activity,
invite children to paint pictures. Then
have them use the Words to Explore to tell
about their painting experience.

What's in a Word? Tell children that adobe is
one material used to build houses. Ask them to
name other materials that can be used to build
houses. If possible, supply pictures of houses
that are built from different materials. Then
have children complete the activity
independently. DEVELOPING VOCABULARY

Classifying Read the words with children
and discuss their meanings. Point out the
illustrations and have children identify the two
groups into which they will classify the words.
(Plants, Animals) Then have them complete
the activity independently. CLASSIFYING

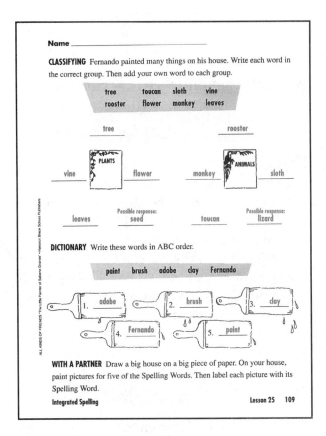

Name _____

CLASSIFYING Fernando painted many things on his house. Write each word in the correct group. Then add your own word to each group.

| tree | toucan | sloth | vine |
| rooster | flower | monkey | leaves |

tree   rooster

PLANTS   ANIMALS

vine   flower   monkey   sloth

leaves   *Possible response:* seed   toucan   *Possible response:* lizard

DICTIONARY Write these words in ABC order.

| paint | brush | adobe | clay | Fernando |

1. adobe   2. brush   3. clay

4. Fernando   5. paint

WITH A PARTNER Draw a big house on a big piece of paper. On your house, paint pictures for five of the Spelling Words. Then label each picture with its Spelling Word.

Integrated Spelling   Lesson 25   109

Dictionary Remind children to look at the first letter of each word to put the words in alphabetical order. Some children may want to circle the first letter of each word to help them isolate and focus on that letter. USING ALPHABETICAL ORDER

 Working Together Have children work in groups of five to use the words from the Dictionary activity to make a dictionary page. Assign one word to each child. Have the child write a definition and sentence for the word. Then have group members compile their work into a dictionary page.

With a Partner Discuss ways to illustrate the Spelling Words. Then have children complete the activity. WORD MEANINGS

Posttest To check children's mastery of the Spelling Words, use the context sentences on page T159 to administer the posttest.

Optional Writing Idea: Opinion Have children look at the houses on Pupil's Edition page 108. Ask children which house they would most like to live in and why. Have them write about the house they chose and why they like it. You might suggest that children begin by listing their ideas in a chart.

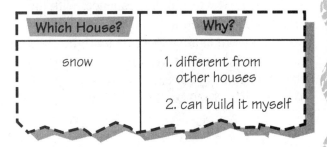

Which House?	Why?
snow	1. different from other houses
	2. can build it myself

Ask children to draw pictures of their houses. Then compile children's work into a group book about houses.

LESSON WRAP-UP

Words to Explore and Context Sentences

1. **artist**   The **artist** paints beautiful pictures.
2. **painting** This **painting** is my favorite.
3. **colors**   My favorite **colors** are red and purple.
4. **finished** I **finished** my picture and put the paints away.

Reteach

 LEARNING DIFFERENCES Cut a window 1/2 inch by 2 inches in a sheet of cardboard. Staple the cardboard to another sheet the same size. On a strip of paper 2 inches wide, write a Spelling Word. Omit one or two letters at a time at 1/2-inch intervals, as follows:

s	t	o	r	e
_	_	o	r	e
_	_	_	_	e
_	_	_	_	_

Place the strip between the sheets of cardboard so that the word *store* shows in the window. Ask the child to spell the word aloud. Then show the next word in the sequence, with the first two letters omitted, and ask the child to spell the word again. Continue until the child has spelled the entire word from memory. Use the same strategy for each of the Spelling Words. VISUAL MODALITY

INTEGRATED CURRICULUM ACTIVITIES

Language Arts

Rhyme Race Have children work in teams of three or four to play this game. Set a time limit, such as five minutes. The object of the game is for each team to use the Spelling Words to make up as many rhymes as possible. Tell children that their rhymes can be silly, but each rhyme must contain at least one Spelling Word. When time is up, have teams read their rhymes aloud. The winning team is the one that made up the most rhymes. Children might also want to vote to choose the funniest or silliest rhyme.

Math

Add or Subtract? Have children work in pairs. Ask each child in a pair to choose five Spelling Words. Then for each word, have children write a math problem whose answer is the number of letters in the word. Suggest that one child write addition problems, and the other subtraction. Ask children to solve each other's problems and to name a Spelling Word that has the same number of letters as the answer. Sample problems for *store* might be:

$$3 + 2 = \underline{\quad}$$

$$13 - 8 = \underline{\quad}$$

Objective

To spell contractions with *not, us,* and *have*

Lesson Planner

Assign words based on the developmental levels of individual children. See the Assignment Guide on page T250.

Informal Assessment

Children's writing may show that they have difficulty spelling contractions with *not, us,* and *have.*

MODEL

we've

I think ⟨wiv⟩ got to stop now.

Use this lesson to introduce the spelling of contractions with *not, us,* and *have.* Encourage children to apply what they have learned to help them spell other contractions of this type. After children have completed the lesson, have them proofread their writing and correct any errors they may have made spelling contractions with *not, us,* and *have.*

SECOND-LANGUAGE SUPPORT Contractions with *not* may present difficulties for Spanish-speaking children. In Spanish, negatives such as *not* are usually placed before the verb rather than after it. Use phrases and corresponding contractions with *not* in sentences to familiarize children with this form. Sample sentences follow:

> I cannot open this window.
> I can't open this window.

FORMING CONTRACTIONS

Pretest/Posttest Context Sentences

You may want to test Semi-Phonetic Spellers on words 1–6 only.

1. **don't**   You **don't** need mittens in summer.
2. **can't**   Cows **can't** climb trees.
3. **let's**   After we finish, **let's** hang up the picture.
*4. **won't**   My feet **won't** get wet if I wear boots.
*5. **I've**   **I've** seen this movie before.
*6. **didn't**   She **didn't** like the book.
7. **wasn't**   The boy **wasn't** ready on time.
*8. **couldn't**   We **couldn't** have a picnic because it rained.
9. **doesn't**   A fish **doesn't** have legs.
10. **wouldn't**   He said he **wouldn't** be late.

*Words appearing in "The Empty Pot."

RESOURCES: HOME ACTIVITIES MASTER 26A

NOTE: Fill in the teacher's note on the Home Activities Master before sending it home with children. See the Assignment Guide on page T250 for assigning lists of words.

INTRODUCTION page 110

Pretest Administer the pretest. Say each word, use it in the sentence provided on page T165, and then repeat the word.
ACCESSING PRIOR KNOWLEDGE

Self-Check Have children check their own pretests by referring to their list of Spelling Words. For each misspelled word on the pretest, remind children to use the **Study Steps to Learn a Word** on pages 8–9 of the Pupil's Edition. STUDENT SELF-ASSESSMENT

Introducing the Lesson To use the open sort, copy Home Activities Master 26A in the Copying Masters section.

Open Sort: Distribute word cards to children and have them individually or cooperatively select criteria for sorting. Ask how children grouped their words and why. You may want to send home the word cards so that children can complete the Home Activities Master.

Closed Sort: Read aloud with children the lesson title and the Spelling Words on Pupil's Edition page 110.
- Write *not, us,* and *have* as headings on the board. As you say each of the following contractions, ask which column it belongs in: *shouldn't, they've, let's, aren't,* and *you've*. Write the words in the appropriate columns.
- Ask children to name other words that could go in the columns for *not* and *have*.
SORTING WORDS

In Summary Have children summarize the lesson. Point out that children should use *n't, 's,* and *'ve* to spell contractions with *not, us,* and *have*.

Your Own Words For homework or practice, have children write in their Spelling Logs other contractions with *not* and *have*. RECOGNIZING PATTERNS

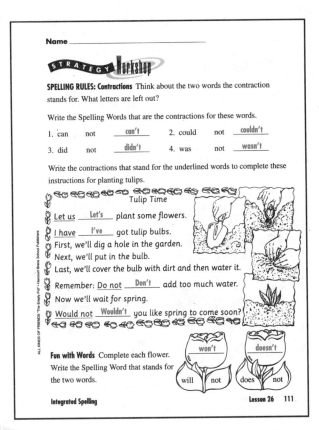

Name _____

STRATEGY Workshop

SPELLING RULES: Contractions Think about the two words the contraction stands for. What letters are left out?

Write the Spelling Words that are the contractions for these words.

1. can not ___can't___   2. could not ___couldn't___

3. did not ___didn't___   4. was not ___wasn't___

Write the contractions that stand for the underlined words to complete these instructions for planting tulips.

Tulip Time

Let us ___Let's___ plant some flowers.

I have ___I've___ got tulip bulbs.
First, we'll dig a hole in the garden.
Next, we'll put in the bulb.
Last, we'll cover the bulb with dirt and then water it.

Remember: Do not ___Don't___ add too much water.

Now we'll wait for spring.

Would not ___Wouldn't___ you like spring to come soon?

Fun with Words Complete each flower. Write the Spelling Word that stands for the two words.

 won't — will / not

 doesn't — does / not

Integrated Spelling

Lesson 26 111

STRATEGY WORKSHOP page 111

Spelling Rules: Contractions
Remind children that most contractions stand for two words and that the apostrophe stands for the letter or letters that were left out when the words were combined. Tell children that thinking about how to spell the words the contraction stands for can help them spell the contraction.
APPLYING SPELLING STRATEGIES

Fun with Words
Call attention to the illustration and have children read aloud the words in the petals. Have them write the correct Spelling Word on the flower.

SECOND-LANGUAGE SUPPORT Help children understand contractions in context by using pairs of sentences. Say the sentence, for example, *This pencil does not have a point.* Then repeat the sentence, substituting the contraction: *This pencil doesn't have a point.* Encourage children to make up sentence pairs for the other contractions. WORD MEANINGS

SEMI-PHONETIC SPELLERS Have children write a list of the Spelling Words that are contractions with *not*. (Note that you may want to treat the word *won't* separately.) Next to each contraction, have children write the words from which it was formed. Tell children to circle each letter that is the same. Then have them cross out the letter or letters that were left out when the contraction was made. Follow a similar procedure for the contractions with *us* and *have*.

Practice Activities

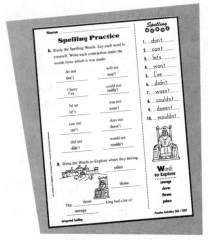

RESOURCES: PRACTICE ACTIVITIES MASTER 26B

Use as extra practice or as a homework activity.

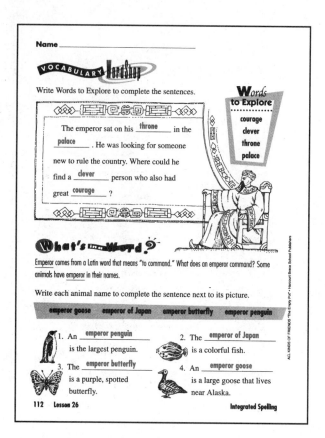

VOCABULARY WORDSHOP pages 112–113

Words to Explore Write the Words to Explore on the board: *courage, clever, throne, palace.* Discuss their meanings with children. Then ask where the emperor in the picture is sitting. (on a throne) Ask who else sits on a throne and which Word to Explore tells where those people might live. (palace)

Spelling Log Have children add the Words to Explore to their Spelling Logs.

TRANSITIONAL SPELLERS Assign the Words to Explore. As a practice activity, have children write the Words to Explore. Challenge them to write a synonym for each one. *(bravery, smart, chair, castle)* Have children use each word and its synonym in a sentence.

What's in a Word? Tell children that some animals, such as the emperor goose, have the word *emperor* in their names. Ask what having *emperor* in its name might tell children about the animal. After children have completed the activity, ask them how a king is similar to an emperor. Challenge them to use a dictionary or an encyclopedia to find animals that have *king* in their names. (Examples include the king cobra, king crab, kingfisher, king salmon, and king snake.) WORD ORIGINS

Flower Words Discuss the time line with
children. Make sure they understand that the
time line progresses from the first event, shown
at the left, to the last event, shown at the right.
Discuss the stages from a seed to a flower.
Then have children complete the activity.
DEVELOPING VOCABULARY

Working Together Have children
work in pairs to discuss and label each
picture with the appropriate word.

Describing Words Write *flower* on the board.
As children name describing words for a
flower, write the words in a web around the
word. Then have children complete the
activity. USING DESCRIBING WORDS

Try This! You may want to have children do
the activity orally before they complete it
independently. FORMING CONTRACTIONS

Posttest To check children's mastery of the
Spelling Words, use the context sentences on
page T165 to administer the posttest.

Optional Writing Idea: Story Have children
look at the illustrations for the What's in a
Word? activity on Pupil's Edition page 112.
Suggest that children choose two of the
animals and imagine what would happen if the
two animals met. Tell children to write a story
that tells what happens when the two animals
meet. You may want to suggest that children
begin by drawing a picture of what they want
to have happen in the story. Then invite
children to read aloud their completed stories.

Vocabulary Activities

LESSON WRAP-UP

Words to Explore and Context Sentences

1. **courage** A brave person has a lot of **courage.**
2. **clever** A **clever** person is smart.
3. **throne** A **throne** is a very fancy chair.
4. **palace** The emperor lived in a huge **palace.**

Reteach

 LEARNING DIFFERENCES Write a Spelling Word on the board and ask children to read it aloud. Have children point out the apostrophe and tell the words from which the contraction was formed. Then tell children to trace over the word with colored chalk. After they have traced the word, have them erase it and write it again from memory. If it is correct, ask children to say the word. If it is not correct, repeat the activity. VISUAL/KINESTHETIC MODALITIES

INTEGRATED CURRICULUM ACTIVITIES

Language Arts

Memory Game Write the Spelling Words on separate word cards. On other cards, write the two words each Spelling Word stands for.

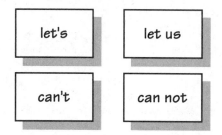

Place all the cards face down on a table. Have a child turn over two cards. If the cards show a contraction and the two words it stands for, the child takes the cards. If the cards don't, the child turns the cards back over. Play continues until all the matches are found.

Physical Education

Spelling Toss Have children work in groups of three or more. After one child reads a Spelling Word, have other children toss a ball or a beanbag back and forth as they spell the word. The first child says the first letter and tosses the ball, the next says the second letter and tosses the ball, and so on. Remind children to include the apostrophe in the spelling. The child who says the last letter changes places with the Reader and reads the next word.

Homophones

Objective
To spell words that are homophones

Lesson Planner
Assign words based on the developmental levels of individual children. See the Assignment Guide on page T250.

Informal Assessment
Children's writing may show that they have difficulty spelling homophones.

MODEL

> bee
> There's a (be) buzzing around.

Use this lesson to introduce the spelling of homophones that children might use in their writing. Encourage them to apply what they have learned to help them spell these words and other homophones. After children have completed the lesson, have them proofread their writing and correct any errors they may have made spelling the homophones in this lesson.

SECOND-LANGUAGE SUPPORT Help children understand the meanings of the Spelling Words by using them in sentences that you write on the board. Write on the board these sample sentences: *Here are four stickers. They are for you.* Point to *four* and have children use it in another sentence to show its meaning. Follow the same procedure with *for.* UNDERSTANDING HOMOPHONES

Pretest/Posttest Context Sentences
You may want to test Semi-Phonetic Spellers on words 1–6 only.

*1. **so**   We laughed because the joke was **so** funny.
*2. **to**   Mike walks **to** school.
*3. **for**   I made this card **for** my mom.
*4. **there** Put the box down over **there.**
5. **sew**   He needs thread to **sew** on the button.
*6. **two**   A bird has **two** wings.

7. **four**   A square has **four** sides.
*8. **their** The children rode **their** bikes.
9. **sow**   Many farmers **sow** their seeds in the spring.
*10. **too**   If you use **too** much salt, the soup won't taste good.

*Words appearing in "Stone Soup." Some additional homophones in the story are *no* and *know.*

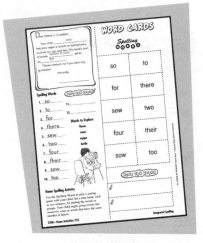

RESOURCES: HOME ACTIVITIES MASTER 27A

NOTE: Fill in the teacher's note on the Home Activities Master before sending it home with children. See the Assignment Guide on page T250 for assigning lists of words.

Name _____

Homophones

Spelling WORDS

Homophones are words that sound alike but have different spellings and meanings. Say each Spelling Word aloud. Can you find the words that sound alike? Write the words in groups of homophones. *Words added by students will vary.*

1. so
2. to
3. for
4. there
5. sew
6. two
7. four
8. their
9. sow
10. too

YOUR OWN WORDS

Look for other words that are homophones. Write them here.

11. _____
12. _____

Homophones are words that sound alike but have different spellings and meanings.

114   Lesson 27   Integrated Spelling

INTRODUCTION page 114

Pretest Administer the pretest. Say each word, use it in the sentence provided on page T171, and then repeat the word. ACCESSING PRIOR KNOWLEDGE

Self-Check Have children work cooperatively in pairs to check their own pretests by referring to their list of Spelling Words. For each misspelled word on the pretest, remind children to use the **Study Steps to Learn a Word** on pages 8–9 of the Pupil's Edition. STUDENT SELF-ASSESSMENT

Introducing the Lesson To use the open sort, copy Home Activities Master 27A in the Copying Masters section.
Open Sort: Distribute word cards to children and have them individually or cooperatively select criteria for sorting. Have children tell how they grouped their words and why. You may want to send home the word cards so that children can complete the Home Activities Master.

Closed Sort: Read aloud with children the lesson title and the Spelling Words on Pupil's Edition page 114.
• Write the words *be, one, our, won, hour,* and *bee* on the board. Have children sort the words into groups of homophones.
• Have children name other homophones. List them in groups on the board. SORTING WORDS

In Summary Ask children what they call words that sound alike but have different spellings and meanings. (homophones) Have children give examples of some homophones.

Your Own Words Encourage children to look for homophones as they read independently. Have them list homophones they find in their Spelling Logs. RECOGNIZING PATTERNS

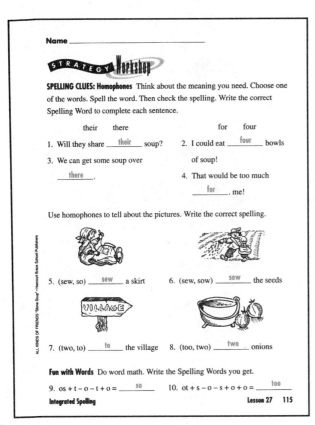

Name _____

STRATEGY Workshop

SPELLING CLUES: Homophones Think about the meaning you need. Choose one of the words. Spell the word. Then check the spelling. Write the correct Spelling Word to complete each sentence.

their   there

1. Will they share ___their___ soup?

3. We can get some soup over ___there___.

for   four

2. I could eat ___four___ bowls of soup!

4. That would be too much ___for___ me!

Use homophones to tell about the pictures. Write the correct spelling.

5. (sew, so) ___sew___ a skirt

6. (sew, sow) ___sow___ the seeds

7. (two, to) ___to___ the village

8. (too, two) ___two___ onions

Fun with Words Do word math. Write the Spelling Words you get.

9. os + t − o − t + o = ___so___

10. ot + s − o − s + o + o = ___too___

Integrated Spelling

Lesson 27   115

All languages that are written alphabetically have homophones, words that sound the same but have different meanings and spellings.

STRATEGY WORKSHOP page 115

Spelling Clues: Homophones Remind children that since homophones have different meanings, they must pay attention to what the words mean in sentences. Tell children to think about the spelling for the meaning of the word that fits a sentence. APPLYING SPELLING STRATEGIES

SECOND-LANGUAGE SUPPORT On the board write the words *so, sew, sow, to, two,* and *too.* As you point to each word, have children use it in a sentence to show its meaning. Then discuss the pictures on Pupil's Edition page 115. Make sure children know what is happening in each one. USING PICTURE CLUES

SEMI-PHONETIC SPELLERS Work with children to develop mnemonics that will help them remember how to spell the homophones in this lesson. You might, for example, point out that the word *four* has four letters or that the word *there,* which is the opposite of *here,* has the word *here* in its spelling. Have children think of ways to help them remember the other Spelling Words.

Fun with Words On the board, work through a sample item, such as the following, to be sure children understand how to add and subtract the letters.

if + o − i + r = for

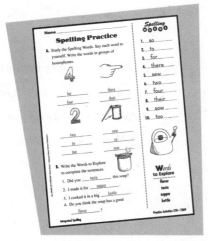

RESOURCES: PRACTICE ACTIVITIES MASTER 27B

Use as extra practice or as a homework activity.

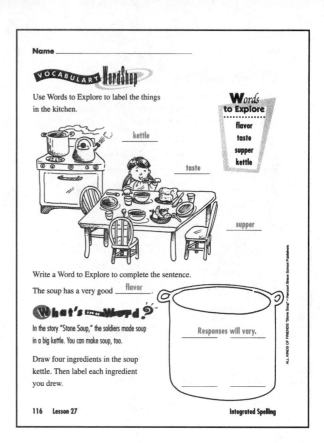

VOCABULARY WORDSHOP pages 116–117

Words to Explore Write the Words to Explore on the board: *flavor, taste, supper, kettle.* Discuss their meanings with children. Ask what all these words have in common. (They tell about supper.) Then ask children to tell what is happening in the picture.

 Spelling Log Have children add the Words to Explore to their Spelling Logs.

TRANSITIONAL SPELLERS Assign the Words to Explore. As a practice activity, distribute graph paper to children so that they can make a word-search puzzle. Ask children to write the Words to Explore, one letter to a square. Have children fill in other squares with any letters they choose. Then have children exchange and solve their puzzles.

What's in a Word? Have children name some of their favorite kinds of soup. Encourage them to tell what ingredients are in the soups. These might include noodles, beans, chicken, or cabbage. Then have children draw and label four ingredients to complete the activity. DEVELOPING VOCABULARY

Antonyms Have children give examples of opposites, such as *up, down; fast, slow; large, small.* Then explain that children will complete the story by writing the opposite of each underlined word. USING ANTONYMS

 Working Together Suggest that one child read aloud the antonyms activity story with the underlined words. Then have another read it with the antonyms. Ask how the meaning changes.

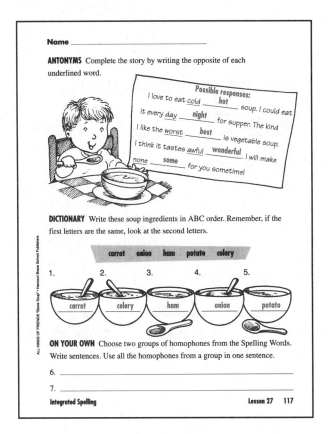

Name _____

ANTONYMS Complete the story by writing the opposite of each underlined word.

Possible responses:

I love to eat <u>cold</u> **hot** soup. I could eat it every <u>day</u> **night** for supper. The kind I like the <u>worst</u> **best** is vegetable soup. I think it tastes <u>awful</u> **wonderful**. I will make <u>none</u> **some** for you sometime!

DICTIONARY Write these soup ingredients in ABC order. Remember, if the first letters are the same, look at the second letters.

carrot   onion   ham   potato   celery

1. carrot   2. celery   3. ham   4. onion   5. potato

ON YOUR OWN Choose two groups of homophones from the Spelling Words. Write sentences. Use all the homophones from a group in one sentence.

6. _____

7. _____

Integrated Spelling   Lesson 27   117

Dictionary Have a volunteer read the list of ingredients aloud. Then have children complete the activity independently. USING ALPHABETICAL ORDER

On Your Own Write this sentence on the board: *I will sew my dress quickly so I can go out and sow the seeds.* Have children find and circle the homophones. Then have them write their own sentences to complete the activity. USING HOMOPHONES

Posttest To check children's mastery of the Spelling Words, use the context sentences on page T171 to administer the posttest.

Optional Writing Idea: Recipe Have children write their own soup recipes. Suggest that they begin by discussing and listing the ingredients they want to include. Point out that they might look over the ingredients they drew for What's in a Word? on Pupil's Edition page 116 and the ones for the Dictionary activity on Pupil's Edition page 117. Remind children to include water in their recipes.

Ingredients
water
chicken
noodles
carrots
salt

Share copies of actual recipes with children. Point out that they should include the following in their recipes: ingredients, how much of each ingredient to use, and how long to cook the soup. After children have completed their recipes, compile them into a class cookbook.

Vocabulary Activities

LESSON WRAP-UP

Words to Explore and Context Sentences

1. **flavor**   Strawberry is my favorite **flavor** of ice cream.
2. **taste**   Did you **taste** the salad yet?
3. **supper**   My family eats **supper** at six o'clock.
4. **kettle**   There is a **kettle** of water on the stove.

Reteach

LEARNING DIFFERENCES Write each homophone group on the board. Use the first word in a simple context sentence, and have children repeat the sentence. Then have children spell the word aloud with you as they trace over the letters on the board. Say the context sentence again and have children repeat it. Follow the same procedure with the other homophone or homophones in the group. AUDITORY/KINESTHETIC MODALITIES

INTEGRATED CURRICULUM ACTIVITIES

Language Arts

Homophone Telephone This game is similar to the familiar game of "Telephone," in which players pass a whispered message along. To begin this game, have children form a circle or a line. Whisper to the first child a phrase with one of the Spelling Words and the spelling of the word. Children pass the phrase along until it reaches the last child, who says aloud what he or she heard. Have children change places and continue the game with a different phrase. Phrases you might want to use include the following:

> two little kittens, *t-w-o*
> sew on buttons, *s-e-w*
> good for you, *f-o-r*
> over there, *t-h-e-r-e*

Math

Two Plus Two Makes Four Have children write two word problems, one for addition and one for subtraction. Tell them to use the Spelling Word *two* in one of their problems and the Spelling Word *four* in the other. Ask children to exchange and solve each other's problems. Use this problem as a sample:

> Corey had two cats. One of them had four kittens. How many cats does Corey have now?

Words That End with -ed and -ing

Objective
To spell words with the ending -ed or -ing

Lesson Planner
Assign words based on developmental levels of individual children. See the Assignment Guide on page T250.

Informal Assessment
Children's writing may show that they have difficulty spelling words with the ending -ed or -ing.

MODEL

walked
We (walkked) to school.

Use this lesson to introduce the spelling of words that have the ending -ed or -ing. Encourage children to apply what they have learned to help them spell other words with these endings. After children have completed the lesson, have them proofread their writing and correct any errors they may have made spelling words with the -ed or -ing ending.

SECOND-LANGUAGE SUPPORT It is sometimes difficult for speakers of other languages to form and pronounce the past tense of regular verbs. Help children become more familiar with this form by having them follow a simple command. Say, for example, "*Look out the window.*" Then ask,"*What did you do?*" Model this response: "*I looked out the window.*" Have children repeat the correct response. Follow a similar procedure with other commands. DEVELOPING VOCABULARY

Pretest/Posttest Context Sentences
You may want to test Semi-Phonetic Spellers on words 1–6 only.

*1. **asked**   Sarah **asked** many questions.
2. **doing**   Are you **doing** that for me?
3. **called**   I **called** my mother on the telephone.
4. **going**   I'm **going** to school today.
5. **looked**   He **looked** at all the pictures.
6. **playing**   The children are **playing** a game.

7. **started**   She **started** to read the book.
8. **trying**   We were **trying** to win the race.
*9. **looking**   They were **looking** at me.
10. **wanted**   The kitten **wanted** some milk.

*Words appearing in "The Night of the Stars." Some additional story words following the generalization are *worked, answered, turned, reached, shouted, climbed, opened, stretching, watering, watching,* and *covering.*

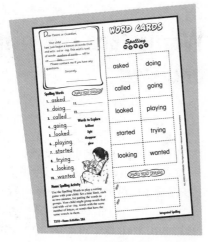

RESOURCES: HOME ACTIVITIES MASTER 28A

NOTE: Fill in the teacher's note on the Home Activities Master before sending it home with children. See the Assignment Guide on page T250 for assigning lists of words.

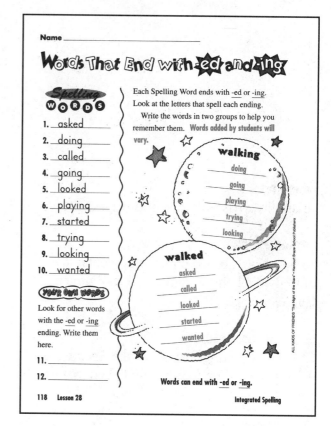

INTRODUCTION page 118

Pretest Administer the pretest. Say each word, use it in the sentence provided on page T177, and then repeat the word. ACCESSING PRIOR KNOWLEDGE

Self-Check Have children check their own pretests by referring to their list of Spelling Words. For each misspelled word on the pretest, remind children to use the **Study Steps to Learn a Word** on pages 8–9 of the Pupil's Edition. STUDENT SELF-ASSESSMENT

Introducing the Lesson To use the open sort, copy Home Activities Master 28A in the Copying Masters section.

Open Sort: Distribute word cards to children and have them individually or cooperatively select criteria for sorting. Have children read their groups of words and discuss how they sorted them. You may want to send home the word cards so that children can complete the Home Activities Master.

Closed Sort: Read aloud with children the lesson title and the Spelling Words on Pupil's Edition page 118.

- Write these words on the board: *played, singing, knocked,* and *asking.* Have children sort the words into groups with the endings *-ed* and *-ing.*
- Ask children to name other words for each group. Write their responses in the correct groups. SORTING WORDS

In Summary Ask children which endings they learned about. Point out that knowing about the endings *-ed* and *-ing* can help them spell words.

Your Own Words Have pairs of children work together to list words that end in *-ed* or *-ing.* Suggest that children choose some words from their lists to include in their Spelling Logs. RECOGNIZING PATTERNS

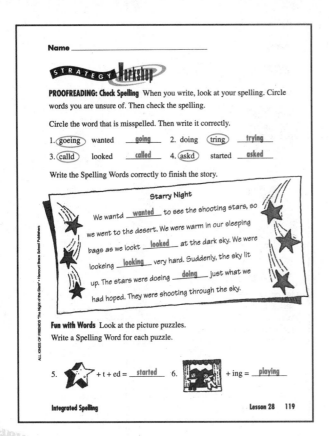

Worksheet content:

Name _____

STRATEGY Workshop

PROOFREADING: Check Spelling When you write, look at your spelling. Circle words you are unsure of. Then check the spelling.

Circle the word that is misspelled. Then write it correctly.

1. (goeing) wanted ___going___ 2. doing (tring) ___trying___
3. (calld) looked ___called___ 4. (askd) started ___asked___

Write the Spelling Words correctly to finish the story.

Starry Night

We wantd ___wanted___ to see the shooting stars, so we went to the desert. We were warm in our sleeping bags as we lookt ___looked___ at the dark sky. We were lookeing ___looking___ very hard. Suddenly, the sky lit up. The stars were doeing ___doing___ just what we had hoped. They were shooting through the sky.

Fun with Words Look at the picture puzzles. Write a Spelling Word for each puzzle.

5. ⭐ + t + ed = ___started___   6. 🎭 + ing = ___playing___

Integrated Spelling

Lesson 28   119

Most past-tense verbs in English are formed by adding *-ed*. The ending may be pronounced in three different ways—with a vowel and the /d/ sound as in *started* and *wanted*, with just the /d/ sound as in *called*, or with the /t/ sound as in *asked* and *looked*.

STRATEGY WORKSHOP page 119

Proofreading: Check Spelling Write on the board the sentence *I am goeing to be late*. Have children look at the words and tell which one is spelled wrong. Then ask how they would spell *going* correctly. APPLYING SPELLING STRATEGIES

SECOND-LANGUAGE SUPPORT Check children's understanding of the Spelling Words. As you say each word, have children use it in a sentence to show its meaning. Then read "Starry Night" on Pupil's Edition page 119 with children. Discuss the meanings of the words *shooting star, desert,* and *sleeping bags.* WORD MEANINGS

Fun with Words Call attention to the illustrations and have children identify the pictures as a star and a play. Tell them to use these picture clues and the letters to figure out the Spelling Word for each puzzle.

SEMI-PHONETIC SPELLERS Have children write their Spelling Words on word cards. Help them cut the words apart before the endings to make puzzle pieces. Have children put the puzzle pieces together to spell the words.

Practice Activities

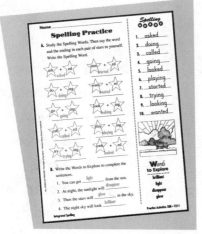

**RESOURCES: PRACTICE
ACTIVITIES MASTER 28B**

Use as extra practice or as a
homework activity.

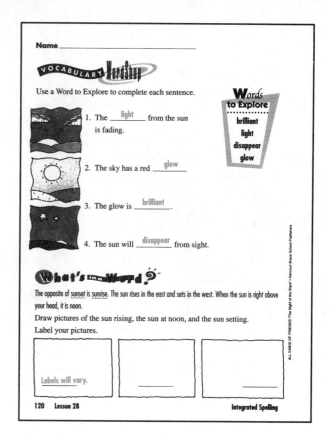

· ·

VOCABULARY WORDSHOP pages 120–121

Words to Explore Write the Words to Explore
on the board: *brilliant, light, disappear, glow.*
Discuss their meanings with children. Then
point out that these words could be used to
describe a sunset. Invite children to describe
sunsets they have seen.

Spelling Log Have children add the
Words to Explore to their Spelling
Logs.

TRANSITIONAL SPELLERS Assign the Words
to Explore. As a practice activity, have
children paint or draw a sunset. Then
have them use the Words to Explore to write
about their sunsets.

What's in a Word? After children have
completed this activity, have them figure out
where east is by finding the sun in the morning
sky and where west is by finding the sun in the
afternoon sky. WORD MEANINGS

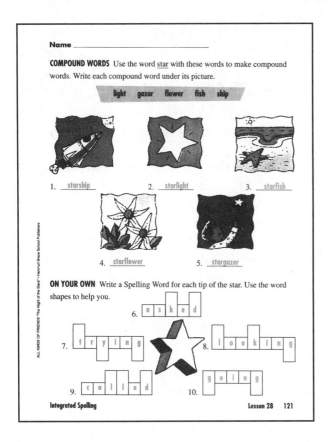

Name_____

COMPOUND WORDS Use the word star with these words to make compound words. Write each compound word under its picture.

| light | gazer | flower | fish | ship |

1. starship   2. starlight   3. starfish

4. starflower   5. stargazer

ON YOUR OWN Write a Spelling Word for each tip of the star. Use the word shapes to help you.

6. a s k e d

7. t r y i n g   8. l o o k i n g

9. c a l l e d   10. g o i n g

Integrated Spelling   Lesson 28   121

- -

Compound Words Remind children that a compound word is made from two smaller words. Have children give examples of compound words. *(playground, sunshine, blueberry)* Then explain that children can make compound words from the word *star* and the words in the box. Have children write the compound words to complete the activity. FORMING COMPOUND WORDS

 Working Together Have children work together using field guides or other reference books to find and illustrate examples of plant and animal names with the word *star* in them. Examples include *star grass, starflower, starwort, starfish, star-nosed mole,* and *starling.*

On Your Own Ask children to complete this activity independently and then to make word shapes for the other Spelling Words. USING SPELLING STRATEGIES

Posttest To check children's mastery of their Spelling Words, use the context sentences on page T177 to administer the posttest.

Optional Writing Idea: Description Tell children that they are going to write a description of a nighttime sky. You may want to provide color photographs and have children choose one to describe. Suggest that they begin by making a web of words and phrases that could describe the sky at night. After children have finished writing, encourage them to illustrate and share their work.

Vocabulary Activities

LESSON WRAP-UP

Words to Explore and Context Sentences

1. **brilliant** He blinked his eyes in the **brilliant** sunlight.
2. **light** The **light** from the sun helps plants grow.
3. **disappear** The magician made the rabbit **disappear.**
4. **glow** The **glow** from the sun is warm and red.

Reteach

LEARNING DIFFERENCES Have children write or copy the words *ask, call, look, start,* and *want* on lined paper. Ask them to skip a line after each word. Have them add *-ed* to each word and then copy the completed word with the ending added on the line below. Follow the same procedure for the words with *-ing* added. VISUAL/KINESTHETIC MODALITIES

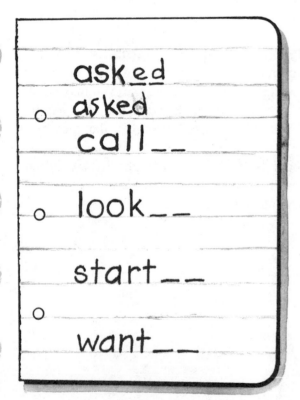

INTEGRATED CURRICULUM ACTIVITIES

Language Arts

Charades Write the Spelling Words *playing, going, trying,* and *looking* on slips of paper. Add other words that can be pantomimed or acted out, such as *reading, singing, jumping, painting, laughing,* and *sleeping.* Have children take turns picking a slip of paper and acting out the word for classmates to guess.

Art

Collage Have children make collages. Tell them to draw or cut out from magazines pictures of people doing things. Have them use words ending in *-ing* to label the pictures in their collages.

Objectives

To review spelling patterns and strategies in Lessons 24–28; to give children the opportunity to recognize and use these spelling patterns and the Spelling Words in their writing

Review of Spelling Strategies

Review with children the spelling strategies presented in Lessons 24–28.

CHECKING SPELLING Write on the board the sentence *He calld me on the phone.* Ask children to read the sentence and identify the misspelled word. Have a volunteer circle the word and spell it correctly. Then ask children how they can check the spelling to see if it is right. (They can ask someone who knows the correct spelling or look up the word in a dictionary.)

USING SPELLING RULES Write *more, corn,* and *floor* on the board. Point out three ways that the /ôr/ sound can be spelled. Then ask how thinking of ways to spell a vowel sound can help children spell a word.

FORMING CONTRACTIONS Write the words *did not* on the board. Ask a volunteer to write the contraction that stands for these two words. *(didn't)* Have children tell which letters are the same in both the two words and the contraction and which letter is left out of the contraction.

USING HOMOPHONES Write the words *for* and *four* on the board. Ask children to tell what each word means and to use it in a sentence. Have children tell how knowing about homophones can help them spell words.

Unit 5 Words

The following words from Unit 5 are reviewed in this lesson.

Lesson 24 Words Like *arm* and *heart:* far, park, start

Lesson 25 Words Like *door* and *more:* corn, sort, more, store, floor, or

Lesson 26 Contractions: can't, I've

Lesson 27 Homophones: to, there, sew

Lesson 28 Words That End with *-ed* and *-ing:* doing

> An integrated program of reading, writing, and word study that allows students to apply knowledge at their appropriate instructional levels offers teachers coherent, manageable tools to augment memory in spelling tasks.
>
> (Janet W. Bloodgood)

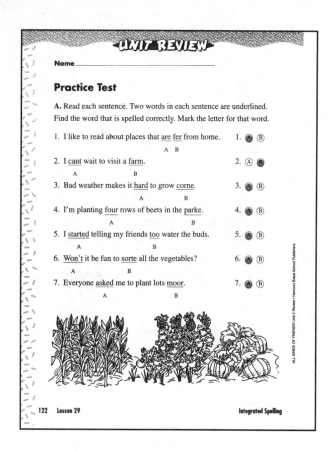

PRACTICE TEST pages 122–123

Options for Administering the Practice Test

The Practice Test provides an opportunity to review Spelling Words and spelling generalizations in a standardized test format.

Option 1: Have children review their **Words to Study** in the Spelling Log for Unit 5. If they need extra help, review the spelling generalizations on Pupil's Edition pages 102, 106, 110, 114, and 118. Then administer both parts of the Practice Test on Pupil's Edition pages 122–123 to determine whether children have mastered the spelling generalizations.

Option 2: Administer both parts of the Practice Test on Pupil's Edition pages 122–123 as a pretest. Have children study the words they misspell. Then, on another day, dictate the Spelling Words from Pupil's Edition pages 122–123 as a posttest.

☑ Options for Evaluation

- Have children check their own Practice Tests by referring to their lists of Spelling Words. The list on the preceding page provides references to the lessons where children will find the words on the Practice Test.
- You may prefer to assign partners and have them check each other's Practice Tests. Refer children to their own lists of Spelling Words to use as they check their partners' tests.

For each word misspelled on the Practice Test, remind children to follow the **Study Steps to Learn a Word** on pages 8–9 of the Pupil's Edition. Be sure to have them write the words they missed in the Unit 5 **Words to Study** box in the Spelling Log. STUDENT SELF-ASSESSMENT

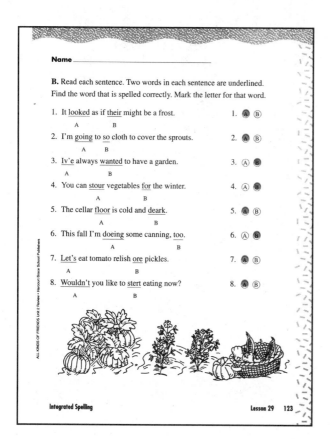

Name _____

B. Read each sentence. Two words in each sentence are underlined. Find the word that is spelled correctly. Mark the letter for that word.

1. It <u>looked</u> as if <u>their</u> might be a frost.   1. Ⓐ Ⓑ
   A   B

2. I'm <u>going</u> to <u>so</u> cloth to cover the sprouts.   2. Ⓐ Ⓑ
     A   B

3. <u>Iv'e</u> always <u>wanted</u> to have a garden.   3. Ⓐ Ⓑ
  A   B

4. You can <u>stour</u> vegetables <u>for</u> the winter.   4. Ⓐ Ⓑ
     A   B

5. The cellar <u>floor</u> is cold and <u>deark</u>.   5. Ⓐ Ⓑ
     A   B

6. This fall I'm <u>doeing</u> some canning, <u>too</u>.   6. Ⓐ Ⓑ
       A   B

7. <u>Let's</u> eat tomato relish <u>ore</u> pickles.   7. Ⓐ Ⓑ
  A   A

8. <u>Wouldn't</u> you like to <u>stert</u> eating now?   8. Ⓐ Ⓑ
  A   B

Integrated Spelling   Lesson 29   **123**

RESOURCES: HOME ACTIVITIES MASTER 29A

Use as an extra activity to reinforce spelling strategies.

Review of Spelling Strategies Review with children the spelling strategies discussed on pages 176–177 of the Pupil's Edition. Then distribute Home Activities Master 29A.

The Reteach section of each Lesson Wrap-Up provides suggestions for helping children who are still having difficulty with the concepts taught in that lesson.

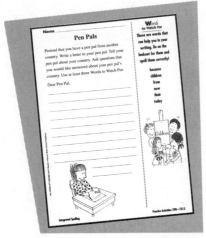

RESOURCES: PRACTICE ACTIVITIES MASTER 29B

Use as an extra activity to provide children an opportunity to combine spelling and writing.

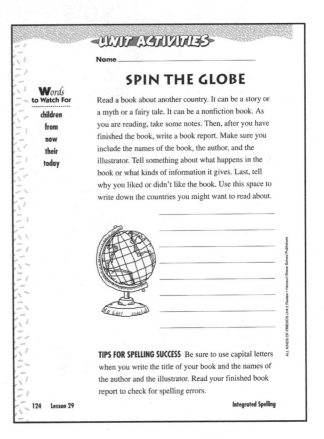

SPIN THE GLOBE

Words to Watch For

children
from
now
their
today

Read a book about another country. It can be a story or a myth or a fairy tale. It can be a nonfiction book. As you are reading, take some notes. Then, after you have finished the book, write a book report. Make sure you include the names of the book, the author, and the illustrator. Tell something about what happens in the book or what kinds of information it gives. Last, tell why you liked or didn't like the book. Use this space to write down the countries you might want to read about.

TIPS FOR SPELLING SUCCESS Be sure to use capital letters when you write the title of your book and the names of the author and the illustrator. Read your finished book report to check for spelling errors.

124   Lesson 29   Integrated Spelling

UNIT 5 ACTIVITIES pages 124–125

Activities on pages 124 and 125 of the Pupil's Edition emphasize reading and writing (Spin the Globe and Playtime) and word play (Word Doodles). The **Tips for Spelling Success** point out the importance of standard spelling and give children hints for proofreading and for applying spelling strategies.

Spin the Globe If possible, have appropriate books available in the classroom or school library for this activity.

Read the directions with children. Discuss the kinds of books that are mentioned. Ask what notes children might take as they read. If necessary, point out that they should note characters' names, important events that occur in a story, or important facts in a nonfiction book. When children are ready to write their book reports, remind them to use the Writing Process.

Have children read aloud the **Tips for Spelling Success.** Then point out the **Words to Watch For.** These are words children often use in writing. Explain that children can use

the list as a reference to help them spell the words correctly.

When children proofread their work, provide them with the following checklist or the proofreading checklist on page 175 of the Pupil's Edition. WRITING/PROOFREADING

Proofreading Checklist
✔ Did I spell words correctly?
✔ Did I write complete sentences?
✔ Did I begin sentences with capital letters?
✔ Did I end sentences with the correct marks?
✔ Did I begin people's names with capital letters?
✔ Did I use capital letters in the book title?

If children need help with writing a book report, refer them to pages 24–25 of the *Language Handbook*.

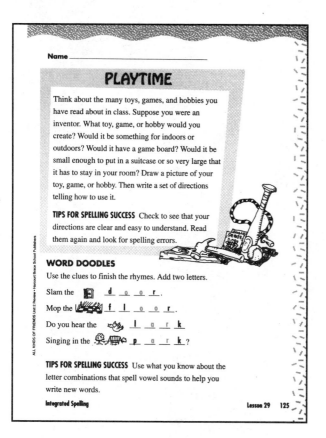

PLAYTIME

Think about the many toys, games, and hobbies you have read about in class. Suppose you were an inventor. What toy, game, or hobby would you create? Would it be something for indoors or outdoors? Would it have a game board? Would it be small enough to put in a suitcase or so very large that it has to stay in your room? Draw a picture of your toy, game, or hobby. Then write a set of directions telling how to use it.

TIPS FOR SPELLING SUCCESS Check to see that your directions are clear and easy to understand. Read them again and look for spelling errors.

WORD DOODLES

Use the clues to finish the rhymes. Add two letters.

Slam the [image] d _o_ _o_ r .

Mop the [image] f l _o_ _o_ r .

Do you hear the [image] l _a_ _r_ k

Singing in the [image] p _a_ _r_ k ?

TIPS FOR SPELLING SUCCESS Use what you know about the letter combinations that spell vowel sounds to help you write new words.

Integrated Spelling   Lesson 29   125

Playtime Read the directions with children. Ask what kinds of toys, games, or hobbies they would create. For each creation, discuss the questions in the directions. List creations and the responses to the questions in a chart on the board. Then have children draw their creations and write their directions for using them.

Have children read the **Tips for Spelling Success** and encourage them to proofread their work. WRITING/PROOFREADING

For help in writing a set of directions or a how-to paragraph, children can refer to pages 28–29 of the *Language Handbook*.

Word Doodles Read the directions for the activity with children. Point out that the pictures will help them figure out the words. If necessary, tell children that the bird in the third item is a lark.

Read the **Tips for Spelling Success** and encourage children to recall and use the strategy. Tell them that they can also use a rhyming strategy to help them spell these words. USING SPELLING RULES

Have children write sentences using one or more of the review words listed on page T183 and draw pictures to illustrate them. Encourage children to include more than one review word in each sentence.

Have children write each of the review words from Lessons 24 and 25 on a word card. (See the list of review words on page T183.) Mix up the cards and have pairs of children work cooperatively to sort the words into two groups according to the vowel sound in each word. Then have children further sort the words in each group according to the spelling pattern in each word.

Form two teams. As you say a review word from the list on page T183, have the first person from each team go to the board and write the word. Each player who spells it correctly scores a point for his or her team. Continue for all the review words.

Have children who need a reteaching activity listen to a tape recording of the review words listed on page T183. Encourage children to make their own tapes on which they say the word and the spelling. Ask children to spell the word on paper as they hear it spelled on the tape.

Words to Remember

Objective
To spell words that are used often

Lesson Planner
Assign words based on the developmental levels of individual children. See the Assignment Guide on page T250.

Informal Assessment
Children's writing may show that they have difficulty spelling some words that are used frequently.

MODEL

and
You (an) I are friends.

Use this lesson to introduce the spelling of words that children might use frequently in their writing. After children have completed the lesson, have them proofread their writing and correct any errors they may have made spelling these words.

 SECOND-LANGUAGE SUPPORT Help children understand the Spelling Words *down, after, out, other,* and *over* by demonstrating the meanings. Ask children to take, for example, crayons *out* of a box or to pick up the *other* book. Encourage children to use the words in sentences to tell what they are doing. Then ask them to demonstrate other actions. ROLE-PLAYING/WORD MEANINGS

Pretest/Posttest Context Sentences
You may want to test Semi-Phonetic Spellers on words 1–6 only.

*1.	**about**	It is just **about** time to leave.
2.	**down**	Mario lives **down** the street.
*3.	**after**	We can go outside **after** lunch.
4.	**how**	He showed us **how** to make a kite.
*5.	**because**	I laughed **because** the joke was funny.
*6.	**out**	She took a toy car **out** of her pocket.
7.	**other**	First I waved one hand and then the **other.**
*8.	**were**	The children **were** in the classroom.
*9.	**very**	I was **very** hungry.
*10.	**over**	The bus went **over** a big bridge.

*Words appearing in "The Goat in the Rug."

RESOURCES: HOME ACTIVITIES MASTER 30A

NOTE: Fill in the teacher's note on the Home Activities Master before sending it home with children. See the Assignment Guide on page T250 for assigning lists of words.

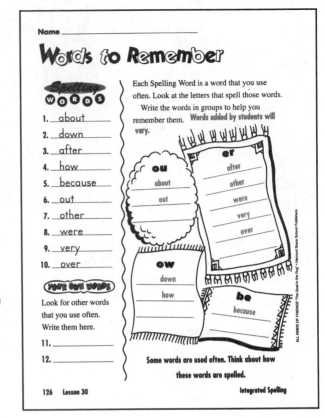

Words to Remember

Each Spelling Word is a word that you use often. Look at the letters that spell those words.

Write the words in groups to help you remember them. *Words added by students will vary.*

1. about
2. down
3. after
4. how
5. because
6. out
7. other
8. were
9. very
10. over

YOUR OWN WORDS

Look for other words that you use often. Write them here.

11. _____
12. _____

ou
about
out

er
after
other
were
very
over

ow
down
how

be
because

Some words are used often. Think about how these words are spelled.

126   Lesson 30

Integrated Spelling

INTRODUCTION page 126

Pretest Administer the pretest. Say each word, use it in the sentence provided on page T189, and then repeat the word. ACCESSING PRIOR KNOWLEDGE

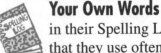 **Self-Check** Have children check their own pretests by referring to their list of Spelling Words. For each misspelled word on the pretest, remind children to use the **Study Steps to Learn a Word** on pages 8–9 of the Pupil's Edition. STUDENT SELF-ASSESSMENT

Introducing the Lesson To use the open sort, copy Home Activities Master 30A in the Copying Masters section.

Open Sort: Distribute word cards to children and have them individually or cooperatively select criteria for sorting. After children group their words, ask them to name their categories. Ask other children to suggest more words that could belong in each category. You may want to send home the word cards so that children can complete the Home Activities Master.

Closed Sort: Read aloud with children the lesson title and the Spelling Words on Pupil's Edition page 126.

- Write the words *her* and *where* on the board. Tell children that the words could be grouped together because they both have *er* in them.
- Write the words *clown* and *now* on the board. Ask why these words could be grouped together. (They both have *ow*.)
- Have children complete the page. SORTING WORDS

In Summary Ask children to name some words they use a lot. Ask why it is helpful for children to know how to spell those words.

Your Own Words Have children list in their Spelling Logs other words that they use often in their writing. RECOGNIZING WORDS

Sorting Activities

LESSON WRAP-UP

Words to Explore and Context Sentences

1. **design** This rug has a blue and white **design.**
2. **weave** Some people **weave** straw into baskets.
3. **wool** This sweater is made of **wool.**
4. **loom** I wove this rug on a **loom.**

Reteach

LEARNING DIFFERENCES Make a tape recording of the Spelling Words. On the tape, say each word, spell it slowly, and say it again. As children listen to the tape, have them use a finger to form the letters of each Spelling Word on a desktop. Then ask them to listen again and to write each word on paper. AUDITORY/KINESTHETIC MODALITIES

INTEGRATED CURRICULUM ACTIVITY

Language Arts

Chain Story Prepare for the activity by writing the Spelling Words on cards.

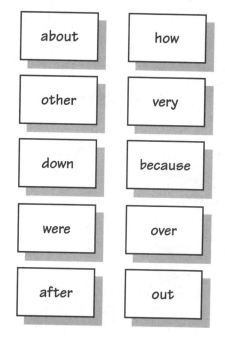

about	how
other	very
down	because
were	over
after	out

Tell children that they are going to make up a chain story. Explain that you will give them the first sentence of the story and each child in turn will add another sentence. The story can be realistic or silly, but each sentence in the story must contain one of the Spelling Words.

Mix up the cards and hold them in a fan shape so children cannot see the words. Begin the story with a sentence such as the following: *One day a goat went for a walk.* Have a volunteer pick a card, read the word, and use that word in the next sentence of the story. Continue in the same fashion, having children take turns picking cards and adding to the story.

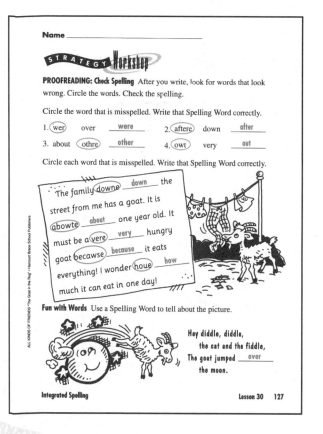

Name _____

PROOFREADING: Check Spelling After you write, look for words that look wrong. Circle the words. Check the spelling.

Circle the word that is misspelled. Write that Spelling Word correctly.

1. wer   over   were
2. aftere   down   after
3. about   othre   other
4. owt   very   out

Circle each word that is misspelled. Write that Spelling Word correctly.

The family downe ___down___ the street from me has a goat. It is abowte ___about___ one year old. It must be a vere ___very___ hungry goat becawse ___because___ it eats everything! I wonder houe ___how___ much it can eat in one day!

Fun with Words Use a Spelling Word to tell about the picture.

Hey diddle, diddle,
the cat and the fiddle,
The goat jumped ___over___
the moon.

Integrated Spelling   Lesson 30   127

> It has been shown that a core of about five thousand words accounts for about 95 percent of the running words in everyday adult writing. Few would question the importance of knowing how to spell correctly words of such impressive utility.
>
> (Edmund H. Henderson)

STRATEGY WORKSHOP page 127

Proofreading: Check Spelling Remind children that after they write, they should check their work and circle words that look wrong. Ask how children can check the spelling of words they have circled. (They can ask someone who knows the correct spelling or look up words in a dictionary.) APPLYING SPELLING STRATEGIES

SEMI-PHONETIC SPELLERS Have children use a different-colored marker or crayon to write each Spelling Word on a strip of paper. Have them use this list to check the spelling of words in the activities on Pupil's Edition page 127.

Fun with Words Say the rhyme "Hey Diddle, Diddle" with children. Ask what jumped over the moon. (cow) Then have children tell what is jumping over the moon in the picture. (goat) Have children read the rhyme and use a Spelling Word to complete it.

SECOND-LANGUAGE SUPPORT Have children read the rhyme in Fun with Words, but ask them to substitute other animals for the word *goat*. Then have them draw pictures for their new rhymes. Children might also enjoy substituting other words for *moon*.

**RESOURCES: PRACTICE
ACTIVITIES MASTER 30B**

Use as extra practice or as a
homework activity.

VOCABULARY WordShop

Use a Word to Explore to tell about each picture.

**Words
to Explore**
design
weave
wool
loom

1. Will you _weave_ a rug
for me?

2. Draw a picture of the _design_
you want.

3. We'll use this _wool_
from one of our sheep.

4. Use a _loom_ to weave the
yarn into a rug!

What's in a Word?

You can *weave* yarn into a rug. You can also
weave your way somewhere by turning or
twisting as you go.

Weave your way through this maze.
Can you find the loom?

128   Lesson 30   Integrated Spelling

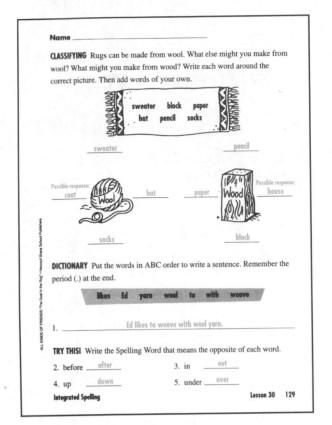

CLASSIFYING Rugs can be made from wool. What else might you make from
wool? What might you make from wood? Write each word around the
correct picture. Then add words of your own.

| sweater | block | paper |
| hat | pencil | socks |

sweater   pencil

Possible response:
coat   _Wool_   hat   paper   _Wood_   Possible response:
                                                                  house

socks   block

DICTIONARY Put the words in ABC order to write a sentence. Remember the
period (.) at the end.

| likes | Ed | yarn | wool | to | with | weave |

1. _____ _Ed likes to weave with wool yarn._

TRY THIS! Write the Spelling Word that means the opposite of each word.

2. before _after_   3. in _out_

4. up _down_   5. under _over_

Integrated Spelling   Lesson 30   129

VOCABULARY WORDSHOP pages 128–129

Words to Explore Write the Words to Explore
on the board: *design, weave, wool, loom.*
Discuss their meanings with children. Ask
what the words have in common. (They are all
weaving words.) Have children use the words
in sentences about weaving a rug. Then have
them complete the activity independently.

Spelling Log Have children add the
Words to Explore to their Spelling
Logs.

TRANSITIONAL SPELLERS Assign the Words
to Explore. As a practice activity, have
children draw pictures for the Words
to Explore. Ask them to label each picture with
the correct word.

What's in a Word? Ask children how
weaving a rug is like weaving through a maze.
Have children demonstrate how they weave
their way through someplace by having them
weave their way through a line of objects
placed on the floor.   UNDERSTANDING IDIOMS

Classifying Display some objects made of
wood, plastic, yarn, or other materials. Have
children identify each object. Then ask
volunteers to put the objects into groups of
things made with the same material.
CLASSIFYING

Working Together Have children
work together to make collages of
things that are alike in some way.
Have them draw or cut from magazines
pictures to put in their collages of items made
of wood, clothing, food, or other things that are
alike in some way.

Dictionary Write these words on the board:
yarn, I, sweaters, knit, with. Help children write
a sentence by putting the words in alphabetical
order. Then have children complete the activity
independently.   USING ALPHABETICAL ORDER

Try This! Ask children the opposite of words
like *off (on)* and *above (below).* Then have
them complete the activity independently.
USING ANTONYMS

Posttest To check children's mastery of the
Spelling Words, use the context sentences on
page T189 to administer the posttest.

Optional Writing Idea: Description Ask what
design children would make if they were
weaving a rug: What colors would they use?
What shapes or pictures would they weave?
Explain that children are going to write
descriptions of the rugs they would weave.
Suggest that they begin by drawing a picture of
the rug and then listing words that describe it.
Then encourage children to display their
finished pictures and descriptions.

Compound Words

Objective
To spell compound words

Lesson Planner
Assign words based on the developmental levels of individual children. See the Assignment Guide on page T250.

Informal Assessment
Children's writing may show that they have difficulty spelling compound words.

MODEL

> football
> I like to watch (foot ball) on TV.

Use this lesson to introduce the spelling of compound words. Encourage children to apply what they have learned to help them spell other words made from two smaller words. After children have completed the lesson, have them proofread their writing and correct any errors they may have made spelling compound words.

 SECOND-LANGUAGE SUPPORT Help children understand the meanings of the Spelling Words by using them in sentences. When you say each sentence, leave out the compound word and have children supply it. Then ask children to use the words in sentences of their own. WORD MEANINGS

Pretest/Posttest Context Sentences
You may want to test Semi-Phonetic Spellers on words 1–6 only.

1. **upon** — The emperor sat **upon** his throne.
*2. **grandma** — I like to visit my **grandma.**
3. **seesaw** — Nancy and Berto sat on the **seesaw.**
4. **sometimes** — I walk to school **sometimes.**
5. **herself** — She looked at **herself** in the mirror.
6. **somewhere** — He lives **somewhere** far away.
7. **classroom** — The children went into their **classroom** at school.
8. **himself** — He solved the puzzle by **himself.**
9. **baseball** — You need a bat and ball to play **baseball.**
10. **something** — She is holding **something** behind her back.

*Word appearing in "Thunder Cake." Some additional story words following the generalization are *tablecloth, barnyard, notepaper, cupboards, farmhouse, overripe, woodstove, teaspoons, anything,* and *doorway.*

RESOURCES: HOME ACTIVITIES MASTER 31A

NOTE: Fill in the teacher's note on the Home Activities Master before sending it home with children. See the Assignment Guide on page T250 for assigning lists of words.

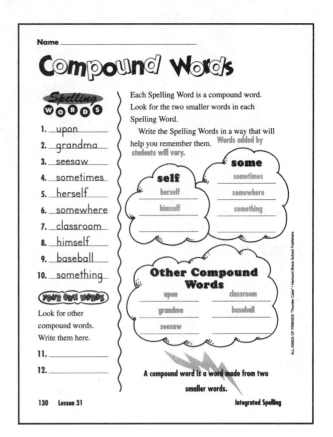

Name _____

Compound Words

Spelling WORDS

Each Spelling Word is a compound word. Look for the two smaller words in each Spelling Word.

Write the Spelling Words in a way that will help you remember them. *Words added by students will vary.*

1. upon
2. grandma
3. seesaw
4. sometimes
5. herself
6. somewhere
7. classroom
8. himself
9. baseball
10. something

self
herself
himself

some
sometimes
somewhere
something

Other Compound Words
upon   classroom
grandma   baseball
seesaw

YOUR OWN WORDS

Look for other compound words. Write them here.

11. _____
12. _____

A compound word is a word made from two smaller words.

130   Lesson 31   Integrated Spelling

ALL KINDS OF FRIENDS "Thunder Cake" • Harcourt Brace School Publishers

- -

INTRODUCTION page 130

Pretest Administer the pretest. Say each word, use it in the sentence provided on page T195, and then repeat the word. ACCESSING PRIOR KNOWLEDGE

✓ Self-Check Have children work cooperatively in pairs to check their own pretests by referring to their list of Spelling Words. For each misspelled word on the pretest, remind children to use the **Study Steps to Learn a Word** on pages 8–9 of the Pupil's Edition. STUDENT SELF-ASSESSMENT

Introducing the Lesson To use the open sort, copy Home Activities Master 31A in the Copying Masters section.

Open Sort: Distribute word cards to children and have them individually or cooperatively select criteria for sorting. Discuss how children sorted their words and why. You may want to send home the word cards so that children can complete the Home Activities Master.

Closed Sort: Read aloud with children the lesson title and the Spelling Words on Pupil's Edition page 130.

- Write the words *football, myself, yourself,* and *basketball* on the board. Have each compound word and the two words in it identified.
- Ask children how they could sort these words into two groups. Have them group the compound words that have the same smaller word in them. SORTING WORDS

In Summary Ask children what a word that is made from two smaller words is called. Then ask children how knowing about compound words can help them become better spellers.

 Your Own Words Ask children to list in their Spelling Logs other compound words. RECOGNIZING PATTERNS

Name ____________________

STRATEGY Workshop

PROOFREADING: Check Spelling After you write, look for words that look wrong. Circle the words. Check the spelling.

Circle the word that is misspelled. Write that Spelling Word correctly.

1. wer over ___were___ 2. aftere down ___after___
3. about othre ___other___ 4. owt very ___out___

Circle each word that is misspelled. Write that Spelling Word correctly.

The family downe ___down___ the street from me has a goat. It is abowte ___about___ one year old. It must be a vere ___very___ hungry goat becawse ___because___ it eats everything! I wonder houe ___how___ much it can eat in one day!

Fun with Words Use a Spelling Word to tell about the picture.

Hey diddle, diddle,
the cat and the fiddle,
The goat jumped ___over___
the moon.

ALL KINDS OF FRIENDS "The Goat in the Rug" • Harcourt Brace School Publishers

Integrated Spelling Lesson 30 127

"It has been shown that a core of about five thousand words accounts for about 95 percent of the running words in everyday adult writing. Few would question the importance of knowing how to spell correctly words of such impressive utility."
(Edmund H. Henderson)

STRATEGY WORKSHOP page 127

Proofreading: Check Spelling Remind children that after they write, they should check their work and circle words that look wrong. Ask how children can check the spelling of words they have circled. (They can ask someone who knows the correct spelling or look up words in a dictionary.) APPLYING SPELLING STRATEGIES

SEMI-PHONETIC SPELLERS Have children use a different-colored marker or crayon to write each Spelling Word on a strip of paper. Have them use this list to check the spelling of words in the activities on Pupil's Edition page 127.

Fun with Words Say the rhyme "Hey Diddle, Diddle" with children. Ask what jumped over the moon. (cow) Then have children tell what is jumping over the moon in the picture. (goat) Have children read the rhyme and use a Spelling Word to complete it.

SECOND-LANGUAGE SUPPORT Have children read the rhyme in Fun with Words, but ask them to substitute other animals for the word *goat*. Then have them draw pictures for their new rhymes. Children might also enjoy substituting other words for *moon*.

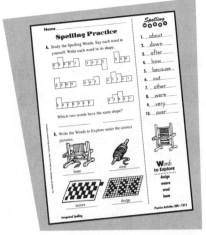

RESOURCES: PRACTICE ACTIVITIES MASTER 30B

Use as extra practice or as a homework activity.

VOCABULARY WORDSHOP pages 128–129

Words to Explore Write the Words to Explore on the board: *design, weave, wool, loom.* Discuss their meanings with children. Ask what the words have in common. (They are all weaving words.) Have children use the words in sentences about weaving a rug. Then have them complete the activity independently.

Spelling Log Have children add the Words to Explore to their Spelling Logs.

TRANSITIONAL SPELLERS Assign the Words to Explore. As a practice activity, have children draw pictures for the Words to Explore. Ask them to label each picture with the correct word.

What's in a Word? Ask children how weaving a rug is like weaving through a maze. Have children demonstrate how they weave their way through someplace by having them weave their way through a line of objects placed on the floor. UNDERSTANDING IDIOMS

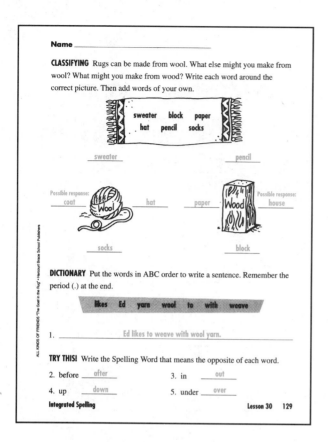

Name _____

CLASSIFYING Rugs can be made from wool. What else might you make from wool? What might you make from wood? Write each word around the correct picture. Then add words of your own.

| sweater | block | paper |
| hat | pencil | socks |

sweater   pencil

Possible response: coat   hat   paper   Possible response: house

socks   block

DICTIONARY Put the words in ABC order to write a sentence. Remember the period (.) at the end.

| likes | Ed | yarn | wool | to | with | weave |

1. _____ Ed likes to weave with wool yarn. _____

TRY THIS! Write the Spelling Word that means the opposite of each word.

2. before ___after___   3. in ___out___

4. up ___down___   5. under ___over___

Integrated Spelling   Lesson 30   129

Classifying Display some objects made of wood, plastic, yarn, or other materials. Have children identify each object. Then ask volunteers to put the objects into groups of things made with the same material. CLASSIFYING

 Working Together Have children work together to make collages of things that are alike in some way. Have them draw or cut from magazines pictures to put in their collages of items made of wood, clothing, food, or other things that are alike in some way.

Dictionary Write these words on the board: *yarn, I, sweaters, knit, with.* Help children write a sentence by putting the words in alphabetical order. Then have children complete the activity independently. USING ALPHABETICAL ORDER

Try This! Ask children the opposite of words like *off (on)* and *above (below)*. Then have them complete the activity independently. USING ANTONYMS

Vocabulary Activities

Posttest To check children's mastery of the Spelling Words, use the context sentences on page T189 to administer the posttest.

Optional Writing Idea: Description Ask what design children would make if they were weaving a rug: What colors would they use? What shapes or pictures would they weave? Explain that children are going to write descriptions of the rugs they would weave. Suggest that they begin by drawing a picture of the rug and then listing words that describe it. Then encourage children to display their finished pictures and descriptions.

LESSON WRAP-UP

Words to Explore and Context Sentences

1. **design** This rug has a blue and white **design.**
2. **weave** Some people **weave** straw into baskets.
3. **wool** This sweater is made of **wool.**
4. **loom** I wove this rug on a **loom.**

Reteach

LEARNING DIFFERENCES Make a tape recording of the Spelling Words. On the tape, say each word, spell it slowly, and say it again. As children listen to the tape, have them use a finger to form the letters of each Spelling Word on a desktop. Then ask them to listen again and to write each word on paper. AUDITORY/KINESTHETIC MODALITIES

INTEGRATED CURRICULUM ACTIVITY

Language Arts

Chain Story Prepare for the activity by writing the Spelling Words on cards.

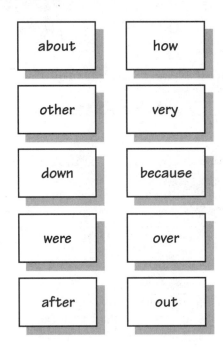

about	how
other	very
down	because
were	over
after	out

Tell children that they are going to make up a chain story. Explain that you will give them the first sentence of the story and each child in turn will add another sentence. The story can be realistic or silly, but each sentence in the story must contain one of the Spelling Words.

Mix up the cards and hold them in a fan shape so children cannot see the words. Begin the story with a sentence such as the following: *One day a goat went for a walk.* Have a volunteer pick a card, read the word, and use that word in the next sentence of the story. Continue in the same fashion, having children take turns picking cards and adding to the story.

Compound Words

Objective
To spell compound words

Lesson Planner
Assign words based on the developmental levels of individual children. See the Assignment Guide on page T250.

Informal Assessment
Children's writing may show that they have difficulty spelling compound words.

MODEL

football
I like to watch (foot ball) on TV.

Use this lesson to introduce the spelling of compound words. Encourage children to apply what they have learned to help them spell other words made from two smaller words. After children have completed the lesson, have them proofread their writing and correct any errors they may have made spelling compound words.

 SECOND-LANGUAGE SUPPORT Help children understand the meanings of the Spelling Words by using them in sentences. When you say each sentence, leave out the compound word and have children supply it. Then ask children to use the words in sentences of their own. WORD MEANINGS

Pretest/Posttest Context Sentences
You may want to test Semi-Phonetic Spellers on words 1–6 only.

1. **upon** — The emperor sat **upon** his throne.
*2. **grandma** — I like to visit my **grandma.**
3. **seesaw** — Nancy and Berto sat on the **seesaw.**
4. **sometimes** — I walk to school **sometimes.**
5. **herself** — She looked at **herself** in the mirror.
6. **somewhere** — He lives **somewhere** far away.
7. **classroom** — The children went into their **classroom** at school.
8. **himself** — He solved the puzzle by **himself.**
9. **baseball** — You need a bat and ball to play **baseball.**
10. **something** — She is holding **something** behind her back.

*Word appearing in "Thunder Cake." Some additional story words following the generalization are *tablecloth, barnyard, notepaper, cupboards, farmhouse, overripe, woodstove, teaspoons, anything,* and *doorway.*

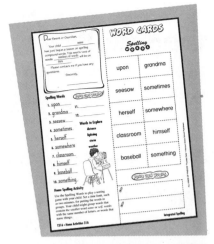

**RESOURCES: HOME
ACTIVITIES MASTER 31A**

NOTE: Fill in the teacher's note on the Home Activities Master before sending it home with children. See the Assignment Guide on page T250 for assigning lists of words.

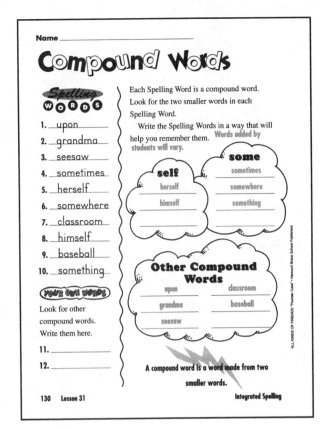

Compound Words

Name _____

Spelling WORDS

1. upon
2. grandma
3. seesaw
4. sometimes
5. herself
6. somewhere
7. classroom
8. himself
9. baseball
10. something

Each Spelling Word is a compound word. Look for the two smaller words in each Spelling Word.

Write the Spelling Words in a way that will help you remember them. *Words added by students will vary.*

self
herself
himself

some
sometimes
somewhere
something

YOUR OWN WORDS

Look for other compound words. Write them here.

11. _____
12. _____

Other Compound Words

upon   classroom
grandma   baseball
seesaw

A compound word is a word made from two smaller words.

130   Lesson 31   Integrated Spelling

INTRODUCTION page 130

Pretest Administer the pretest. Say each word, use it in the sentence provided on page T195, and then repeat the word. ACCESSING PRIOR KNOWLEDGE

 Self-Check Have children work cooperatively in pairs to check their own pretests by referring to their list of Spelling Words. For each misspelled word on the pretest, remind children to use the **Study Steps to Learn a Word** on pages 8–9 of the Pupil's Edition. STUDENT SELF-ASSESSMENT

Introducing the Lesson To use the open sort, copy Home Activities Master 31A in the Copying Masters section.

Open Sort: Distribute word cards to children and have them individually or cooperatively select criteria for sorting. Discuss how children sorted their words and why. You may want to send home the word cards so that children can complete the Home Activities Master.

Closed Sort: Read aloud with children the lesson title and the Spelling Words on Pupil's Edition page 130.

• Write the words *football, myself, yourself,* and *basketball* on the board. Have each compound word and the two words in it identified.

• Ask children how they could sort these words into two groups. Have them group the compound words that have the same smaller word in them. SORTING WORDS

In Summary Ask children what a word that is made from two smaller words is called. Then ask children how knowing about compound words can help them become better spellers.

Your Own Words Ask children to list in their Spelling Logs other compound words. RECOGNIZING PATTERNS

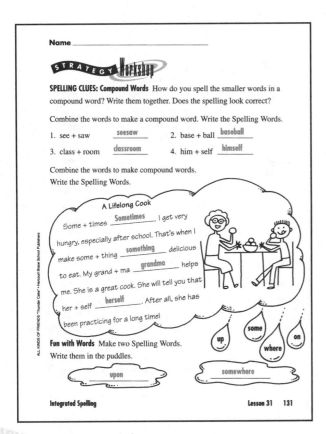

Name _____

STRATEGY Workshop

SPELLING CLUES: Compound Words How do you spell the smaller words in a compound word? Write them together. Does the spelling look correct?

Combine the words to make a compound word. Write the Spelling Words.

1. see + saw   _seesaw_   2. base + ball   _baseball_

3. class + room   _classroom_   4. him + self   _himself_

Combine the words to make compound words. Write the Spelling Words.

A Lifelong Cook

Some + times _Sometimes_ I get very hungry, especially after school. That's when I make some + thing _something_ delicious to eat. My grand + ma _grandma_ helps me. She is a great cook. She will tell you that her + self _herself_. After all, she has been practicing for a long time!

Fun with Words Make two Spelling Words. Write them in the puddles.

puddle: _upon_

raindrops: up, some, where, on

puddle: _somewhere_

Integrated Spelling   Lesson 31   131

Many new words have been invented in the English language by combining two smaller words into a compound word. The word *basketball* was invented around 1891 to name a brand new game that involved a ball and a basket.

STRATEGY WORKSHOP page 131

SPELLING CLUES: Compound Words
Write the words *mail* and *box* on the board. Tell children that you can put these words together to make a compound word. Write *mailbox.* Explain that thinking about how to spell the two words a compound word is made from will help children spell the compound word.

SEMI-PHONETIC SPELLERS Write on separate word cards the two words for each compound Spelling Word. Have children put the cards together to make the Spelling Words. Ask them to write the words they make.

Fun with Words
Read the words in the raindrops. Explain that two of these words can be put together to make one of the Spelling Words and the other two can be put together to make another Spelling Word. Have children figure out the compound words and write them in the puddles.

SECOND-LANGUAGE SUPPORT Tell children that *up* is the first part of one of the Spelling Words. Have them find and write the Spelling Word. Follow a similar procedure with *some*.

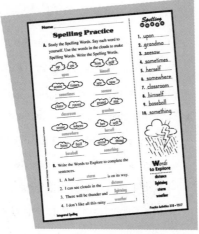

RESOURCES: PRACTICE ACTIVITIES MASTER 31B

Use as extra practice or as a homework activity.

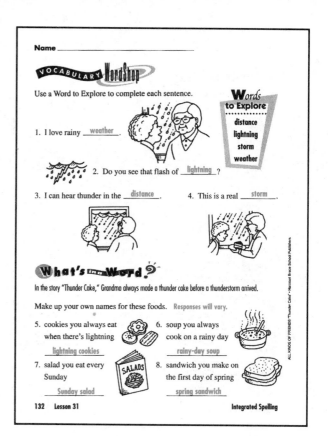

· ·

VOCABULARY WORDSHOP pages 132–133

Words to Explore Write the Words to Explore on the board: *distance, lightning, storm, weather.* Discuss their meanings with children. Then have children discuss storms they have been in. Ask them to tell about their favorite kind of weather.

Spelling Log Have children add the Words to Explore to their Spelling Logs.

TRANSITIONAL SPELLERS Assign the Words to Explore. As a practice activity, ask children to write a paragraph about a lightning storm. Tell them to use all the Words to Explore in their writing.

What's in a Word? Have children identify the kind of food shown in each picture. Explain that children should read the description of each food and then make up a name for it based on that description. Encourage children to be creative. Accept all reasonable names, such as "rain soup" or "first-day-of-spring sandwich." USING DESCRIBING WORDS

Describing Words Ask children to look happy. Then ask them to look sad. Discuss how children look different when they are happy and when they are sad. Encourage children to show different feelings and have others guess what the feelings are. USING DESCRIBING WORDS

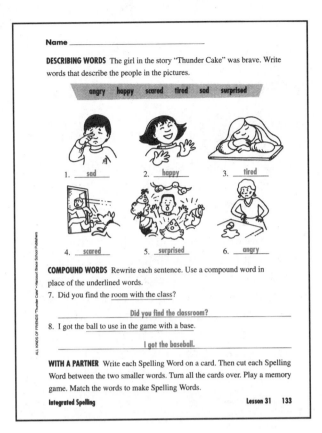

Name _____

DESCRIBING WORDS The girl in the story "Thunder Cake" was brave. Write words that describe the people in the pictures.

| angry | happy | scared | tired | sad | surprised |

1. _sad_   2. _happy_   3. _tired_

4. _scared_   5. _surprised_   6. _angry_

COMPOUND WORDS Rewrite each sentence. Use a compound word in place of the underlined words.

7. Did you find the room with the class?

_____ Did you find the classroom? _____

8. I got the ball to use in the game with a base.

_____ I got the baseball. _____

WITH A PARTNER Write each Spelling Word on a card. Then cut each Spelling Word between the two smaller words. Turn all the cards over. Play a memory game. Match the words to make Spelling Words.

Integrated Spelling   Lesson 31   133

- -

Compound Words Write on the board the word *thunderstorm* and the definition "a storm in which there is thunder." Have children point out in the definition the two smaller words from which the compound word was made. Then have them complete the activity. USING COMPOUND WORDS

Working Together Suggest that children work together to think of compound words that name things around school. Examples might include *wastebasket, playground, flagpole, wheelchair, lunchroom,* and *paintbrush.* Have children write sentences like those in the Compound Words activity. Ask them to exchange and rewrite each other's sentences.

With a Partner Provide ten cards for each pair of children. Help them cut between the words.

Posttest To check children's mastery of their Spelling Words, use the context sentences on page T195 to administer the posttest.

Optional Writing Idea: Personal Story Ask children to write about a favorite food that they eat on a special occasion. Encourage them to make up a special name for their food. Explain that they should tell what makes the food special and why they like it. Suggest that they begin by making a chart to organize their ideas. Children may enjoy illustrating their finished stories and sharing their work in small groups.

Name	Snowy-Day Hot Chocolate
When I Like It	when it snows
Why I Like It	warms me up

Vocabulary Activities   **Lesson 31   T199**

Words to Explore and Context Sentences

1. **distance**   The airplane I see looks very small in the **distance.**
2. **lightning**   The flash of **lightning** lit up the dark sky.
3. **storm**   We ran inside to get out of the **storm.**
4. **weather**   I like winter **weather** the best.

Reteach

 LEARNING DIFFERENCES Say a Spelling Word aloud. Then dictate the spelling as children write the word. Next, spell the word aloud with children as they write it again. Have children trace the word for additional reinforcement. Finally, have children spell the word aloud and write it from memory. AUDITORY/KINESTHETIC MODALITIES

INTEGRATED CURRICULUM ACTIVITIES

Language Arts

Wordplay On self-stick notes, write the smaller words that make up some familiar compound words. Distribute the notes and have children stick them on their clothing. Have children find other children whose words can be put together with their own to form compound words. When all the pairs have been matched, have children read their compound words aloud. You may want to use words such as the following: *everything, upset, jigsaw, myself, bedroom, football, grandfather, beehive, sunshine, raincoat, goldfish, popcorn.*

Science

Weather Display or have children draw pictures of different weather. Pictures might be of lightning, snow, a blizzard, rain, a cloudy day, a sunny day, a tornado, or a hurricane. As you discuss the pictures, introduce the weather terms. Then have children use the Spelling Words *sometimes, somewhere,* and *something* in a story about one of the pictures.

Words Like *dropped* and *running*

Objective

To spell words in which the final consonant is doubled before the ending *-ed* or *-ing* is added

Lesson Planner

Assign words based on the developmental levels of individual children. See the Assignment Guide on page T250.

Informal Assessment

Children's writing may show that they have difficulty spelling words in which they must double the final consonant before adding the ending *-ed* or *-ing*.

MODEL

humming
We are ⟨huming⟩ a tune.

Use this lesson to introduce the spelling of words in which the final consonant was doubled before the ending *-ed* or *-ing* was added. Encourage children to apply what they have learned to help them spell similar words. After children have completed the lesson, have them proofread their writing and correct any errors they may have made spelling words in which a consonant was doubled before the *-ed* or *-ing* ending was added.

SECOND-LANGUAGE SUPPORT It is sometimes difficult for speakers of other languages to form and pronounce the past tense of regular verbs by adding *-ed*. Help children become more familiar with this form by having them follow a simple command. Say, for example, "Stop writing now." Then ask, "What did you do?" Model the response: "I stopped writing." Have children repeat the correct response. Follow a similar procedure with other commands.
DEVELOPING VOCABULARY

Pretest/Posttest Context Sentences

You may want to test Semi-Phonetic Spellers on words 1–6 only.

1. **dropped** The book **dropped** to the floor.
2. **putting** We are **putting** the toys away.
3. **stopped** The car **stopped** at the red light.
4. **getting** They are **getting** their coats.
5. **planned** The children **planned** the puppet show.
*6. **running** The dog was **running** fast.

7. **slipped** He **slipped** and fell on the ice.
8. **sitting** I am **sitting** in my chair.
9. **grabbed** The boy **grabbed** his jacket and ran out.
10. **popping** I am **popping** popcorn.

*Word appearing in "Ant Cities." Some additional story words following the generalization are *digging, rotting, leaf-cutting,* and *round-topped.*

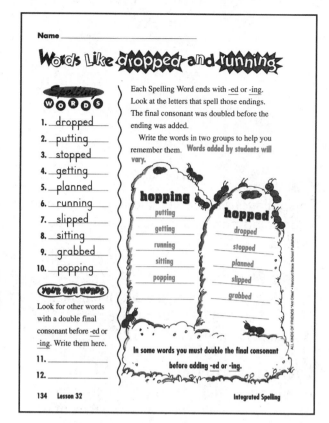

RESOURCES: HOME ACTIVITIES MASTER 32A

NOTE: Fill in the teacher's note on the Home Activities Master before sending it home with children. See the Assignment Guide on page T250 for assigning lists of words.

INTRODUCTION page 134

Pretest Administer the pretest. Say each word, use it in the sentence provided on page T201, and then repeat the word. ACCESSING PRIOR KNOWLEDGE

Self-Check Have children check their own pretests by referring to their list of Spelling Words. For each misspelled word on the pretest, remind children to use the **Study Steps to Learn a Word** on pages 8–9 of the Pupil's Edition. STUDENT SELF-ASSESSMENT

Introducing the Lesson To use the open sort, copy Home Activities Master 32A in the Copying Masters section.

Open Sort: Distribute word cards to children and have them individually or cooperatively select criteria for sorting. Have children read their groups of words. Ask why they grouped the words as they did. You may want to send home the word cards so that children can complete the Home Activities Master.

Closed Sort: Read aloud with children the lesson title and the Spelling Words on Pupil's Edition page 134.

- Write the endings *-ed* and *-ing* as headings on the board. Have children tell in which column you should write each of these words: *hopping, hummed, napped,* and *hitting.*
- Ask how the words in one group are different from the words in the other. (different endings) Then ask how all the words in both groups are alike. (all doubled the final consonant) SORTING WORDS

In Summary Have children summarize the lesson. Remind them that the final consonant in some words is doubled before the ending *-ed* or *-ing* is added.

Your Own Words Encourage children to look through magazines, newspapers, or brochures to find and write in their Spelling Logs other words that have a doubled final consonant before the *-ed* or *-ing* ending. RECOGNIZING PATTERNS

STRATEGY Workshop

SPELLING CLUES: Spelling Rules Think about the rule for doubling the final consonant. Try spelling the word. Does it look right?

Add the ending to each word. Remember to double the final consonant. Write the Spelling Word.

1. drop **(ed)** _dropped_   2. grab **(ed)** _grabbed_

3. put **(ing)** _putting_   4. stop **(ed)** _stopped_

Add the ending to each underlined word to tell about the ant fair. Write the Spelling Word.

Under the Magnifying Glass

There's a fair going on at Anthill. Balloons are pop(ing) _popping_ . One ant is get(ing) _getting_ on the merry-go-round. Another is sit(ing) _sitting_ on the Ferris wheel. The ants have plan(ed) _planned_ a great day!

Fun with Words Unscramble the letters to write a Spelling Word that tells about each picture.

nnruing   edippsl

5. _running_   6. _slipped_

Integrated Spelling   Lesson 32   135

- -

STRATEGY WORKSHOP page 135

Spelling Clues: Spelling Rules Write *hum* on the board. Ask volunteers to go to the board and write *hummed* and *humming*. Then ask children to check the spellings: Were the final consonants doubled? Do the words look right? If necessary, have children correct the spellings. APPLYING SPELLING STRATEGIES

SEMI-PHONETIC SPELLERS For each base word in the activities on Pupil's Edition page 135, write out the equation for adding the ending as follows:

drop + p + ed = _____

Write these equations in a list on the board or in individual lists for children to use as a reference as they complete the page.

Fun with Words Ask what the ants in the pictures are doing. Then, as a hint, you might remind children that the Spelling Words all end in *-ed* or *-ing*.

SECOND-LANGUAGE SUPPORT Reinforce meanings of the Spelling Words. Have children draw pictures of or act out the words. Encourage them to write a sentence to go with the picture for each Spelling Word. WORD MEANINGS

Practice Activities

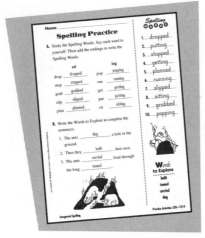

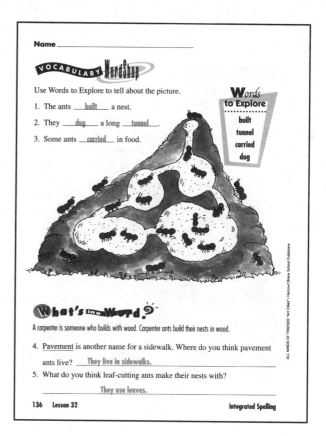

RESOURCES: PRACTICE ACTIVITIES MASTER 32B

Use as extra practice or as a homework activity.

VOCABULARY WORDSHOP pages 136–137

Words to Explore Write the Words to Explore on the board: *built, tunnel, carried, dug*. Discuss their meanings with children. Then have children name insects or other animals to which these words could refer. (ants, chipmunks, moles) Ask why these animals might have dug holes and built tunnels in the ground. Then have children complete the activity.

Spelling Log Have children add the Words to Explore to their Spelling Logs.

TRANSITIONAL SPELLERS Assign the Words to Explore. As a practice activity, have children choose an animal that digs holes and builds tunnels. Ask them to draw the animal in its tunnel. Then have children use the Words to Explore in a paragraph that tells about their picture.

What's in a Word? Invite children to share what they know about carpenters and the kind of work they do. Then ask how children think carpenter ants got their name and whether they think it is a good name for ants who build their nests in wood. When children have completed the activity, encourage them to discuss what they wrote. BUILDING VOCABULARY

Action Words Have children read the action words and pantomime the actions. Then ask children to complete the activity independently. USING ACTION WORDS

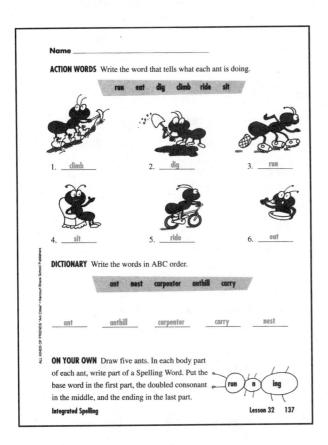

Name _____

ACTION WORDS Write the word that tells what each ant is doing.

| run | eat | dig | climb | ride | sit |

1. climb   2. dig   3. run

4. sit   5. ride   6. eat

DICTIONARY Write the words in ABC order.

| ant | nest | carpenter | anthill | carry |

ant   anthill   carpenter   carry   nest

ON YOUR OWN Draw five ants. In each body part of each ant, write part of a Spelling Word. Put the base word in the first part, the doubled consonant in the middle, and the ending in the last part.

Integrated Spelling

Lesson 32   137

ALL KINDS OF FRIENDS "Ant Cities" • Harcourt Brace School Publishers

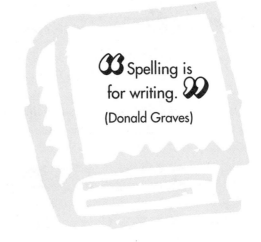

"Spelling is for writing."
(Donald Graves)

Dictionary Write *dog* and *doghouse* on the board. Have children explain why *dog* comes before *doghouse* in alphabetical order. Then write *tunnel* and *tune*. Ask what letter children must look at to put these words in alphabetical order. (fourth) Then have children complete the activity independently. USING ALPHABETICAL ORDER

Working Together Have children work in groups of five. Tell each child to choose a different word from the Dictionary activity and to write it on a card. Then have children arrange themselves in alphabetical order. They might enjoy picking other words and repeating this activity.

On Your Own You might want to draw and then duplicate the ants for children to use. Discuss the example with children to make sure they understand what to write in each section of the ants. APPLYING SPELLING STRATEGIES

Posttest To check children's mastery of the Spelling Words, use the context sentences on page T201 to administer the posttest.

Optional Writing Idea: Ant's Diary Entry
Have children look again at the illustration on Pupil's Edition page 136. Ask them to imagine what a day in the life of an ant might be like. Tell them that they are going to write a diary entry that an ant might write on a typical day. Suggest that children prewrite by listing some things they might do in a day if they were ants. Then have them draft, revise, proofread, and publish their diary entries.

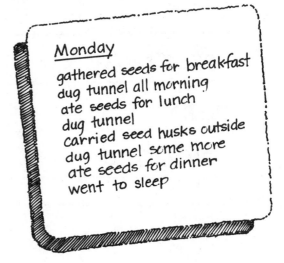

Monday
gathered seeds for breakfast
dug tunnel all morning
ate seeds for lunch
dug tunnel
carried seed husks outside
dug tunnel some more
ate seeds for dinner
went to sleep

Vocabulary Activities

LESSON WRAP-UP

Words to Explore and Context Sentences

1. **built** — The carpenters **built** a new house.
2. **tunnel** — Who made this **tunnel** in the ground?
3. **carried** — We **carried** our books to school.
4. **dug** — My dog **dug** a big hole in the yard.

Reteach

LEARNING DIFFERENCES Have children write or copy the words *drop, stop, plan, slip, grab,* and *pop* on lined paper, skipping a line after each word. Have them double the final consonant and add *-ed* to each word. Then have them copy the complete word on the line below. Follow the same procedure for the Spelling Words with *-ing* added. VISUAL/KINESTHETIC MODALITIES

drop
dropped
stop
stopped
plan
planned

INTEGRATED CURRICULUM ACTIVITIES

Language Arts

Riddle Time Have children write riddles for the Spelling Words. Ask them to give at least three clues in each riddle. Then invite children to tell their riddles for classmates to guess. Share a sample riddle with children:

> This word has seven letters.
> It has a doubled *t*.
> It means the opposite of *standing*.
> What word is it? *(sitting)*

Science

Popcorn Pop some popcorn with children. Discuss why the corn pops and the sound it makes while popping. Then have children use the popcorn to spell their Spelling Words. Have each child spell two words. They can glue the popcorn in letter shapes on paper, or they can spell the words on napkins on their desks and then eat the words!

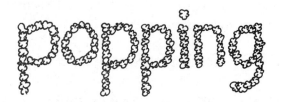

Words Like *loved* and *moving*

Objective

To spell words in which the final *e* is dropped before the ending *-ed* or *-ing* is added

Lesson Planner

Assign words based on the developmental levels of individual children. See the Assignment Guide on page T250.

Informal Assessment

Children's writing may show that they have difficulty spelling words in which the final *e* is dropped before the ending *-ed* or *-ing* is added.

MODEL

having

We are (haveing) lunch.

Use this lesson to introduce the spelling of words in which the final *e* was dropped before the ending *-ed* or *-ing* was added. Encourage children to apply what they have learned to help them spell other words with these endings. After children have completed the lesson, have them proofread their writing and correct any errors they may have made spelling words in which the final *e* was dropped before *-ed* or *-ing* was added.

 SECOND-LANGUAGE SUPPORT It is sometimes difficult for speakers of other languages to form and pronounce the past tense of regular verbs by adding *-ed*. Help children become more familiar with this form by asking such questions as *Did you smile?* Model the response: *Yes, I smiled.* Have children repeat the correct response. Follow a similar procedure with other questions. DEVELOPING VOCABULARY

Pretest/Posttest Context Sentences

You may want to test Semi-Phonetic Spellers on words 1–6 only.

1. **saved**   The mother cat **saved** the kitten.
2. **giving**   Are you **giving** your mom a gift?
*3. **liked**   Everyone **liked** this soup best.
4. **taking**   We are **taking** these books home.
5. **used**   Max **used** a red crayon to draw a heart.
6. **riding**   She was **riding** her new bike.
7. **placed**   The teacher **placed** the pencil on her desk.
*8. **moving**   The fish were **moving** fast in the water.
*9. **loved**   I **loved** the movie we just saw.
10. **living**   We are **living** on a farm.

*Words appearing in "Ibis: A True Whale Story." Some additional story words following the generalization are *lived, tired, stared, named, dived, scared, dazzling, circling, waving, coming,* and *diving.*

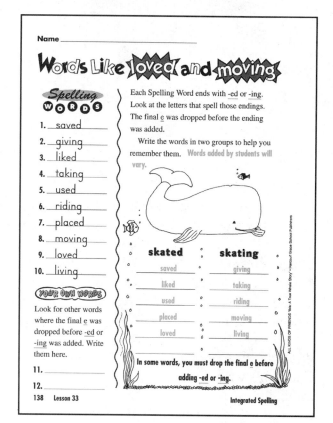

RESOURCES: HOME ACTIVITIES MASTER 33A

NOTE: Fill in the teacher's note on the Home Activities Master before sending it home with children. See the Assignment Guide on page T250 for assigning lists of words.

INTRODUCTION page 138

Pretest Administer the pretest. Say each word, use it in the sentence provided on page T207, and then repeat the word. ACCESSING PRIOR KNOWLEDGE

Self-Check Have children check their own pretests by referring to their list of Spelling Words. For each misspelled word on the pretest, remind children to use the **Study Steps to Learn a Word** on pages 8–9 of the Pupil's Edition. STUDENT SELF-ASSESSMENT

Introducing the Lesson To use the open sort, copy Home Activities Master 33A in the Copying Masters section.

Open Sort: Distribute word cards to children and have them individually or cooperatively select criteria for sorting. Ask how they sorted the words and why. You may want to send home the word cards so that children can complete the Home Activities Master.

Closed Sort: Read aloud with children the lesson title and the Spelling Words on Pupil's Edition page 138.

- Write the endings *-ed* and *-ing* as headings on the board. Have children tell in which column you should write each of these words: *skated, smiling, waving,* and *raced.*
- Have children note how the words in each group end alike. Then point out that in all the words in both groups, the final *e* was dropped before *-ed* or *-ing* was added. SORTING WORDS

In Summary Ask children what letter is sometimes dropped before the ending *-ed* or *-ing* is added. (final *e*)

Your Own Words For homework or practice, have children list in their Spelling Logs other words in which the final *e* was dropped before *-ed* or *-ing* was added. RECOGNIZING PATTERNS

Name _____

STRATEGY Workshop

SPELLING CLUES: Spelling Rules Think about the rule for dropping final e. Try spelling the word. Does it look right?

Add the ending to each word. Remember to drop the final e. Write the Spelling Word.

1. give (ing) _____giving_____   2. place (ed) _____placed_____

3. like (ed) _____liked_____   4. live (ing) _____living_____

Finish the story. Add the ending to each word. Then write the Spelling Word.

A Whale of a Dream

I had a dream last night! A whale was move (ing) _____moving_____ through the water. I was ride (ing) _____riding_____ on its back! It was take (ing) _____taking_____ me for quite a ride! I love (ed) _____loved_____ flying through the water. I hated waking up from my dream!

Fun with Words Write the Spelling Words that fit in each shape to complete the sentences.

5. The whale s a v e d its baby.

6. It u s e d its nose to push the baby up for air.

Integrated Spelling   Lesson 33   139

> **❝** Writers come to recognize, or are taught to recognize, certain spelling patterns in English. They learn, for example, that verbs with a final e _(like)_ drop the e when adding _-ing (liking)_ and look strange if the e is not dropped _(likeing)._ **❞**
>
> (Patricia J. McAlexander, Ann B. Dobie, Noel Gregg)

STRATEGY WORKSHOP page 139

Spelling Clues: Spelling Rules As a warm-up activity, write the word _dance_ on the board. Have children think about the rule for dropping the final _e._ Then ask volunteers to write _danced_ and _dancing_ on the board. Ask whether the spellings look right. If necessary, have other children correct the spellings. APPLYING SPELLING STRATEGIES

SECOND-LANGUAGE SUPPORT Review the meanings of the Spelling Words. Have children use in sentences or demonstrate _moving, riding, taking,_ and _loved._ WORD MEANINGS

Fun with Words Have children look at the word shapes. Ask if they can tell by looking at the word shapes which ending each Spelling Word has.

SEMI-PHONETIC SPELLERS Prepare letter cards and have children match the letter shapes with the shapes of the letters in the Spelling Words in the Fun with Words activity. You may want to extend this activity for all the Spelling Words. APPLYING SPELLING STRATEGIES

Practice Activities   **Lesson 33   T209**

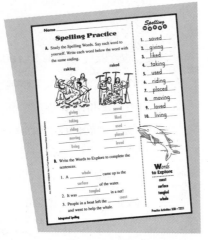

RESOURCES: PRACTICE ACTIVITIES MASTER 33B

Use as extra practice or as a homework activity.

VOCABULARY WORDSHOP pages 140–141

Words to Explore Write the Words to Explore on the board: *coast, surface, tangled, whale.* Discuss their meanings with children. Then have children tell what they see in the picture. Explain that children will complete the activity by labeling things they see in the picture.

Spelling Log Have children add the Words to Explore to their Spelling Logs.

TRANSITIONAL SPELLERS Assign the Words to Explore. As a practice activity, have each child write the Words to Explore on word cards. Then on sentence strips, have him or her write sentences for the words. Tell children to leave a space for each Word to Explore. Have children work in pairs to play a memory game in which they match the words to the sentences. Each pair will use eight word cards (four words each) and eight sentence strips.

What's in a Word? Ask if children have heard the expression *a whale of a time.* Then ask why people might mention a whale when they talk about something big or special. Encourage children to think of big or special events in their lives, such as a party or a trip, that they can use in their own *whale of a* phrases. UNDERSTANDING IDIOMS

Synonyms Remind children that synonyms are words that have almost the same meaning. Point out the words in the box on Pupil's Edition page 141. Explain that these are the words children will write in the puzzle. Then have a volunteer read aloud the clue for *2 Across* and identify the underlined word. Tell children to begin the puzzle by finding the synonym for the underlined word. Help them to write it next to the number *2* in the puzzle. Make sure they understand that the answers for clues under the heading *Across* are written from left to right, while those for clues under *Down* are written from top to bottom. USING SYNONYMS

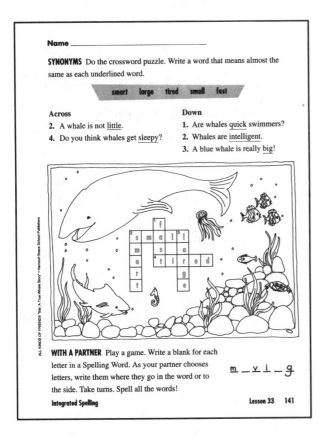

Name _____

SYNONYMS Do the crossword puzzle. Write a word that means almost the same as each underlined word.

| smart | large | tired | small | fast |

Across
2. A whale is not <u>little</u>.
4. Do you think whales get <u>sleepy</u>?

Down
1. Are whales <u>quick</u> swimmers?
2. Whales are <u>intelligent</u>.
3. A blue whale is really <u>big</u>!

WITH A PARTNER Play a game. Write a blank for each letter in a Spelling Word. As your partner chooses letters, write them where they go in the word or to the side. Take turns. Spell all the words!

m _ v i _ g

Integrated Spelling

Lesson 33   141

Working Together Have children work in pairs to create their own crossword puzzles. Point out that the clues might be synonyms, word meanings, or pictures. Encourage children to exchange and solve each other's puzzles.

With a Partner Use the sample on Pupil's Edition page 141 to model playing the game with children. Ask why *d* or *g* might be a good letter to guess. (Every Spelling Word ends with one of the letters.) Ask why *b, x,* or *w* would not be a good letter to guess. (None of the Spelling Words contains those letters.)
APPLYING SPELLING STRATEGIES

Posttest To check children's mastery of the Spelling Words, use the context sentences on page T207 to administer the posttest.

Optional Writing Idea: Personal Story Refer children to the *whale of a* phrases they wrote for the What's in a Word? activity on Pupil's Edition page 140. Tell them to choose one of the phrases to write about. Suggest that children begin by making a chart to help them remember important details to include.

A Whale of a Hit			
Where	When	What	How I felt
park	last fall	first baseball hit home run	happy excited proud

Have children copy their finished stories onto whale shapes. Then display the stories for children to read.

LESSON WRAP-UP

Words to Explore and Context Sentences

1. **coast** — The **coast** is where the sea meets the land.
2. **surface** — Fish swim below the **surface** of the water.
3. **tangled** — Sometimes whales get **tangled** in fishing nets.
4. **whale** — A **whale** is a huge animal that lives in the sea.

Reteach

 LEARNING DIFFERENCES Have children write or copy the words *save, like, use, place,* and *love* on lined paper, skipping a line after each word. Have them cross out final *e* and add *-ed* to each word. Then have them copy the completed word on the line below. Follow the same procedure for Spelling Words with *-ing.* VISUAL/ KINESTHETIC MODALITIES

> Sav̶e̶ed
> Saved
> Lik̶e̶ed
> Liked
> Us̶e̶ed
> Used

INTEGRATED CURRICULUM ACTIVITIES

Language Arts

Charades Write the Spelling Words *giving, taking, riding,* and *moving* on slips of paper. Add similar words that can be pantomimed or acted out, such as *smiling, dancing, waving, writing, diving,* and *skating.* Have children take turns picking slips of paper and silently acting out the words for classmates to guess.

Math

Break the Code Give children the following code:

o = 9 – 8	g = 16 – 9	u = 7 + 6
s = 11 – 9	i = 17 – 9	r = 9 + 5
a = 10 – 7	n = 14 – 5	p = 8 + 7
v = 13 – 9	l = 5 + 5	c = 7 + 9
e = 12 – 7	k = 7 + 4	m = 9 + 8
d = 12 – 6	t = 6 + 6	

Tell children to solve the math problems to find out the value of each letter. Then have children use the values to break a secret code. Have them write in the letters to spell the Spelling Words. Use the following secret codes or ones you make up for other Spelling Words.

(l)	(o)	(v)	(e)	(d)
10	1	4	5	6

(m)	(o)	(v)	(i)	(n)	(g)
17	1	4	8	9	7

(p)	(l)	(a)	(c)	(e)	(d)
15	10	3	16	5	6

(l)	(i)	(k)	(e)	(d)
10	8	11	5	6

Plurals

Objective
To spell plurals formed by adding *-s* or *-es*

Lesson Planner
Assign words based on the developmental levels of individual children. See the Assignment Guide on page T250.

Informal Assessment
Children's writing may show that they have difficulty spelling plurals that are formed by adding *-s* or *-es*.

MODEL

peaches
Mom got some (peachs) at the store.

Use this lesson to introduce the spelling of plurals formed by adding *-s* or *-es*. Encourage children to apply what they have learned to help them spell other plurals. After children have completed the lesson, have them proofread their writing and correct any errors they may have made spelling plurals with *-s* or *-es*.

 SECOND-LANGUAGE SUPPORT Children may have difficulty forming plurals by adding *-s* or *-es* to a noun, especially when plurals in their first languages are formed in a different way. Pronouncing a consonant plus *-s* at the end of a word may also be difficult. Give children practice with plurals. Say the word *boy,* for example, and have one boy stand. Then say the word *boys* and have several boys stand. Encourage children to repeat each word. Follow similar procedures to show the meanings of other words, such as *girl* and *girls, toy* and *toys, book* and *books, box* and *boxes,* and *dish* and *dishes.* UNDERSTANDING PLURALS

Pretest/Posttest Context Sentences
You may want to test Semi-Phonetic Spellers on words 1–6 only.

*1.	**girls**	Two **girls** won the race.
2.	**boxes**	What is in those big **boxes**?
3.	**toys**	Which **toys** do you like to play with best?
4.	**dishes**	We washed the **dishes** after dinner.
5.	**times**	How many **times** have you been to the zoo?
6.	**inches**	There are twelve **inches** in one foot.
*7.	**boys**	Three **boys** rode their bikes to the park.
8.	**wishes**	Do you make many **wishes** on your birthday?
*9.	**days**	There are seven **days** in a week.
10.	**things**	Greg showed us all the **things** he found at the beach.

*Words appearing in "Sam the Sea Cow." Some additional story words following the generalization are *whales, dolphins, rivers, plants, manatees, eyes, trees, miles, bananas,* and *places.*

RESOURCES: HOME
ACTIVITIES MASTER **34A**

NOTE: Fill in the teacher's note on the
Home Activities Master before sending it
home with children. See the Assignment
Guide on page T250 for assigning lists
of words.

Name _____

Plurals

W O R D S

1. girls
2. boxes
3. toys
4. dishes
5. times
6. inches
7. boys
8. wishes
9. days
10. things

YOUR OWN WORDS

Look for other words
that are plurals. Write
them here.

11. _____
12. _____

142   Lesson 34

Each Spelling Word is a plural, or means
"more than one." Look at the letter or letters,
s or es, that were added to make the plurals.

Write the words in two groups to help you
remember them. Words added by students will
vary.

s

girls
toys
times
boys
days
things

es

boxes
dishes
inches
wishes

You can make plurals by adding -s or -es.

Integrated Spelling

INTRODUCTION page 142

Pretest Administer the pretest. Say each
word, use it in the sentence provided on page
T213, and then repeat the word. ACCESSING
PRIOR KNOWLEDGE

✓ Self-Check Have children check their
own pretests by referring to their list of
Spelling Words. For each misspelled word on
the pretest, remind children to use the **Study
Steps to Learn a Word** on pages 8–9 of the
Pupil's Edition. STUDENT SELF-ASSESSMENT

Introducing the Lesson To use the open sort,
copy Home Activities Master 34A in the
Copying Masters section.

Open Sort: Distribute word cards to children and
have them individually or cooperatively select
criteria for sorting. Ask them to name their
categories. Ask other children to name more
words that could belong in each category. You
may want to send home the word cards so that
children can complete the Home Activities
Master.

Closed Sort: Read aloud with children the lesson
title and the Spelling Words on Pupil's Edition
page 142.

• Write the letters s and es on the board. Then
write these words: *cars, beaches, foxes,
dogs, roses,* and *bushes.*
• Have children sort the words into groups
under s or es. Point out that *rose* ends with
the letter e and that only s was added to
make the plural. SORTING WORDS

In Summary Ask what letter or letters children
can add to words to spell plurals. (*s* or *es*) Then
have children spell the plurals of some known
words, like *cat* or *dog.*

Your Own Words Encourage
children to think of and write in their
Spelling Logs other plurals that were
formed by adding -*s* or -*es* to a word.
RECOGNIZING PATTERNS

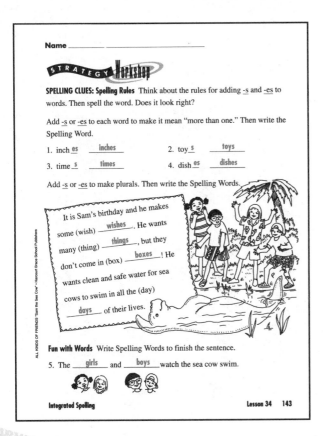

Name _____

STRATEGY Workshop

SPELLING CLUES: Spelling Rules Think about the rules for adding -s and -es to words. Then spell the word. Does it look right?

Add -s or -es to each word to make it mean "more than one." Then write the Spelling Word.

1. inch _es_ _____inches_____   2. toy _s_ _____toys_____

3. time _s_ _____times_____   4. dish _es_ _____dishes_____

Add -s or -es to make plurals. Then write the Spelling Words.

It is Sam's birthday and he makes some (wish) _____wishes_____. He wants many (thing) _____things_____, but they don't come in (box) _____boxes_____! He wants clean and safe water for sea cows to swim in all the (day) _____days_____ of their lives.

Fun with Words Write Spelling Words to finish the sentence.

5. The _____girls_____ and _____boys_____ watch the sea cow swim.

Integrated Spelling   Lesson 34   143

---

66 There is not much point in learning to spell if you have little intention of writing. 99
(Frank Smith)

STRATEGY WORKSHOP page 143

Spelling Clues: Spelling Rules
Have children look at the plurals formed by adding -es. Ask them to name the last letter of each noun to which -es was added. Explain that -es is added to form the plurals of words that end with *x, sh,* or *ch.* APPLYING SPELLING STRATEGIES

SEMI-PHONETIC SPELLERS Make word cards for the Spelling Words and for their singular forms. Have children match the word pairs and tell what ending was added to make each base word plural.

Fun with Words
Call attention to the illustrations below the blanks. Explain that the pictures will help children figure out which word to write in each blank.

SECOND-LANGUAGE SUPPORT Use the illustrations in Fun with Words to reinforce the meanings of *girls* and *boys.* Say each word aloud and have children point to the correct picture. Then have children repeat the correct word as they point to themselves. USING PICTURE CLUES

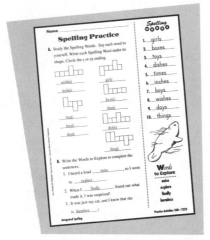

RESOURCES: PRACTICE ACTIVITIES MASTER 34B

Use as extra practice or as a homework activity.

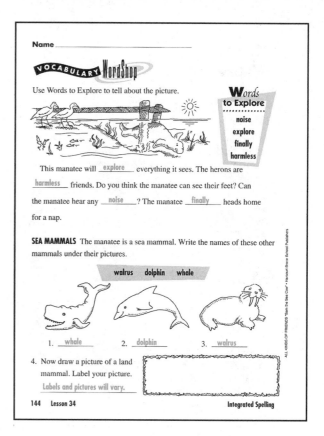

VOCABULARY WORDSHOP pages 144–145

Words to Explore Write the Words to Explore on the board: *noise, explore, finally, harmless.* Discuss their meanings with children. Then point out that the manatee in the picture is exploring. Ask children what they like to explore.

 Spelling Log Have children add the Words to Explore to their Spelling Logs.

 TRANSITIONAL SPELLERS Assign the Words to Explore. As a practice activity, ask children to write riddles for each of the Words to Explore. Have them share and answer each other's riddles.

Sea Mammals Invite children to share what they know about mammals. Ask whether fish, crabs, and clams that live in the sea are mammals. (no) Then ask children to name some sea animals that are mammals. (walrus, dolphin, whale)

What's in a Word? Ask children how they think manatees might have come to be called "sea cows." Point out that the name makes a comparison between an animal that lives in the sea and one that lives on land. Tell children that they will read about some "sea" names that other animals can have. When children have completed the activity, discuss the "sea" names with them. DEVELOPING VOCABULARY

 Working Together Provide appropriate reference books for children to find pictures of other sea animals. Encourage children to compare the sea animals to land animals with which they are familiar. Have children make up names for the sea animals. They might, for example, call a shark a "sea wolf" or "sea tiger." A manta ray might be a "sea bat" and a shrimp might be a "sea centipede."

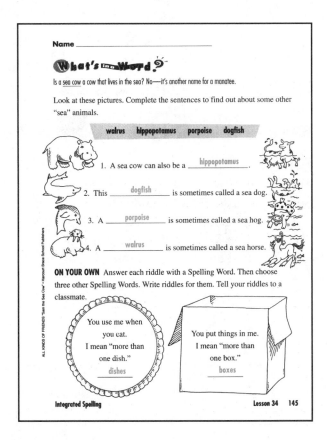

Name _____

What's the Word?

Is a sea cow a cow that lives in the sea? No—it's another name for a manatee.

Look at these pictures. Complete the sentences to find out about some other "sea" animals.

| walrus | hippopotamus | porpoise | dogfish |

1. A sea cow can also be a ___*hippopotamus*___ .

2. This ___*dogfish*___ is sometimes called a sea dog.

3. A ___*porpoise*___ is sometimes called a sea hog.

4. A ___*walrus*___ is sometimes called a sea horse.

ON YOUR OWN Answer each riddle with a Spelling Word. Then choose three other Spelling Words. Write riddles for them. Tell your riddles to a classmate.

You use me when you eat.
I mean "more than one dish."
___*dishes*___

You put things in me.
I mean "more than one box."
___*boxes*___

Integrated Spelling Lesson 34 145

On Your Own Suggest that children model their own riddles on those in the activity. Provide time for children to share their riddles. WORD MEANINGS

Posttest To check children's mastery of the Spelling Words, use the context sentences on page T213 to administer the posttest.

Optional Writing Idea: Description Tell children that they are going to write a description of a noise. Have children brainstorm different kinds of noises they might describe. Then have each child choose a noise to write about. Suggest that they begin by making a web of words and phrases that describe how the noise sounds and how it makes them feel.

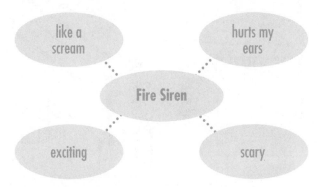

Suggest that children read their descriptions without identifying the noise. Encourage classmates to guess what noise is being described.

LESSON WRAP-UP

Words to Explore and Context Sentences

1. **noise** — I jumped when I heard the loud **noise.**
2. **explore** — Anna likes to **explore** new places.
3. **finally** — We walked all day and **finally** reached the end of the trail.
4. **harmless** — Many insects are **harmless.**

Reteach

LEARNING DIFFERENCES Have children make a tape recording of their Spelling Words. Ask them to say each word, spell it slowly, and say it again. Then as children listen to their tapes, have them write each word. When they are done, ask them to write over the *s* or *es* in another color.
AUDITORY/VISUAL MODALITIES

INTEGRATED CURRICULUM ACTIVITIES

Language Arts

Plurals in a Row Distribute nine-square grids to children. Have them write nine of the Spelling Words in the squares. Provide beans or small paper squares as markers. Then as you say a Spelling Word, children cover it on their grid. The first child to cover three words in a row wins.

boxes	wishes	times
girls	days	dishes
things	toys	inches

Math

Inch by Inch Have children measure classmates or classroom objects to find out how many inches long they are. Ask them to make a chart. Have them draw each object measured and write how many inches long it is. Then have children write about their findings. Encourage them to use these Spelling Words in their writing: *girls, boys, times, inches,* and *things.*

Objectives

To review spelling patterns and strategies in Lessons 30–34; to give children the opportunity to recognize and use these spelling patterns and the Spelling Words in their writing

Review of Spelling Strategies

Review with children the spelling strategies presented in Lessons 30–34.

CHECKING SPELLING Write the sentence *It was a verey cold day* on the board. Ask children to read the sentence and identify the misspelled word. Have a volunteer circle the word and spell it correctly. Then ask children how they can check the spelling to see if it is right. (ask someone who knows the correct spelling or look it up in a dictionary)

ANALYZING COMPOUND WORDS Write the words *some* and *thing* on the board and have children identify them. Ask how knowing the spellings of these two words can help children spell the compound word *something.* Have a volunteer write the compound word *something* on the board.

APPLYING SPELLING RULES Write the words *dropped, liked,* and *days* on the board. Circle the base word in each one. Ask what ending has been added to each word and how the spelling changed. Then write the words *slip, use,* and *box.* Have children tell what spelling rules can help them spell *slipped, used,* and *boxes.* Ask children to write the words on the board. Point out that the *p* was doubled in *slipped* and the *e* was dropped in *used.*

Unit 6 Review Words

The following words from Unit 6 are reviewed in this lesson.

Lesson 30 Words to Remember: down, out, because, after

Lesson 31 Compound Words: grandma, upon, baseball, somewhere

Lesson 32 Words Like *dropped* and *running:* stopped, popping

Lesson 33 Words Like *loved* and *moving:* riding, giving

Lesson 34 Plurals Ending with *s* or *es*: boxes, wishes, dishes, inches

> **❝**It is possible to spell a word correctly by chance, or because someone prompts you, but you are a scholar only if you spell it correctly because you know how.**❞**
>
> (Aristotle)

Pupil's Edition page reproduction:

◄UNIT REVIEW►

Name _____

Practice Test

A. Read each word list. Choose the correctly spelled word that fits in the blank. Mark the letter next to that word.

1. fall _____
   - Ⓐ down
   - Ⓑ donw
   - Ⓒ downe

2. balloons _____
   - Ⓐ poping
   - Ⓑ popping
   - Ⓒ popeing

3. visit _____
   - Ⓐ grandmae
   - Ⓑ grandma
   - Ⓒ granma

4. moving _____
   - Ⓐ oute
   - Ⓑ owt
   - Ⓒ out

5. toy _____
   - Ⓐ boxs
   - Ⓑ boxis
   - Ⓒ boxes

6. once _____ a time
   - Ⓐ upon
   - Ⓑ unpo
   - Ⓒ upone

7. going _____
   - Ⓐ riding
   - Ⓑ rideing
   - Ⓒ ridding

8. three _____
   - Ⓐ wishs
   - Ⓑ wishes
   - Ⓒ wises

146   Lesson 35   Integrated Spelling

ALL KINDS OF FRIENDS Unit 3 Review • Harcourt Brace School Publishers

---

PRACTICE TEST pages 146–147

Options for Administering the Practice Test

The Practice Test provides an opportunity to review Spelling Words and spelling generalizations in a standardized test format.

Option 1: Have children review their **Words to Study** in the Spelling Log for Unit 6. If they need extra help, review the spelling generalizations on Pupil's Edition pages 126, 130, 134, 138, and 142. Then administer both parts of the Practice Test on Pupil's Edition pages 146–147 to determine whether children have mastered the spelling generalizations.

Option 2: Administer Part A of the Practice Test on Pupil's Edition page 146 as a pretest. Have children check their pretests and study the words they misspelled. On another day, administer Part B of the Practice Test on Pupil's Edition page 147 as a posttest.

☑ Options for Evaluation

- Have children check their own Practice Tests by referring to their lists of Spelling Words. The list on page T219 provides references to the lessons in which children will find the words on the Practice Test.

- You may prefer to assign partners and have them check each other's Practice Tests. Refer children to their own lists of Spelling Words as they check their partners' tests.

For each word misspelled on the Practice Test, remind children to follow the **Study Steps to Learn a Word** on pages 8–9 of the Pupil's Edition. Be sure to have them write the misspelled words in the Unit 6 **Words to Study** box in the Spelling Log. STUDENT SELF-ASSESSMENT

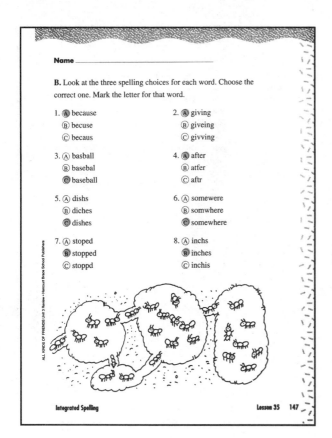

Name_____

B. Look at the three spelling choices for each word. Choose the correct one. Mark the letter for that word.

1. Ⓐ because
   Ⓑ becuse
   Ⓒ becaus

2. Ⓐ giving
   Ⓑ giveing
   Ⓒ givving

3. Ⓐ basball
   Ⓑ basebal
   Ⓒ baseball

4. Ⓐ after
   Ⓑ atfer
   Ⓒ aftr

5. Ⓐ dishs
   Ⓑ diches
   Ⓒ dishes

6. Ⓐ somewere
   Ⓑ somwhere
   Ⓒ somewhere

7. Ⓐ stoped
   Ⓑ stopped
   Ⓒ stoppd

8. Ⓐ inchs
   Ⓑ inches
   Ⓒ inchis

Integrated Spelling   Lesson 35   147

**RESOURCES: HOME
ACTIVITIES MASTER 35A**

Use as an extra activity to reinforce spelling strategies.

Review of Spelling Strategies Review with children the spelling strategies discussed on pages 176–177 of the Pupil's Edition. Then distribute Home Activities Master 35A.

The Reteach section of the Lesson Wrap-Up provides suggestions for helping children who are still having difficulty with the concepts taught in that lesson.

Practice Test

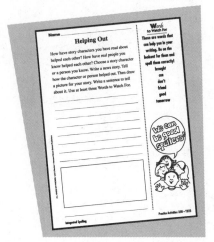

RESOURCES: PRACTICE ACTIVITIES MASTER 35B

Use as an extra activity to provide children an opportunity to combine spelling and writing.

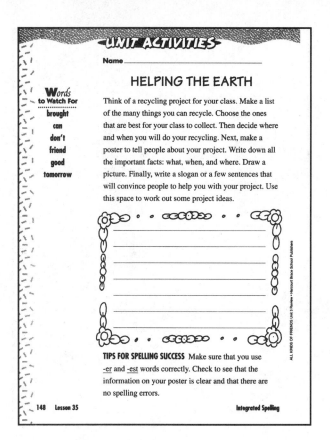

Name

HELPING THE EARTH

Think of a recycling project for your class. Make a list of the many things you can recycle. Choose the ones that are best for your class to collect. Then decide where and when you will do your recycling. Next, make a poster to tell people about your project. Write down all the important facts: what, when, and where. Draw a picture. Finally, write a slogan or a few sentences that will convince people to help you with your project. Use this space to work out some project ideas.

Words to Watch For

brought
can
don't
friend
good
tomorrow

TIPS FOR SPELLING SUCCESS Make sure that you use -er and -est words correctly. Check to see that the information on your poster is clear and that there are no spelling errors.

148   Lesson 35   Integrated Spelling

UNIT 6 ACTIVITIES pages 148–149

Activities on pages 148 and 149 of the Pupil's Edition emphasize writing (Helping the Earth and Medal Winner), reading (Medal Winner), and word play (Word Doodles). The **Tips for Spelling Success** point out the importance of standard spelling and give children hints for proofreading and for applying spelling strategies.

Helping the Earth Read the directions with children. Help them brainstorm a list of things they can recycle. Write their responses on the board. Choose things that are able to be recycled in the community. Encourage children to work in small groups to create their posters. Remind children to draw pictures and to write slogans. Then arrange to have posters displayed in the school lunchroom, lobby, or other appropriate locations if you plan to collect and recycle the items.

Have children read aloud the **Tips for Spelling Success.** Then point out the **Words to Watch For.** These are words children often use in writing. Explain that children can use the list as a reference to help them spell the words correctly. When children proofread their work, provide them with the following checklist or with the proofreading checklist on page 175 of the Pupil's Edition. WRITING/PROOFREADING

Proofreading Checklist

✔ Did I spell words correctly?

✔ Did I begin each sentence with a capital letter?

✔ Did I end each sentence with the correct end mark?

✔ Did I begin special words with capital letters?

If children need help in creating a poster that persuades, refer them to pages 32–33 of the *Language Handbook.*

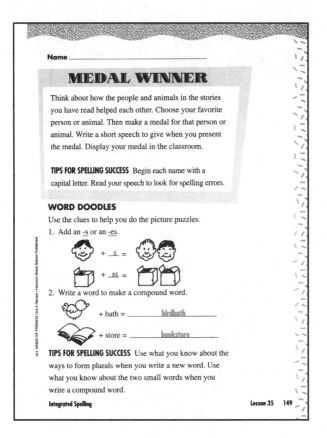

MEDAL WINNER

Think about how the people and animals in the stories you have read helped each other. Choose your favorite person or animal. Then make a medal for that person or animal. Write a short speech to give when you present the medal. Display your medal in the classroom.

TIPS FOR SPELLING SUCCESS Begin each name with a capital letter. Read your speech to look for spelling errors.

WORD DOODLES

Use the clues to help you do the picture puzzles.

1. Add an -s or an -es.

2. Write a word to make a compound word.

+ bath = _____ birdbath _____

+ store = _____ bookstore _____

TIPS FOR SPELLING SUCCESS Use what you know about the ways to form plurals when you write a new word. Use what you know about the two small words when you write a compound word.

Integrated Spelling   Lesson 35   149

Medal Winner Read the directions with children. As they name story characters that have helped each other, list the names on the board. Encourage children to discuss why the helpful characters might deserve medals. Provide materials such as tagboard, foil, or ribbons for children to use to make their medals. After children have written their speeches, have them present the medals and speeches. Children can work in pairs to present and accept the medals.

Have children read the **Tips for Spelling Success** and encourage them to proofread their work. WRITING/PROOFREADING

Word Doodles Draw on the board a picture of one flower and a picture of two flowers. Ask what letter children would add to *flower* to spell *flowers*. Follow a similar procedure for *dish*.

Write the word *mail* and draw a picture of a box. Ask children to put the two together to spell a compound word. Then have children complete the activity independently.

Read the **Tips for Spelling Success** and encourage children to recall and use the strategies. USING SPELLING RULES AND COMPOUND WORDS

Write the review words, listed on page T219, on self-stick notes and stick them around the room. Have children number their papers from 1 to 16. Then send them on a review-word hunt. When children find a self-stick note, they leave the note where it is but write the word on their list.

Make a set of word cards for the review words listed on page T219. Spell some of the words correctly and the others incorrectly. Then organize two teams of children. As you flash a card, the first child on each team must say *Right* or *Wrong* to tell whether the word is spelled correctly. The first child to answer correctly scores a point for the team. Challenge children to spell incorrect words correctly to score an additional point.

For children who need a reteaching activity, have them draw pictures for the review words listed on page T219. (They probably won't be able to draw *because* or *somewhere*.) On the back of each picture, have them write the review word. Then ask children to work in pairs. As one child shows a picture, the other guesses and spells the word.

Children may enjoy making up their own Word Doodles like the ones on page 149 of the Pupil's Edition.

Spelling Dictionary

The Spelling Dictionary, which appears on pages 150–172 of the Pupil's Edition, contains all the Spelling Words and Words to Explore from the spelling lessons. After each entry, a number in square brackets appears. This is the number of the spelling lesson in which that word appears.

Features of the Dictionary

The information on page 150 introduces the Spelling Dictionary to children. The features of a dictionary are pointed out and explained:

✓ Entry word

✓ Other forms of the word (plural, past tense)

✓ Meaning(s) of the word

✓ Context sentence in which the word is used

In addition to these standard dictionary features, the Spelling Dictionary may include synonyms for the entry word.

Introducing the Spelling Dictionary

Remind children that a dictionary shows the meaning and spelling of words and that the words are listed in alphabetical order. Then read and discuss page 150 with children. Invite volunteers to point out each feature of the Spelling Dictionary and explain why that feature is useful. Questions such as these may be used to guide discussion:

• Why do you think a dictionary lists more than one meaning of a word?

• How can you tell which meaning is the one you are looking for? (Make sure children understand that sentence context, or the way they use a word in a sentence, helps them know which meaning is the right one.)

• Why do you think the dictionary includes synonyms?

• How can synonyms for a word be useful when you write?

Next, ask children when they think they should use the Spelling Dictionary. Help them understand these points:

✓ A dictionary can be used when reading to look up the meaning of unfamiliar words.

✓ A dictionary can be used when writing to check the spelling of words.

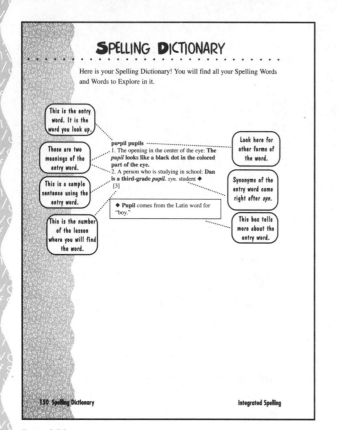

Page 150

Page 151

Referring to the Spelling Table

Discuss the Spelling Table on page 151 with children. Read the paragraph above the table to them. Then ask them how they think this table can help them. (The third column shows examples of the different ways that sounds can be spelled.) Encourage children to provide additional examples of words they know that have spellings which reflect the different sounds shown.

Page 152

A

a•bout 1. being near a certain amount; almost: **It is *about* one mile from our house to my school. 2.** having something to do with: **Charlotte's Web is a book *about* animals on a farm.** [30]
a•bove in a higher place; over: **There was a sign *above* the door that said "EXIT."** [10]
add 1. to put one thing with another; combine: **Put the soup in the pot, and *add* one can of water.** 2. to put numbers together: **When you *add* the numbers 4 and 6, you get 10.** [15]
ad•ven•ture something that is exciting or unusual: **Going across the ocean from England to America was a real *adventure* in the days of sailing ships.** [10]
af•ter 1. at a later time; after now: **June is the month that comes *after* May.** 2. along with and behind: **Tim went out the door, and his dog ran *after* him.** [30]
a•gainst 1. in the other direction; opposite: **Our team played a softball game *against* the Redbirds.** 2. so as to touch; in contact with: **She leaned her bicycle *against* the wall.** [22]
all every one of something; the whole thing: ***All* fish live in water.** [15]
an a special word used before a noun or adjective that begins with the sound of *a, e, i, o,* or *u*: **I had *an* apple for lunch, and she had *an* orange. *An* elephant is *an* enormous animal.** [1] ♦

♦ **An, a,** and **the** are special words called *articles*. We use articles to point out a certain thing. **An** goes before a word with a *vowel sound* **(a, e, i, o, u).**

an•gry very mad: **The man was *angry* when he spilled grape juice all over his new white rug.** [18]
are a special word used when talking about more than one person or thing: **These shoes *are* new. Karen and Rosa *are* friends of mine.** [24]
arm 1. the part of the body between the shoulder and the hand: **Keesha's *arm* was tired after she pitched in the baseball game.** 2. something that looks or works like an arm: **The cat was sleeping on the *arm* of the chair.** [24]
ar•tist a person who draws or paints: **A person who paints pictures is an *artist*.** [25]
asked used words to try to find out something: **I didn't hear the teacher, so I *asked* my friend what she said.** [28]
a•void to stay away from: **That road always has a lot of traffic, so we *avoid* it and take another road.** [22]
aw•ful very bad: **There was an *awful* flood and many people had to leave their homes.** [18]

B

bad 1. not good; not as is wanted or as it should be: **He had only two answers right, so he got a *bad* score on the test.** 2. causing a problem or difficulty: **She was sick in bed with a *bad* cold.** [1]
ball 1. a round object: **The cat plays with a *ball* of yarn.** 2. a thing with a round shape that is used to play certain games: **In soccer you try to kick the *ball* into the goal.** [15]
bal•loon a small rubber bag filled with air: **On my birthday, I got a big red *balloon* that said "Happy Birthday."** [16]

Page 153

base•ball 1. a game that is played on a field in which one team tries to hit the ball and run around the bases to score a run. The other team tries to catch the ball to get the runners out: ***Baseball* is a popular game in the United States.** 2. the ball that is used in this game: **A *baseball* is hard, and players wear gloves when they try to catch it.** [31]
bat 1. a long stick that is made of wood or metal, used to hit a baseball: **A wooden *bat* makes a loud cracking sound when it hits the ball.** 2. a small mouselike animal that has wings made of very thin skin: **A *bat* sleeps during the day and flies at night.** [1]
bath a washing of the body with water: **He takes a *bath* every night before he goes to bed.** [18]

bath

be•cause for the reason that: **I woke up late *because* my alarm clock did not go off.** [30]
be•gan set off to do something; started: **She *began* her speech by saying, "Good morning, everyone."** [2]
bet to feel strongly that something will happen: **The sky looks really dark. I *bet* it will rain today.** [2]
bike a shorter word for **bicycle,** a vehicle with two wheels that people ride on: **I ride my *bike* to school every day.** [2]
bit 1. a very small amount: **He couldn't hear the radio, so he turned up the sound a *bit*.** 2. something very small: **She tore up the paper into tiny *bits*.** 3. grabbed or cut with the teeth: **Tara *bit* into the apple.** [3]
black a color that is the opposite of white; the darkest color: **A killer whale is *black* with white markings.** [19]
blow to send air out strongly, as from the mouth: **You will have to *blow* very hard to put out all the candles.** [14]
boat a thing that floats on water and moves by means of oars, sails, or an engine: **Jason likes to sail his toy *boat* on the pond.** ♦ [10]

♦ **Boat** and **ship** are two words that are close in meaning. Boats and ships both carry people on the water. A boat is small and carries a few people, usually for a short distance. A ship is much larger and can carry many people across an ocean.

bone one of the hard white parts that make up the skeleton of a person's or animal's body: **Cory broke a *bone* in his arm.** [13]
book a set of pages with words printed on them, held together inside a cover: **A dictionary is a *book* that tells how to spell words and what they mean.** [19]
bor•ing not interesting; not fun: **They thought the movie was *boring*, so they left the theater before it was over.** [20]
born brought into life: **My grandmother was *born* in 1928.** [25]
both the two together: **Here and hear are different words, but they *both* have the same sound.** [7]
box a container that is used to hold things: **When we got our new computer home, we had to take it out of the *box*. Some kinds of food are sold in *boxes*, such as cereal, crackers, and candy.** [4, 34]

Page 154

boys male children; children who are not girls: **There are twelve *boys* and fifteen girls in my class at school.** [34]
brave facing danger with courage: **The *brave* woman jumped into the water to save a baby.** [2]
bright 1. giving off much light; shining with a strong light: **She had to put on her sunglasses because the sun was very *bright*.** 2. having a good mind; smart: **Maria is a *bright* child who gets A's in all her subjects.** [22]
bril•liant 1. very bright; glowing: **The diamond sparkled with a *brilliant* light.** 2. having a very good mind; very smart: **Dr. Seuss was a *brilliant* writer who wrote some of the world's funniest books for children.** [28]
brought took along from one place to another: **She thought it might rain, so she *brought* an umbrella with her.** [16]
built made something; put something together: **Some American pioneers lived in cabins that they *built* with logs.** [32]
bur•row 1. a hole made in the ground by an animal: **A mole lives in a *burrow*.** 2. to make a hole in the ground: **The mole can *burrow* for many feet underground.** [19]
bus a large motor vehicle with many rows of seats for carrying a large number of people: **The school *bus* stops at our corner at 7:45 each morning.** ♦ [6]

♦ **Bus** comes from the word **omnibus.** The word *omni* means "all." The idea is that a bus is for all people. A car is owned by one person or family, but anyone can pay to ride on a bus.

by 1. by means of; through: **They sent the package *by* mail.** 2. next to; near: **Mom told us to wait for her *by* the door.** 3. not later than: **Our book reports have to be finished *by* Friday.** [7]

C

call to talk to a person on the telephone: **I'm going to *call* Kevin to find out if he can play later.** [15]
called said something in a loud voice: **I *called* to my friend when I saw him across the street.** [28]
can't cannot; is not able to: **My brother is only three, and he *can't* read yet.** [26]
car a four-wheeled motor vehicle that carries people: **A *car* is also called an "automobile."** [19]
care 1. to look after; watch over: **A mother bear will *care* for her cubs until they are about two years old.** 2. to have feelings for or about: **It rained at our picnic, but I didn't *care* because we had fun anyway.** [19]
car•ried held and taken from one place to another: **He *carried* his books to school in his backpack.** [32]
cat a small furry animal with pointed ears, sharp claws, and a long tail, often kept as a pet: **A *cat* makes a fine indoor pet.** [1]

cat

caught 1. got, became infected: **Maria Elena *caught* a cold at camp.** 2. took hold of something moving: **He reached up and *caught* the ball in his hand.** [12]
cel•e•brate to have a good time or do certain things because of a special time: **People like to *celebrate* Thanksgiving by getting the whole family together for a big dinner.** [15]

Page 155

change 1. to make or become different: **I asked the teacher to *change* my seat so that I would be closer to the board.** 2. money given back when a person pays more than something costs: **She gave the clerk one dollar for a fruit drink that cost 75 cents and got 25 cents in *change*.** [16, 21]
chest 1. a box with a lid attached, used to store things: **Billy put his blocks into the toy *chest*.** 2. the part of the body where the heart is: **The *chest* is between the shoulders and the waist.** [16]
child 1. a young boy or girl: **When my mother was a *child*, she lived on a farm.** 2. someone's son or daughter: **Abraham Lincoln was the *child* of a poor Kentucky farmer.** [7]
class•room a room in a school where classes are held: **Our *classroom* has pictures of animals on the walls.** [31]
clev•er smart; good at doing things: **Our coach had a *clever* idea for what we could do to win the game.** [26]
coal a black material that is dug out of the ground and used for fuel: **When *coal* is burned in a furnace, it gives off a great amount of heat.** [10]
coast 1. the land at the edge of a sea or ocean: **San Francisco is a city on the Pacific *coast*.** 2. to ride on a bicycle or in a car without using power: **He took his feet off the pedals so that he could *coast* down the hill.** [10, 33]
coat 1. a piece of clothing with sleeves, worn over other clothes to keep warm: **In winter, I wear a wool *coat* almost every day.** 2. the hair or fur of an animal: **Our pet bunny has a very soft *coat*.** 3. a thin layer or covering: **The outside of our house needs a new *coat* of paint.** [10]
cold 1. having a very low temperature; not hot: **It sometimes snows when the weather is very *cold*.** 2. an illness with sneezing, coughing, and a runny nose: **I stayed home from school yesterday because I had a *cold*.** [7] ♦

♦ **Cold** might seem to be the wrong name for a kind of sickness. When you are sick with this, you often feel hot, not cold. The name comes from the idea that people get colds more often in the winter. This is the time of the year when it is cold.

col•or the different ways we see the light from something; red, blue, yellow, and so on: **My favorite *colors* are purple and blue.** [25]
com•pa•ny 1. someone who comes to visit; a guest or guests: **We're having *company* for dinner tonight.** 2. a group of people who work together; a business: **That *company* sells computers.** [7]
cook•ies small, sweet cakes that are usually flat and round: **He had a snack of milk and oatmeal *cookies*.** [6]
corn a kind of tall plant that is often eaten as a vegetable: **The parts of *corn* that we eat are the kernels, which are usually yellow or white.** [25]
cough a rough sound made by sending air out through the mouth from the chest: **My baby sister has a *cough*.** [12]
could•n't could not; was or were not able to: **We kept playing until it got so dark that we *couldn't* see the ball.** [26]
cour•age bravery when facing something dangerous or when afraid: **A firefighter has to have *courage* to enter a burning building.** [26]
co•zy warm and comfortable: **The dog found a *cozy* spot near the fireplace and went to sleep.** [19]
cry to have tears coming out from the eyes: **The movie about the lost little dog made Abby so sad that she began to *cry*.** [22]

Page 156

cup a small round container used for drinking: **People often drink hot chocolate from a *cup*.** [6]

cup

cut 1. to make an opening in something using a sharp tool: **She used a knife to *cut* the piece of string.** 2. to be hurt by something sharp going through the skin: **Marty *cut* his foot when he stepped on some broken glass.** [6]

cute nice to look at; pretty: **Our dog was so *cute* when she was a puppy.** [13] ♦

♦ **Cute** is usually used to talk about something that is small and young: **That is a very *cute* picture of the baby because of the smile on his face.**

D

D

dad a friendly name for a father: **My *dad* said I did a good job on my book report.** [1]

dark having little or no light: **He turned off the TV, and the screen was *dark*.** [24]

days the time when the sun is out; the time that is not night: **Many people work or go to school five *days* each week.** [34]

de•cide to make up one's mind what to do: **I like both shirts, and I just can't *decide* which one to wear.** [13]

deep going far down from the top or the surface: **The water is very *deep* in the middle of the ocean.** [9]

de•li•cious very good to eat; tasting very good: **The strawberries are fresh and *delicious*.** [6]

de•sign 1. a plan or sketch to be used as a pattern for making something: **This is the *design* I will use for my costume.** 2. a pattern of form or color: **The sweater's *design* is made of green and blue fish.** 3. to form a thing in a certain way: **to *design* a dress, to *design* a new computer.** [30]

did•n't a shorter way to say **did not: He was late and *didn't* get to the bus stop in time for his bus.** [26]

dis•ap•pear to go away or become hidden: **He does a magic trick in which he holds up a coin and then makes it *disappear*.** [28]

dis•cov•er to find out about something: **Scientists are still trying to *discover* a way to prevent the common cold.** [12]

dish•es plates or other objects used to serve food: **She helps out at home by washing the *dishes* after dinner.** [34]

dis•tance 1. a point or place far away: **We could see the tallest buildings in the *distance*.** 2. how far it is between one place and another: **The *distance* from my house to school is about one mile.** [31]

does•n't a shorter way to say **does not: She stays out of the water because she *doesn't* know how to swim.** [26]

do•ing carrying on some action: **Laura is *doing* her homework in her room.** [28]

doll a toy that looks like a person: **Missy likes to pretend that her *doll* is a real baby.** [4]

dol•lar a unit of money that is the same as one hundred pennies: **Four quarters make one *dollar*.** [3]

don't a shorter way to say **do not: I *don't* watch TV on school nights.** [26]

door a part that moves so that you can go into or out of something: **You need a key to open the front *door* of our house.** [25]

down from a higher place to a lower one: **The ball rolled *down* the hill.** [30]

Page 157

dress 1. a one-piece top and skirt that is worn by women and girls: **Janie got a new *dress* for her birthday.** 2. to put clothes on: **My little sister has learned to *dress* herself.** [15]

drew made a picture with a pen, pencil, or crayon: **In art class today, Gene *drew* a picture of his pet rabbit.** [21]

dropped to let fall; let go down: **I *dropped* a glass, and it broke on the floor.** [32]

dry 1. having very little water; not wet: **The Sahara Desert is a very *dry* place.** 2. to make dry: **She used a big towel to *dry* her hair after she had washed it.** [14]

duck

duck a water bird with webbed feet and a broad bill: **A *duck* has feathers that keep off water.** [6]

dug broke up the ground; made a hole in the ground: **We *dug* holes in the garden to plant our new rose bushes.** [6, 32]

E

each one of two or more people or things: ***Each* question that you get right adds ten points to your score.** [9]

earn 1. to get money by doing work: **She can *earn* $6.00 per hour working at that store.** 2. to get what is deserved: **You will have to work hard to *earn* an A in that subject.** [3]

eat to take in food; chew and swallow food: **They usually *eat* lunch at noon.** [9]

egg a cell or cells produced by some female animals from which a young animal develops: **Birds, fish, and reptiles hatch from *eggs*.** [2]

ex•cit•ed full of feeling: **The girls on the team were very *excited* when they scored the goal that won the game.** [20]

ex•plore to go into new or unknown places: **The U.S. has sent spacecraft to *explore* the planet Mars.** [34]

F

fair 1. giving everyone the same chance: **Our teacher is *fair* and treats each student the same way.** 2. clear and sunny: **a *fair* spring day.** 3. a show where things are on display: **We all showed our science projects at the school science *fair*.** [9]

fall 1. the season of the year between summer and winter: ***Fall* is also called autumn.** 2. to go down suddenly from a higher place or position: **Be careful on those steps, or you will *fall*.** [15]

E F

fa•mil•iar well-known; often seen or heard: **All the people in this snapshot are *familiar* to me.** [7]

fam•i•ly a group of people forming a household: **A new *family* just moved into the house across the street from us.** [7]

far not near; at a great distance: **The road sign was too *far* away for her to read.** [24]

farm land where plants or animals are raised for food: **My uncle has a *farm* in Iowa where he grows corn.** [24]

fast moving quickly; going at a high speed: **Erin is a *fast* runner, and she wins all the races at school.** [14]

fav•o•rite a person or thing that is liked the best: **When Li gets the newspaper, the first thing he reads is his *favorite* comic strip.** [16]

Page 158

feel 1. to find out about by touching: **I can *feel* cold air coming in; there must be a window open somewhere.** 2. to have a certain sense in the body or mind: **to *feel* sick, to *feel* happy.** [9]

feet 1. the body parts at the end of the legs, used for standing and moving: **Humans and some animals stand on two *feet*.** 2. units of length, equal to 12 inches each: **Val's dad is over 6 *feet* tall.** [9]

fes•ti•val a big party that takes place on a holiday or at another special time: **In the summer, our town has a *festival* of the arts with plays, concerts, and art shows.** [15]

field a piece of land used for sports: **Football is played on a *field* 100 yards long.** [1]

fi•es•ta a day or time to celebrate something: **In Mexico a *fiesta* can be held to celebrate a religious holiday.** [15] ♦

♦ **Festival** and **fiesta** both mean the same thing. *Festival* is an English word, and *fiesta* is a Spanish word. Another word that means the same thing is **feast.** All these words go back to a Latin word meaning "a special holiday."

F

fight an attack with force or words: **Scott had a *fight* with his brother Ted after Ted called him a bad name.** [22]

fi•nal•ly at last: **I looked all over for my watch and *finally* found it next to the kitchen sink.** [34]

fin•ished completed: **When he *finished* writing his story, he checked it for spelling mistakes.** [25]

fire the flames, heat, and light given off by burning: **Someone dropped a match in the dry grass, and it started a *fire*.** [12]

fish 1. any of a large group of animals that live in the water: ***Fish* have fins to help them swim.** 2. to catch fish for food or as a sport: **We walked along the river looking for a good place to *fish*.** [16]

five the number that is one more than four; 5. [12]

fix to bring back to the proper condition; repair: **We had to *fix* Kevin's bicycle because the chain was broken.** [3]

fla•vor the seasoning of food; taste: **Chocolate ice cream has a wonderful *flavor*.** [27]

flew moved through the air by the use of wings: **The birds *flew* over the lake.** [21]

floor the bottom surface of a room: **There was a small rug on the *floor*.** [25]

fly 1. to move through the air by the use of wings: **Hawks *fly* high above the earth.** 2. a small insect with one pair of wings: **The *fly* is a common pest.** [14]

food what people and animals eat to keep them alive: **Pizza is a *food* that people often eat for lunch.** [21]

for 1. directed to a certain person or thing: **This picture book is *for* children.** 2. to a certain distance, time, or amount: **I slept *for* nine hours last night.** [27]

four the number that is one more than three; 4. [27]

fox a wild animal with a bushy tail and thick fur: **The *fox* is closely related to the wolf and the dog.** [4]

fox

from used to show a starting point or time: **I'll race you *from* here to our house. The store is open *from* nine o'clock in the morning until six o'clock at night.** [14]

Page 159

fur•i•ous very angry: **He was *furious* when he found out someone had picked all the flowers in the garden.** [22]

G

game something that is done to have fun: **a *game* of cards, a *game* of checkers, a *game* of soccer.**[12]

gath•er to come together at one place: **Even before the tickets went on sale, people began to *gather* around the ticket booth.** [14]

gen•tle soft or mild: **She didn't get angry or upset but just spoke in a quiet, *gentle* voice.** [4]

get•ting 1. going onto or into: **Manuel tripped as he was *getting* on the bus.** 2. coming to have: **I'm *getting* a new bike because my old one is too small.** 3. becoming: **It was *getting* dark, and they had to stop the game.** [32]

gi•gan•tic very big; huge: **Many dinosaurs were *gigantic* animals.** [8]

girls female children; children who are not boys: **There are fifteen *girls* in the fourth-grade class.** [34]

giv•ing letting have as a present: **What are you *giving* Maria for her birthday?** [33]

glass 1. a hard material that can be seen through and breaks easily: ***Glass* is made by melting together sand and certain other materials.** 2. a container made of this material, used for drinking: **I'd like a *glass* of milk, please.** [15]

glide to move in a smooth, easy way: **Some kinds of planes can *glide* through the air without using power.** [10]

glow to shine with a soft, clear light: **The eyes of a cat seem to *glow* in the dark when light hits them.** [28]

go•ing moving from one place to another: **What time are you *going* to see the movie?** [28]

grabbed took something in a sudden way: **Before anyone else could take the last piece of candy, Jerry *grabbed* it and put it in his mouth.** [32]

grand•ma the mother of a person's mother or father: ***Grandma* is a name that children call their grandmother.** [31]

grass any of a large family of green plants with long, thin leaves: ***Grass* is a plant that grows all over the world.** [14]

grew became bigger: **Andrew *grew* five inches taller in the past year.** [21]

group a number of persons or things together: **Tigers usually live alone, but lions live together in a *group*.** [21]

H

had the form of the word **have** we use to tell about the past: **Willy *had* to leave school early yesterday.** [1]

hard 1. not easy to do or understand: **The science test was *hard*, and no one got an 'A' on it.** 2. solid and firm; not easy to push in or bend: **Diana hurt her knee when she fell on the *hard* sidewalk.** [24]

G H

harm•less not causing harm or damage: **That looks like a real sword, but it is actually just a *harmless* toy made of rubber.** [34]

heart the large muscle that pumps blood to all parts of the body: **Your *heart* is in your chest.** [24] ♦

♦ **Heart** is the muscle that pumps blood to the body. The word also has many other meanings coming from the idea that the heart is the most important part of the body. For example, the *heart* of a city is the most important part of the city.

Page 160

her•self her own self: **She's old enough now to cross the street by *herself*.** [31]
he's a shorter way to say he is: **If Eric doesn't hurry, *he's* going to be late for school.** [20]
hid put out of sight: **Mark *hid* the present for Susan in the back of his closet.** [3]
high going far above the ground; not low: **That mountain looks very *high* from here.** [22]
hill a piece of ground that is higher than the land around it but smaller than a mountain: **When it snows, we ride sleds down the *hill* behind our house.** [3]
him a male person who is being talked about: **I called Chuck on the phone and asked *him* about our math homework.** [3]
him•self his own self: **Josh is lucky he didn't hurt *himself* when he fell down the stairs.** [31]
hope to want something to happen or be true: **I *hope* the weather will be nice for our picnic tomorrow.** [13]
horse a large animal that has four legs: **A *horse* is strong and can run very fast.** [25]
how in what way: **Can you tell me *how* to get to Main Street from here?** [30]
huge very large: **The whale is a *huge* animal.** [13]

I

if in the event that: ***If* it rains today, the game will be put off until Tuesday.** [3]
I'll a shorter way to say I will: **I have to go now, or *I'll* be late for dinner.** [20]
I'm a shorter way to say I am: ***I'm* sorry that I stepped on your foot.** [20]
im•por•tant worth extra attention: **Eating good foods is *important* if you want to stay healthy.** [15]
inch•es small units of length: **There are twelve *inches* in one foot.** [34]
I've a shorter way to say I have: **I like that movie, and *I've* seen it twice.** [26]

J

job work for which a person is paid: **The *job* of a firefighter is to put out fires.** [4]
join 1. to become a member of a group: **Bobby wants to *join* the Boy Scouts.** 2. to get together with someone: **She told all the children to *join* hands in a circle.** [14]
jump to use the legs to move up in the air: **Basketball players *jump* high to catch or shoot the ball.** [6]

K

keep 1. to continue or maintain: ***Keep* your hands on the handlebars to be safe.** 2. to have and hold onto: **She's just going to borrow the book, not *keep* it.** [9]
ket•tle a large pot used to heat liquids or cook food: **a *kettle* of soup.** [27]
kick to hit with the foot: **Soccer players try to *kick* the ball into the goal.** [19]
kind 1. wanting to help others; friendly: **Helping Mrs. Smith with her packages was a *kind* thing to do.** 2. a group of things that are the same in some way; a type: **Owls are one *kind* of bird.** [7]

L

laid 1. produced an egg: **We gathered the eggs the duck had *laid*.** 2. put down on a surface: **When he was finished digging, he *laid* his shovel on the ground.** [8]

I J K L

Page 161

larg•er bigger: **Your feet are *larger* than mine.** [21]
last 1. coming after all others: **December is the *last* month of the year.** 2. to stay in good condition: **That battery should *last* for at least one year.** [14]
late not on time: **He missed the bus and was *late* for school.** [12]
lay to place or put down on a surface: **You can *lay* the box down on the table.** [8]
leg 1. one of the body parts used to walk or run: **The knee is part of the *leg*.** 2. a part that supports something: **the *leg* of a table.** [2]
less not as much: **His dad wants him to spend *less* time watching TV and more time studying.** [15]
let's a shorter way to say let us: ***Let's* take the bus home.** [26]
life the quality that makes people, animals, and plants able to grow and produce new living things like themselves: **Rocks and machines do not have *life*.** [12]
light 1. the opposite of darkness: **The sun gives off a very bright *light*.** 2. to make burn: **I used a match to *light* the candles.** 3. not heavy: **A paper towel is very *light*.** [22, 28]

lightning

light•ning a sudden flash of light in the sky that happens during a storm: ***Lightning* is actually a form of electricity.** [31]
liked felt good about; enjoyed: **I *liked* the book and want to read another one by the same author.** [33]
lis•ten to pay attention to a sound: **Mom likes to *listen* to the news on the radio.** [4]
live•ly active; full of life: **Our new puppy is very *lively* and loves to run and play.** [19]
liv•ing having life: **Although many dinosaurs were bigger, the elephant is the largest *living* land animal.** [33]
long 1. having great length; not short: **Our dog has a *long* tail.** 2. being a great distance from one end to the other: **It is a *long* way across the Atlantic Ocean.** [18]
looked used the eyes to see: **He *looked* out the window and saw his friend coming up the street.** [28]
look•ing using the eyes for seeing: **If you are *looking* for your book, I saw it on the kitchen table.** [28]
loom a machine or frame used to make cloth: **Cotton cloth is made by a huge machine called a power *loom*.** [30]
lot 1. a large amount: **A *lot* of people watch the Super Bowl football game on TV.** 2. a piece of land: **They are going to build a house on that empty *lot*.** [4]
loved had a strong feeling of caring for someone or something; liked very much: **The story of Little Red Riding Hood tells how she *loved* her grandmother.** [33]
low 1. near to the ground or another surface: **The plane was flying very *low*, just over the houses below.** 2. not high in amount: **Ninety cents is a *low* price for a gallon of gas.** [10]

M

mad feeling anger; angry: **Joey is *mad* at Susan because she didn't invite him to her party.** [1]
made formed into something: **Jamala *made* a whistle out of clay.** [12]

M

Page 162

M

make to form into something: **She is going to *make* a pie for dessert.** [12
mam•mal the name used in science for an animal that has a backbone, is warm-blooded, and has hair or fur on the body: **A female *mammal* gives birth to live young and feeds them with her milk.** [21]

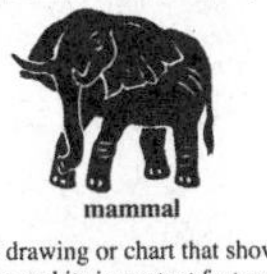
mammal

map a drawing or chart that shows a certain place and its important features: **When we drove to Florida, we used a road *map* to tell us where to go.** [1]
ma•ter•i•al cloth: **Cotton is a *material* that is often used for clothing.** [24]
math a shorter word for **mathematics**, the study of numbers: **In *math* class, students learn to add and subtract.** [18]
may a helping verb that means: 1. it is more or less likely: **We *may* get there by lunchtime; it depends on how much traffic there is.** 2. it is allowed: **Students *may* play outside after they eat lunch.** [8]
me the person who is speaking or writing: **I asked Jed to call *me* at home later.** [7]
med•i•cine something that is taken into or put on the body to bring back good health: **When people are sick, they often take *medicine* to get better.** [12]
mem•ber a person or animal that belongs to a certain group: **Heather is a *member* of the Girl Scouts.** [21]
men more than one man: ***Men* who work in a business office usually wear a necktie to work.** [2]
mess a place that is dirty and has things scattered about: **His room was a big *mess*, with dirty clothes and toys all over the floor.** [2]
might 1. a helping verb that means something more or less likely: **Peggy *might* come for dinner, so Mom bought some extra meat.** 2. strength or power: **Lily kicked the ball with all her *might*.** [22]
milk a white liquid that comes from mother animals to feed their young: **People use *milk* to make cheese and butter.** [19]
miss to not do, see, or know: **In baseball it is a strike if you swing and *miss* the ball.** [15]
mom a friendly name for a mother: **My *mom* leaves my breakfast for me before she goes to work.** [4]
more greater than another in number or amount: **In baseball the team that scores *more* runs wins the game.** [25]
most 1. greatest in number or amount: **California has the *most* people of any state in the U.S.** 2. to a great amount; nearly all: ***Most* of the children I know like to play tag.** [7]
move to go to a new place: **Please *move* your car because it is blocking our driveway.** [13]
mov•ing going from one place to another: **The people in line were *moving* very slowly.** [33]
much being a large amount: **I'd rather watch a movie in the theater than on TV because the screen is *much* bigger.** [6]
mud dirt that is wet and sticky: **Get the *mud* off your shoes before you come into the house.** [6]

mule

mule an animal that is part horse and part donkey: **A *mule* has longer ears than a horse.** [13]

Page 163

must a helping verb that means something is certain or likely: **These footprints *must* belong to our dog.** [6]
my belonging to me: ***My* brother and I sleep in the same bedroom.** [7]

N

neck the body part that connects the head to the body: **A swan has a long, graceful *neck*.** [19]
need to want or require something: **Plants *need* water and light to grow.** [9]
new made or done now or a short time ago; not old: **She bought a *new* dress at the store. When spring comes, trees grow *new* leaves.** [21]
nice good or pleasing in some way: **Our soccer coach is a *nice* woman who never yells at us.** [12]
night the time when it is dark; the time between sunset and sunrise: **Some animals sleep during the day and come out to hunt at *night*.** [22]
noise a sound: **The saw made a loud *noise* as it cut through the wood.** [34]
nose the part of the face or head that is used for breathing and smelling: **A dog depends on its *nose* to find things.** [13]
note a short letter or message: **Mom left us a *note* to say that she went to the store to buy milk.** [13]

O

once one time: **My favorite TV show is on *once* a week, on Friday afternoon.** [2]
or a special word used to show a choice: 1. one of a group of things: **Would you like a red, a blue, *or* a green ribbon on your package?** 2. the second of two things: **Send the card today, *or* it won't get there in time.** [25]
oth•er not this one: **Our team had six points in the game, and the *other* team had five.** [30]
out away from the inside: **It was a nice day, and Lisa went *out* to play.** [30]
o•ver 1. higher than; above: **The ball went *over* the fence.** 2. at the end: **We left the theater when the movie was *over*.** [30]
own 1. belonging to oneself or itself: **The puppy sleeps in its *own* little bed.** 2. to have something belong to one: **Mr. and Mrs. Davis *own* a store where they sell toys and games.** [10]

N O P

P

pack 1. a large bundle, to be carried on a person or animal: **Gina's *pack* was full of books.** 2. to put something into a box or suitcase: **Be sure to *pack* some warm clothes for your trip.** 3. a group of things that belong together: **a *pack* of cards, a *pack* of wolves.** [19]
pack•age something packed, wrapped up, or tied together: **Teri got a *package* in the mail from our uncle.** [8]
paint•ing completed picture done with paint: **I used watercolor paints when I made this *painting*.** [25]
pal•ace a huge building in which a king or other ruler lives. **Queen Elizabeth of Great Britain lives in a *palace* in London.** ♦ [26]

♦ **Palace** is a word that comes from a place in the ancient city of Rome. The Palatine Hill Hill was a hill at the center of the city of Rome. The ruler of Rome lived there in a large building. *Palace* meant "the house of the ruler on Palatine Hill."

Page 164

park 1. an area of land set aside for everyone to use: **I like to go to the *park* after school to play ball or ride my bike.** 2. to leave a car for a time in a special place: **Dad didn't stop at the store because he couldn't find a place to *park*.** [24]
part something that belongs to a thing but is not all of it: **The first *part* of the movie was good, but it got boring later on.** [24]
pass to go beyond: **He drove faster to *pass* the car in front of him.** [15]
pay to give money to buy something or for work done: **Mom is going to *pay* me five dollars to shovel all the snow off the driveway.** [8]
peo•ple more than one person; a group of persons: **About 10,000 *people* live in this town.** [13]
per•fect as good as it can be: **Tyrone drew a *perfect* picture of his kitten.** ♦ [6]

♦ **Perfect** means that something is as good as it can possibly be. Sometimes people use the word just to mean "very good," as in: **That was really a *perfect* meal we had for dinner last night.** But to be really correct, you should use *perfect* to mean "the best that it can ever be."

phone a shorter word for **telephone: I want to call Mom on the *phone* to ask if I can eat dinner at Stacy's house.** [3]
pin a short length of metal with a point at one end and a flat head at the other: **She put her name tag on with a *pin*.** [3]
placed put something in a certain position: **He *placed* the bowl of flowers in the center of the table.** [33]
plan ideas about what to do or how to do something: **The coach has a *plan* for how we can win the game.** [13]
planned worked out how to do something: **The trip went just as they had *planned*, and they arrived right on time.** [32]
play 1. to make music on an instrument: **to *play* the piano, to *play* the guitar.** 2. to have fun: **We love to *play* outside at recess.** [14]
play•ing doing something for fun: **The children were in the yard, *playing* a game of tag.** [28]
pond a small, shallow body of water: **Fish, frogs, and ducks live in the little *pond* near our house.** [4]

pond

pop•ping making a short, sudden sound: **The engine made a funny *popping* sound, but it wouldn't start.** [32]
prac•tice to do something over and over to get better at it: **to *practice* the piano, to *practice* throwing a baseball.** [1]
prob•lem something that is hard to figure out or that causes trouble: **We had a *problem* when we brought the new sofa home, because it was too big to fit through the front door.** [8]
put•ting placing in a certain spot: **Katie spends hours *putting* toy blocks into her wagon and then dumping them out.** [32]

R

rain 1. drops of water that fall from clouds: **We had more than an inch of *rain* from last night's storm.** 2. to fall as water in this way: **Those dark clouds make me think it's going to *rain* today.** [8]

Page 165

reach 1. to stretch out the arm to try to touch or hold something: **Can you *reach* the top shelf to get down that bowl?** 2. to go as far as a certain place: **Our plane should *reach* Chicago at about two o'clock.** [16]
read to look at something that is written and understand it: **Children usually learn to *read* when they are about six years old.** [9] ♦

♦ **Read** is an unusual word because the same word is used to talk about the present (now) and about the past (then): **I like to *read* books about animals.** (now) **Last week I *read* a book about lions.** (then) The two words are spelled the same but have different sounds. Now I read a book has a sound like "need." Then I read a book has a sound like "red."

rich having a lot of money: **Movie stars can get *rich* from the films they make.** [16]
rid•ing sitting on or in something and making it move: **Carrie was *riding* her bike in the park when she got a flat tire.** [33]
right 1. on the side opposite the left: **Most people write with their *right* hand.** 2. without a mistake; correct: **Sandy had all the *right* answers on the test.** [22]
ring 1. a band in the shape of a circle that is worn on a finger: **Maggie has a gold *ring* that she wears on her right hand.** 2. to make a sound like a bell: **We have to go in from recess when we hear the bell *ring*.** [18]
road a smooth strip of ground that has been cleared so that cars or other vehicles can go on it: **Route 5 is the main *road* across the state of Kansas.** [10]
rock 1. to move back and forth or side to side: **If you *rock* the cradle, the baby will fall asleep.** 2. the solid material that makes up part of the earth's crust: **The house is built on solid *rock*.** 3. a small piece of this material: **He threw a *rock* into the water, and it made a big splash.** [4]
room 1. an area in a building that is set aside for a particular use: **Our school has a computer *room* where we can do word processing.** 2. the space that is needed for something: **There is enough *room* in the garage to park two cars.** [21]
rope a thick, strong cord made of twisted or woven strands of wire or fiber: **A *rope* can be used to pull heavy things.** [13]
round shaped like a circle or ball: **An orange is a *round* fruit.** [16]
row 1. to use oars to move a boat: **It took us about twenty minutes to *row* across the lake.** 2. a straight line of people or things: **We sat in the last *row* of the theater to watch the movie.** [10]
run•ning faster than when walking; going by moving the legs quickly: **In baseball after you hit the ball, you start *running* to first base.** ♦ [32]

♦ **Run** is probably the word in English with the most different meanings. If you look in a large dictionary, you will find that **run** has as many as one hundred meanings. Some of these are a *run* in baseball, a *run* of bad luck, a *run* on a bank, to *run* a business, to *run* a computer, and to *run* a story in a newspaper.

S

sad not happy; feeling bad: **Rashon was *sad* when his new toy broke the first time he played with it.** [1]

Page 166

sat got into a still position in a chair: **When Mom said dinner was ready, I went and *sat* at the table.** [1]
saved kept for a later time: **They didn't eat all the meat, so they *saved* the rest to use for sandwiches.** [33]
say to speak words out loud: **People usually *say* "Hello" when they answer the telephone.** [8]
school a place for learning and teaching: **Children go to *school* to learn to read and write.** [21]
scis•sors a tool with two blades used for cutting: **He used a pair of *scissors* to cut the piece of string.** [24]
seat a place to sit: **The teacher changed my *seat*, and now I sit next to Juan.** [9]

seesaw

see•saw a long board that is balanced on a bar: **Children play on a *seesaw* in a playground.** [31]
set 1. to put something in a certain place: ***Set* those packages down on the kitchen table.** 2. a group of things that belong together: **a *set* of dishes.** [2]
sew to make clothes or other things with a needle and thread: **She had to *sew* a button on her jacket.** [27]
sew•ing the act of someone who sews: **This machine is used for *sewing* clothes.** [24]
shape the outer form of something: **These cookies have a round *shape*.** [16]
she's a shorter way to say **she is: Jessie called and said that *she's* on her way home.** [20]

ship

ship 1. a large boat that goes on the ocean: **The Titanic is a famous *ship* that sank the first time it ever went to sea.** 2. to send a thing from one place to another: **Farmers grow oranges in Florida and *ship* them to other parts of the country.** [16]
shoot 1. to try to score a goal in games such as basketball, soccer, or hockey: **When players are fouled in basketball, they sometimes *shoot* a basket.** 2. to fire a gun or other weapon: **She knows how to *shoot* arrows with a bow.** [9]
shop 1. a small store: **We get our cat's food at the pet *shop* in our neighborhood.** 2. to go to stores to look at and buy things: **Theresa loves to *shop* for clothes.** [16]
short not tall or long: **Two seconds is a *short* time.** [25]
show 1. to bring into sight: **Mr. Gray is going to *show* a movie in class tomorrow.** 2. something that is seen by people: **We're going to the auto *show* to see what next year's cars will look like.** [10]
side a part of something that is not the top, bottom, front, or back: **The driver of a car gets in and out of a car on the left *side*.** [12]

Page 167

sight 1. something to see: **The clowns in the circus were a funny *sight* in their odd costumes.** 2. the power to see: **Dad got glasses for reading because his *sight* isn't as good as it used to be.** [22]
sit to be in a position in which the body rests on the hips: **Please *sit* still in your chair. Danny was *sitting* on the bench waiting for a chance to get into the game.** [3, 32]
six the number that is one more than five; 6. [3]
sky the space above the earth: **The clouds floated across the *sky*.** [22]
sled a plastic disk or wooden vehicle with runners that carries people over the snow: **Pablo rode his *sled* down the snowy hill.** [14]
slipped moved suddenly or slid out of control: **Amy *slipped* on the ice and sat down hard.** [32]
slow going at a low speed; not fast: **Five miles an hour is a fast speed for walking, but it is a *slow* speed for a car.** ♦ [10]

♦ **Slow** can be used in several different ways without any change in the word. It can tell about a person or a thing: **He is a *slow* eater and is always the last one to finish his lunch.** It can show action: **Cars had to *slow* down because of the heavy traffic.** And it can tell how an action happens: **Go *slow* when you get to the corner.** This last use can also be written as **slowly: Go *slowly* when you get to the corner.**

snore to make a loud, rough noise while sleeping: **I thought Dad was just resting until I heard him start to *snore*.** [18]
so 1. in the same way: **I liked the movie, and *so* did my friends.** 2. with the result that: **All the seats were taken, *so* we had to stand.** [27]
soar to fly quickly and easily: **A hawk can *soar* high above the earth.** [10]
some•thing a thing that is not known or named: ***Something* got stuck in the sink, and now the water won't run out.** [31]
some•times now and then: ***Sometimes* we eat breakfast in the dining room.** [31]
some•where in or to a place that is not known or named: **When we go to the beach, we like to put our blanket down *somewhere* near the water.** [31]
soon before long: **I'm really hungry, and I hope dinner will be ready *soon*.** [21]
sort 1. a group of things that are somewhat alike: **What *sort* of books do you like to read?** 2. to arrange by kind: **After she washed the socks, she had to *sort* them into pairs.** [25]
sound something that is sensed by the ears: **Did you hear the *sound* of thunder?** [4]
sow to plant or scatter seeds in order to grow plants: **The farmer will *sow* wheat in his fields.** [27]
squawk•ing making a loud, sharp cry: **Alex says his parrot is talking, but it sounds to me like *squawking*.** [20]
start 1. to go into action; begin: **The game will *start* at two o'clock and end at about four o'clock.** 2. the first part; the beginning: **Let's sit here so that we can see the *start* of the race.** [24]
start•ed to make a beginning; set out: **The hikers *started* on their trip in the rain.** [28]
stew a thick soup: **Beef *stew* is made with small pieces of beef and vegetables.** [6]
stick a long, thin piece of wood: **I threw the *stick*, and my dog ran after it.** [19]
still 1. without movement or sound; quietly: **The rabbit heard a noise and stood *still*, listening for where it came from.** 2. as before; even now: **Do you *still* want to go, even though it might rain?** [14]

Page 168

stood stayed in one place on the feet: **Marta *stood* up to make her speech.** [14]
stop to keep from moving or doing something: **Could you please *stop* talking?** [4]
stopped kept from moving or doing something: **The car *stopped* when the light turned red.** [32]
store a place where things are sold: **I got this shirt at a *store* in the mall.** [25]
storm a heavy rain or snow with strong winds: **More than six inches of snow fell during last night's *storm.*** [31]

storm

stretch 1. to extend the body or a part of it: **Kim likes to *stretch* her legs before she runs.** 2. to make longer: **You can *stretch* a rubber band so that it becomes much longer.** [18]
sup•per a meal eaten in the evening: **We had dinner in the afternoon and then a light *supper* at night.** [27]
sur•face 1. the top of the water, where the water meets the air: **There are bugs on the *surface* of the pond.** 2. the outside or top of something: **The car wash does not use brushes because brushes can scratch the *surface* of a car.** [33]

T

tail a movable part of an animal's body that sticks out from the rear: **Our dog wags his *tail* whenever he is happy.** [8]
take 1. to travel by: **Do you *take* a bus to school?** 2. to get hold of: ***Take* my hand when we cross the street.** [12]
tak•ing carrying: **My little brother is *taking* his favorite toy along on our trip.** [33]
tan•gled twisted and trapped: **When she got out of bed, her hair was all *tangled*, and she had a hard time combing it.** [33] ♦

♦ **Tangle** once had a different meaning than the meaning it has now. It meant a kind of seaweed. This may appear to have no connection with the present meaning, but actually it isn't as far off as it seems. This seaweed grew in a wild, tangled way, and people began to use *tangle* to talk about other things that looked like this.

tape 1. to fasten or bind with tape: **Ask Andrew to *tape* this ripped book cover.** 2. a long, narrow strip of plastic, paper, or cloth that is sticky on one side: ***Tape* is used to wrap packages or close boxes.** [8]
taste 1. to get the flavor of something: **She has to *taste* the sauce to see whether it is ready.** 2. flavor; what makes food different and special in your mouth: **Strawberries have a sweet *taste.*** [27]
team a group of people who play on the same side in a game: **The Boston Red Sox is a famous baseball *team.*** [1, 9]
ten the number that is one more than nine; 10. [2]
than a word used to compare one thing with another or others: **I like pizza better *than* any other food.** [18]
that's a shorter way to say **that is**: ***That's* our car parked across the street from the school.** [20]
their belonging to them: **The people who live next door to us have a big oak tree in *their* yard.** [27]

Page 169

them the people or things being talked or written about: **The Smiths asked us whether we wanted to go with *them* to the zoo.** [18]
there 1. at that place: **You sit here, and I'll sit over *there* by the window.** 2. it is true; it is a fact: ***There* are thirty days in the month of June.** [27]
there's a shorter way to say **there is**: ***There's* a strange dog in our yard.** [20]
they the people or things being talked or written about: **The children got wet when *they* were playing out in the rain.** [18]
they're a shorter way to say **they are**: **There is a For Sale sign on their lawn, so I guess *they're* going to move.** [20]
things 1. objects or items: **Books, pencils, and paper are *things* you use in school.** 2. subjects or ideas: **From that movie, I learned a lot of interesting *things* about how whales live.** [34]
those showing the people or things that are being talked or written about: **We want to save *those* papers in the box.** [18]
thread a very thin string or cord that is used in sewing: **Elias used black *thread* to sew the rip in his black sweater.** [24]
throne a large, decorated chair that a king or queen sits on: **The queen sat on a *throne* when she met with her court.** [26]
throw•ing tossing: **The pitcher starts the play in baseball by *throwing* the ball to the batter.** [20]
times 1. certain points or periods in history; occasions: **He's already seen that movie three *times* before, but he still likes to watch it.** 2. multiplied by: **Two *times* three is six.** [34]
to in the direction of: **The bus takes them *to* school. Please take this note *to* the teacher.** [27]
told made known to someone: **My uncle *told* me a funny joke about a dog that could talk.** [7]
too in addition to; also: **I'd like an apple, and Craig wants one, *too.*** [27]
took 1. got hold of; came to have: **When I passed around the cookies, Debbie *took* two.** 2. carried or went along with: **He *took* the garbage out and put it in the garbage can.** [19]
top the highest part of something: **There was snow on the *top* of the mountain.** [4]
toss to throw: **I'll *toss* this ball in the air, and you try to catch it.** [9]
touch 1. to feel something by using a part of the body: **Don't *touch* that wall with your hand because the paint is still wet.** 2. to put one thing up against something else: **The desk should be very close to the wall but should not *touch* it.** [4]
to•ward in the direction of; near: **At night many kinds of insects will go *toward* a bright light and fly around it.** [9]
toys things that children play with for fun: **Charlie has a big box in his room to put all his *toys* in.** [34]
track 1. a mark or footprint left on the ground by an animal or person as it moves: **If you look closely, you can see a *track* in the snow that was left by a deer.** 2. the rails that a train runs on: **The trains that run on this *track* go to the city.** [19]
train 1. a line of railroad cars joined together and pulled by an engine: **At this station, you can get a *train* that will take you all the way to California.** 2. to teach how to do something: **Michael wants to *train* his dog to bring in the newspaper.** [8]
trou•ble 1. problem; difficulty: **Jeff got in *trouble* at school because he was teasing a younger boy.** 2. extra work or effort: **I hope Mom likes this present, because I went to a lot of *trouble* to find it.** [22]
try 1. to make an effort to do something;

Page 170

attempt: **We *try* to learn a new word every day.** 2. an effort to do something; an attempt: **Jill didn't get the ball in the goal, but it was a good *try* anyway.** [7]
try•ing making an effort to do something: **My baby sister is *trying* to learn to walk.** [28]
tune simple songs that are easy to remember: **Our teacher made up a class song to the *tune* of "Mary Had a Little Lamb."** [14]

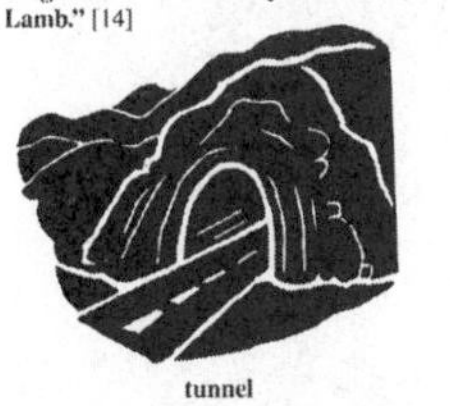

tunnel

tun•nel a long, narrow passage under the ground or the water: **Cars can drive under the river by going through a *tunnel.*** [32]
turn 1. a chance for one person to do something: **Each child was given one *turn* in the game.** 2. to move in a circle or part of a circle: **You *turn* this knob to the right to make the radio louder.** 3. to change in some way: **As the sun went down, the air began to *turn* cold.** 4. a movement in a circle or part of a circle: **Make a left *turn* at the next corner.**
two the number that is more than one and less than three: 2. [27]

U

un•cle the brother of someone's mother or father: **The husband of your aunt is also called your *uncle.*** [7]
up•on touching and held up by; on: **She placed the vase of flowers *upon* the table.** [31]
us the persons who are speaking or writing: **Dad drove *us* to the movies.** [6]
use 1. to put into action or service for some purpose: **We will *use* the good dishes for dinner tonight, since we are having company.** 2. the act or fact of being in service: **All the pay phones were in *use*, and he had to wait to make his call.** [13]
used 1. put into action for some purpose: **She *used* a knife to cut open the package.** 2. not new: **A *used* car is one that has already been owned by some other person.** [33]

V

ver•y more than usual: **In most of the U.S., it gets cold in the winter; in Alaska it gets *very* cold.** [30]

W

wait 1. to stay in a place until someone comes or something happens: **We will *wait* right here until the next bus comes.** 2. the time spent doing this: **They had a long *wait* before the bus finally came.** [8]
want•ed wished to have or do something: **Barbara has *wanted* to be an airplane pilot ever since she was a child.** [28]
wash 1. to get rid of dirt or stains with water, or with soap and water: **It's your turn to *wash* the dishes tonight.** 2. the clothes or other things that are cleaned at one time: **She put a large load of *wash* into the washing machine.** [16]
was•n't a shorter way to say **was not**: **I**

Page 171

called my friend Li on the phone, but she *wasn't* at home. [26]
way 1. a certain method to do or get something: **My coach showed me the right *way* to pitch a ball so that I wouldn't hurt my arm.** 2. a road or path that leads from one place to another: **Route 7 is the fastest *way* to drive to the city from here.** [8]
weath•er the way things are outside; sunny, rainy, cold, hot, and so on: **Southern California usually has warm, dry *weather* during the summer.** ♦ [31]

♦ **Weather** comes from a word that means "storm." We now use the word for nice, sunny days as well as for rainy or snowy days. But in early times, it was during storms that people really noticed what the weather was like. So they used **weather** as another word for **storm.**

weave to make cloth by lacing threads over and under each other: **A Native American visitor taught us how to *weave* baskets out of thin strips of wood.** [30]
were a form of the word be that we use to talk about more than one person or thing in the past: **We are now learning about fish in our science class; last week we *were* studying insects.** [30]
we're a shorter way to say **we are**: **Mom promised me that *we're* going to take a vacation trip this summer.** [20]
wet covered or soaked with water or another liquid: **The streets were *wet* after the sudden heavy rain.** [2]
whale a very large animal that lives in water: **A *whale* is actually a mammal, not a fish.** [33]
what's a shorter way to say **what is** or **what has**: ***What's* the name of that boy who's in your car pool?** [20]
which what one or ones: ***Which* of the books do you want to read first?** [18]
while 1. a short period of time: **They got tired of walking and sat down to rest for a *while.*** 2. during the time that: **We don't like to get phone calls *while* we're eating dinner.** [18]
win 1. to be first or best in a game or contest: **Karen has to spell one more word correctly to *win* the spelling bee.** 2. to get as a prize in a game or contest: **The person who guesses the number will *win* two free tickets to the play.** [3]
wish 1. to hope very much for something: **I *wish* the rain would stop because I want to go out to play.** 2. something that a person hopes for: **If you could have just one *wish*, what would you choose? In the fairy tale, the prince was given three *wishes.*** [16, 34]
woke went from sleeping to not sleeping: **She *woke* early in the morning and dressed quickly.** [13]
won't a shorter way to say **will not**: **If you can be there by five o'clock, you *won't* be late.** [26]
wool the thick, soft hair taken from sheep or some kinds of goats and used to make clothing: ***Wool* is used to make warm sweaters and coats.** [30]

whale

wool

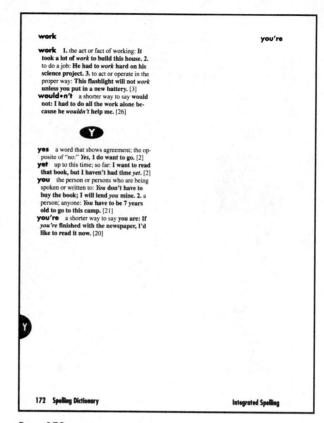

work

you're

work 1. the act or fact of working: It took a lot of *work* to build this house. 2. to do a job: He had to *work* hard on his science project. 3. to act or operate in the proper way: This flashlight will not *work* unless you put in a new battery. [3]

would•n't a shorter way to say would not: I had to do all the work alone because he *wouldn't* help me. [26]

Y

yes a word that shows agreement; the opposite of "no:" *Yes,* I do want to go. [2]

yet up to this time; so far: I want to read that book, but I haven't had time *yet.* [2]

you the person or persons who are being spoken or written to: *You* don't have to buy the book; I will lend *you* mine. 2. a person; anyone: *You* have to be 7 years old to go to this camp. [21]

you're a shorter way to say you are: If *you're* finished with the newspaper, I'd like to read it now. [20]

Y

Page 172

The Writing Process

Using the writing process can help children not only in thinking about, creating, revising, and polishing original written works but also in improving their spelling. Producing an error-free piece of writing involves a combination of creative thinking, critical evaluation, and checking for errors in spelling and mechanics. Although the writing process is a recursive one in which children may move back and forth between stages as necessary, it also allows children to focus on one task at a time.

The basic stages of the writing process are:

▶ **Prewriting** Children identify their task, audience, and purpose for writing. Then they select a topic and organize their information. Pictures, lists, charts, and webs are effective graphic organizers for the prewriting stage.

▶ **Drafting** Children try to get all their ideas on paper. They focus on the message rather than on correct spelling, punctuation, usage, and mechanics at this stage.

▶ **Responding and Revising** Children reread their writing and make changes. They might also ask for an evaluation or suggestions from a partner or a group.

▶ **Proofreading** Children find and correct errors in spelling, usage, mechanics, and punctuation.

▶ **Publishing** Children prepare their writing to share with others.

Spelling as Part of Writing

Learning correct spelling in the context of their writing encourages children to focus on the relationships between words as well as the spelling of individual words. As children learn about written language, they apply that knowledge to words they wish to use in their writing.

Practice Through Proofreading

The proofreading stage of the writing process provides an excellent opportunity for children to learn spelling skills. Children will more readily understand the need for correct spelling when they recognize misspellings in their own writing. Teaching spelling as part of the writing process, together with the direct teaching of reading vocabulary and problem words taken from children's own writing, is both natural and effective. Such teaching works because it is based on the desire of children as writers to communicate clearly.

Introducing the Writing Process

Ask children to name some things they like to write. Explain that they will learn about a plan that will help them become better writers. Then read Pupil's Edition pages 173–175 to the children. Next, help volunteers reread the different stages of the writing process aloud. Use questions such as these to discuss the writing process with children:

- How can the writing process help you write?
- Why do you think it is important to make changes to your writing? How can other children help you with this part?

Help children to understand that every piece of writing they produce need not be constructed according to the stages of the writing process. The writing process is intended for writing they want to share with others, such as stories or reports, and works they hope to develop into finished form.

Suggestions for Using the Writing Process

Here are suggestions for helping children to become familiar with and use the writing process to improve their spelling:

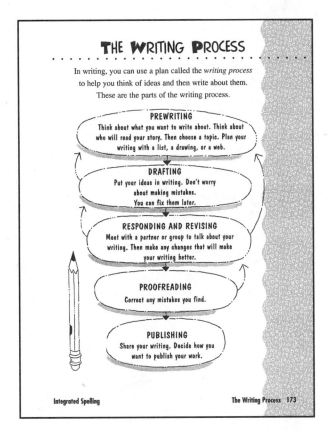

Page 173

Prewriting Children can sometimes benefit from group brainstorming sessions. Write idea webs on the board to help children consider a variety of topics before selecting a topic to write about. Children may need some guidance in identifying their purpose and audience. Use these questions to guide them:

- Who will read your writing?

- What can you do to make your writing interesting to your readers?

Drafting Remind children that when they use the stages of the writing process, they can go back to what they have written as many times as they like and make changes. As children write their first draft, encourage them to write freely. Remind them that they will have the chance to correct their work later.

Note that children acquiring English may need some assistance with writing a first draft. You might encourage them to draw pictures to show story events and then work with a peer to dictate a caption for each picture.

Responding and Revising Have children work with a partner to revise their writing. At this stage of the writing process, children add, delete, move, or replace information. Encourage children to ask one another for feedback and offer helpful responses. Also, ask children to begin checking for spelling. However, note that it is at the proofreading stage that children will concentrate on making sure spelling is correct.

Proofreading Discuss with children the importance of proofreading as a way to prepare their writing for their readers. Point out that correct spelling is important because their writing will be shared with others, and misspelled words can make their message hard for their readers to understand.

Proofreading instruction may be carried out in small or whole-class groups. Suggest these procedures to help children proofread for spelling errors:

- Children should proofread their writing twice. The first time they should circle any

Page 174

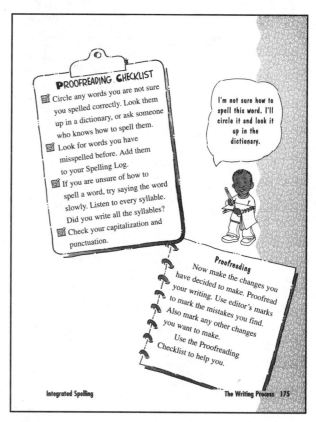

Page 175

words they know are misspelled. The second time they should circle words they suspect are misspelled.

- Children can work with a partner to correct spellings by using a dictionary and other resources, by referring to their Spelling Logs, and by applying spelling generalizations.
- Help children understand that words that are most commonly misspelled, such as *too, to,* and *two,* can be determined by their meaning in a sentence.
- Have children add the words they have misspelled to their Spelling Logs. Remind them that a Spelling Log is a useful resource for recording the spelling of words they have trouble with.

Publishing You might give children an opportunity to generate creative ideas for publishing their work and allow them to choose from among these and other ideas when they share their writing:

- Help children organize an "author's circle" in which classroom authors read their work aloud. Afterwards, have children discuss the spelling errors they found and how and when they corrected them.
- Children can collect stories and bind them together into books for the classroom library.
- Children might create a graphic display of their writing.

Spelling Strategies

The lessons in *Integrated Spelling* are designed around and utilize two major strategies of instruction: (a) phonology— consistent spelling patterns based on sound-letter relationships; and (b) analogy— common characteristics of words as the basis for predicting the spelling of unfamiliar words.

To aid children in developing the tools to become competent independent spellers, spelling strategies are provided to maximize their learning. The strategies help children think about spelling as a skill they can develop through a variety of processes such as these:

- Utilizing a five-step strategy can help them learn the spelling of new words.
- Using a variety of spelling strategies can help them remember the spelling of troublesome words.
- Using possible spellings, thinking about word families, and using the dictionary can help them figure out how to spell new words.
- Proofreading will help them identify spelling errors in their own writing.

Specific Strategies for Spelling

These specific strategies and others are presented in *Integrated Spelling*:

✓ *Study Steps to Learn a Word*   Children are encouraged to use the five study steps to help them learn the spelling of new words.

✓ *Picture a Word and Sound It Out*   In this strategy, children picture a word they want to write and think about the sounds the letters stand for.

✓ *Try Different Spellings*   Children think about the vowel sound in a word, consider different ways this sound can be represented by letters, and try different spellings until the word looks right.

✓ *Guess and Check*   Children guess the spelling of a word and then check its spelling in the dictionary.

✓ *Rhyming Words/Word Families*   By thinking about word families or rhyming words that share the same spelling pattern and letter-sound relationship, children often figure out the spelling of a word.

✓ *Use the Dictionary*   Children can simply look up the spelling of a word in a dictionary.

✓ *Homophones*   Children pay particular attention to context clues and make sure homophones are spelled correctly.

✓ *Compound Words*   Children break compound words into two smaller words and check the spelling of each word.

✓ *Mnemonic Devices/Memory Clues*   Good spellers develop and use memory clues, including mnemonic devices, to help them remember the spelling of words.

Strategies for Identifying Spelling Errors in Writing

These particular strategies are helpful to children as they proofread:

- *Proofread Twice*   By proofreading their writing twice, children identify spelling errors they know they have made as well as possible misspellings.
- *Proofread with a Partner*   Using this strategy, children work with a partner to check and discuss each other's spelling.
- *Proofread Backward*   By beginning with the last word in a paragraph and reading each word in isolation, children are apt to notice misspellings because the words are not in context.

Introducing the Strategies

Ask children to name some things they can do to help them figure out how to spell a word that is new to them and remember the spelling of words they know. List their suggestions on the board. Explain that children will learn about some additional spelling strategies they can use as they write and proofread. Read

Page 176

Page 177

pages 176 and 177 with the children. Then invite individual volunteers to read aloud the strategies in the speech balloons.

Encourage children to summarize the strategies by asking questions such as these:

- Which strategies might you use when you are trying to figure out how to spell a word you don't know?
- Imagine that you want to spell the word *top*. How can thinking about the words *hop* and *pop* help you?

- How can proofreading your written work two times help you find spelling errors?

Invite children to share mnemonic devices they have heard or made up themselves that help them remember the spelling of new words.

Discuss with children when to use spelling strategies. Point out that these strategies are also useful as they are writing. Encourage children to refer to pages 176 and 177 as they write.

Suggestions for Using the Spelling Log

The Spelling Log is located on pages 179–192 of the Pupil's Edition. There are three parts to the Spelling Log:

• Words to Study
• Words to Explore
• My Own Word Collection

Words to Study

Spelling Log pages 180–183 correspond to the six units in *Integrated Spelling*. There is one section for each unit. Each page presents "chalkboards" for the five or six lessons in that unit. Children can use this space to write words they misspelled on the pretest, words they have misspelled in writing assignments, and words with spellings they are unsure of.

Remind children to check the spelling of words before writing those words in the Spelling Log. Also encourage children to use the Study Steps to Learn a Word on pages 8 and 9 to help them learn the spelling of these words.

Words to Explore

Spelling Log pages 184-187 correspond to the Words to Explore section of the spelling lessons. Children can group the Words to Explore any way they like, but they should place the words on the pages where they belong. These pages are organized according to the following categories:

Language Words: page 184

Social Studies Words: page 185

Math and Science Words: page 186

Art and Music Words: page 187

After children complete each spelling lesson, have them write the Words to Explore on the pages where they belong. Encourage children to use the category heads along the margins to help them group words.

Some words might be placed in more than one category. Encourage children to discuss reasons a word fits in both categories. Children can write the word in both categories.

My Own Word Collection

The last five pages of the Spelling Log provide space for children to record words they have gathered from other sources and want to remember. Make sure children understand that they can create their own word lists on these pages. Encourage children to categorize the words they collect.

Suggestions for how to group words are provided along the margins of pages 188–192. Children can choose from among these ideas or think of their own ways to group words.

Point out the last page of the Spelling Log, and explain that this space is for words that do not immediately fit into any of the categories children have created.

From time to time, invite volunteers to share the words they have written in this section of the Log. Children can read words aloud and explain how they have chosen to group them. Encourage children who have created the same groups to compare the words they have included.

Reviewing the Spelling Logs

You might want to monitor children's progress in using their Spelling Logs. At the end of each unit, encourage children to share with you what they have written in each section of the Log. Discuss with children their reasons for grouping and categorizing different words. Encourage children to use the words they have gathered from other sources and the words they have written in the Words to Study and Words to Explore sections of their Spelling Log.

Page 179

Page 180

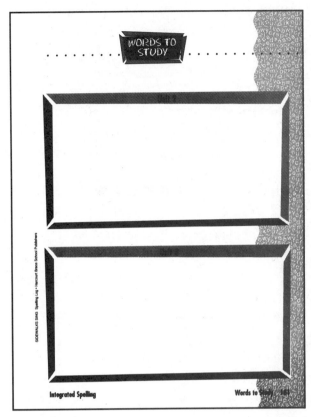

Page 181

Page 182

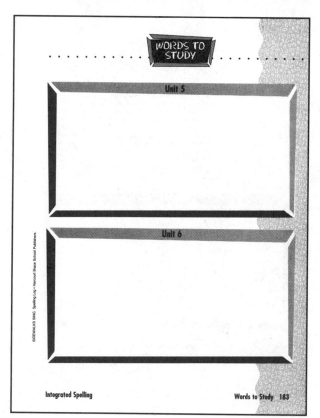

Page 183

Page 184

Page 185

Page 186

Page 187

Page 188

Page 189

Page 190

Page 191

Page 192

Each lesson in the Teacher's Edition provides research-based support and teaching strategies to help meet the individual needs of children.

LEARNING DIFFERENCES

Many features of *Integrated Spelling* encourage application of different learning modalities:

- Study Steps to Learn a Word is a systematic approach to learning the spelling of individual words that includes auditory, visual, and kinesthetic involvement with words.
- Reteach activities in the Reteach section of each lesson are designated for visual, auditory, or kinesthetic learners.
- Self-Check activities and Open and Closed Sort Activities are other elements of each lesson that address varying modalities.

SECOND-LANGUAGE SUPPORT

Each Teacher's Edition lesson includes Second-Language Support notes. These notes

- identify patterns and spelling skills that are transferable from certain languages to English.
- describe phonemic elements that differ between some children's first language and English.
- suggest ways to reinforce and convey the meaning of unfamiliar words and phrases.
- encourage children acquiring English to work with peer tutors who can model correct usage and answer questions.

The many oral language activities in *Integrated Spelling* are also of great benefit to children who are acquiring English.

DEVELOPMENTAL LEVELS

Integrated Spelling recognizes that today's classroom includes children at different developmental levels. The Spelling Placement Inventory and pretests/posttests provide insight into each child's developmental level, and each lesson includes suggestions for adapting instruction.

Developmental Levels of Spellers, Grades 1-8

Emergent Spellers	Semi-Phonetic Spellers	Phonetic Spellers
• Children first begin to use alphabet symbols to represent words or messages, but they don't always know what sounds match the letters.	• Children use invented spellings.	• Children refine their invented spellings.
• Spelling attempts are often not readable by anyone other than the child who produced them because the letters don't consistently represent sounds.	• They conceptualize that letters represent the sounds in words, but they may omit major sounds (often vowel sounds) in words, such as in *BT* for *boat*.	• They use a phonetic or letter-name system of spelling in which they make a one-to-one match between the sequential sounds they hear in words (/m/ /ā/ /k/) and alphabet letter names that represent these sounds (*MAK*).
• Children may or may not have the concept of word. The letters are strung together at random, sometimes in left-to-right fashion.	• They understand the concept of word and of left-to-right progression.	• Children spell words the way the words sound, and although the spelling may be unconventional, the words are usually readable.
• Children frequently mix uppercase and lowercase letter forms, although they generally show a preference for uppercase, such as in *IEOOS*.		• Children may or may not be aware of word segmentation, breaking words into smaller parts.
		• The matching of letters to sounds is systematic and perceptually accurate, such as in *shuts* for *shoots* and *ses* for *says*.

Note: Developmental levels of spellers are determined using placement inventories.

Transitional Spellers

- Children move from concrete to more abstract representation, which requires greater reliance on visual memory—spelling words the way they look rather than the way they sound.

- By reading, writing, and thinking about spelling, children develop a sense of when a particular spelling looks correct.

- Children may still invent spellings, but they have learned many of the conventions of English spelling. They put vowels in every syllable, use e-marker and vowel digraph patterns, spell inflectional endings correctly, and use letter sequences that occur frequently in English.

- Transitional spellers may include all the appropriate letters in a word, but they may reverse some letters, such as in *TAOD* for *toad* or *FETE* for *feet.*

Syntactic-Semantic Spellers

- Children are competent and correct spellers. They understand the English spelling system and its basic rules.

- Children understand the accurate spelling of prefixes, suffixes, contractions, compound words, and many irregular spellings; they usually use silent letters and double consonants correctly; they are able to distinguish between homophones.

- Through understanding the principles of syllable juncture and applying what they know about one-syllable words, children are able to spell multisyllabic words accurately.

- When spelling a new word, children think of alternative spellings and visualize the word.

- Children begin to recognize word origins and use this information to make meaningful associations as they accumulate a large corpus of known spellings.

Strategic Spellers

- Children have already mastered basic spelling patterns and are able to apply them automatically.

- Children have developed a "spelling consciousness" that allows them to adapt and integrate spelling strategies as a natural part of the writing process.

- Their understanding of meaning relationships enables children to be confident language users and serves as a powerful spelling resource.

Assignment Guide

Use this assignment guide to adjust assignments to the developmental levels of children.

3-Day Plan	5-Day Plan	Materials	Developmental Levels
Day 1 Pretest and/or Sorting Activity Strategy Workshop	**Day 1** Pretest and/or Sorting Activity	First Page of Pupil Edition Lesson Home Activities Master A	Semi-Phonetic Spellers (Below Level): Introduce Spelling Words 1–6 Phonetic Spellers (On Level): Pretest Spelling Words 1–10 Transitional Spellers (Above Level): Pretest Spelling Words 1–10
	Day 2 Strategy Workshop	Second Page of Pupil Edition Lesson	
Day 2 Vocabulary WordShop	**Days 3 & 4** Vocabulary WordShop	Third and Fourth Pages of Pupil Edition Lesson Practice Activities Master B	Transitional Spellers (Above Level): Assign Words to Explore
Day 3 Posttest	**Day 5** Posttest		Semi-Phonetic Spellers (Below Level): Test Spelling Words 1–6 Phonetic Spellers (On Level): Test Spelling Words 1–10 Transitional Spellers (Above Level): Test Spelling Words 1–10 and Words to Explore

Copying Masters

This section of the Teacher's Edition contains the following reproducible record-keeping charts and copying masters for the home and practice activities.

PERCENT CONVERSION CHART ....page T253

The Percent Conversion Chart indicates percentage scores on tests that have from 4 to 24 test items. The vertical row of numbers that runs along the left side of the chart represents the number of items in a test. The horizontal row of numbers across the top of the chart represents the number of items answered correctly. To find the percentage score a particular child has earned, find the box where the appropriate horizontal and vertical rows meet. The percent score appears in that box.

SPELLING PROGRESS RECORD ....page T254

The Spelling Progress Record may be used to track individual children's scores for the pretest, posttest, and Practice Test over the course of six units. Make one photocopy of the Spelling Progress Record for each child. Keep a copy of this chart in each child's portfolio and refer to it during student-and-teacher conferences. If you prefer, you may want to allow the children themselves to help record and keep a copy of the record to monitor their own progress as a form of self-assessment.

The Practice Test at the end of each unit is designed to give children practice with the standardized test format and help them become comfortable with test-taking procedures. The number of correctly spelled words should be recorded in the appropriate column of the chart.

CLASS RECORD-KEEPING CHART ....page T255

Use the Class Record-Keeping Chart to keep track of the progress of your class. This copying master can hold all children's scores for the pretest, the posttest, and Practice Test. Make six copies of this page. Use one copy with each unit.

COPYING MASTERS ....pages T256–T325

Two copying masters, labeled A and B, are provided for each developmental and Review lesson in *Integrated Spelling*. The Answer Key for the copying masters appears on pages T327-T329.

Using the Copying Masters

For Developmental Lessons

After children complete the Strategy Workshop, copy Home Activities
Master A. Distribute the word cards to children and guide them in an "open
sort" activity. In open sort, children group the word cards according to a
criterion they select themselves. They might group words that share the
same beginning or middle sound, words that are related by topic, or words
that have a similar shape. Alternately, have children take home Master A
with the word cards and complete the activity with a family member.

Practice Activities

Master B provides additional practice. If you are following the three-day
plan, use Practice Activities Master B on Day 2. If you are following the
five-day plan, use Practice Activities Master B on Day 4. This master may
be completed during class or assigned as homework.

For Review Lessons

Use Home Activities Master A as an extra activity to reinforce spelling
strategies. Begin by having children review the spelling strategies in the
Pupil's Edition. Use Practice Activities Master B as an extra activity to provide children with an opportunity to combine spelling and writing.

PERCENT CONVERSION CHART

Use the matrix below to convert the raw score for each test to a percentage.

Number of Test Items	Number Correct																						
	2	3	4	5	6	7	8	9	10	11	12	13	14	15	16	17	18	19	20	21	22	23	24
For 4-item tests	50	75	100																				
For 5-item tests	40	60	80	100																			
For 6-item tests		50	67	83	100																		
For 7-item tests		43	57	71	86	100																	
For 8-item tests			50	63	75	88	100																
For 9-item tests			44	56	67	78	89	100															
For 10-item tests				50	60	70	80	90	100														
For 11-item tests				45	55	64	73	82	91	100													
For 12-item tests					50	58	67	75	83	92	100												
For 13-item tests					46	54	62	69	77	85	92	100											
For 14-item tests						50	57	64	71	79	86	93	100										
For 15-item tests						47	53	60	67	73	80	87	93	100									
For 16-item tests							50	56	63	69	75	81	88	94	100								
For 17-item tests							47	53	59	65	71	76	82	88	94	100							
For 18-item tests								50	56	61	67	72	78	83	89	94	100						
For 19-item tests								47	53	58	63	68	74	79	84	89	95	100					
For 20-item tests									50	55	60	65	70	75	80	85	90	95	100				
For 21-item tests									48	52	57	62	67	71	76	81	86	90	95	100			
For 22-item tests										50	55	59	64	68	73	77	82	86	91	95	100		
For 23-item tests										48	52	57	61	65	70	74	78	83	87	91	96	100	
For 24-item tests											50	54	58	63	67	71	75	79	83	88	92	96	100

Name _____

Spelling Progress Record

	LESSON	NUMBER OF WORDS CORRECTLY SPELLED		HOW WELL I DID	
		Pretest	Posttest	Showed Improvement	Mastered Words
UNIT 1	Lesson 1			☺	☺
	Lesson 2			☺	☺
	Lesson 3			☺	☺
	Lesson 4			☺	☺
	Lesson 5	Practice Test		☺	☺
UNIT 2	Lesson 6			☺	☺
	Lesson 7			☺	☺
	Lesson 8			☺	☺
	Lesson 9			☺	☺
	Lesson 10			☺	☺
	Lesson 11	Practice Test		☺	☺
UNIT 3	Lesson 12			☺	☺
	Lesson 13			☺	☺
	Lesson 14			☺	☺
	Lesson 15			☺	☺
	Lesson 16			☺	☺
	Lesson 17	Practice Test		☺	☺
UNIT 4	Lesson 18			☺	☺
	Lesson 19			☺	☺
	Lesson 20			☺	☺
	Lesson 21			☺	☺
	Lesson 22			☺	☺
	Lesson 23	Practice Test		☺	☺
UNIT 5	Lesson 24			☺	☺
	Lesson 25			☺	☺
	Lesson 26			☺	☺
	Lesson 27			☺	☺
	Lesson 28			☺	☺
	Lesson 29	Practice Test		☺	☺
UNIT 6	Lesson 30			☺	☺
	Lesson 31			☺	☺
	Lesson 32			☺	☺
	Lesson 33			☺	☺
	Lesson 34			☺	☺
	Lesson 35	Practice Test		☺	☺

Directions: Write in pretest, posttest, and Practice Test scores. If a child shows improvement but has missed one or more items, circle the smiling face under *Showed Improvement.* For perfect scores, circle the smiling face under *Mastered Words.*

Harcourt Brace School Publishers

Class Record-Keeping Chart

NAME	LESSON		LESSON		LESSON		LESSON		LESSON		REVIEW LESSON	
	Pretest	Posttest	Pretest	Posttest	Pretest	Posttest	Pretest	Posttest	Pretest	Posttest	Practice	Test
1.												
2.												
3.												
4.												
5.												
6.												
7.												
8.												
9.												
10.												
11.												
12.												
13.												
14.												
15.												
16.												
17.												
18.												
19.												
20.												
21.												
22.												
23.												
24.												
25.												
26.												
27.												
28.												
29.												
30.												
31.												
32.												
33.												
34.												
35.												

Directions: Make six copies of this page, and use one copy with each unit.

Harcourt Brace School Publishers

Spelling Words

1. an
2. bad
3. bat
4. map
5. had
6. dad
7. sat
8. sad
9. cat
10. mad

YOUR OWN WORDS

11. _____
12. _____

Words to Explore

field

practice

team

turn

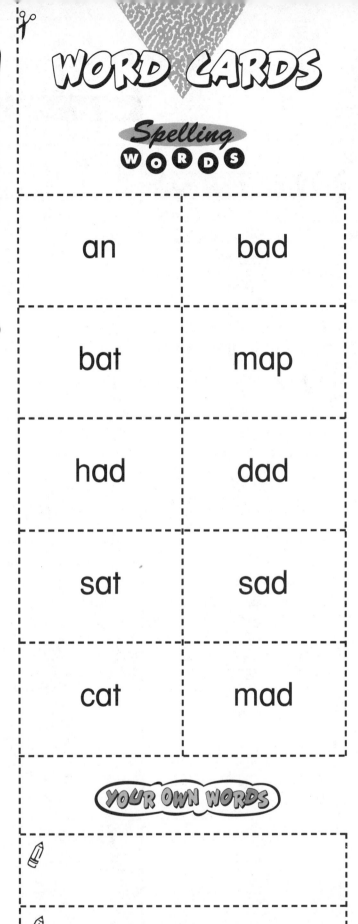

Home Spelling Activity

Use the Spelling Words to play a sorting
game with your child. Set a time limit, such
as two minutes, for putting the words in
groups. Your child might make groups of
words that rhyme or groups of words that
begin or end with the same letter.

WORD CARDS

Spelling WORDS

an	bad
bat	map
had	dad
sat	sad
cat	mad

YOUR OWN WORDS

SIDEWALKS SING "Ronald Morgan Goes to Bat" • Harcourt Brace School Publishers

Name _____

Spelling Practice

A. Study the Spelling Words. Say each word to yourself. Write the words that rhyme with <u>pad</u> under the pad. Write the other words under the pencil. Circle the letter that spells the vowel sound in each word.

_____   _____

_____   _____

_____   _____

_____   _____

_____   _____

B. Write the Words to Explore in the correct places.

1. 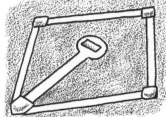   2.

_____   _____

3. The children _____ baseball.

4. Each one gets a _____ to bat.

Spelling WORDS

1. an
2. bad
3. bat
4. map
5. had
6. dad
7. sat
8. sad
9. cat
10. mad

Words to Explore

field

practice

team

turn

Spelling Words

1. bet
2. men
3. egg
4. yes
5. ten
6. mess
7. wet
8. leg
9. set
10. yet

YOUR OWN WORDS

11. _____
12. _____

Words to Explore

began

bike

brave

once

Home Spelling Activity

Use the Spelling Words to play a sorting
game with your child. Set a time limit, such
as two minutes, for putting the words in
groups. Your child might group words that
rhyme, words that begin or end with the same
letter, words with double letters, or words that
name things.

WORD CARDS

Spelling WORDS

bet	men
egg	yes
ten	mess
wet	leg
set	yet

YOUR OWN WORDS

SIDEWALKS SING "Matthew and Tilly" • Harcourt Brace School Publishers

Name _____

Spelling Practice

A. Study the Spelling Words. Say each word to yourself. Then circle and write the Spelling Word hidden in each group of letters.

1. sewett _____

2. beggen _____

3. menett _____

4. tetyes _____

5. ssette _____

6. messen _____

7. bgtenn _____

8. eegleg _____

9. bbette _____

10. eyetel _____

B. Write the Words to Explore to complete the sentences.

1. I have a red _____ .

2. I went riding with my friend _____ .

3. We felt _____ and rode all day.

4. When it _____ to get dark, we went home.

SIDEWALKS SING "Matthew and Tilly" • Harcourt Brace School Publishers

1. bet
2. men
3. egg
4. yes
5. ten
6. mess
7. wet
8. leg
9. set
10. yet

Words to Explore

began

bike

brave

once

Dear Parent or Guardian,

Your child _____
has just begun a lesson on spelling words
with the short *i* vowel sound. This week's
test of words _____ will be
on _____ .

Please contact me if you have any
questions.

Sincerely,

_____

Spelling Words

1. pin
2. sit
3. if
4. fix
5. hid
6. him
7. hill
8. six
9. win
10. bit

YOUR OWN WORDS

11. _____

12. _____

Words to Explore

dollar

earn

phone

work

Home Spelling Activity

Use the Spelling Words to play a sorting
game with your child. Set a time limit, such
as two minutes, for putting the words in
groups. Your child might group words that
rhyme, words that name things, or words that
tell actions you can do.

WORD CARDS

Spelling WORDS

pin	sit
if	fix
hid	him
hill	six
win	bit

YOUR OWN WORDS

SIDEWALKS SING "Arthur's Pet Business" • Harcourt Brace School Publishers

Spelling Practice

A. Study the Spelling Words. Say each word to yourself. Write the words in the correct shapes. Then answer the questions.

1.

2.

3.

4.

Which two words have this shape?

5. _____   6. _____

Which two words have this shape?

7. _____   8. _____

Which other two words have the same shape?

9. _____   10. _____

B. Write the Words to Explore to answer the questions.

Which word . . .

1. names a kind of money? _____

2. is short for <u>telephone</u>? _____

3. rhymes with <u>turn</u>? _____

4. tells what you do to make money? _____

SIDEWALKS SING "Arthur's Pet Business" • Harcourt Brace School Publishers

Integrated Spelling

Spelling WORDS

1. pin
2. sit
3. if
4. fix
5. hid
6. him
7. hill
8. six
9. win
10. bit

Words to Explore

dollar

earn

phone

work

Dear Parent or Guardian,

Your child _____
has just begun a lesson on spelling words
with the short o vowel sound. This week's
test of words _____ will be
on _____ .

Please contact me if you have any
questions.

Sincerely,

_____

Spelling Words

YOUR OWN WORDS

1. top
2. lot
3. mom
4. doll
5. rock
6. box
7. stop
8. pond
9. job
10. fox

11. _____

12. _____

Words to Explore

listen

sound

touch

gentle

Home Spelling Activity

Use the Spelling Words to play a sorting
game with your child. Set a time limit, such
as two minutes, for putting the words in
groups. Your child might make groups of
words that rhyme, words that have the same
number of letters, or words that name things.

WORD CARDS

Spelling WORDS

top	lot
mom	doll
rock	box
stop	pond
job	fox

YOUR OWN WORDS

Spelling Practice

A. Study the Spelling Words. Say each word to yourself. Use the letters in the musical notes to write Spelling Words.

1. top
2. lot
3. mom
4. doll
5. rock
6. box
7. stop
8. pond
9. job
10. fox

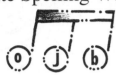

_____

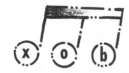

_____

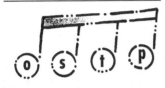

_____

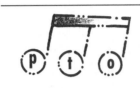

_____

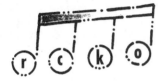

_____

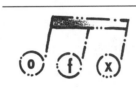

_____

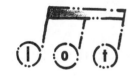

_____

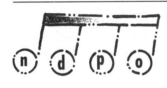

_____

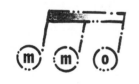

_____

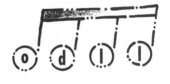

_____

B. Write the Words to Explore to complete the sentences.

1. I _____ to the wind.

2. It makes a whistling _____ .

3. I wish I could _____ the wind.

4. Would it be _____ in my hands?

Words
to Explore
· · · · · · · · · · · · ·
listen
sound
touch
gentle

Rhyme Time

Use a rhyming word strategy to spell the names for the pictures.

1.     2.

   ten   _____   stop   _____

3.     4.

   peg   _____   net   _____

Find the misspelled word in each rhyme. Circle it. Then write it correctly.

1. The day I had
   was very bade.

   _____

2. I'll give you a pin
   if you wen.

   _____

3. We have a lat
   of things to jot.

   _____

4. Can you site
   and stay a bit?

   _____

5. If you are sixe,
   you have to mix.

   _____

6. My name is Rob.
   I do my jeb.

   _____

SIDEWALKS SING Unit 1 Review • Harcourt Brace School Publishers

A Special Treat

You worked all month and saved a lot of money.
Now you can treat yourself to a special prize.
Your mom takes you to a store and . . .

Write about where you go and what you buy
there. Use at least three of the Words to Watch For.

_____

_____

_____

_____

_____

_____

_____

_____

_____

Words
to Watch For

**These are words that
can help you in your
writing. Be on the
lookout for them and
spell them correctly!**

aunt

bought

people

snow

store

time

Dear Parent or Guardian,

Your child _____
has just begun a lesson on spelling words
with the short *u* vowel sound. This week's
test of words _____ will be
on _____ .

Please contact me if you have any
questions.

Sincerely,

_____

Spelling Words

1. us
2. cup
3. dug
4. much
5. duck
6. mud
7. bus
8. cut
9. must
10. jump

YOUR OWN WORDS

11. _____
12. _____

Words to Explore

delicious

stew

perfect

cookies

Home Spelling Activity

Use the Spelling Words to play a sorting
game with your child. Set a time limit, such
as two minutes, for putting the words in
groups. Your child might group words that
have the same number of letters, words that
begin with the same letter, words that name
things, or words that tell actions you can do.

WORD CARDS

Spelling WORDS

us	cup
dug	much
duck	mud
bus	cut
must	jump

YOUR OWN WORDS

Spelling Practice

A. Study the Spelling Words. Say each word to yourself. Write the words with the CVC pattern under <u>CVC</u>. Write the other words in the column at the right. Circle the letter that spells the vowel sound in each word.

CVC	Other
_____	_____
_____	_____
_____	_____
_____	_____
_____	_____

1. __us__
2. __cup__
3. __dug__
4. __much__
5. __duck__
6. __mud__
7. __bus__
8. __cut__
9. __must__
10. __jump__

B. Label each picture with a Word to Explore. Then use the other Words to Explore in sentences about the pictures.

1. _____

2. _____

3. _____

_____

4. _____

_____

Words to Explore
....
delicious
stew
perfect
cookies

Spelling Words

1. by
2. told
3. me
4. try
5. kind
6. cold
7. my
8. most
9. child
10. both

YOUR OWN WORDS

11. _____
12. _____

Words to Explore

family

company

uncle

familiar

Home Spelling Activity

Use the Spelling Words to play a sorting game
with your child. Set a time limit, such as two
minutes, for putting the words in groups. Your
child might group words that have the same
number of letters, words that begin with the
same letter, or words with the same vowel sound.

WORD CARDS

Spelling WORDS

by	told
me	try
kind	cold
my	most
child	both

YOUR OWN WORDS

SIDEWALKS SING "Everett Anderson's Friend" • Harcourt Brace School Publishers

Spelling Practice

SIDEWALKS SING "Everett Anderson's Friend" • Harcourt Brace School Publishers

A. Study the Spelling Words. Say each word to yourself. Write each word where it belongs. Circle the letter that spells the vowel sound in each word.

long i spelled y

_____

_____

_____

long i spelled i

_____

long o

_____

_____

_____

long e

_____

B. Write the Words to Explore to complete the puzzles.

1. <u>Across</u>
   to be known
   <u>Down</u>
   group of people

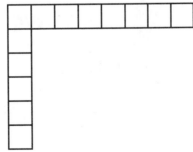

2. <u>Across</u>
   people visiting
   <u>Down</u>
   parent's brother

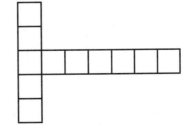

Integrated Spelling

Spelling WORDS

1. by
2. told
3. me
4. try
5. kind
6. cold
7. my
8. most
9. child
10. both

Words to Explore
....
family
company
uncle
familiar

Spelling Words

1. may
2. rain
3. say
4. wait
5. pay
6. train
7. lay
8. laid
9. way
10. tail

YOUR OWN WORDS

11. _____

12. _____

Words to Explore

package

gigantic

tape

problem

Home Spelling Activity

Use the Spelling Words to play a sorting
game with your child. Set a time limit, such
as two minutes, for putting the words in
groups. Your child might group words with
ay and *ai*, words that begin with the same
letter, words that rhyme, or action words.

WORD CARDS

Spelling WORDS

may	rain
say	wait
pay	train
lay	laid
way	tail

YOUR OWN WORDS

SIDEWALKS SING "Mitchell Is Moving" • Harcourt Brace School Publishers

Name _____

Spelling Practice

A. Study the Spelling Words. Say each word to yourself. Write each word in the web that has the same spelling for long <u>a</u>. Circle the letters that spell the vowel sound in each word.

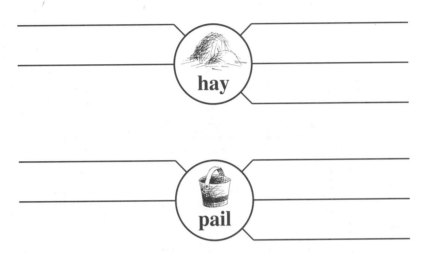

hay

pail

B. Look at the pictures. Write each Word to Explore next to the correct picture.

_____

_____

_____

_____

Spelling
W O R D S

1. may
2. rain
3. say
4. wait
5. pay
6. train
7. lay
8. laid
9. way
10. tail

Words
to Explore
· · · · · · · · · · · ·
package

gigantic

tape

problem

Dear Parent or Guardian,

Your child _____
has just begun a lesson on spelling words
with the long e vowel sound. This week's
test of words _____ will be
on _____ .

Please contact me if you have any
questions.

Sincerely,

_____

Spelling Words

1. need
2. read
3. deep
4. eat
5. keep
6. team
7. feet
8. each
9. feel
10. seat

YOUR OWN WORDS

11. _____
12. _____

Words to Explore

toss

toward

fair

shoot

Home Spelling Activity

Use the Spelling Words to play a sorting
game with your child. Set a time limit, such
as two minutes, for putting the words in
groups. Your child might group words with *ee*
and *ea*, words that begin with the same letter,
action words, or naming words.

WORD CARDS

Spelling WORDS

need	read
deep	eat
keep	team
feet	each
feel	seat

YOUR OWN WORDS

SIDEWALKS SING "Jamaica Tag-Along" • Harcourt Brace School Publishers

Name _____

Spelling Practice

A. Study the Spelling Words. Say each word to yourself. Write each word below the word that has the same spelling for long e. Circle the letters that spell the vowel sound in each word.

weed

bean

_____   _____

_____   _____

_____   _____

_____   _____

_____   _____

B. Write the Words to Explore to complete the sentences.

1. First you dribble _____ the basket.

2. Then you _____ the ball to a teammate.

3. Your teammate will _____ for a basket.

4. You play by the rules so the game is _____.

SIDEWALKS SING "Jamaica Tag-Along" • Harcourt Brace School Publishers

Spelling W O R D S

1. need
2. read
3. deep
4. eat
5. keep
6. team
7. feet
8. each
9. feel
10. seat

Words **to Explore**

toss

toward

fair

shoot

Practice Activities 9B • T273

Dear Parent or Guardian,

Your child _____
has just begun a lesson on spelling words
with the long *o* vowel sound. This week's
test of words _____ will be
on _____.

Please contact me if you have any
questions.

Sincerely,

_____

Spelling Words

YOUR OWN WORDS

1. boat
2. row
3. show
4. coal
5. coat
6. slow
7. coast
8. own
9. low
10. road

11. _____
12. _____

Words to Explore

above

adventure

glide

soar

Home Spelling Activity

Use the Spelling Words to play a sorting
game with your child. Set a time limit, such
as two minutes, for putting the words in
groups. Your child might group words with
oa and *ow,* words that rhyme, naming words,
or words with the same number of letters.

WORD CARDS

Spelling WORDS

boat	row
show	coal
coat	slow
coast	own
low	road

YOUR OWN WORDS

SIDEWALKS SING "Abuela" • Harcourt Brace School Publishers

Spelling Practice

A. Study the Spelling Words. Say each word to yourself. Write each word below the word that has the same spelling for long <u>o</u>. Circle the letters that spell the vowel sound in each word.

bow

goat

_____   _____

_____   _____

_____   _____

_____   _____

B. Write the Words to Explore to complete the sentences. Use the word shapes to help you.

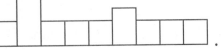

1. We will go on an _____ .

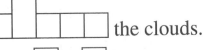

2. We will _____ into the sky.

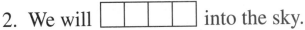

3. We will fly _____ the clouds.

4. Then we will _____ down to land in a tree.

What are we? _____

Spelling
W O R D S

1. boat
2. row
3. show
4. coal
5. coat
6. slow
7. coast
8. own
9. low
10. road

Words to Explore
....
above
adventure
glide
soar

SIDEWALKS SING "Abuela" • Harcourt Brace School Publishers

Rhyme Time

Write a review word from the box to complete each rhyme.

The bus is late.
We have to

_____ .

Would you like a peach?
We can have one

_____ .

Touch this peel.
How does it

_____ ?

Read the note. Circle each misspelled word. Write the words
correctly on the lines.

Dear Diary,
Today we went to the coaste. For mste of the day,
we had a lot of fun. But then it started to rane.
We had to jomp up and run to the car. Then Mom
and Dad took me out to eet. They tolde me I could
have whatever I wanted. I got the best kynd of
food. We mai go back to the beach next week!

_____   _____   _____   _____

_____   _____   _____   _____

SIDEWALKS SING Unit 2 Review • Harcourt Brace School Publishers

Integrated Spelling

I'm on Vacation!

You are on a vacation with your family. Write a letter to your friend. Tell where you are. Then tell about all the fun things you are doing. Use at least three of the Words to Watch For.

_____

_____

_____

_____

_____

_____

_____

_____

Now draw a picture of you and your family.

Words to Watch For

These are words that can help you in your writing. Be on the lookout for them and spell them correctly!

always

am

brother

father

mother

writing

Now I will always remember how to spell <u>brother</u>!

Dear Parent or Guardian,

   Your child _____
has just begun a lesson on spelling words
with the long a and long i vowel sounds.
This week's test of words _____
will be on _____.

   Please contact me if you have any
questions.

                   Sincerely,

                   _____

Spelling Words

1. take
2. fire
3. made
4. five
5. game
6. life
7. late
8. nice
9. make
10. side

YOUR OWN WORDS

11. _____

12. _____

Words to Explore

caught

discover

cough

medicine

Home Spelling Activity

Use the Spelling Words to play a sorting
game with your child. Set a time limit, such
as two minutes, for putting the words in
groups. Your child might group words with
long *a* and long *i,* words that begin with the
same letter, or action words.

WORD CARDS

Spelling WORDS

take	fire
made	five
game	life
late	nice
make	side

YOUR OWN WORDS

SIDEWALKS SING "Six-Dinner Sid" • Harcourt Brace School Publishers

Spelling Practice

A. Study the Spelling Words. Say each word to yourself. Write each word below the word that has the same vowel sound.

cake   **bike**

_____   _____

_____   _____

_____   _____

_____   _____

_____   _____

B. Write the Words to Explore in the sentences.

1. I had a bad _____, so I went to the doctor.

2. What did I _____?

3. I had _____ a bad cold.

4. The doctor gave me _____ and sent me home.

Spelling WORDS

1. take
2. fire
3. made
4. five
5. game
6. life
7. late
8. nice
9. make
10. side

Words to Explore

caught

discover

cough

medicine

Spelling Words

1. bone
2. mule
3. nose
4. huge
5. use
6. note
7. rope
8. cute
9. woke
10. hope

YOUR OWN WORDS

11. _____

12. _____

Words to Explore

decide

plan

move

people

Home Spelling Activity

Use the Spelling Words to play a sorting game
with your child. Set a time limit, such as two
minutes, for putting the words in groups. Your
child might group words with long *o* and
long *u,* words that begin with the same letter,
or words that are the same part of speech.

WORD CARDS

Spelling WORDS

bone	mule
nose	huge
use	note
rope	cute
woke	hope

YOUR OWN WORDS

Name _____

Spelling Practice

A. Study the Spelling Words. Say each word to yourself. Write the long <u>o</u> words in the home and the long <u>u</u> words in the tulips.

1. _bone_
2. _mule_
3. _nose_
4. _huge_
5. _use_
6. _note_
7. _rope_
8. _cute_
9. _woke_
10. _hope_

B. Use the Words to Explore to complete the puzzles.

1. <u>Across</u>
   more than one person
   <u>Down</u>
   idea

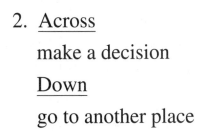

2. <u>Across</u>
   make a decision
   <u>Down</u>
   go to another place

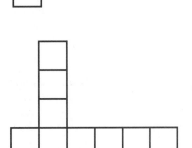

Words
to Explore
· · · · · · · · ·
decide

plan

move

people

Dear Parent or Guardian,

Your child _____ has just begun a lesson on spelling words that have consonant clusters with *l*, *r*, and *t*. This week's test of words _____ will be on _____.

Please contact me if you have any questions.

Sincerely,

_____

Spelling Words

1. from
2. dry
3. still
4. fast
5. blow
6. grass
7. sled
8. stood
9. last
10. fly

YOUR OWN WORDS

11. _____
12. _____

Words to Explore

gather

join

tune

play

Home Spelling Activity

Use the Spelling Words to play a sorting game with your child. Set a time limit, such as two minutes, for putting the words in groups. Your child might group words that begin or end with clusters with *l*, *r*, or *t*.

WORD CARDS

Spelling WORDS

from	dry
still	fast
blow	grass
sled	stood
last	fly

YOUR OWN WORDS

Spelling Practice

A. Study the Spelling Words. Say each word to yourself. Use the letters from the penguins to make Spelling Words. Write the words.

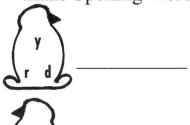 _____

 _____

 _____

 _____

 _____

 _____

 _____

 _____

B. Write the Words to Explore to complete the sentences.

1. The pigs will _____ under the tree.

2. They will _____ their instruments.

3. Why don't you _____ in?

4. You can play a _____ on your flute.

SIDEWALKS SING "Little Penguin's Tale" • Harcourt Brace School Publishers

Integrated Spelling

Spelling WORDS

1. from
2. dry
3. still
4. fast
5. blow
6. grass
7. sled
8. stood
9. last
10. fly

Words to Explore
....
gather

join

tune

play

Dear Parent or Guardian,

Your child _____
has just begun a lesson on spelling words
with final double consonants. This week's
test of words _____ will be
on _____.

Please contact me if you have any
questions.

Sincerely,

_____

Spelling Words

1. ball
2. add
3. miss
4. all
5. dress
6. fall
7. less
8. call
9. pass
10. glass

YOUR OWN WORDS

11. _____
12. _____

Words to Explore

celebrate

festival

important

fiesta

Home Spelling Activity

Use the Spelling Words to play a sorting game
with your child. Set a time limit, such as two
minutes, for putting the words in groups. Your
child might group words that end with the
double consonants *ll, ss,* or *dd;* naming words;
or action words.

WORD CARDS

Spelling WORDS

ball	add
miss	all
dress	fall
less	call
pass	glass

YOUR OWN WORDS

SIDEWALKS SING "Fiesta!" • Harcourt Brace School Publishers

Spelling Practice

A. Study the Spelling Words. Say each word to yourself. Write the words below the picture whose name ends with the same double consonants.

_____   _____

_____   _____

_____   _____

_____   _____

_____

What Spelling Word is left? _____

B. Write the Words to Explore to complete the sentences.

1. The Spanish word _____

   means "_____."

2. People come together to _____

   on _____ holidays.

Spelling
W O R D S

1. ball
2. add
3. miss
4. all
5. dress
6. fall
7. less
8. call
9. pass
10. glass

Words
to Explore
. . . .
celebrate
festival
important
fiesta

Spelling Words

1. ship
2. rich
3. wash
4. change
5. shop
6. chest
7. fish
8. reach
9. wish
10. shape

YOUR OWN WORDS

11. _____

12. _____

Words to Explore

favorite

balloon

brought

round

Home Spelling Activity

Use the Spelling Words to play a sorting
game with your child. Set a time limit, such
as two minutes, for putting the words in
groups. Your child might group words that
begin with *sh*, end with *sh*, begin with *ch*, or
end with *ch*.

WORD CARDS

Spelling WORDS

ship	rich
wash	change
shop	chest
fish	reach
wish	shape

YOUR OWN WORDS

SIDEWALKS SING "Miss Eva and the Red Balloon" • Harcourt Brace School Publishers

Spelling Practice

A. Study the Spelling Words. Say each word to yourself. Circle the Spelling Word in each group of letters. Then write the Spelling Word.

shchest

_____

ocshoph

_____

cshiphi

_____

washcha

_____

schange

_____

richsh

_____

wicwish

_____

ficfish

_____

ereachr

_____

cshapeh

_____

B. Write the Words to Explore in the correct place.

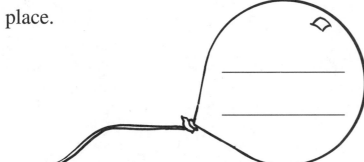

_____

_____

1. The clown _____ balloons to my party.

2. The purple one was my _____ .

Spelling
W O R D S

1. ship
2. rich
3. wash
4. change
5. shop
6. chest
7. fish
8. reach
9. wish
10. shape

Words **to Explore**
. . . .
favorite
balloon
brought
round

This Old Mule

Read the sentences that tell about the pictures. Circle each misspelled word. Write the words correctly on the lines at the bottom.

It is lat.

The man will mak a firr.

Bobo the mul wants to eat.

_____   _____

_____   _____

Bobo can reash fiv bags.

Bobo's nos is in one of them.

_____   _____   _____

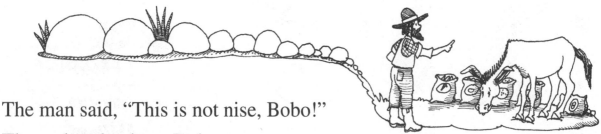

The man said, "This is not nise, Bobo!"

Then a bug lands on Bobo.

Bobo will yuse its tail to get the fli.

_____   _____   _____

SIDEWALKS SING Unit 3 Review • Harcourt Brace School Publishers

Block Party

Your neighborhood had a huge block party. Your job is to write a story for a newspaper telling about the party. Write the news story. Tell about the party! Make sure to tell why the neighborhood had the party, what fun things you did at the party, and what the neighborhood looked like during the party. Use at least three Words to Watch For.

_____

_____

_____

_____

_____

_____

_____

Last Saturday my neighborhood had a block party. It was a huge party!

SIDEWALKS SING Unit 3 Review • Harcourt Brace School Publishers

Words to Watch For

These are words that can help you in your writing. Be on the lookout for them and spell them correctly!

and
balloon
cousin
house
make
Thanksgiving

Dear Parent or Guardian,

Your child _____
has just begun a lesson on spelling
words with *th, wh,* and *ng*. This week's
test of words _____ will be
on _____.

Please contact me if you have any
questions.

Sincerely,

_____

Spelling Words

1. long
2. they
3. which
4. bath
5. ring
6. them
7. while
8. math
9. those
10. than

YOUR OWN WORDS

11. _____

12. _____

Words to Explore

stretch

angry

awful

snore

Home Spelling Activity

Use the Spelling Words to play a sorting game
with your child. Set a time limit, such as two
minutes, for putting the words in groups. Your
child might group words that begin with *th,*
end with *th,* begin with *wh,* or end with *ng.*

WORD CARDS

Spelling WORDS

long	they
which	bath
ring	them
while	math
those	than

YOUR OWN WORDS

Spelling Practice

A. Study the Spelling Words. Say each word to yourself. Write each word below the word that begins or ends with the same letters. Circle the letters <u>th</u>, <u>wh</u>, or <u>ng</u> in each word.

there

_____

_____

_____

_____

path

_____

_____

wing

_____

_____

whale

_____

_____

B. Write each Word to Explore under the picture it best describes.

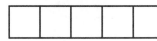

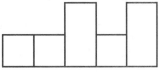

ALL KINDS OF FRIENDS "Awful Aardvark" • Harcourt Brace School Publishers

1. long
2. they
3. which
4. bath
5. ring
6. them
7. while
8. math
9. those
10. than

Words **to Explore**

stretch

angry

awful

snore

Dear Parent or Guardian,

Your child _____
has just begun a lesson on spelling
words with *c*, *k*, and *ck*. This week's test
of words _____ will be
on _____.

Please contact me if you have any
questions.

Sincerely,

_____

Spelling Words

1. car
2. book
3. stick
4. kick
5. took
6. care
7. track
8. black
9. neck
10. pack

11. _____
12. _____

Words to Explore

cozy

milk

lively

burrow

Home Spelling Activity

Use the Spelling Words to play a sorting
game with your child. Set a time limit, such
as two minutes, for putting the words in
groups. Your child might group words that
begin with *c*, end with *k*, or end with *ck*.

WORD CARDS

Spelling WORDS

car	book
stick	kick
took	care
track	black
neck	pack

YOUR OWN WORDS

Spelling Practice

A. Study the Spelling Words. Say each word to yourself. Use the Spelling Words to complete the puzzles. The letters already in the puzzles will help you.

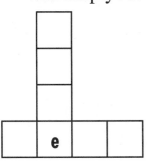

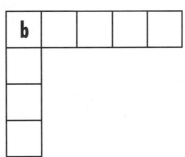

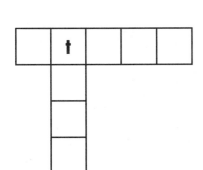

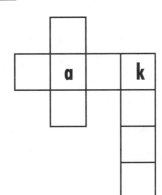

What Spelling Word is left? _____

B. Write the Words to Explore to complete the sentences.

1. The sleeping kitten looks _____.

2. The playful kitten is _____.

3. The hungry kitten drinks _____.

4. The curious kitten sticks its paw in the animal's _____.

Spelling WORDS

1. car
2. book
3. stick
4. kick
5. took
6. care
7. track
8. black
9. neck
10. pack

Words to Explore

cozy

milk

lively

burrow

Dear Parent or Guardian,

Your child _____
has just begun a lesson on spelling
contractions with *is, are, will,* and *am.* This
week's test of words _____
will be on _____.

Please contact me if you have any
questions.

Sincerely,

_____

Spelling Words

1. he's
2. we're
3. I'm
4. she's
5. they're
6. I'll
7. you're
8. that's
9. there's
10. what's

YOUR OWN WORDS

11. _____
12. _____

Words to Explore

throwing

squawking

boring

excited

Home Spelling Activity

Use the Spelling Words to play a sorting
game with your child. Set a time limit, such
as two minutes, for putting the words in
groups. Your child might group contractions
with *is* and *are,* words with the same number
of letters, contractions with *I,* or contractions
that begin with the same letters.

WORD CARDS

he's	we're
I'm	she's
they're	I'll
you're	that's
there's	what's

YOUR OWN WORDS

✏ _____

✏ _____

ALL KINDS OF FRIENDS "The Day Jimmy's Boa Ate the Wash" • Harcourt Brace School Publishers

Spelling Practice

A. Study the Spelling Words. Say each word to yourself. Write each contraction below the word from which it was formed.

is	are
_____	_____
_____	_____
_____	_____
_____	
_____	

will	am
_____	_____

B. Write the Words to Explore to complete the sentences.

1. The chickens are _____ loudly.

2. The children are _____ baseballs.

3. The farmer is jumping up and down because he is _____ .

4. Life on the farm is not _____ !

Spelling WORDS

1. he's
2. we're
3. I'm
4. she's
5. they're
6. I'll
7. you're
8. that's
9. there's
10. what's

Words to Explore

throwing
squawking
boring
excited

Dear Parent or Guardian,

Your child _____
has just begun a lesson on spelling
words with *oo, ew,* and *ou.* This week's
test of words _____ will be
on _____.

Please contact me if you have any
questions.

Sincerely,

_____

Spelling Words

YOUR OWN WORDS

1. soon
2. grew
3. you
4. room
5. new
6. group
7. school
8. flew
9. food
10. drew

11. _____
12. _____

Words to Explore

change

larger

member

mammal

Home Spelling Activity

Use the Spelling Words to play a sorting
game with your child. Set a time limit, such
as two minutes, for putting the words in
groups. Your child might group words that
are spelled with *oo, ew,* and *ou;* words with
the same number of letters; or words that
begin or end the same.

WORD CARDS

Spelling WORDS

soon	grew
you	room
new	group
school	flew
food	drew

YOUR OWN WORDS

ALL KINDS OF FRIENDS "A Dinosaur Named after Me" • Harcourt Brace School Publishers

Integrated Spelling

Spelling Practice

A. Study the Spelling Words. Say each word to yourself. Write each Spelling Word below the word that has the vowel sound spelled the same way. Circle the letters that spell the vowel sound in each word.

blew 　　　　**moon**

_____　　_____

_____　　_____

_____　　_____

_____　　_____

soup

_____

B. Write the Words to Explore to complete the sentences.

1. An elephant is a _____.

2. It is _____ than a hare.

3. A hare is a _____ of the mammal family, too.

4. Some hares _____ color in winter.

ALL KINDS OF FRIENDS "A Dinosaur Named after Me" • Harcourt Brace School Publishers

Integrated Spelling

Spelling WORDS

1. soon
2. grew
3. you
4. room
5. new
6. group
7. school
8. flew
9. food
10. drew

Words to Explore

change

larger

member

mammal

Dear Parent or Guardian,

Your child _____
has just begun a lesson on spelling words
with long *i* spelled *igh* and *y*. This week's
test of words _____ will be
on _____.

Please contact me if you have any
questions.

Sincerely,

_____

Spelling Words

YOUR OWN WORDS

1. high
2. cry
3. night
4. sky
5. fight
6. right
7. light
8. sight
9. bright
10. might

11. _____
12. _____

Words to Explore

against

avoid

furious

trouble

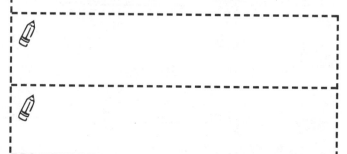

Home Spelling Activity

Use the Spelling Words to play a sorting game
with your child. Set a time limit, such as two
minutes, for putting the words in groups. Your
child might group words that are spelled with
igh and *y*, words with the same number of
letters, words that rhyme, or words that are the
same part of speech.

WORD CARDS

Spelling WORDS

high	cry
night	sky
fight	right
light	sight
bright	might

YOUR OWN WORDS

Spelling Practice

A. Study the Spelling Words. Say each word to yourself. Write each word below its shape. Circle the letter or letters that spell the long <u>i</u> sound in each word.

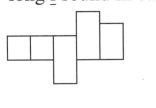

_____

_____

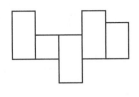

_____

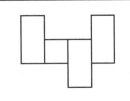

_____

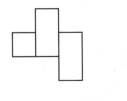

_____

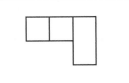

_____

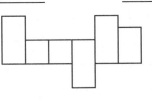

_____

B. Write the Words to Explore to complete the sentences.

1. If I'm very angry, I'm _____.

2. Then you should _____ me.

3. Don't try to fight _____ me.

4. We will both get into _____!

Integrated Spelling

ALL KINDS OF FRIENDS "Tyrone the Horrible" • Harcourt Brace School Publishers

Spelling WORDS

1. high
2. cry
3. night
4. sky
5. fight
6. right
7. light
8. sight
9. bright
10. might

Words to Explore

against

avoid

furious

trouble

Dog Talk

In each sentence, circle the two words that can be made into a contraction. Then write the contraction.

1. What is Karen doing with five dogs? _____

2. I think she is taking them for a walk. _____

3. Five dogs! I think I will go and help her! _____

Read the words. Circle the one that is spelled correctly. Then write it to complete the sentence.

 bath   baff   schewl   school

Woof takes a _____.   Patches goes to _____.

 pak   pack    night   nite

Barker carries my _____.   Spot sings every _____.

            Integrated Spelling

ALL KINDS OF FRIENDS Unit 4 Review • Harcourt Brace School Publishers

Lost and Found

You lost your pet! Make a poster to hang up. Draw a picture of your pet. Then write about your pet. Tell what kind of pet you lost, where you lost it, and what it looks like. Be creative. Choose an unusual pet! Use at least three Words to Watch For.

ALL KINDS OF FRIENDS Unit 4 Review • Harcourt Brace School Publishers

Words **to Watch For**

These are words that can help you in your writing. Be on the lookout for them and spell them correctly!

didn't
dog
everybody
fun
know
that's

Integrated Spelling

Dear Parent or Guardian,

Your child _____
has just begun a lesson on spelling
words with the vowel sound heard in *arm*
and *heart*. This week's test of words
_____ will be on _____.
Please contact me if you have any
questions.

Sincerely,

_____

Spelling Words

1. arm

2. are

3. far

4. heart

5. dark

6. hard

7. farm

8. park

9. start

10. part

YOUR OWN WORDS

11. _____

12. _____

Words to Explore

material

sewing

scissors

thread

Home Spelling Activity

Use the Spelling Words to play a sorting
game with your child. Set a time limit, such
as two minutes, for putting the words in
groups. Your child might group words that
have the letters *ar* at the beginning, in the
middle, and at the end; words with the same
number of letters; or words that rhyme.

WORD CARDS

Spelling WORDS

arm	are
far	heart
dark	hard
farm	park
start	part

YOUR OWN WORDS

ALL KINDS OF FRIENDS "The Chalk Doll" • Harcourt Brace School Publishers

Integrated Spelling

Name _____

Spelling Practice

A. Study the Spelling Words. Say each word to yourself. Use the letters in each heart to spell a Spelling Word.

 _____

 _____

_____

 _____

 _____

 _____

 _____

_____   _____

 _____

ALL KINDS OF FRIENDS "The Chalk Doll" • Harcourt Brace School Publishers

B. Write the Words to Explore under their pictures.

_____   _____

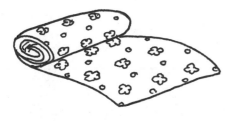

_____   _____

1. __arm__
2. __are__
3. __far__
4. __heart__
5. __dark__
6. __hard__
7. __farm__
8. __park__
9. __start__
10. __part__

Words
to Explore
. . . .
material
sewing
scissors
thread

Spelling Words

1. store
2. or
3. door
4. more
5. corn
6. horse
7. floor
8. short
9. born
10. sort

YOUR OWN WORDS

11. _____

12. _____

Words to Explore

artist

painting

colors

finished

Home Spelling Activity

Use the Spelling Words to play a sorting
game with your child. Set a time limit, such
as two minutes, for putting the words in
groups. Your child might group words that
have the letters *ore, or,* and *oor;* words with
the same number of letters; or words that are
the same part of speech.

WORD CARDS

Spelling WORDS

store	or
door	more
corn	horse
floor	short
born	sort

YOUR OWN WORDS

ALL KINDS OF FRIENDS "The Little Painter of Sabana Grande" • Harcourt Brace School Publishers

Name _____

Spelling Practice

A. Study the Spelling Words. Say each word to yourself. Then use the Spelling Words to complete the puzzle. The letters will help you.

B. Write the Words to Explore where they belong.

_____ _____

She is using many _____.

When she is _____, she'll put the paints away.

Integrated Spelling

Spelling
W O R D S

1. _store_

2. _or_

3. _door_

4. _more_

5. _corn_

6. _horse_

7. _floor_

8. _short_

9. _born_

10. _sort_

Words
to Explore
· · · · · · · · · · · ·
artist

painting

colors

finished

Dear Parent or Guardian,

Your child _____
has just begun a lesson on spelling
contractions with *not, us,* and *have.* This
week's test of words _____
will be on _____ .

Please contact me if you have any
questions.

Sincerely,

_____

Spelling Words

1. don't
2. can't
3. let's
4. won't
5. I've
6. didn't
7. wasn't
8. couldn't
9. doesn't
10. wouldn't

YOUR OWN WORDS

11. _____
12. _____

Words to Explore

courage

clever

throne

palace

Home Spelling Activity

Use the Spelling Words to play a sorting
game with your child: Set a time limit, such
as two minutes, for putting the words in
groups. Your child might group contractions
with *not, us,* and *have;* words with the same
number of letters; or words that begin with
the same letter.

WORD CARDS

Spelling WORDS

don't	can't
let's	won't
I've	didn't
wasn't	couldn't
doesn't	wouldn't

YOUR OWN WORDS

ALL KINDS OF FRIENDS "The Empty Pot" • Harcourt Brace School Publishers

Spelling Practice

A. Study the Spelling Words. Say each word to yourself. Write each contraction under the words from which it was made.

do not   will not

_____   _____

I have   could not

_____   _____

let us   was not

_____   _____

can not   does not

_____   _____

did not   would not

_____   _____

B. Write the Words to Explore where they belong.

_____

_____

The _____ king had a lot of

_____ .

ALL KINDS OF FRIENDS "The Empty Pot" • Harcourt Brace School Publishers

Integrated Spelling

Spelling
W O R D S

1. _don't_
2. _can't_
3. _let's_
4. _won't_
5. _I've_
6. _didn't_
7. _wasn't_
8. _couldn't_
9. _doesn't_
10. _wouldn't_

Words
to Explore
• • • • • • • • • • •
courage
clever
throne
palace

Dear Parent or Guardian,

Your child _____
has just begun a lesson on homophones,
such as to, too, and two. This week's test
of words _____ will be
on _____.

Please contact me if you have any
questions.

Sincerely,

_____

Spelling Words

1. so
2. to
3. for
4. there
5. sew
6. two
7. four
8. their
9. sow
10. too

YOUR OWN WORDS

11. _____
12. _____

Words to Explore

flavor

taste

supper

kettle

Home Spelling Activity

Use the Spelling Words to play a sorting
game with your child. Set a time limit, such
as two minutes, for putting the words in
groups. Your child might group words that
sound the same or words that have the same
number of letters.

WORD CARDS

Spelling WORDS

so	to
for	there
sew	two
four	their
sow	too

YOUR OWN WORDS

Spelling Practice

A. Study the Spelling Words. Say each word to yourself. Write the words in groups of homophones.

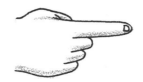

_____   _____

_____   _____

_____   _____

_____   _____

_____

1. __so__
2. __to__
3. __for__
4. __there__
5. __sew__
6. __two__
7. __four__
8. __their__
9. __sow__
10. __too__

B. Write the Words to Explore to complete the sentences.

1. Did you _____ this soup?

2. I made it for _____ .

3. I cooked it in a big _____ .

4. Do you think the soup has a good

_____ ?

Words
to Explore
· · · · · · · · · · · ·
flavor

taste

supper

kettle

Dear Parent or Guardian,

Your child _____
has just begun a lesson on words that
end with -ed or -ing. This week's test
of words _____ will be
on _____.

Please contact me if you have any
questions.

Sincerely,

_____

Spelling Words

1. asked
2. doing
3. called
4. going
5. looked
6. playing
7. started
8. trying
9. looking
10. wanted

YOUR OWN WORDS

11. _____
12. _____

Words to Explore

brilliant

light

disappear

glow

Home Spelling Activity

Use the Spelling Words to play a sorting
game with your child. Set a time limit, such
as two minutes, for putting the words in
groups. Your child might group words that
end with -ed or -ing, words with the same
number of letters, or words that have the
same vowels in them.

WORD CARDS

Spelling WORDS

asked	doing
called	going
looked	playing
started	trying
looking	wanted

YOUR OWN WORDS

Name _____

Spelling Practice

A. Study the Spelling Words. Then say the word and the ending in each pair of stars to yourself. Write the Spelling Word.

ask + ed _____

start + ed _____

do + ing _____

want + ed _____

go + ing _____

look + ing _____

call + ed _____

play + ing _____

try + ing _____

look + ed _____

B. Write the Words to Explore to complete the sentences.

1. You can get _____ from the sun.

2. At night, the sunlight will _____.

3. Then the stars will _____ in the sky.

4. The night sky will look _____.

Integrated Spelling

1. asked
2. doing
3. called
4. going
5. looked
6. playing
7. started
8. trying
9. looking
10. wanted

Words to Explore

brilliant
light
disappear
glow

ALL KINDS OF FRIENDS "The Night of the Stars" • Harcourt Brace School Publishers

Rhyme Time

Write a review word from the box to complete each rhyme.

It fell on the _____.

We'll go to the _____.

We'll buy some _____!

Write the correct spelling to complete each sentence.

to   two   too

One, _____, three, four.

I think the shoes will run _____ the store.

their   there

Look over _____!

The cat's on the chair.

sow   so   sew

I think I will _____

these pants for Joe.

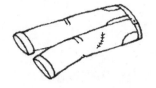

ALL KINDS OF FRIENDS Unit 5 Review • Harcourt Brace School Publishers

Integrated Spelling

Pen Pals

Pretend that you have a pen pal from another country. Write a letter to your pen pal. Tell your pen pal about your country. Ask questions that you would like answered about your pen pal's country. Use at least three Words to Watch For.

Dear Pen Pal,

_____

_____

_____

_____

_____

_____

_____

_____

Words to Watch For

These are words that can help you in your writing. Be on the lookout for them and spell them correctly!

because
children
from
now
their
today

Spelling Words

1. about
2. down
3. after
4. how
5. because
6. out
7. other
8. were
9. very
10. over

11. _____
12. _____

Words to Explore

design

weave

wool

loom

Home Spelling Activity

Use the Spelling Words to play a sorting
game with your child. Set a time limit, such
as two minutes, for putting the words in
groups. Your child might group words that
contain the letters *er, ow, ou,* or *be;* words
with the same number of letters; or words that
begin with the same letter.

WORD CARDS

Spelling WORDS

about	down
after	how
because	out
other	were
very	over

YOUR OWN WORDS

Spelling Practice

A. Study the Spelling Words. Say each word to yourself. Write each word in its shape.

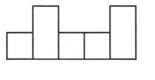
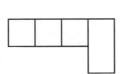

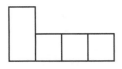

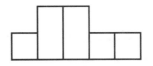

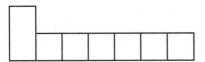

Which two words have the same shape?

_____   _____

B. Write the Words to Explore under the correct pictures.

_____   _____

_____   _____

Spelling WORDS

1. about
2. down
3. after
4. how
5. because
6. out
7. other
8. were
9. very
10. over

Words to Explore

design

weave

wool

loom

Dear Parent or Guardian,

Your child _____ has just begun a lesson on spelling compound words. This week's test of words _____ will be on _____.

Please contact me if you have any questions.

Sincerely,

_____

Spelling Words

YOUR OWN WORDS

1. upon
2. grandma
3. seesaw
4. sometimes
5. herself
6. somewhere
7. classroom
8. himself
9. baseball
10. something

11. _____
12. _____

Words to Explore

distance

lightning

storm

weather

Home Spelling Activity

Use the Spelling Words to play a sorting game with your child. Set a time limit, such as two minutes, for putting the words in groups. Your child might group words that contain the smaller word *some* or *self,* words with the same number of letters, or words that name things.

WORD CARDS

Spelling WORDS

upon	grandma
seesaw	sometimes
herself	somewhere
classroom	himself
baseball	something

YOUR OWN WORDS

ALL KINDS OF FRIENDS "Thunder Cake" • Harcourt Brace School Publishers

Spelling Practice

A. Study the Spelling Words. Say each word to yourself. Use the words in the clouds to make Spelling Words. Write the Spelling Words.

_____   _____

_____   _____

_____   _____

_____   _____

_____   _____

Spelling WORDS

1. upon
2. grandma
3. seesaw
4. sometimes
5. herself
6. somewhere
7. classroom
8. himself
9. baseball
10. something

B. Write the Words to Explore to complete the sentences.

1. A bad _____ is on its way.

2. I can see clouds in the _____.

3. There will be thunder and _____.

4. I don't like all this rainy _____!

Words to Explore

distance

lightning

storm

weather

Dear Parent or Guardian,

Your child _____
has just begun a lesson on spelling words
in which the final consonant was doubled
before the ending -ed or -ing was added.
This week's test of words _____
will be on _____.

Please contact me if you have any
questions.

Sincerely,

_____

Spelling Words

1. dropped
2. putting
3. stopped
4. getting
5. planned
6. running
7. slipped
8. sitting
9. grabbed
10. popping

YOUR OWN WORDS

11. _____
12. _____

Words to Explore

built

tunnel

carried

dug

Home Spelling Activity

Use the Spelling Words to play a sorting
game with your child. Set a time limit, such
as two minutes, for putting the words in
groups. Your child might group words that
end with *-ed* or *-ing,* words that begin with
the same letter, or words that have the same
double letters.

WORD CARDS

Spelling
WORDS

dropped	putting
stopped	getting
planned	running
slipped	sitting
grabbed	popping

YOUR OWN WORDS

ALL KINDS OF FRIENDS "Ant Cities" • Harcourt Brace School Publishers

Spelling Practice

A. Study the Spelling Words. Say each word to yourself. Then add the endings to write the Spelling Words.

ed	ing
drop _____	pop _____
stop _____	run _____
grab _____	get _____
slip _____	put _____
plan _____	sit _____

B. Write the Words to Explore to complete the sentences.

1. The ants _____ a hole in the ground.

2. Then they _____ their nest.

3. The ants _____ food through the long _____.

Spelling WORDS

1. dropped
2. putting
3. stopped
4. getting
5. planned
6. running
7. slipped
8. sitting
9. grabbed
10. popping

Words to Explore

built

tunnel

carried

dug

Spelling Words

1. saved
2. giving
3. liked
4. taking
5. used
6. riding
7. placed
8. moving
9. loved
10. living

YOUR OWN WORDS

11. _____
12. _____

Words to Explore

coast

surface

tangled

whale

Home Spelling Activity

Use the Spelling Words to play a sorting game with your child. Set a time limit, such as two minutes, for putting the words in groups. Your child might group words that end with -ed or -ing, words that begin with the same letter, words with the letter *v* in them, or words that have the same number of letters.

WORD CARDS

Spelling WORDS

saved	giving
liked	taking
used	riding
placed	moving
loved	living

YOUR OWN WORDS

Spelling Practice

A. Study the Spelling Words. Say each word to yourself. Write each word below the word with the same ending.

ALL KINDS OF FRIENDS "Ibis: A True Whale Story" • Harcourt Brace School Publishers

raking    **raked**

_____   _____

_____   _____

_____   _____

_____   _____

_____   _____

B. Write the Words to Explore to complete the sentences.

1. A _____ came up to the

   _____ of the water.

2. It was _____ in a net!

3. People in a boat left the _____

   and went to help the whale.

Spelling
W O R D S

1. saved
2. giving
3. liked
4. taking
5. used
6. riding
7. placed
8. moving
9. loved
10. living

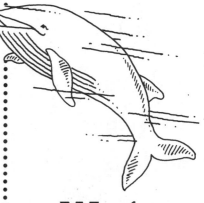

Words
to Explore
• • • • • • • • • • •
coast
surface
tangled
whale

Dear Parent or Guardian,

Your child _____ has just begun a lesson on spelling plurals. This week's test of words _____ will be on _____.

Please contact me if you have any questions.

Sincerely,

_____

Spelling Words

1. girls
2. boxes
3. toys
4. dishes
5. times
6. inches
7. boys
8. wishes
9. days
10. things

YOUR OWN WORDS

11. _____

12. _____

Words to Explore

noise

explore

finally

harmless

Home Spelling Activity

Use the Spelling Words to play a sorting game with your child. Set a time limit, such as two minutes, for putting the words in groups. Your child might group words that end with *s* or *es,* words with the same number of letters, or words that begin with the same letter.

WORD CARDS

Spelling WORDS

girls	boxes
toys	dishes
times	inches
boys	wishes
days	things

YOUR OWN WORDS

ALL KINDS OF FRIENDS "Sam the Sea Cow" • Harcourt Brace School Publishers

Name _____

Spelling Practice

A. Study the Spelling Words. Say each word to yourself. Write each Spelling Word under its shape. Circle the <u>s</u> or <u>es</u> ending.

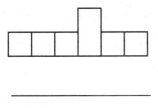

_____

_____

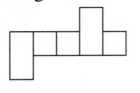

_____

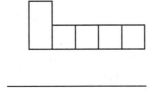

_____

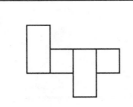

_____

_____

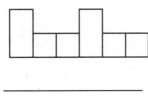

_____

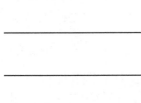

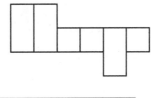

_____

B. Write the Words to Explore to complete the sentences.

1. I heard a loud _____, so I went

   to _____.

2. When I _____ found out what made it, I was surprised!

3. It was just my cat, and I know that she

   is _____!

Integrated Spelling

Spelling WORDS

1. girls
2. boxes
3. toys
4. dishes
5. times
6. inches
7. boys
8. wishes
9. days
10. things

Words to Explore

noise

explore

finally

harmless

Rabbit Talk

Read what the rabbits say.

Circle each misspelled word.

Write the words correctly on the lines.

_____   _____   _____

_____   _____

Use the words to make compound words. Write the compound words.

_____   _____

ALL KINDS OF FRIENDS Unit 6 Review • Harcourt Brace School Publishers

Helping Out

How have story characters you have read about helped each other? How have real people you know helped each other? Choose a story character or a person you know. Write a news story. Tell how the character or person helped out. Then draw a picture for your story. Write a sentence to tell about it. Use at least three Words to Watch For.

_____

_____

_____

_____

_____

_____

_____

[blank drawing box]

_____

Words to Watch For

These are words that can help you in your writing. Be on the lookout for them and spell them correctly!

brought

can

don't

friend

good

tomorrow

We can be good spellers!

1B
A. *(column 1)* b<u>a</u>d, h<u>a</u>d, d<u>a</u>d, s<u>a</u>d, m<u>a</u>d
(column 2) <u>a</u>n, b<u>a</u>t, m<u>a</u>p, s<u>a</u>t, c<u>a</u>t

B. **1.** field **2.** team
3. practice **4.** turn

2B
A. **1.** wet **2.** egg **3.** men
4. yes **5.** set **6.** mess **7.** ten
8. leg **9.** bet **10.** yet

B. **1.** bike **2.** once **3.** brave
4. began

3B
A. **1.** pin **2.** sit **3.** if **4.** hill
5. bit **6.** hid **7.** fix **8.** him
9. six **10.** win

B. **1.** dollar **2.** phone
3. earn **4.** work

4B
A. *(left to right)* job, box, stop, top, rock, fox, lot, pond, mom, doll

B. **1.** listen **2.** sound
3. touch **4.** gentle

5A
Rhyme Time: **1.** men **2.** top
3. leg **4.** wet

1. bad **2.** win **3.** lot **4.** sit
5. six **6.** job

6B
A. CVC pattern: c<u>u</u>p, d<u>u</u>g, m<u>u</u>d, b<u>u</u>s, c<u>u</u>t
Other: <u>u</u>s, m<u>u</u>ch, d<u>u</u>ck, m<u>u</u>st, j<u>u</u>mp

B. **1.** cookies **2.** stew

7B
A. *(column 1)* b<u>y</u>, tr<u>y</u>, m<u>y</u>; k<u>i</u>nd, ch<u>i</u>ld
(column 2) t<u>o</u>ld, c<u>o</u>ld, m<u>o</u>st, b<u>o</u>th; m<u>e</u>

B. **1.** ACROSS: familiar; DOWN: family
2. ACROSS: company; DOWN: uncle

8B
A. *hay:* w<u>ay</u>, m<u>ay</u>, s<u>ay</u>, p<u>ay</u>, l<u>ay</u>
pail: l<u>ai</u>d, r<u>ai</u>n, w<u>ai</u>t, tr<u>ai</u>n, t<u>ai</u>l

B. package, gigantic, tape, problem

9B
A. *weed:* n<u>ee</u>d, d<u>ee</u>p, k<u>ee</u>p, f<u>ee</u>t, f<u>ee</u>l
bean: r<u>ea</u>d, <u>ea</u>t, t<u>ea</u>m, <u>ea</u>ch, s<u>ea</u>t

B. **1.** toward **2.** toss
3. shoot **4.** fair

10B
A. *bow:* r<u>ow</u>, sh<u>ow</u>, sl<u>ow</u>, <u>ow</u>n, l<u>ow</u>
goat: b<u>oa</u>t, c<u>oa</u>l, c<u>oa</u>t, c<u>oa</u>st, r<u>oa</u>d

B. **1.** adventure **2.** soar
3. above **4.** glide

birds

11A
Rhyme Time *(left to right):* wait, each, feel

coast, most, rain, jump, eat, told, kind, may

12B
A. *cake:* take, made, game, late, make
bike: fire, five, life, nice, side

B. **1.** cough **2.** discover
3. caught **4.** medicine

13B
A. long *o:* bone, nose, note, rope, woke, hope
long *u:* mule, huge, use, cute

B. **1.** ACROSS: people; DOWN: plan **2.** ACROSS: decide; DOWN: move

14B
A. *(column 1)* dry, grass, from, stood, blow
(column 2) fly, sled, last, still, fast

B. **1.** gather **2.** play **3.** join
4. tune

15B
A. *grass:* miss, dress, less, pass, glass
bell: ball, all, fall, call

add

B. **1.** fiesta, festival
2. celebrate, important

16B
A. *(left to right)* chest, rich, shop, wish, ship, fish, wash, reach, change, shape

B. round balloon; **1.** brought
2. favorite

17A
This Old Mule: late, make, fire, mule; reach, five, nose; nice, use, fly

18B
A. *there:* <u>th</u>ey, <u>th</u>em, <u>th</u>ose, <u>th</u>an
path: ba<u>th</u>, ma<u>th</u>
wing: lo<u>ng</u>, ri<u>ng</u>
whale: <u>wh</u>ich, <u>wh</u>ile

B. *(left to right)* snore, awful, stretch, angry

19B
A. *(left to right)*
ACROSS: neck;
DOWN: care
ACROSS: black;
DOWN: book
ACROSS: stick;
DOWN: took
ACROSS: pack;
DOWN: car, kick

track

B. **1.** cozy **2.** lively **3.** milk **4.** burrow

20B
A. *is:* he's, she's, that's, there's, what's; *will:* I'll
are: we're, they're, you're
am: I'm

B. **1.** squawking **2.** throwing **3.** excited **4.** boring

21B
A. *blew:* g<u>rew</u>, n<u>ew</u>, fl<u>ew</u>, d<u>rew</u>
soup: y<u>ou</u>, gr<u>ou</u>p
moon: s<u>oo</u>n, r<u>oo</u>m, sch<u>oo</u>l, f<u>oo</u>d

B. **1.** mammal **2.** larger **3.** member **4.** change

22B
A. *(column 1)* ni<u>ght</u>, ri<u>ght</u>, si<u>ght</u>, mi<u>ght</u>; sky
(column 2) li<u>ght</u>, fi<u>ght</u>; hi<u>gh</u>; cry; bri<u>ght</u>

B. **1.** furious **2.** avoid **3.** against **4.** trouble

23A
Dog Talk: **1.** What's **2.** she's **3.** I'll

(left to right) bath, school, pack, night

24B
A. *(left to right)* heart, arm, start, are, part, dark, far, park, hard, farm

B. *(left to right)* scissors, thread, material, sewing

25B
A. *(top to bottom)*
ACROSS: corn, sort, short, more; DOWN: door, floor, store, horse, born

B. *(left to right)* artist, painting, colors, finished

26B
A. *(left to right)* don't, won't, I've, couldn't, let's, wasn't, can't, doesn't, didn't, wouldn't

B. palace, throne, clever, courage

27B
A. *(column 1)* for, four; two, to, too
(column 2) there, their; sew, so, sow

B. **1.** taste **2.** supper

3. kettle **4.** flavor

28B
A. *(left to right)* asked, started, doing, wanted, going, looking, called, playing, trying, looked

B. **1.** light **2.** disappear **3.** glow **4.** brilliant

29A
Rhyme Time: floor, store, more

two, to; there; sew

30B
A. *(left to right)* about, very, how, down, out, other, because, after

were, over

B. loom, wool, weave, design

31B
A. upon, sometimes, classroom, himself, seesaw, somewhere, baseball, herself, something, grandma

B. **1.** storm **2.** distance **3.** lightning **4.** weather

32B
A. *(left to right)* dropped, popping, stopped, running, grabbed, getting, slipped, putting, planning, sitting

B. **1.** dug **2.** built **3.** carried, tunnel

33B
A. *raking:* giving, taking, riding, moving, living
raked: saved, liked, used, placed, loved

B. 1. whale, surface
2. tangled **3.** coast

34B
A. *(column 1)* wish<u>es</u>,
inch<u>es</u>; toy<u>s</u>, boy<u>s</u>, day<u>s</u>
(column 2) girl<u>s</u>; box<u>es</u>,
tim<u>es</u>; dish<u>es</u>; thing<u>s</u>

B. 1. noise, explore
2. finally **3.** harmless

35A
Rabbit Talk *(left to right):*
boxes, giving, wishes,
Because, baseball, dishes

somewhere, upon

INFORMAL ASSESSMENT OPTIONS

Writing Activity Error Analysis

Each lesson in the *Integrated Spelling* Teacher's Edition includes a writing model that contains common grade-level error patterns. Children's daily writing can be compared to these models to determine which lessons will be of greatest benefit and interest.

Error Analysis Chart for Writing Activities

The chart on page T332 of this Teacher's Edition enables you to record and analyze the words children misspell as they complete writing activities in each unit. It is designed to help you analyze the nature of children's spelling errors and thereby customize instruction to meet individual needs.

Portfolio Conferences

Periodic conferences give children, teachers, and family members a chance to reflect on each child's writing and developing knowledge of spelling. An evaluation portfolio should be created for each child. See the section Guidelines for Portfolio Conferences on page T337 for suggestions of items to include in each evaluation portfolio.

FORMAL ASSESSMENT OPTIONS

Spelling Placement Inventory

See pages T333–T336 for administering and interpreting the Spelling Placement Inventory. The Inventory will help you devise an instructional plan for each child by assessing his or her developmental level.

Pretest/Posttest/Practice Test

The pretest/posttest for each lesson provides a set of numbered context sentences for the Spelling Words. Children are asked to write each Spelling Word after hearing the word and context sentence read aloud.

The pretest should be given at the beginning of each lesson, encouraging children to draw on their prior knowledge. It determines which spelling patterns or generalizations have been mastered and which areas need improvement. The Self-Check activities encourage children to play an active role in evaluating their work. Assign or have children choose partners for assessing children's own words.

The posttest given at the end of each lesson is an effective diagnostic tool for determining if extra practice is needed. In addition, the Practice Test at the end of each unit may be used to assess each child's progress.

Informal Assessment in *Integrated Spelling*

Research has shown that spelling instruction is most effective when it is linked to authentic writing tasks. For children to develop the skills and habits of proficient spellers, they need to view correct spelling within the broader context of reading, writing, and the communication of ideas. Therefore, the natural starting point for the assessment of spelling awareness is the written work that children complete in all subject areas as part of their daily assignments.

Error Analysis Chart

Integrated Spelling supports you in the ongoing informal assessment of each child's developing spelling skills. The Error Analysis Chart on page T332 provides space for recording the misspellings that appear in children's writing. Use the chart to help you identify recurring spelling errors, analyze the nature of the misspellings, and determine error patterns. These findings will help you determine which lessons in *Integrated Spelling* will be of greatest benefit.

At the beginning of each lesson are models of student writing that contain common grade-level error patterns. You can compare these models to the error patterns you find and record on children's Error Analysis Charts. As children work through each lesson, mastering spelling and acquiring skills, update the charts. This process will enable you to identify areas of achievement and informally assess areas that need improvement.

Integrated Activities

The lessons in *Integrated Spelling* are designed to engage children actively in integrated listening, speaking, reading, and writing activities and help them develop a "spelling consciousness." All of the writing activities provide excellent opportunities for ongoing performance-based assessment. Clues to children's developing word knowledge and attitudes toward spelling may also be revealed in oral summarizing activities. Throughout the lessons, children are encouraged to assess their progress and to help their classmates evaluate their work.

Portfolio Assessment

To develop independent spelling awareness, *Integrated Spelling* teaches spelling as part of the writing process. Writing samples, including unfinished work and proofread drafts, should be included in an evaluation portfolio and reviewed periodically. The proofreading phase provides important clues to student progress. For informal assessment during this stage, children can work independently, in pairs, or in small groups.

You may want to monitor children's performance, observing how effectively they edit their work and how successfully they select resources to confirm spellings. Children's personalized Spelling Logs are another useful measure of their growth as independent, competent spellers.

A Comprehensive Assessment Program

Integrated Spelling offers a comprehensive, holistic assessment program. The components of informal assessment, combined with the formal assessment of the Spelling Placement Inventory and the pretests/ posttests, ensure that every child receives individualized instruction and is recognized for his or her achievements.

Name _____

Error Analysis Chart for Writing Activities

Misspelling	Correct Spelling	Where the Error Appears in the Word			Substitutions, Omissions, Insertions, Reversals					Other		
		Beginning	Middle	End	Vowel	Consonant	Silent Letters	Double Letters	Compounds, Homophones, Contractions	Irregular Words	Inflectional Endings and Suffixes	

Directions: Make as many copies of this chart as necessary.

Harcourt Brace School Publishers

Directions for Administering the Spelling Placement Inventory

Administer the Spelling Placement Inventory on pages T335–T336 at the beginning of second grade. Follow these directions.

1. Dictate the 20 words to children by pronouncing each word, using it in a sentence, and then pronouncing the word again.

2. Collect children's papers and score each Spelling Inventory by writing the correct spelling beside each incorrect spelling. For example:

1.	sied	side
2.	must	✓
3.	thoes	those
4.	glas	glass
5.	stik	stick

By correcting the Spelling Inventories in this manner, you will gain valuable knowledge of each child's developmental understanding of one-syllable spelling words and the patterns they represent.

3. Although a numerical score can be assigned to each child's spelling test (0 percent to 100 percent range, with 5 points taken off for each incorrect spelling), it is more appropriate at the beginning of the second-grade year to note the child's stage of spelling development.

Note in the example above that the child's misspellings place him in the Transitional stage of spelling. In one-syllable words, he or she represents short vowels correctly (*must, glas,* and *stik*), and puts in an extra vowel letter or "marker" in long-vowel spellings such as *sied* and *thoes*.

Although the child only spelled one of the five words correctly, his or her pattern of marking long vowels and representing short vowels conventionally shows good spelling knowledge for a beginning second grader.

4. By administering the same 20-word Spelling Inventory at the end of second grade and scoring it in the manner described, you will be able to document, for each child, pretest-posttest gains in the number of correct spellings—and also qualitative gains in spelling knowledge (e.g., movement from the Phonetic stage to the Transitional stage).

By the end of the second-grade year, an achieving student should score at least 70 percent accuracy on the test and his or her errors should cluster in the Transitional stage of development.

Grade 2 Spelling Placement Inventory

Follow the directions on pages T333–T334 for administering this Placement Inventory.

WORDS	STAGES		
	ON LEVEL *Phonetic*	BELOW LEVEL *Semi-Phonetic*	ABOVE LEVEL *Transitional*
1. side	sid, sod	sd	sied
2. must	moct, most	mt	must*
3. those	thoz, thos	os	thoes
4. glass	gas, glas	gs	glass*
5. stick	stec, ctek	ck	stik
6. light	lit, lot	lt	lite, ligt
7. train	tran, chran	hn	trane
8. don't	dot	dt	dont
9. hard	hrd	hd	hard*
10. deep	dep	dp	deap, depe

continued

	STAGES		
WORDS	ON LEVEL *Phonetic*	BELOW LEVEL *Semi-Phonetic*	ABOVE LEVEL *Transitional*
11. new	nu	n	noo, noow
12. chest	hact, chast	ht	chest*
13. rock	roc, rik	rk	rock*
14. call	col	kl	coll, caul
15. floor	for, flor	fr	flore
16. couldn't	codent	cdt	coudnt
17. dishes	dechiz	dss	dishis
18. getting	gateng	gtn	geting
19. saved	savd	sd	savved
20. toys	toz, tos	tz	toyes, toies

*A correct spelling. There are few Transitional stage possibilities for this particular word.

Guidelines for Portfolio Conferences

Since spelling occurs naturally within the context of writing, a portfolio provides an effective way of illustrating children's development as spellers. This section provides suggestions for including indicators of spelling progress in children's portfolios. It also offers guidelines for discussing spelling progress in conferences with children and with family members.

Incorporating Spelling Samples into the Portfolio

Help each child organize the contents of the portfolio. Several methods of organization are suggested in the *Portfolio Assessment Teacher's Guide* that accompanies *Treasury of Literature.*

After children have decided on an order, suggest that they think about ways they can include examples of their spelling work. Help them to decide how their spelling work best fits in with other categories in the portfolio.

If a child has organized a portfolio by topic, he or she may want to place topic-related Spelling Words in the appropriate sections of the portfolio. If a child's portfolio is organized chronologically, spelling-related work might be placed in the portfolio according to when the work was done. Some children may want you to help them create a separate section just for spelling work.

Items to Include in a Portfolio

In addition to selecting several examples of completed spelling assignments, children might include the following items in their portfolios:

 Writing Samples Encourage children to add writing samples that show spelling corrections they have made. Drafts that show errors which children have discovered and corrected while proofreading are good indicators of their spelling progress.

 Pretests and Posttests You may want to have children include pretests and posttests in their portfolios to show the progress they have made with particular groups of words. Such items should not be included as part of a formal assessment or as a means of judging children's weaknesses. Rather they should be used as a method of demonstrating progress and as a way for children to assess their own achievements.

 Spelling Logs If children are keeping individual Spelling Logs of unusual and interesting words, encourage them to photocopy some of these pages and add them to the portfolio. These pages provide insight into a child's interests.

Language Discovery Sheets From time to time children will discover a language fact or pattern that proves especially useful. Encourage students to record their facts or patterns on a "Language Discovery Sheet" and add the sheet to their portfolios.

 Optional Writing Activity Children may want to include in their portfolios the Optional Writing Activity that is suggested at the end of each spelling lesson.

Conferences Between a Family Member and a Teacher

Discuss with the family member how the child has incorporated indicators of his or her spelling progress into the portfolio. Then share examples of the child's work that reveal spelling development, such as process writing activities, Spelling Log pages, and pretest-posttest pages. The following checklist may be used to help you emphasize the progress individual children have made and point out areas that need improvement.

✓ Awareness of spelling patterns

✓ Ability to apply knowledge of known words to unfamiliar words that share a similar pattern or origin

✓ Developmental level of the child

Conferences Between a Teacher and a Child

Try to conduct the conference so that the child does most of the talking. Prompts such as these will help generate discussion:

- Let's look at a piece of writing that shows some corrections you made in spelling. How did you find the mistakes?
- How did you figure out how to spell the words correctly in your writing?
- What helps you the most when you are trying to spell new words?
- How often do you use a dictionary?
- How is the dictionary helpful?
- In what ways have you become a better speller?

The child's responses to questions such as these will provide valuable insight into her or his attitudes, habits, and strengths. Help the child set goals that will develop increased proficiency in spelling. These goals might include using a dictionary more often when proofreading, consulting with peers when troublesome words are encountered, or referring to spelling strategies more often.

Conferences Between Two Students

Peer portfolio conferences offer a valuable opportunity for children to discuss their progress, share the things they find most challenging, and compare problem-solving strategies with one another. The questions below can help children get their peer conferences off the ground. You might want to duplicate a set of questions for each pair of children to use as a guide during the conference.

- How did you put things together in your portfolio?
- Where did you put your spelling work? What kinds of things did you include?
- What do you like about spelling? What is hard about spelling for you?
- What do you do when you want to write a word but don't know how to spell it?
- What are some difficult words you can spell? How did you learn to spell them?

Encourage children to share the strategies they have discovered that are the most useful for spelling new words and remembering the spelling of troublesome words. Ask children to try to be as specific as they can. For example, a child who has trouble with certain consonant clusters spellings may have developed a mnemonic device for remembering which spelling to use.

Also, encourage children to become resources for one another in sharing their solutions and strategies. Encourage them or help them to take notes during their peer conferences and add them to the portfolio. Each child's name, his/her partner's name, the date of the conference, and any valuable information learned during the conference should be included.

Integrating Spelling and Literature

Each spelling lesson in *Integrated Spelling* corresponds to an anthology selection in *Treasury of Literature*. Every spelling lesson features a list of Spelling Words and a list of Words to Explore. The spelling words include words taken from the corresponding anthology selection. Each list of Words to Explore includes Key Words and other story words.

At the end of each unit in the Teacher's Edition of *Integrated Spelling* is a review lesson with activities that reflect the writing forms and language skills featured in the corresponding *Treasury of Literature* unit.

LESSON	SPELLING GENERALIZATION	CORRESPONDING LITERATURE
1	Words with Short *a*	"Ronald Morgan Goes to Bat"
2	Words with Short *e*	"Matthew and Tilly"
3	Words with Short *i*	"Arthur's Pet Business"
4	Words with Short *o*	"I Have a Sister—My Sister Is Deaf"
5	REVIEW	
6	Words with Short *u*	"The Wolf's Chicken Stew"
7	Words with Long *e*, Long *i*, and Long *o*	"Everett Anderson's Friend"
8	Words Like *may* and *wait*	"Mitchell Is Moving"
9	Works Like *keep* and *team*	"Jamaica Tag-Along"
10	Words Like *boat* and *show*	"Abuela"
11	REVIEW	
12	Words Like *make* and *five*	"Six-Dinner Sid"
13	Words Like *note* and *cute*	"Old Henry"
14	Consonant Clusters	"Little Penguin's Tale"
15	Final Double Consonants	"Fiesta!"

LESSON	SPELLING GENERALIZATION	CORRESPONDING LITERATURE
16	Words with *sh* and *ch*	"Miss Eva and the Red Balloon"
17	REVIEW	
18	Words with *th, wh,* and *ng*	"Awful Aardvark"
19	Words Like *car, book,* and *track*	"It's an Armadillo!"
20	Words Like *she's* and *you're*	"The Day Jimmy's Boa Ate the Wash"
21	Words Like *food* and *new*	"A Dinosaur Named After Me"
22	Words Like *fight* and *sky*	"Tyrone the Horrible"
23	REVIEW	
24	Words Like *arm* and *heart*	"The Chalk Doll"
25	Words Like *door* and *more*	"The Little Painter of Sabana Grande"
26	Words Like *I've* and *won't*	"The Empty Pot"
27	Homophones	"Stone Soup"
28	Words That End with *-ed* and *-ing*	"The Night of the Stars"
29	REVIEW	
30	Words to Remember	"The Goat in the Rug"
31	Compound Words	"Thunder Cake"
32	Words Like *dropped* and *running*	"Ant Cities"
33	Words Like *loved* and *moving*	"Ibis: A True Whale Story"
34	Plurals	"Sam the Sea Cow"
35	REVIEW	

Spelling Word List Development

Integrated Spelling is a complete and developmentally founded spelling program that integrates with *Treasury of Literature*. The lists of words to be taught in *Integrated Spelling* were compiled after careful consideration of lists of words children use in their writing and reading.

Words are grouped in accordance with the natural developmental flow of written language acquisition, and lists reflect common and consistent spelling patterns based on sound-letter relationships (phonology), word structures (affixes, inflections, syllable patterns, common roots, compound words), and word meaning.

Over the past sixty years, researchers have identified the words that students at different grade levels are most likely to encounter when reading and the words they use most often in writing. These words, along with selected words children encounter in *Treasury of Literature* anthology selections, form the basis of the spelling word lists in *Integrated Spelling*.

Word-list selection used in developing the database for *Integrated Spelling* is one of the most systematic and comprehensive ever developed because it is based on data not from a single word study but on the different sources shown on the next page—in addition to selected words from *Treasury of Literature*.

Integrated Spelling

Writing

 Rinsland List (1945, Grades 1–8)
25,632 words

 Hillerich List (1966, Grades 2–6)
10,446 words

 Smith & Ingersoll (1984, Grades 1–8)
500,000 words from 4,000 compositions

 Farr List (1990, Grades 2–8)
3,080,831 running words from 21,697 essays

Reading

 Morris List (1987–88, 1993, Grades 2–adult)
10.2 million words from 1,500 publications

 Dolch List (1939, Grades 1–3)
220 words

 Kucera and Francis (1964, adult)
50,406 words from 500 samples

Success Rate

 New Iowa Spelling Scale
5,507 words

 Farr Survey
3,080,831 running words

This alphabetical list of 2,991 words includes all the spelling words that appear in Grades 1–8 of *Integrated Spelling*. Each word in the list is followed by two numbers. The first number indicates the grade in which the word appears. The second number indicates the lesson. Therefore, the listing "able 3 31" indicates that the word *able* appears in Grade 3, Lesson 31.

Word	Lesson	Word	Lesson	Word	Lesson	Word	Lesson	Word	Lesson	Word	Lesson
abilities	8 3	advance	6 1	anecdote	8 5	around	4 14	awe	8 4
ability	6 19	adventure	7 34	angel	6 10	arrange	7 10	awesome	7 11
able	3 31	advertise	7 18	angle	6 10	arrangements	7 10	awful	8 4
abolished	8 17	advice	8 6	animal	4 25	array	7 10	awfully	8 4
about	2 30	advise	7 20	animals'	4 21	arrest	7 10	awkward	7 11
abrupt	6 33	advocate	8 18	announced	7 10	arrested	8 6	babies	3 21
absence	6 18	affair	6 20	announcement	8 6	arrived	7 10	baby-sitter	5 19
absent	6 22	affect	6 10	annoy	7 10	artist	7 35	back	3 1
absolute	8 17	affection	6 20	annoyed	4 14	artistic	5 32	background	5 19
abstract	8 17	affectionate	8 6	answer	4 24	as	1 27	backup	5 34
accelerate	7 10	afford	5 25	answered	6 16	ask	5 1	backward	7 11
acceleration	7 33	Africa	7 9	antidote	8 5	asked	2 28	backyard	4 18
accent	7 10	African	7 9	antique	7 23	aspirin	7 29	bacon	4 32
accept	6 10	after	2 30	any	3 26	assembly	6 20	bacteria	6 26
acceptable	8 31	afternoon	4 18	anyone	4 18	assign	6 20	bad	2 1
acceptance	8 31	age	4 7	anything	4 18	assistance	6 20	badly	3 20
accepted	7 10	agent	6 15	anyway	4 18	assistant	6 22	bag	3 1
access	8 5	agreeable	8 6	apart	6 4	association	6 20	bait	6 2
accident	6 20	agreement	4 28	apologizing	7 32	assurance	6 18	baker	4 32
accidentally	6 30	agricultural	7 33	apparent	6 20	asterisk	8 28	bakery	7 14
accommodate	7 10	aimlessly	8 35	appear	5 25	astronaut	7 27	balance	7 21
accompany	6 20	air	3 13	appearance	6 18	astronauts	8 28	ball	2 15
accompanying	7 10	airplane	3 28	applause	6 20	astronomer	7 27	ballet	7 23
accomplish	7 10	airport	4 26	apple	3 31	astronomy	7 27	balloon	4 8
accomplished	8 6	all	2 15	applicable	8 33	at	1 27	banjo	7 5
account	6 3	alley	4 20	applications	5 34	ate	3 18	bankrupt	6 33
accumulation	7 33	allied	6 12	applied	4 16	athlete	5 33	banner	6 25
accurate	6 20	alligator	7 4	applies	6 12	athletes	7 29	banquet	8 32
accuse	6 20	allow	4 14	apply	4 20	athletic	5 33	barbecue	8 27
accustomed	6 20	allowance	6 18	appoint	7 10	atmosphere	8 12	bard	8 2
achieve	6 7	almost	3 9	appointed	6 20	attendance	7 21	barefoot	6 8
acquired	8 3	alphabet	8 11	appreciate	6 20	attended	8 31	barefooted	8 9
act	3 1	also	3 9	approach	6 20	attention	5 16	bark	5 8
action	5 16	although	6 6	approaching	7 10	attitude	7 15	barn	5 8
actively	6 30	altimeter	8 28	approve	7 10	attract	7 22	barometer	7 27
activities	6 12	altitude	8 28	approved	8 6	attractive	6 27	barred	8 2
activity	6 19	alto	8 28	April	5 23	audience	6 18	barrier	7 15
adapt	6 10	always	3 9	apron	6 15	Australia	7 9	baseball	2 31
add	2 15	am	1 27	archaeologist	8 26	Australian	7 9	basic	4 32
addition	5 16	amateur	8 8	archaic	8 26	authority	6 19	basin	5 27
adjective	7 29	amazing	5 20	architectural	8 35	autobiography	7 33	basis	6 15
adjust	8 31	ambulance	6 18	architecture	8 11	autograph	7 27	basketball	4 18
adjustments	8 31	American	6 13	archives	8 26	automatically	8 26	bat	2 1
administration	7 33	among	6 6	arctic	7 12	automobile	7 30	bath	2 18
admire	6 14	amount	6 3	are	2 24	automobiles	8 26	batter	3 23
admission	5 16	an	2 1	area	4 10	autumn	7 25	battle	5 23
admit	6 1	analogy	7 32	argument	6 19	autumnal	7 25	bazaar	8 5
admits	7 22	analyze	7 18	arithmetic	8 11	available	5 17	be	1 34
admitted	6 16	ancient	5 11	arm	2 24	avoid	4 14	beach	4 2
adopt	6 10	and	1 27	aroma	8 11	aware	4 10	bear	3 13

Word	Lesson	Word	Lesson	Word	Lesson	Word	Lesson	Word	Lesson	Word	Lesson
beat	3 4	bottle	4 25	cactus	6 26	chaos	6 25	clock	3 2
beaten	6 13	bottom	3 23	cafeteria	7 4	chapter	5 22	close	4 6
beautiful	4 28	bought	5 5	cake	3 5	characteristic	7 33	closed	3 19
beautifully	6 30	boulder	6 6	calculate	7 18	charge	5 8	closer	3 25
beauty	4 20	boundary	7 12	calendar	4 24	chasing	4 15	closet	5 28
beaver	5 27	bouquet	7 23	call	2 15	chattering	8 21	cloth	5 5
because	2 30	box	2 4	called	2 28	chauffeur	8 8	clothes	5 10
becoming	5 20	boxes	2 34	calves	4 23	cheating	7 3	cloud	3 12
bed	1 30	boycott	8 30	came	1 38	check	4 2	clover	5 27
bedroom	3 28	boyfriend	6 7	camouflage	7 23	cheeks	5 2	clown	4 14
bedtime	6 8	boy's	3 17	can	1 22	cheerful	4 28	club	3 2
been	5 13	boys	2 34	cannon	4 30	cheese	5 2	clue	5 4
before	4 10	boys'	4 21	cannot	3 23	cheetah	6 15	coach	4 6
beginning	4 15	bracelet	8 32	can't	2 26	chemical	8 12	coal	2 10
belief	6 7	bragged	6 16	canyon	5 22	chemicals	4 23	coarse	5 13
believe	4 12	Braille	8 30	cap	3 1	cherries	4 23	coast	2 10
berries	4 23	brain	5 2	capable	5 17	chest	2 16	coat	2 10
berth	7 2	brake	5 13	capital	8 2	chew	4 4	cocoa	7 4
best	3 1	bread	3 1	Capitol	8 2	chewing	4 15	coin	4 14
bet	2 2	breadth	8 5	captain	3 30	chicken	5 22	cold	2 7
better	4 29	break	5 13	capture	5 31	chief	4 12	collar	4 24
beverage	7 12	breakfast	3 28	car	2 19	child	2 7	colonial	7 24
bicycle	7 28	breath	8 5	caravan	7 30	childish	7 11	colonies	6 12
big	1 21	breathe	6 2	carbohydrate	7 32	children's	4 21	colony	7 24
bigger	3 25	bride	6 2	card	4 10	child's	4 21	color	3 29
biggest	3 25	bridge	4 7	cardboard	5 19	chili	7 4	colored	4 15
bike	3 5	brief	5 2	care	2 19	chimney	4 20	colorful	4 28
bin	5 13	bright	2 22	careful	3 20	chipmunk	8 27	comb	5 3
binoculars	7 28	brilliant	7 21	carefully	6 30	chocolate	7 29	combination	8 15
biography	7 27	bring	4 3	careless	4 28	choice	4 14	combine	8 15
biologist	7 35	broken	3 30	carelessly	8 35	choose	3 8	come	1 32
biology	7 32	brook	5 5	cargo	8 27	chop	4 6	comfortable	5 17
bird	3 15	brother's	4 21	carnival	8 27	chorus	8 11	comic	6 24
birth	7 2	brought	5 5	carried	3 21	chose	5 3	coming	3 19
birthday	3 28	brown	3 12	carrying	7 3	chosen	5 27	command	5 34
biscuit	6 6	brush	4 4	cassette	8 32	church	3 15	commanded	6 21
bit	2 3	bubble	3 31	cat	2 1	chute	7 2	commander	6 21
bizarre	8 5	buffalo	7 15	catalog	7 32	cider	5 27	commence	6 21
black	2 19	buffet	7 23	catch	4 1	cinnamon	7 15	comment	6 1
blanket	4 30	bug	1 29	cattle	5 23	circle	5 9	commercial	6 21
blew	3 18	bugle	7 5	caucus	8 34	circles	7 16	commission	5 32
block	3 2	build	5 1	caught	5 5	circuit	8 25	commit	6 21
blouse	8 8	building	6 6	cause	3 9	circular	7 16	commitment	7 22
blow	2 14	bun	1 20	cedar	4 31	circulation	8 25	committed	6 16
blue	3 18	bunch	4 4	ceiling	4 12	circumference	8 25	committee	6 21
board	4 9	buried	3 21	celebrate	7 18	circumstances	8 25	commonly	6 21
boarder	8 2	burn	4 13	cellar	4 24	circus	5 25	commotion	6 21
boat	2 10	burnt	6 4	Celsius	8 30	cities	6 12	communicate	6 21
bodies	4 23	burro	8 2	cent	4 9	city	4 7	communication	6 21
bodyguard	6 8	burrow	8 2	center	4 7	civil	5 23	communities	6 21
boil	5 7	burst	4 13	centimeters	7 27	civilian	7 35	community	6 19
bold	5 3	bus	2 6	central	5 26	clapped	3 19	companion	7 24
bone	2 13	bush	5 5	centuries	6 12	clarinet	7 5	company	7 24
book	2 19	busiest	4 16	century	7 14	class	4 1	compare	5 9
booklet	8 32	busy	6 6	certain	3 30	classical	7 5	compelled	7 3
boot	3 10	but	1 29	chair	3 13	classroom	2 31	complicated	8 33
border	8 2	butter	4 24	chairperson	7 1	clay	3 4	component	5 34
bored	4 9	button	4 25	champion	7 30	clean	3 4	composer	7 5
born	2 25	by	2 7	championship	6 19	clever	6 25	composition	7 20
both	2 7	cabin	5 28	change	2 16	client	5 29	compromise	7 18
bothering	7 3	cabinet	8 32	channel	4 30	climate	6 24	computer	5 34

Word	Lesson		Word	Lesson		Word	Lesson		Word	Lesson		Word	Lesson		Word	Lesson	
concentrate	8	18	county	6	3	debate	8	18	dictionaries	8	14	documentary	7	14
concert	7	5	coup	8	8	debris	8	8	dictionary	7	14	does	5	1
conducted	8	31	couple	5	23	decade	7	28	did	1	26	doesn't	2	26
conductor	7	5	coupon	7	23	decades	4	23	didn't	2	26	doing	2	28
confederate	8	9	courage	6	6	decay	7	8	die	3	3	doll	2	4
conference	6	18	course	5	13	deceived	8	31	died	5	20	dollar	3	29
confidence	7	21	court	4	10	December	7	28	diet	5	29	done	1	32
confident	6	22	cousin	5	10	decent	6	10	difference	6	18	don't	2	26
confined	8	33	covered	5	21	decide	5	10	different	7	12	door	2	25
confusing	6	21	cow	3	12	decided	5	20	dig	1	21	doorway	5	19
confusion	5	16	coyote	7	4	decimal	7	28	digging	4	15	double	5	23
congratulate	7	18	crawled	6	3	decision	5	15	dinner	3	23	doubt	7	17
Congress	5	26	creak	6	9	declare	6	4	diplomacy	7	24	doubtful	7	17
conjunction	8	33	cream	5	2	decline	7	8	diplomatic	7	24	doubtless	7	17
conscience	8	5	create	5	29	decorate	8	18	direction	5	16	dough	6	6
conscious	8	5	creative	6	27	deduct	5	15	directory	5	34	down	2	30
conservation	8	14	creature	5	31	deduction	7	8	dirt	5	9	downtown	4	18
considerable	5	17	credit	5	28	deep	2	9	disability	5	15	dozen	5	22
considered	6	21	creek	6	9	defeat	7	8	disabled	7	8	dragon	5	22
constant	7	21	crew	4	4	defects	7	8	disadvantage	5	15	drama	8	4
constitution	6	21	cried	3	21	defense	5	15	disadvantages	7	8	dramatic	8	4
constructing	7	20	criminal	6	13	define	5	33	disagree	3	24	dramatically	8	4
contact	6	1	crisis	5	27	definitely	8	33	disagreeable	6	28	draw	3	9
contained	8	3	critical	6	13	definition	5	33	disagreement	6	28	dream	5	2
container	8	31	criticism	8	22	degree	5	15	disappear	4	19	dress	2	15
contented	8	9	criticize	7	18	dehydrated	7	32	disappeared	7	8	drew	2	21
contest	4	30	crochet	8	8	delegate	8	18	disappointed	5	15	dried	4	3
continue	8	4	crooked	8	9	delicious	6	27	disappointment	7	8	drive	5	33
continued	6	21	croquet	8	8	demand	5	15	disastrous	7	29	drive-in	4	18
continuous	8	4	cross	6	3	democratic	8	9	discharge	5	15	driven	5	33
continuously	8	4	crowd	4	14	demonstrate	8	18	discomfort	4	19	driving	4	15
contract	6	1	cruel	5	29	denied	6	12	discount	5	15	drop	3	2
contracted	7	22	cruelty	8	22	deny	4	20	discover	3	24	dropped	2	32
control	5	26	cry	2	22	dependent	7	8	discovered	7	8	drove	3	5
controlled	5	21	crystal	6	25	depends	7	34	discovery	7	14	drown	5	7
controlling	7	3	culture	5	31	depositing	7	20	discussion	5	16	drowned	7	29
convention	7	34	cup	2	6	depot	8	8	disease	5	10	dry	2	14
conviction	6	21	cupboard	6	8	depth	6	1	disguise	7	8	duck	2	6
convince	6	14	curb	6	4	descent	6	10	dishes	2	34	dug	2	6
cook	3	10	cure	4	13	describe	5	15	diskette	8	32	duke	5	4
cookie	3	26	curiosity	6	19	description	6	32	dislike	3	24	duplicate	8	33
cool	3	10	curious	6	27	descriptive	6	32	disliked	7	8	dust	4	4
cooling	6	16	current	6	22	desert	3	15	dismissed	7	22	duties	4	32
cooperate	7	18	curve	4	13	design	5	15	disobey	3	24	each	2	9
cooperation	7	33	custom	6	10	designated	7	25	disorder	5	15	eager	6	15
copied	4	16	cut	2	6	designed	7	25	display	6	25	earlier	4	16
copies	4	23	cute	2	13	despair	8	4	dispose	7	8	earliest	3	25
copper	4	29	cutting	3	19	desperate	7	29	disposed	8	15	earn	4	13
corn	2	25	cycle	8	10	desperately	8	4	disposition	8	15	earnings	5	9
corner	4	24	cyclone	8	10	destroy	5	15	disrupting	6	33	earth	4	13
corral	7	4	dad	2	1	destroyed	7	8	disruption	6	33	earthquake	5	19
corridor	7	15	dairy	5	9	destruction	7	20	dissatisfied	5	15	easier	3	25
corrupt	6	33	dance	5	1	detail	4	31	dissolved	7	8	easiest	4	16
cosmonauts	8	28	dare	3	13	detained	8	31	distance	5	25	easy	5	10
cost	5	5	dark	2	24	detention	5	32	distract	7	22	eat	2	9
costume	6	10	data	5	34	develop	5	15	distribute	8	15	economically	8	35
cotton	3	23	daughter	5	22	device	6	10	distribution	8	15	ecstatic	7	29
couldn't	2	26	day	1	38	devise	6	10	divide	5	33	edge	4	7
council	5	23	daylight	7	1	dialogue	7	23	dividend	5	33	editor	7	24
count	6	3	days	2	34	diameter	7	27	do	1	31	editorial	7	24
country	4	20	dead	5	1	dictator	8	14	doctor	4	24	educate	8	31

Word	Lesson		Word	Lesson		Word	Lesson		Word	Lesson		Word	Lesson		Word	Lesson	
education	5	16	escape	6	14	famous	6	15	floor	2	25	funny	4	20
effect	6	10	especially	7	17	fan	1	22	flow	4	6	fur	4	13
effective	6	27	estimate	8	18	fantastic	7	24	flower	3	12	further	6	14
effort	5	25	ethnic	6	1	fantasy	7	24	flute	5	4	furthermore	8	1
egg	2	2	even	5	27	far	2	24	fly	2	14	futile	8	5
eight	3	18	eventually	8	35	farm	2	24	focus	4	31	future	4	32
eighteen	4	12	ever	3	29	farmer	3	20	folk	5	3	gallery	7	15
eighth	6	6	evergreen	8	1	farther	5	26	follow	3	23	game	2	12
eighty	4	12	everybody	4	26	fast	2	14	following	7	3	garden	3	30
either	4	12	everyone	4	26	faster	3	25	food	2	21	gasoline	7	30
eject	6	33	everything	4	26	fatal	6	25	foolish	7	11	gather	6	25
election	5	16	evil	6	15	father's	4	21	foot	3	10	gathered	7	3
electric	5	32	exaggerated	8	21	fatigue	7	23	football	3	28	gathering	5	21
electrical	8	12	examination	7	30	fault	3	9	for	2	27	gave	1	38
electricity	6	19	example	4	25	favor	3	29	forbidding	8	3	general	5	32
electronic	8	9	exceed	7	7	favorable	5	17	force	3	14	generation	8	10
elegant	7	21	excel	7	7	favorably	8	35	foreign	6	7	generator	8	10
element	6	22	excellent	6	22	feature	5	31	forgetting	5	21	genes	8	10
elephant	6	22	except	6	10	February	7	12	form	3	14	genius	8	10
eleven	4	25	exceptionally	7	33	federal	5	32	formal	5	23	genuine	7	11
eliminate	8	18	excess	8	5	feel	2	9	formation	7	34	geographic	8	28
elite	8	8	exchange	7	7	feet	2	9	formula	7	34	geography	7	27
else	4	2	excited	5	10	fellow	5	25	fortunate	7	17	geology	8	28
elsewhere	5	19	excitement	7	7	female	4	31	fortunately	8	35	geometry	8	28
embarrassed	8	8	exclaim	7	7	feminine	7	11	fortune	7	17	German	6	13
embassy	8	21	exclude	7	7	fence	5	10	forty	5	8	gesture	5	31
emigrate	8	14	excuse	5	10	feudal	8	5	forward	4	30	get	1	19
employed	4	14	execute	5	34	fever	4	31	fought	5	5	getting	2	32
employee	5	7	executive	6	27	few	4	4	foul	8	2	giant	5	29
employer	5	7	exercise	7	18	fiber	6	15	found	4	14	gift	4	3
empty	6	25	existence	7	21	fiddle	7	5	four	2	27	gingerbread	8	1
enclose	7	7	exit	7	7	field	4	12	fourth	3	14	girlfriend	6	7
encourage	7	7	expand	7	7	fierce	6	7	fowl	8	2	girl's	3	17
encyclopedia	7	33	experience	7	21	fifteen	6	14	fox	2	4	girls	2	34
end	3	1	experiments	8	12	fifth	4	3	fracture	5	31	give	1	32
endless	4	28	explain	5	26	fight	2	22	France	7	9	given	3	30
endurance	7	21	explode	7	7	file	5	3	frankfurter	8	30	giving	2	33
enemies	6	12	explore	5	8	final	3	31	frantic	6	14	glad	4	1
enemy	5	32	explorer	6	13	finally	8	5	free	4	2	glance	6	1
engine	6	14	exported	8	14	finance	5	27	freight	6	7	glass	2	15
engineer	7	35	express	7	7	financial	8	33	French	7	9	globe	6	2
England	7	9	extend	7	7	find	1	37	frequent	7	21	glue	5	4
English	7	9	extra	5	26	fine	3	5	fresh	3	8	go	1	35
enjoy	3	12	extraordinary	8	17	finely	8	5	Friday	6	15	goal	3	3
enjoying	7	7	extraterrestrial	8	17	finger	5	25	fried	4	3	goalie	7	35
enormous	6	27	extravagant	8	17	finish	5	28	friend	4	12	goat	3	3
enough	6	6	eye	4	3	fire	2	12	friendship	6	19	going	2	28
entered	5	21	fabulous	6	27	firefighter	4	26	fright	3	3	gold	4	6
enthusiasm	7	7	face	3	5	fireplace	4	26	frigid	6	24	golden	4	25
entrance	6	18	fact	5	1	fireworks	6	8	from	2	14	goldfish	6	26
envelope	7	7	factor	5	22	firm	5	9	front	5	1	good	3	10
environment	8	12	factory	7	14	first	3	15	frozen	5	22	good-bye	4	18
episode	8	11	Fahrenheit	8	30	fish	2	16	fruit	5	4	good-natured	8	1
equal	4	31	fair	4	10	five	2	12	fuel	5	29	goods	4	8
equality	8	20	fairy tales	6	8	fix	2	3	full	5	5	gopher	6	24
equation	8	20	faithfully	6	30	flashlight	5	19	fun	1	20	gorilla	7	15
equator	8	20	fall	2	15	flavor	5	22	function	5	11	got	1	18
equipped	5	21	familiar	7	24	flew	2	21	fungi	6	26	gotten	6	14
equivalent	8	20	families	6	12	flies	3	21	fun-loving	6	8	governmental	8	35
error	5	34	family	7	24	flight	3	3	funnel	6	25	grabbed	2	32
erupt	6	33	family's	4	21	float	4	6	funniest	4	16	gracefully	6	30

Word	Lesson	Word	Lesson	Word	Lesson	Word	Lesson	Word	Lesson	Word	Lesson
ladies	3 21	little	3 31	masculine	7 11	misfortune	7 17	musical	6 13		
laid	2 8	lived	5 20	massacre	7 15	miss	2 15	musician	7 35		
landscape	8 27	living	2 33	master	4 29	missed	7 2	must	2 6		
large	3 13	load	5 3	math	2 18	mission	5 11	my	2 7		
large-scale	8 1	local	6 15	mathematics	7 30	missionary	7 14	mysterious	6 27		
largest	3 25	lock	4 6	matinee	8 8	misspelled	4 19	mysteriously	8 35		
larvae	6 26	logic	7 32	matter	4 24	mist	7 2	mythology	7 32		
laser	8 12	loneliness	8 35	may	2 8	mistake	4 19	name	1 38		
last	2 14	lonesome	7 11	mayor	3 29	misunderstand	4 19	named	5 20		
late	2 12	long	2 18	me	2 7	mixture	5 31	narrative	8 21		
later	6 10	long-term	8 1	mean	4 2	moccasins	7 15	narrow	5 25		
latter	6 10	look	1 36	measure	5 31	model	5 23	nation	4 32		
laugh	3 7	looked	2 28	mechanism	8 22	moist	5 7	national	4 25		
laughing	3 7	looking	2 28	medal	5 28	moisture	5 31	native	4 32		
laughs	5 1	loose	4 8	media	6 26	molecules	8 12	natural	4 25		
launched	6 3	lose	5 4	medical	5 32	mom	2 4	naturalization	8 35		
law	3 9	lost	3 9	medicinal	8 15	moment	5 27	naturally	6 30		
lay	2 8	lot	2 4	medicine	8 15	money	3 26	nature	4 32		
layer	6 13	loud	3 12	meet	3 4	monitor	5 34	nautical	8 28		
leader	3 20	loudspeaker	8 1	melancholy	8 11	monkey	3 26	navigation	8 28		
leadership	6 19	love	5 1	melody	5 32	monologue	7 32	nearby	4 26		
leaflet	8 32	loved	2 33	melon	5 28	monopoly	7 28	necessary	7 20		
league	7 23	low	2 10	member	4 29	monotonous	7 28	necessity	6 19		
learn	4 13	loyal	4 14	memorandum	7 30	monsoon	8 27	neck	2 19		
least	4 2	loyalty	8 22	memories	4 23	monster	6 14	necktie	7 30		
leaves	4 23	luck	4 4	memorize	7 18	moon	3 10	need	2 9		
lecture	5 31	lumber	4 29	memory	5 34	moonlight	7 1	needle	5 23		
left	3 1	luncheon	7 30	men	2 2	moose	6 26	negative	6 27		
leg	2 2	luncheonette	8 32	men's	4 21	moral	5 23	negotiate	8 18		
legal	4 31	luxury	7 14	mention	5 11	more	2 25	neighbors	4 12		
legislative	6 27	macaroni	8 27	menu	5 34	morning	4 10	neither	4 12		
lemon	4 25	machine	5 11	merchant	5 26	mosquito	7 4	nervous	6 4		
length	7 12	machinery	7 14	mercury	7 11	most	2 7	nervously	6 30		
less	2 15	mackintosh	8 30	mess	2 2	mother's	4 21	nest	4 2		
lesson	4 30	mad	2 1	met	1 19	motion	4 31	network	5 19		
let	1 19	made	2 12	metal	5 23	motive	6 15	never	3 29		
let's	2 26	magnetic	8 9	metallic	8 9	motor	4 24	nevertheless	4 26		
letter	4 24	magnificent	7 21	meter	6 15	motorcycle	4 26	new	2 21		
letting	7 3	magnificently	8 20	meters	7 27	mountain	6 3	newspaper	4 18		
level	5 23	magnify	8 20	metropolitan	8 26	mouse	5 7	New Year	6 8		
liar	5 29	magnitude	8 20	microcomputer	8 20	mouth	5 7	next	4 2		
librarian	7 35	mail	4 1	microorganism	8 20	move	5 4	nice	2 12		
library	7 12	main	3 4	microphone	8 10	moved	4 15	niece	5 2		
lie	3 3	major	4 32	microscope	7 32	movement	4 28	night	2 22		
life	2 12	majority	6 19	microscopic	8 20	movie	3 26	nightmare	6 4		
lifeguard	5 19	make	2 12	microwave	8 20	moving	2 33	nine	5 3		
life jackets	7 1	make-believe	5 19	middle	3 31	much	2 6	no	1 35		
lifted	6 16	making	3 19	middle-aged	6 8	mud	2 6	nobody	4 18		
light	2 22	malapropism	8 30	middle-class	6 8	mule	2 13	noise	4 14		
lightning	7 29	mammoth	1 22	might	2 22	multicolored	8 20	noisy	5 7		
like	1 37	man	1 22	migrate	8 14	multicultural	8 20	nonsense	6 1		
liked	2 33	mandate	8 18	milk	3 2	multimedia	8 20	noon	3 10		
limit	5 28	manner	4 24	million	5 25	multiplication	8 20	normal	3 31		
limousine	7 30	manual	5 32	mind	4 3	multiplied	4 16	north	3 14		
line	1 37	many	3 26	mine	4 3	multiply	4 20	nose	2 13		
linen	6 24	map	2 1	minor	4 31	multitude	8 20	not	1 18		
lion	5 29	marathon	8 11	minus	4 31	mummies	6 12	note	2 13		
liquid	6 1	march	5 8	mirror	3 29	murder	5 9	notebook	4 18		
listen	4 25	marine	7 11	misbehave	4 19	muscle	7 16	notice	4 31		
listening	7 3	mark	3 13	mischief	6 7	muscular	7 16	noun	5 7		
literature	7 12	market	4 29	miserable	5 17	music	4 32	novel	6 24		

Word	Lesson		Word	Lesson		Word	Lesson		Word	Lesson		Word	Lesson		Word	Lesson	
novelty	8	22	opportunity	8	23	pass	2	15	photography	7	27	popping	2	32			
now	1	31	opposite	7	20	passionate	8	9	physical	8	11	popular	7	16			
nowhere	4	26	opposition	8	23	pasteurize	8	30	physician	7	35	population	7	16			
nuclei	6	26	optic	8	26	pasture	5	31	pianist	7	5	porch	5	8			
nucleus	6	26	optical	8	26	patience	5	11	piano	8	27	portable	8	14			
number	3	29	optimism	8	22	patient	4	32	pick	3	2	portion	5	11			
nurse	3	15	optometrist	8	26	patio	7	4	picked	3	19	portrait	7	23			
nursery	7	14	or	2	25	patriotic	8	15	picnic	4	29	position	7	20			
nutrients	8	3	orange	4	7	patriotism	8	22	picnic basket	8	1	positive	6	27			
oak	5	3	orchard	5	26	patriots	8	15	picture	5	31	possibility	7	33			
obedience	6	18	order	5	8	pattern	5	25	piece	4	9	possible	4	25			
object	5	25	ordered	5	21	pay	2	8	pier	6	7	pot	1	18			
objected	6	33	ore	5	8	payment	4	28	pig	1	21	potatoes	8	3			
objection	8	23	organization	7	33	peace	4	9	pigeon	8	8	pounds	6	3			
objections	6	33	organize	7	18	peacefully	6	30	pillow	6	14	poverty	8	22			
objective	8	23	original	6	13	peacefulness	8	35	pilot	4	31	power	5	7			
obligation	8	15	orphan	6	25	peach	6	2	pin	2	3	powerful	3	20			
oblige	8	15	other	2	30	peanut	5	27	pinnacle	7	15	practice	5	10			
oblong	8	23	our	3	18	pear	4	9	pioneer	7	35	practicing	5	20			
obscure	8	23	out	2	30	pearl	5	9	pirate	4	32	prairie	7	23			
observation	8	23	outdoors	5	19	pencil	4	7	place	4	1	praise	6	2			
observatory	8	14	outside	3	28	pending	7	34	placed	2	33	precaution	5	14			
obsessions	8	23	oval	6	25	penetrate	7	29	plains	4	9	precious	5	11			
obstacle	8	23	over	2	30	pennies	4	23	plan	4	1	predict	5	14			
obtained	8	23	overnight	7	1	penniless	8	21	planes	4	9	predicting	8	14			
obvious	6	27	owl's	3	17	people's	4	21	planet	5	28	prefer	5	14			
obviously	8	23	own	2	10	perceived	8	31	planned	2	32	preferred	6	16			
occasion	5	32	owner	3	20	percent	5	10	planning	3	19	prehistoric	4	19			
occasionally	8	23	ownership	6	30	perception	8	25	plant	4	1	prejudice	7	17			
occupant	8	23	pack	2	19	perfect	5	25	plaque	7	23	prepaid	4	19			
occupation	8	23	packet	8	32	perfectly	8	25	plastic	4	30	preparation	5	14			
occupied	6	12	page	4	7	perform	7	34	plateau	8	8	prepare	5	14			
occurred	5	21	paid	3	4	performance	7	5	platform	6	25	prescribed	6	32			
occurring	5	21	pain	7	2	perfume	8	8	platinum	7	29	presence	6	18			
ocean	5	11	paint	5	2	perimeter	8	25	play	1	38	present	5	10			
October	7	28	pair	4	9	periodic	8	25	played	5	20	preservation	8	14			
octopus	7	28	palace	6	24	peripheral	8	25	player	3	20	president	6	22			
odd	4	6	palette	8	2	periscope	7	32	playground	3	28	pressure	5	11			
odometer	8	28	pallet	8	2	permanent	6	22	playing	2	28	pretend	5	14			
odor	5	22	pamphlet	8	32	permanently	8	25	plays	4	23	prettier	4	16			
odyssey	8	30	pane	7	2	permission	5	16	pleasant	6	24	prettiest	4	16			
of	1	31	panther	5	26	permit	7	22	please	5	10	pretty	3	26			
off	1	31	paper	4	24	permitted	5	21	pleasure	5	31	pretzel	8	34			
offensive	8	23	parachute	7	30	permitting	7	3	plenty	4	20	prevent	5	14			
offered	7	22	paragraph	7	27	persecuted	8	5	plot	4	6	preview	5	14			
offering	8	23	parakeet	8	27	persimmon	8	34	pneumonia	8	11	previous	5	14			
offshore	7	1	parallel	8	21	person	3	15	poem	5	29	prime	6	2			
often	4	25	paralyze	7	18	personal	5	32	poet	5	29	principal	8	2			
oil	3	12	pare	4	9	personality	6	19	poetic	8	9	principle	8	2			
old	1	35	parent	4	10	perspective	8	25	point	3	12	prior	5	29			
older	3	25	parents'	4	21	persuaded	8	25	pointed	6	16	prison	6	24			
omit	7	22	park	2	24	pet	1	19	polar	4	31	private	5	27			
omitted	8	3	parka	8	34	petals	5	28	police	4	7	prize	5	3			
on	1	31	part	2	24	petrified	8	3	policy	8	26	probability	8	12			
once	4	7	participate	8	18	phenomenon	8	11	political	6	13	probably	7	12			
one	3	18	particle	8	32	philosopher	8	26	politician	7	35	proceed	5	33			
only	3	26	particles	7	16	philosophy	8	11	politics	8	26	proceeds	8	16			
opening	5	21	particular	7	16	phone	3	7	polluted	8	21	process	5	14			
opera	8	27	parties	4	23	phonograph	8	10	pond	2	4	procession	5	33			
opossum	7	15	partner	5	26	phosphate	8	18	pony	4	20	processor	5	34			
opponent	6	22	partnership	6	19	photograph	7	27	pool	3	10	produce	5	14			

Word	Lesson	Word	Lesson	Word	Lesson	Word	Lesson	Word	Lesson
produced	8 3	rapid	6 1	repeated	8 15	running	2 32	sensible	5 17
product	5 14	rare	3 13	repetition	8 15	rupture	6 33	sensitive	6 27
productive	8 31	rather	5 22	replacement	6 28	sack	6 1	sensory	8 31
profession	8 4	ray	5 2	replied	3 21	sad	2 1	sent	4 9
professionally	8 4	razor	6 15	report	4 10	sadness	4 28	sentence	5 10
profit	6 24	reach	2 16	reproduction	6 28	said	1 36	sentimental	8 31
profitable	8 16	react	5 29	research	5 9	sail	5 13	separate	7 12
program	5 14	reaction	6 28	reservation	8 14	sailboat	7 1	separating	8 3
programming	8 3	read	2 9	resign	7 25	salad	5 28	sequoia	8 30
project	5 14	reader	6 13	resignation	7 25	sale	5 13	servant	6 22
projected	6 33	real	7 2	resources	8 3	salmon	6 26	session	5 11
projections	6 33	realism	8 22	respectively	6 30	salt	6 3	set	2 2
promise	5 28	realize	7 18	respiration	7 34	same	3 5	seven	3 30
proof	6 3	reason	3 30	responsibilities	7 33	sandwich	8 30	several	4 25
proper	5 28	reasonable	5 17	responsibility	6 19	sapling	8 32	sew	2 27
propose	8 15	rebuild	3 24	responsible	5 17	sat	2 1	shape	2 16
proposition	8 15	receipt	7 25	rest	3 1	satellite	8 21	share	4 10
prosecuted	8 5	receive	6 7	restaurant	7 29	Saturn	6 25	shark	5 8
prosperity	8 16	received	4 12	return	4 13	saucer	6 3	sharp	3 8
protect	5 14	receiver	6 7	returned	6 16	saved	2 33	she	1 34
protested	8 16	reception	7 25	revised	7 20	saw	1 36	she'd	3 17
proud	5 7	recess	7 20	revolutionary	7 14	say	2 8	shelves	4 23
prove	5 4	recognize	7 18	reward	6 4	says	5 1	she's	2 20
provide	5 14	recommendation	7 33	rhythm	8 11	scarce	6 4	shield	5 2
provisions	8 16	reconstruction	6 28	rhythmically	8 35	scare	3 13	ship	2 16
psychiatrist	7 35	rectangle	7 16	ribbon	4 25	scared	4 15	shirt	3 8
psychology	7 32	rectangular	7 16	rich	2 16	scattering	8 21	shoe	3 10
public	4 29	recycle	8 10	ride	1 37	scene	3 18	shone	7 2
pulled	3 19	red	1 30	riding	2 33	scenery	7 14	shook	3 8
pupil	4 32	reddish	7 11	right	2 22	scenic	6 15	shoot	7 2
puppet	4 29	reduce	5 33	rigid	8 9	scent	4 9	shop	2 16
puppies	3 21	reduction	5 33	ring	2 18	scholarship	8 26	shopping	3 19
purchase	5 26	reel	7 2	riot	5 29	scholastic	8 26	shore	3 14
pure	4 13	refer	7 22	rival	6 15	school	2 21	short	2 25
purple	3 31	reference	7 12	rivalry	8 22	science	4 7	shot	5 1
purpose	5 9	references	7 22	river	3 29	scientist	7 35	should	5 5
purse	6 4	referred	5 21	road	2 10	scientists	8 12	shout	6 3
push	3 8	referring	6 16	roar	6 4	scope	7 32	show	2 10
putting	2 32	refining	8 33	roast	6 2	score	3 14	shower	5 7
qualified	6 12	reform	7 34	robber	4 30	scribbled	6 32	shown	7 2
qualify	4 20	refrigerator	7 30	robbery	8 22	scribe	6 32	shut	4 4
quart	7 28	refused	8 3	robin	5 28	script	6 32	sick	3 2
quarter	5 8	region	4 7	rock	2 4	scrubbed	6 16	side	2 12
quarters	7 28	regular	7 16	rodeo	7 4	scuba	8 12	sidewalk	4 18
quartet	7 28	regulate	8 18	Roman	6 13	sculpture	5 31	sight	2 22
question	5 16	regulation	7 16	room	2 21	search	4 13	sign	7 25
quickly	3 20	rehabilitation	7 33	rope	2 13	seashore	6 8	signal	4 30
quiet	5 29	rehearsal	7 5	rose	3 5	season	3 30	signature	7 25
quietly	3 20	reins	6 7	rotten	6 13	seat	2 9	significant	6 22
quit	5 1	reject	6 33	rough	6 6	seaweed	7 1	significantly	8 35
quite	4 3	rejected	6 33	round	5 7	section	5 16	silence	4 32
rabbit	4 29	relationship	6 30	route	4 8	secure	4 13	silent	4 31
raccoon	4 8	relied	4 16	row	2 10	see	1 34	silver	4 29
radar	8 12	relief	6 7	royal	4 14	seen	3 18	simple	3 31
radius	6 26	reluctant	7 21	royalty	8 22	seesaw	2 31	simultaneously	7 33
ragged	8 9	remarkable	5 17	rude	5 4	seismometer	8 28	since	4 7
railroad	3 28	remember	4 24	ruin	5 29	seldom	4 29	sing	4 3
rain	2 8	renewal	6 28	ruined	7 3	selection	5 32	single	5 23
raise	3 4	repair	5 9	rule	5 4	selfish	7 11	siren	6 24
ran	1 22	repay	3 24	rumors	6 3	sensation	8 31	sister's	4 21
range	5 2	repayment	6 28	run	1 20	sensationally	8 35	sit	2 3

Word	Lesson		Word	Lesson		Word	Lesson		Word	Lesson		Word	Lesson		Word	Lesson	
sitting	2	32	spaceship	3	28	still	2	14	summit	6	1	telegraph	8	16	telegraph	8	16
six	2	3	spaghetti	8	27	stimuli	6	26	summoned	8	21	telephone	3	7			
sixth	4	3	Spain	7	9	stimulus	6	26	sun	1	20	telephones	8	10			
skating	4	15	Spanish	7	9	stock	4	6	sunken	3	30	telescope	7	32			
skeleton	8	27	spare	5	9	stolen	5	27	supercold	8	28	telescopes	8	16			
sketch	6	1	sparkling	6	4	stone	3	5	supermarket	8	28	televised	7	20			
skirt	5	9	speak	4	2	stood	2	14	supervision	8	28	television	5	16			
sky	2	22	speaker	6	13	stop	2	4	supper	3	23	tell	1	36			
sled	2	14	speaking	6	16	stopped	2	32	supplied	4	16	temper	4	30			
sleep	3	4	special	4	25	store	2	25	supplies	6	12	temperature	7	12			
sleigh	6	6	specialist	7	17	storm	3	14	supply	4	20	ten	2	2			
slept	4	2	specialty	8	22	story	4	10	support	5	25	tennis	5	25			
slice	6	2	species	6	26	straight	6	6	supported	8	14	tentatively	7	29			
slide	5	3	specific	7	17	strain	8	4	suppose	3	23	terminal	5	34			
slight	5	3	specifications	7	17	strange	3	8	sure	5	11	terrace	8	33			
slipped	2	32	spectacle	6	32	strategic	7	24	surely	3	20	terrible	5	17			
slope	6	2	spectacular	6	32	strategy	7	24	surgeon	8	8	terrific	8	21			
slow	2	10	spectators	6	32	strawberry	7	1	surprise	5	10	terrified	4	16			
small	3	9	spectrum	6	32	street	4	2	surprised	5	20	territorial	8	33			
smart	5	8	speech	3	8	strength	7	12	suspect	6	32	territories	8	33			
smell	4	2	spelling	6	16	strenuous	8	4	suspended	7	34	territory	7	14			
smiled	3	19	spied	4	16	strenuously	8	4	suspense	6	25	than	2	18			
smoke	3	5	spike	6	2	stretcher	6	13	swallowed	7	3	thank	4	1			
smooth	4	8	spiral	6	24	string	3	8	swam	4	1	thankful	3	20			
snake	5	2	spirit	5	28	stroke	6	2	swayed	7	2	Thanksgiving	5	19			
snow	3	3	splendid	6	1	strong	3	8	swimming	4	15	that	1	24			
so	2	27	spoil	5	7	structure	5	31	swung	4	4	that's	2	20			
soap	3	3	spoke	3	5	structures	7	20	syllable	7	15	the	1	24			
soar	6	9	spoonerism	8	30	stuck	4	4	symbolic	8	10	their	2	27			
so-called	6	8	sport	3	14	student	4	8	sympathetic	8	10	them	2	18			
social	5	11	spot	3	2	studied	3	21	symphony	8	10	themselves	4	26			
socks	4	6	spotted	4	15	studying	7	3	symptoms	8	10	then	1	24			
sofa	4	32	spray	5	2	stuff	4	4	synonyms	8	10	there	2	27			
soft	3	9	spring	4	3	stupid	8	9	synthetic	8	10	therefore	4	10			
softened	7	25	square	3	13	subdued	8	17	system	6	6	there's	2	20			
softly	7	25	squeeze	6	2	subject	4	30	table	3	31	thermometer	7	27			
software	5	34	squirrel	4	30	subjected	8	17	tablet	8	32	these	3	5			
soil	3	12	stadium	8	11	submarine	7	30	tail	2	8	they	2	18			
solar	4	31	stagecoach	8	1	submerged	8	17	take	2	12	they're	2	20			
solid	5	28	stairs	4	10	submit	7	22	taken	3	30	thief	4	12			
solve	4	6	stake	6	9	submitted	8	3	taking	2	33	thieves	6	7			
some	1	32	stampede	7	4	subscription	6	32	talent	6	24	thigh	6	2			
somebody	4	18	stand	4	1	substance	7	21	talk	3	9	thing	5	1			
somehow	4	26	star	4	10	subtract	5	26	tall	5	5	things	2	34			
someone	3	28	stare	5	9	subtracting	8	17	taste	5	2	think	3	2			
something	2	31	start	2	24	subtraction	7	22	taught	5	5	third	3	15			
sometimes	2	31	started	2	28	subway	8	17	taxable	5	17	thirsty	5	9			
somewhere	2	31	state	4	1	succeeded	7	20	teach	3	4	thirty	5	9			
sonar	8	12	statement	6	19	successfully	6	30	teacher's	3	17	this	1	24			
song	3	9	station	5	11	such	3	2	teachers'	4	21	those	2	18			
soon	2	21	stationary	8	2	sudden	4	29	teaching	5	20	though	6	6			
sophisticated	8	26	stationery	8	2	suede	7	2	team	2	9	thought	5	5			
sophomore	8	26	statuette	8	32	suffer	7	22	teams'	4	21	thoughtfully	6	30			
sore	6	9	stay	4	1	suffered	5	21	technician	7	35	thousands	6	3			
sort	2	25	steak	6	9	sufficient	6	22	technique	7	23	threatened	6	16			
sound	5	7	steal	6	9	sugar	3	29	technological	8	12	three	3	4			
soup	3	10	steel	6	9	suit	5	4	technology	7	32	threw	4	4			
source	6	4	step	4	2	suitable	5	17	teenager	6	8	throne	5	13			
south	4	14	stepped	4	15	suite	8	8	teenagers	7	30	through	4	8			
sow	2	27	stew	4	4	summary	5	32	teeth	4	2	throw	3	3			
space	4	1	stick	2	19	summer	4	29	telegram	8	16	thrown	5	13			

Word	Lesson		Word	Lesson		Word	Lesson		Word	Lesson		Word	Lesson		Word	Lesson	
thunder	5	22	tries	3	21	unpredictable	6	28	wallet	4	29	windshield	4	26
thunderstorm	6	8	triggered	8	21	unseen	4	19	walrus	8	27	winning	4	15
tide	7	2	trio	7	28	unsuccessful	6	28	want	5	1	winter	3	29
tie	3	3	trip	4	3	untie	4	19	wanted	2	28	wisdom	5	33
tied	7	2	triple	7	28	unusual	4	19	war	3	14	wise	5	33
tiger	4	31	triumph	5	29	unusually	6	28	warm	3	14	wish	2	16
tight	3	3	trouble	4	25	up	1	29	warmth	5	8	wishes	2	34
time	1	37	trout	6	26	upon	2	31	warn	5	8	with	1	24
times	2	34	truck	3	2	upright	6	8	warrant	6	4	woke	2	13
tiny	4	20	true	5	4	upstairs	5	19	was	1	29	wolf	5	5
tired	4	15	truly	4	8	us	2	6	wash	2	16	wolves	4	23
tissue	5	11	trumpet	7	5	use	2	13	wasn't	2	26	woman	5	22
to	2	27	truth	4	8	used	2	33	waste	5	13	women's	4	21
toast	5	3	try	2	7	useful	3	20	watching	5	20	won	3	18
tobacco	7	15	trying	2	28	useless	4	28	water	3	29	wonder	4	24
toboggan	8	34	tube	5	4	usual	5	32	watermelon	7	1	wondered	6	16
toes	4	6	tundra	8	34	uttered	8	21	way	2	8	wonderful	4	28
token	6	24	tune	5	4	vacant	5	27	we	1	34	wonderfully	6	30
told	2	7	tunnel	4	30	vacation	5	16	weak	6	9	wondering	5	21
tomato	7	4	turkey	3	26	vaccination	8	21	weapon	6	24	won't	2	26
tomorrow	7	15	turn	3	15	vague	7	23	wear	3	13	wood	3	10
too	2	27	turned	5	20	valley	3	26	weather	6	9	wooden	4	8
took	2	19	turtle	6	4	valuable	5	17	week	6	9	wool	4	8
tooth	4	8	tuxedo	8	30	vanilla	7	4	weekend	4	18	word	3	15
top	2	4	twelfth	7	12	vapor	5	27	weigh	4	12	wore	3	14
tore	5	8	twice	5	3	varied	6	12	weighed	6	7	work	3	15
tornado	7	4	two	2	27	various	6	27	weight	4	12	worker	4	13
torrential	8	21	type	4	3	vegetable	7	12	weird	4	12	world	4	13
tortillas	7	4	typewriter	7	1	vehicles	7	16	welcome	5	25	world's	4	21
total	3	31	umbrella	7	15	vehicular	7	16	well	1	30	worm	4	13
totem pole	4	26	unable	3	24	velvet	6	14	well-dressed	8	1	worried	3	21
tourism	8	22	unburned	3	24	verdict	8	14	went	1	30	worse	6	4
tower	5	7	uncertain	4	19	very	2	30	we're	2	20	worst	4	13
town	3	12	uncertainty	8	22	vice-president	5	19	were	2	30	wouldn't	2	26
toys	2	34	uncle	3	31	victory	7	14	wet	2	2	write	3	7
track	2	19	uncomfortable	6	28	Vietnam	7	9	we've	3	17	writing	5	20
trade	5	2	under	5	22	Vietnamese	7	9	whale	5	13	written	3	23
traffic	4	30	underground	8	1	violin	7	5	what	1	25	wrong	3	7
train	2	8	underlying	8	16	virus	5	27	what's	2	20	wrote	3	7
transaction	8	17	underneath	8	16	visible	5	17	wheat	3	8	yacht	8	27
transcripts	6	32	undersized	8	9	vision	7	20	wheel	4	2	yard	3	13
transfer	7	22	undertake	8	16	visit	5	10	when	1	25	yearling	8	32
transferred	8	17	underwater	7	1	visiting	5	21	where	1	25	years	5	10
transformed	7	34	undoubtedly	7	17	visitors	7	20	whether	6	9	yellow	3	23
transient	8	17	unemployment	6	28	vital	6	15	which	2	18	yes	2	2
translation	8	17	uneven	4	19	vocabulary	8	33	while	2	18	yet	2	2
transmission	7	22	unexpected	4	19	vocal	8	33	white	3	8	you	2	21
transportation	8	17	unexpectedly	6	28	vocational	8	33	who	1	25	young	6	6
travel	5	28	unfair	3	24	voice	4	7	whole	4	9	your	3	14
treason	6	24	unfortunate	7	17	volcanic	5	33	wholesome	7	11	you're	2	20
treasure	5	31	unfortunately	6	28	volcano	5	33	whom	4	8	yours	4	10
treasury	7	14	unhappy	3	24	volunteer	7	35	who's	5	13	youth	6	3
tree	3	4	uniform	7	34	vote	4	6	whose	5	13	you've	3	17
tremendous	6	27	unique	7	23	voyage	7	23	why	1	25	zeppelin	8	30
trial	5	23	united	4	15	waffle	8	34	wig	1	21	zoo	3	10
triangle	7	16	universe	8	12	wagon	3	30	wild	4	3			
triangles	7	28	unknown	3	24	wail	5	13	wilderness	4	28			
triangular	7	16	unlike	3	24	waist	5	13	wildlife	7	1			
trick	4	3	unlikely	6	28	wait	2	8	will	1	26			
tricycle	7	28	unlocked	4	19	walk	5	5	win	2	3			
tried	3	21	unlucky	4	19	walked	5	20	window	5	25			

Scope and Sequence

Grade	1	2	3	4	5	6	7	8
SPELLING GENERALIZATIONS								
Sound-Letter Relationships								
Consonants	■	■	■	■	■	■	■	■
Consonant Digraphs	■	■	■	■	■	■	■	■
Consonant Clusters	■	■	■	■	■	■	■	■
Short Vowels	■	■	■	■	■	■	■	■
Long Vowels	■	■	■	■	■	■	■	■
Vowel Diphthongs/Vowel Digraphs/Variant Vowels		■	■	■	■	■	■	■
R-Controlled Vowels		■	■	■	■	■	■	■
Silent Letters	■	■	■	■	■	■	■	■
Schwa			■	■	■	■	■	■
Double Letters	■	■	■	■	■	■	■	■
Spelling Patterns	■	■	■	■	■	■	■	■
Word Structure								
Contractions	■	■	■	■	■	■	■	■
Plurals/Possessives		■	■	■	■	■	■	■
Inflected Forms/Comparatives/Superlatives		■	■	■	■	■	■	■
Prefixes			■	■	■	■	■	■
Suffixes		■	■	■	■	■	■	■
Greek and Latin Word Parts					■	■	■	■
Word Analysis								
Invented Spelling	■	■						
Phonograms	■	■	■	■				
Compound Words		■	■	■	■	■		
Syllable Patterns					■	■	■	■
Letter Patterns					■	■	■	■
Pronunciation					■	■	■	■

Grade	1	2	3	4	5	6	7	8
SPELLING STRATEGIES								
Rhyming Words	■	■	■	■	■	■	■	■
Word Shapes	■	■	■	■	■	■	■	■
Word Families	■	■	■	■	■	■	■	■
Study Steps to Learn a Word		■	■	■	■	■	■	■
Picture/Sound Out a Word		■	■	■	■	■	■	■
Related Words		■	■	■	■	■	■	■
Mnemonic Devices		■	■	■	■	■	■	■
Spell/Proofread with a Partner		■	■	■	■	■	■	■
Try Different Spellings/Best Guess		■	■	■	■	■	■	■
Dictionary/Definitions		■	■	■	■	■	■	■
Proofread Twice		■	■	■	■	■	■	■
Apply Spelling Rules			■	■	■	■	■	■
VOCABULARY DEVELOPMENT								
Classify/Categorize Words	■	■	■	■	■	■	■	■
Antonyms	■	■	■	■	■	■	■	■
Content-Area Words	■	■	■	■	■	■	■	■
Synonyms		■	■	■	■	■	■	■
Homophones		■	■	■	■	■	■	■
Multiple Meanings/Homographs		■	■	■	■	■	■	■
Dictionary (for meaning)		■	■	■	■	■	■	■
Word Origins		■	■	■	■	■	■	■
Analogies			■	■	■	■	■	■
Idioms			■	■	■	■	■	■
Denotation/Connotation					■	■	■	■
Parts of Speech					■	■	■	■
Root Words			■	■	■	■	■	■
WRITING								
The Writing Process	■	■	■	■	■	■	■	■
Proofreading	■	■	■	■	■	■	■	■
Frequently Misspelled Words	■	■	■	■	■	■	■	■

BIBLIOGRAPHY

Professional List For Teachers

Bear, Donald R. "'Learning to Fasten the Seat of My Union Suit Without Looking Around': The Synchrony of Literacy Development." *Theory Into Practice* 30, No. 3 (Summer 1991): 149–157.

Bear, Donald R., and Diane Barone. "Using Children's Spellings to Group for Word Study and Directed Reading in the Primary Classroom." *Reading Psychology: An International Quarterly* 10 (1989): 275–292.

Bolton, Faye, and Diane Snowball. *Teaching Spelling: A Practical Resource.* Portsmouth: Heinemann, 1993.

Buchanan, Ethel. *Spelling for Whole-Language Classrooms.* Winnipeg, Canada: Blue Frog Books, 1992.

Chomsky, Carol. "Invented Spelling in the Open Classroom." New England Kindergarten Conference (1973): 499–518. Portions of this article first appeared in "Beginning Reading Through Invented Spelling" in *Quality Education Makes a Difference* (1–8) and are reprinted by permission of Lesley College.

Cunningham, Patricia M., and James W. Cunningham. "Making Words: Enhancing the Invented Spelling-Decoding Connection." *The Reading Teacher* 46, No. 2 (October 1992): 106–115.

Farr, Roger, Cheryl Kelleher, Katherine Lee, and Caroline Beverstock. "An Analysis of the Spelling Patterns of Children in Grades Two Through Eight: Study of a National Sample of Children's Writing." Center for Reading and Language Studies, Indiana University, 1990.

Fry, Edward, Ph.D. *Spelling Book: Words Most Needed Plus Phonics for Grades 1–6.* Laguna Beach, CA: Laguna Beach Educational Books, N.d.

Gentry, J. Richard. *SPEL . . . Is a Four-Letter Word.* Portsmouth: Heinemann, 1987.

Gentry, J. Richard, and Jean W. Gillet. *Teaching Kids to Spell.* Portsmouth: Heinemann, 1983.

Gill, J. Thomas Jr. "Focus on Research: Development of Word Knowledge As It Relates to Reading, Spelling, and Instruction." *Language Arts* 69 (October 1992): 444–453.

Goodman, Yetta M. "Language and the English Curriculum," *Education in the 80's: English.* Edited by R. Baird Shuman. N.p.: National Education Association, 1981.

Graves, Donald H. *Writing: Teachers and Children at Work.* Portsmouth: Heinemann, 1983.

Hillerich, Robert L. *Teaching Children to Write, K–8: A Complete Guide to Developing Writing Skills.* New York: Prentice-Hall, Inc., 1985. (excerpts)

Hodges, Richard E. *Learning to Spell.* Urbana, Illinois: ERIC Clearinghouse on Reading and Communication Skills and National Council of Teachers of English, 1981.

———. "The Conventions of Writing" in *Handbook of Research on Teaching the English Language Arts,* 775–786. N.p., 1991.

Holdaway, Don. "Shared Book Experience: Teaching Reading Using Favorite Books." In *Early Literacy: A Constructivist Foundation for Whole Language.* Edited by Constance Kamiij, Maryann Manning, and Gary Manning, 91–109. N.p. National Education Association, 1991.

Jongsma, Kathleen Stumpf. "Reading-Spelling Links." *The Reading Teacher* (April 1990): 608–610.

———. "Editorial Comment: Developmental Spelling Theory Revisited." *Reading Psychology: An International Quarterly* 10 (1989): iii–x.

———. "Meeting the Needs of Poor Spellers in the Elementary School: A Developmental Perspective." *National College of Education Occasional Paper* No. 14 (November 1986): 3–30.

McAlexander, Patricia J., Ann B. Dobie, and Noel Gregg, *Beyond the "SP" Label: Improving the Spelling of Learning Disabled and Basic Writers.* National Council of Teachers of English, 1992.

Morris, Darrell. "The Relationship Between Children's Concept of Word in Text and Phoneme Awareness in Learning to Read: A Longitudinal Study." *Research in the Teaching of English* 27, No. 2 (May 1993): 132–154.

———. "'Word Sort': A Categorization Strategy for Improving Word Recognition Ability." *Reading Psychology: An International Quarterly* 3: (1982): 247–259.

Routman, Regie. *Invitations: Changing as Teachers and Learners K–12.* Portsmouth: Heinemann, 1991. (excerpts)

———. "The Uses and Abuses of Invented Spelling." *Instructor* (May/June 1992): 35–39.

Schlagal, Robert C., and Joy Harris Schlagal. "The Integral Character of Spelling." *Language Arts* 69 (October 1992): 418–424.

Strickland, Dorothy S. "Emergent Literacy: How Young Children Learn to Read." *Educational Leadership* (March 1990): 18–23.

Swisher, Karen. "An Action Model for Research in the Classroom: Developmental Spelling K–2." Paper presented at the annual meeting of the College Reading Association, Crystal City, VA, October 31, 1991 to November 3, 1991.

Templeton, Shane. "New Trends in an Historical Perspective: Old Story, New Resolution—Sound and Meaning in Spelling." *Language Arts* 69 (October 1992): 454–466.

——. "Teaching and Learning the English Spelling System: Reconceptualizing Method and Purpose." *The Elementary School Journal* 92, No. 2 (1991): 185–201.

Texas Education Agency. *Spelling Instruction: A Proper Perspective.* N.p.: Texas Education Agency, Spring, 1991.

Wilde, Sandra. "An Analysis of the Development of Spelling and Punctuation in Selected Third and Fourth Grade Children": 1–47. Department of Language, Reading, and Culture, College of Education, University of Arizona, N.d.

——. "A Proposal for a New Spelling Curriculum." *The Elementary School Journal* 90, No. 3 (1990): 275–289.

——. "Spelling Textbooks: A Critical Review." *Linguistics and Education* 2 (1990): 259–280.

——. *You Kan Red This!* Portsmouth: Heinemann, 1992.

Zutell, Jerry, and Timothy Rasinski. "Children's Spelling Strategies and Their Cognitive Development." In *Developmental and Cognitive Aspects of Learning to Spell: A Reflection of Word Knowledge.* Edited by Edmund H. Henderson and James W. Beers, 52–73. N.p.: International Reading Association, 1980.

——. "Reading and Spelling Connections in Third and Fifth Grade Students." *Reading Psychology: An International Quarterly* 10 (1989): 137–155.

Word Play and Language-Related List for Students

Adler, David A. *Bunny Rabbit Rebus.* New York: Crowell, 1983.

Bayer, Jane. *A My Name Is Alice.* New York: Dial, 1984, 1987.

Benjamin, A. *Rat-a-Tat, Pitter Pat.* New York: Crowell, 1987.

Brown, Ruth. *Alphabet Times Four: An International ABC.* New York: Dutton, 1991.

Dragonwagon, Crescent. *Alligator Arrived with Apples: A Potluck Alphabet Feast.* New York: Macmillan, 1987, 1992.

Ehlert, Lois. *Feathers for Lunch.* San Diego: Harcourt Brace Jovanovich, 1990.

Emberly, Rebecca. *City Sounds.* Boston: Little, Brown, 1989.

——. *Jungle Sounds.* Boston: Little, Brown, 1989.

Falwell, Cathryn. *Clowning Around.* New York: Orchard Books, 1991.

Geisert, Arthur. *Pigs from A to Z.* Boston: Houghton Mifflin, 1986.

Hoban, Tana. *I Read Signs.* New York: Morrow, 1987.

Keller, Charles. *Tongue Twisters.* New York: Simon & Schuster, 1989.

McMillan, Bruce. *Play Day: A Book of Terse Verse.* New York: Holiday House, 1991.

Most, Bernard. *Zoodles.* San Diego: Harcourt Brace Jovanovich, 1992.

Spier, Peter. *Gobble, Growl, Grunt.* New York: Doubleday, 1988.

Van Allsburg, Chris. *The Z Was Zapped: A Play in Twenty-Six Acts.* Boston: Houghton Mifflin, 1987.

A

a, **short,** T15–T20, T256–T257

a-e, T81–T86, T278–T279

ai, ay, T57–T62, T270–T271

/är/ar, ear, T153–T158, T302–T303

Accessing prior knowledge, T16, T22, T28, T34, T46, T52, T58, T64, T70, T82, T88, T94, T100, T106, T118, T124, T130, T136, T142, T154, T160, T166, T172, T178, T190, T196, T202, T208, T214

Alphabetical order, T19, T49, T67, T85, T90, T97, T108, T121, T127, T133, T163, T175, T193, T205

Antonyms

See Vocabulary.

Applying spelling strategies, T17, T23, T25, T29, T35, T37, T39, T41, T42, T47, T53, T59, T65, T71, T75, T77, T78, T83, T89, T95, T101, T107, T111, T113, T114, T119, T125, T131, T137, T143, T147, T149, T150, T155, T161, T167, T173, T179, T183, T185, T191, T197, T203, T205, T209, T211, T215, T219, T221, T222, T237–T238

See also Strategy workshop.

Assessment

informal, T15, T21, T27, T33, T45, T51, T57, T63, T69, T81, T87, T93, T99, T105, T117, T123, T129, T135, T141, T153, T159, T165, T171, T177, T189, T195, T201, T207, T213, T330–T331

placement tests, T333–T336

portfolio conference, T337–T339

posttest, T19, T25, T31, T37, T49, T55, T61, T67, T73, T76, T85, T91, T97, T103, T109, T112, T121, T127, T133, T139, T145, T157, T163, T169, T175, T181, T193, T199, T205, T211, T217

practice test, T40, T76, T112, T148, T184, T220

pretest, T16, T22, T28, T34, T46, T52, T58, T64, T70, T76, T82, T88, T94, T100, T106, T112, T118, T124, T130, T136, T142, T154, T160, T166, T172,

T178, T190, T196, T202, T208, T214

reading/writing portfolio, T337–T339

self-assessment, T16, T22, T28, T34, T40, T46, T52, T58, T64, T70, T76, T82, T88, T94, T100, T106, T112, T118, T124, T130, T136, T142, T148, T154, T160, T166, T172, T178, T184, T190, T196, T202, T208, T214, T220

testing, T19, T25, T31, T37, T49, T55, T61, T67, T73, T85, T91, T97, T103, T109, T121, T127, T133, T139, T145, T157, T163, T169, T175, T181, T193, T199, T205, T211, T217

Assignment guide, T250

Auditory modality, T20, T26, T38, T50, T56, T62, T86, T92, T98, T104, T110, T122, T146, T158, T176, T194, T200, T218

C

Classifying

See Sorting; Vocabulary.

Compound words, T66, T181, T195–T200, T316–T317

Consonant clusters *(l, r, t),* T93–T98, T282–T283

Consonants, final double, T99–T104, T284–T285

Context clues, T18, T24, T36, T59, T84, T90, T131, T144, T153, T159, T167, T168, T171, T189, T195

Contractions

is, are, am, will, T129–T134, T294–T295

not, us, have, T165–T170, T306–T307

Cooperative learning

See Working together.

Copying masters, T251–T328

Cumulative word list, T346–T355

D

Describing words

See Vocabulary.

Developmental levels

semi-phonetic spellers, T17, T23, T29, T35,

T47, T53, T59, T65, T71, T83, T89, T95,
T101, T107, T119, T125, T131, T137,
T143, T155, T161, T167, T173, T179,
T191, T197, T203, T209, T215
transitional spellers, T18, T24, T30, T36,
T48, T54, T60, T66, T72, T84, T90, T96,
T102, T108, T120, T126, T132, T138,
T144, T156, T162, T168, T174, T180,
T192, T198, T204, T210, T216

Dictionary
alphabetical order, T49, T67, T97, T108,
T121, T133, T163, T175, T193, T205
definitions, T65, T108
for spelling, T23, T39, T75, T111, T191

Digraphs
sh, ch, T105–T110, T286–T287
th, wh, T117–T122, T290–T291

Drafting
See Process writing steps.

e, **long,** T51–T56, T268–T269
e, **short,** T21–T26, T258–T259
ea, ee, T63–T68, T272–T273

Encoding strategies
See Spelling strategies.

Endings
-ed, -ing, T177–T182, T310–T311
-ed, -ing, (double consonant), T201–T206,
T318–T319
-ed, -ing, (drop *e*), T207–T212, T320–T321

English words from other languages, T24,
T54
Greek, T60
Spanish, T73, T102, T126, T127

Error analysis chart, T332

Etymology
See Vocabulary, word origins.

Evaluation
See Assessment.

Extra help
See Meeting individual needs; Second-
language support.

Figurative language, T48, T84

Frequently misspelled words, T42, T78,
T114, T150, T186, T222, T265, T277,
T289, T301, T313, T325

Fun with words, T17, T23, T29, T35, T47,
T53, T59, T65, T71, T83, T89, T95, T101,
T107, T119, T125, T131, T137, T143,
T155, T161, T167, T173, T179, T191,
T197, T203, T209, T215

Graphic organizers
chart, T31, T37, T67, T92, T103, T133,
T146, T163, T199, T211
diagram, T91
list, T49, T85, T109, T139, T175, T205
map, T115
speech balloon, T145, T169
web, T19, T24, T73, T85, T121, T139,
T157, T181, T217, T271

Home activities masters
See Resources.

Homonyms, T19
See also Vocabulary.

Homophones, T171–T176, T308–T309
See also Vocabulary.

i, **long,** T51–T56, T141–T146, T268–T269,
T298–T299
i, **short,** T27–T32, T260–T261
i-e, T81–T89, T278–T279

Idioms
See Vocabulary.

Informal assessment
See Assessment, informal.

Integrated curriculum activities
art, T128, T182
language arts, T20, T26, T32, T38, T50,
T56, T68, T74, T86, T92, T98, T104,
T110, T122, T128, T134, T140, T146,
T158, T164, T170, T176, T182, T194,
T200, T206, T212, T218
math, T32, T56, T140, T164, T176,

T107, T111, T115, T119, T125, T137,
T147, T237–T238, T276, T288, T300
spelling rules, T35, T65, T75, T107,
T161, T183, T203, T209, T215, T219,
T237–T238

Structural analysis

See Compound words; Contractions.

Student self-assessment

See Self-check.

Students acquiring English

See Second-language support.

Study steps to learn a word, T14

Synonyms

See Vocabulary.

Teacher's corner, T44, T80, T116, T152,
T188, T224

Testing

See Assessment.

Tips for spelling success, T42, T43, T78,
T79, T114, T115, T150, T151, T186, T187,
T222, T223

Transitional spellers

See Developmental levels.

u, short, T45–T50, T266–T267
u-e, T87–T92, T280–T281

Visual modality, T32, T50, T56, T68, T74,
T86, T92, T128, T164, T182, T206, T212,
T218

Vocabulary

action words, T31, T55, T132, T204, T270,
T272, T284

antonyms, T53, T54, T145, T174, T193

classifying, T25, T67, T92, T96, T120,
T139, T146, T162, T193

compound words

See Compound words.

context clues

See Context clues.

contractions, T129–T134, T147–T152,
T165–T170, T183–T188, T294–T295,
T300–T301, T306–T307

definitions, T65, T90, T97, T108, T133,
T138, T143, T145, T153, T157, T171,
T189, T192, T195

describing words, T37, T85, T139, T144,
T169, T198

figurative language, T48, T84

high-frequency words, T189–T194,
T314–T315

homonyms, T19

homophones, T36, T97, T171

idioms, T30, T84, T192, T210

multiple-meaning words, T19, T157

nouns, T31, T61, T102, T169, T216

number words, T32

palindromes, T35

question words, T127

season words, T90

sense words, T37

size words, T139

synonyms, T24, T31, T73, T168, T210

word meanings, T31, T35, T47, T65, T91,
T101, T103, T133, T135, T157, T159,
T163, T167, T179, T180, T189, T195,
T203, T209, T217

word origins, T24, T60, T73, T120, T126,
T138, T144, T156, T168

Vocabulary wordshop, T18–T19, T24–T25,
T30–T31, T36–T37, T48–T49, T54–T55,
T60–T61, T66–T67, T72–T73, T84–T85,
T90–T91, T96–T97, T102–T103, T108–T109,
T120–T121, T126–T127, T132–T133,
T138–T139, T144–T145, T156–T157,
T162–T163, T168–T169, T174–T175,
T180–T181, T192–T193, T198–T199,
T204–T205, T210–T211, T216–T217

What's in a word?, T19, T24, T30, T36,
T48, T54, T60, T66, T73, T84, T91, T97,
T102, T109, T120, T126, T132, T138,
T144, T156, T162, T168, T174, T180,
T192, T198, T204, T210, T216

Word configuration, T18, T37, T90, T181,
T209, T261, T275, T291, T299, T323

Word games, T18, T20, T30, T32, T38, T44,
T47, T55, T60, T62, T65, T68, T72, T84,
T86, T96, T98, T110, T116, T133, T152,
T170, T176, T182, T188, T200, T206,
T212, T218, T224